JEWISH SYMBOLS AND SECRETS

Jewish Symbols and Secrets

A Fifteenth-century Spanish Jewish Carpet

ANTON FELTON

VALLENTINE MITCHELL
LONDON • PORTLAND, OR

First published in 2012 by Vallentine Mitchell

Middlesex House, 920 NE 58th Avenue, Suite 300
29/45 High Street, Edgware, Portland, Oregon,
Middlesex, HA8 7UU, UK 97213-3786 USA

www.vmbooks.com

Copyright © 2012 Anton Felton

British Library Cataloguing in Publication Data

Felton, Anton.
Jewish symbols and secrets : a fifteenth-century Spanish carpet.
1. Jewish rugs--Spain--History--To 1500. 2. Jewish art and symbolism--Spain--History--To 1500. 3. Jews, Spanish--History--To 1500. 4. Marranos--Spain--History--To 1500. 5. Weavers--Spain--History--To 1500. 6. Sephardim--History--To 1500.
I. Title
746.7'9'0089924-dc23

978 0 85303 834 4 (cloth)

Library of Congress Cataloging-in-Publication Data

All rights reserved. No part of this publication may be reproduced, stored in or introduced into a retrieval system, or transmitted, in any form or by any means, electronic, mechanical, photocopying, recording or otherwise without the prior written permission of the publisher of this book.

Printed by Short Run Press Ltd, Exeter, Devon

This book is dedicated to June:

Belsize Park 1957

I never saw so sweet a face
As that I stood before
My heart did leave its dwelling place
And could return no more

(after John Clare)

Stanmore 2011

Oh June, my love, my darling wife
I love you more than my own life:
Fifty three years have flown so fast,
Time earned, time spent, time gone, time past,
Still love-struck now I was then –
Gladly would I you wed again.

(A.F.)

Contents

List of Plates ... ix

Acknowledgements ... xiii

Introduction: Does It Really Matter? ... xv

PART 1. BACKGROUND HISTORIES

1. Weaving in Spain and Murcia ... 3
2. The Jews of Spain ... 11
3. The Role of Carpets in Jewish Culture ... 23
4. The Jewish Weavers of Spain and North Africa ... 33

PART 2. THE CARPETS

5. The Vizcaya Carpet ... 65
6. The Spanish Synagogue Carpet ... 71

PART 3. THE TURN OF EVENTS

7. The Enriquez ... 81
8. 1391–1492: Action and Reaction ... 101
9. Where, and by whom, was the Vizcaya Carpet Woven? ... 129
10. 'For Things Are Never What They Seem' ... 147

PART 4. THE SYMBOLS

11. Symbols ... 157

12.	The Star of David	167
13.	The Menorah and The *Hamsa* (The Hand)	203
14.	Pomegranates and Walnuts	209
15.	Birds	213
16.	Sheep	219
17.	Torah Arks	221
18.	Other Symbols, Numerology and Orant Figures	224

PART 5. SUMMING UP

19.	Conclusion	231
20.	Postscript	239

Appendix: *A Summary of the Main References to Stars, Rosettes and Star Forms in the Text*	241
Glossary	247
Bibliography	253
Index	271

Plates

1. Israelite ship on a seal, eighth century BCE.
2. A Spanish, possibly Jewish, weaver's tombstone, Roman era.
3. Hebrew, Latin and Greek inscriptions on a Spanish sarcophagus, fifth–sixth century.
4. Spanish Jewish weavers at work, Bezalel and Aholiab, fifteenth century.
5. *Parokhet* hanging before the Ark, detail from the mosaic floor of the Beth Shean Synagogue, sixth century.
6. Stars of David decorating the Passover table, the Barcelona Haggadah, fourteenth century.
7. Jewish weavers in Hellenist Alexandria.
8. Jewish Egyptian weave with Star of David and menorah, eighth–ninth century.
9. The Jewish Quarter, Murcia, 1481.
10. Copy of a Sephardi carpet, early seventeenth century.
11. The Vizcaya carpet.
12. Star-studded carpet in a fresco by Matteo di Giovanetti da Viterbo (c.1300–68) in the Palace of the Popes, Avignon.
13. The Spanish synagogue carpet (thirteenth–fourteenth century) as originally presented.
14. The Spanish synagogue carpet (thirteenth–fourteenth century) as restored, post-Second World War.
15. Synagogue carpet (thirteenth–fourteenth century) as published in 1923.
16. Stars of David on the Ark, fourteenth–fifteenth century.
17. Geese or ducks guarding the Ark. Detail from the mosaic floor of the Beth Alpha Synagogue, sixth century.
18. Draped hanging before the Ark. Detail from the mosaic floor of the Beth Hammath Synagogue, fourth century.
19. Ark form in an Egyptian Hebrew Bible, tenth century.
20. Star of David on a tallit, identifying the designer or possibly the player, in the 'Book of Games', Castile, thirteenth century.
21. Map of Granada and Murcia, sixteenth century.

22. Dragged down to Hell, French School, fifteenth century.
23. In Hell, from *De Civitate Dei* by St Augustine, French School, fifteenth century.
24. St Dominic presiding over the Burning of Heretics, Pedro Berruguete (c.1450–1504).
25. A *converso* Hannukiah, Spain, fifteenth century.
26. The Menorah on the Triumphal Arch of the Emperor Titus, first century.
27. The Star and the Hand on a Spanish salt dish, fourteenth–fifteenth century.
28. The private chapel in Buckingham Palace.
29. Star of David, the Capernaum Synagogue, third–fourth century.
30. Two Stars of David, the menorah and the Eternal Light in a child's workbook, tenth century.
31. Stars of David and the menorah, on the Vizcaya carpet.
32. Star of David in an eleventh-century Bible.
33. Star of David in a fifteenth-century Bible from Yemen.
34. Star of David in a signature, Spain, thirteenth century.
35. Star of David in a signature, Barcelona, Middle Ages.
36. Star of David in a Bible, thirteenth–fourteenth century.
37. Star of David in the Golden Haggadah, 1320.
38. Stars of David identifying a Jew's room, thirteenth century.
39. Star of David protecting a rabbit, in a Haggadah, fourteenth century.
40. Stars of David on four seals, thirteenth–fourteenth century.
41. Star of David on a signet ring, early medieval.
42. Star of David in a synagogue window, thirteenth century.
43. Star of David on the flag in the Prague Synagogue, copy of the fifteenth-century flag.
44. Star of David on a mezuzah, fifteenth–sixteenth century.
45. Two triangles in a Hebrew script, Spain, fourteenth century.
46. Stars of David in a book of medieval Jewish magic.
47. Star of David in a book of medieval Jewish magic.
48. Stars of David on the teacher's chair, Maimonides, *Guide to the Perplexed*, fourteenth century.
49. Hexagram in the Qur'an, twelfth century.
50. Four Stars of David.
51. Sephirotic tree.
52. Menorot–*Hamsa* on the Vizcaya carpet.
53. The Hand of God in a Haggadah, Germany, thirteenth century.

Plates

54. The Hand of God, a ram and sheep in a Haggadah, Spain, fourteenth century.
55. The Hand of God delivering the Tablets of the Law to Moses, in a prayer book, Germany, fifteenth century.
56. A praying figure on the Vizcaya carpet.
57. Kabbalist Hands.
58. Section of a pomegranate? The Vizcaya carpet.
59. Two peacocks on the Vizcaya carpet.
60. Peacocks, menorah and Temple façade on a magic mirror plaque, Byzantine period.
61. A dove on the Vizcaya carpet.
62. A rooster in a medieval Haggadah.
63. Roosters on the Vizcaya carpet.
64. A goose or duck, the Vizcaya carpet.
65. Demon birds on the Vizcaya carpet.
66. Kabbalist demon birds.
67. Demon bird and the Hand, Kabbalist images.
68. Sheep on the Vizcaya carpet.
69. More sheep on the Vizcaya carpet.
70. Triangular roof forms on the Vizcaya carpet.
71. Ark and menorah on a Roman tomb, second–third century.
72. Menorot, Ark, temple instruments and lions in a gold glass base, fourth century.
73. Sephardi carpet, fifteenth–sixteenth century.

PICTURE CREDITS

Permission has been granted for the reproduction of the illustrations, as listed below. Every effort has been made to contact the copyright holders, but if any new information comes to light following the publication of this book, credit will be given in any future reprints.

Archivo de la Corona de Aragon, 35
Beth Hatefutsoth, photo archive, Tel Aviv, 7
Bodleian Library, 39
Biblioteca Palatina, S.U. Concessione del Ministero per i Beni Culturali e Ambientali, 54

Bibliotheque Inguimbertine archiveo et Musees de Carpentras, 41
Boralevi, Alberto, 73
Bridgeman Art Library, 22, 23, 24
British Library, 4, 6, 33, 37, 54, 55, 62
Cambridge University Library, 30
Carta, Courtesy of Carta, 34
Collection Israel Museum, Jerusalem. Photo Israel Museum by David Harris, 72
Editions Gaud, 12
Einhorn, Yitzhak, 25
HarperCollins, 40
Institute of Archaeology of the Hebrew University (10.2472), 60
Israel Museum, 5
Jewish Museum, London, Courtesy of, 44
Jewish Museum/Art Resource, New York, 10. 73
Jewish Museum, Prague, 16, 42, 43
Jewish National and University Library, Jerusalem, 49, 66, 67
Keats, Victor, 20
Library of the Jewish Theological Seminary, USA, 46
Minesterio de Cultura, Madrid, 27
National Library, St Petersburg, 19, 32
Patrimonio National, 38
Royal Library, Denmark, 48
Sonia Halliday Photographs, 18
Staatliche Museen zu Berlin – Preubischer Kulturbesitz, Museum fur Kunst. Photo Dietrich Graf, 13, 14
Universidad de Murcia, Spain, 9
Vizcaya Museum and Gardens, Florida, 11, 31, 52, 56, 58, 59, 61, 63, 64, 68, 69, 70

Acknowledgements

It is to the late John Klier, Professor at the Department of Hebrew and Jewish Studies at University College, London, that I am most indebted, for his response to an early outline was that the book would be an important and an original contribution to Jewish Studies. Then, when Walter Denny, Professor of Art History and adjunct Professor of Middle Eastern Studies at the University of Massachusetts, and the towering figure in carpet studies today, was equally encouraging, I felt empowered to proceed.

Nor can I adequately thank Rabbi Professor Marc Saperstein, Professor David Jacobson, Michael Franses and Dr John Mills who, so generously reading an early draft, made numerous corrections and suggestions – all of which (with one exception) have been incorporated in the text. My thanks to Lenard Harrow, guide, philosopher and friend; Joanna Lawson, my erudite and assiduous editor and Heather Marchant, my brave and patient publisher. It is also to the authors, the editors and illustrators of the five hundred or so books I have poured over these past few years to whom I am deeply indebted – and to whom I apologize when I have failed fully to understand or to give due credit. Whilst I have made every effort to track all copyrights, in cases where I have not been successful would any such owners please contact me.

Finally to Francis Bacon (1561–1624), to whom I am indebted for his advice, 'Read not to contradict and refute, nor to believe and take for granted, nor to find talk and discourse, but to weigh and consider'.

INTRODUCTION

Does It Really Matter?

Does it really matter whether a fifteenth-century Spanish carpet was commissioned or created by Jews or by Christians or by Muslims?

I think it does. Memory does matter. Without it, what is there to restrain the powerful, to comfort the weak, to make the young think twice and the old to think generously? Human achievement relies on memory, and the study of textiles, albeit somewhat neglected, but holding its store of many memories, offers us a unique perspective on the history, culture and development of society.

Seeing a carpet as a cultural chronicle with its own social logic, studying it within the context of its own times, recalling those memories and asking how and why it was woven, for whom and when and where, we enter into another world and gain insights and understandings that otherwise we might not have. Key historical milestones and important cultural shifts are there to be seen – if you look. The carpets of a culture, be it Islamic, Christian, Chinese, Indian or Jewish, in demonstrating the essence of that culture, in explaining its uniqueness and in connecting us to our pasts, may, in illuminating our present, cast light upon our future.

What astonishes me is that the substantial contribution of the Jews to textiles, a vouchsafing taking us far further afield in place and far further back in time than does the weaving of almost any other culture, has been allowed to be forgotten. Textiles, no less than language or architecture, help define and illuminate a culture, but little enough information about Jewish weavings, especially of carpets, is to be found in the otherwise voluminous literature of either Jewish or textile studies. I think this is mainly because, in Judaism, carpets – not being ritual artefacts – do not attract the attention they would otherwise merit as cultural objects. And as to carpet studies, it matters not if an Islamic carpet – in a geographical or cultural sense – is woven by a Muslim, a Christian, a Zoroastrian or a Jew, for it is the design, the style, the motifs, the patterns, the overall cultural manifestation of the carpet that determines its type. In this work I am looking at a society through the prism of one of its few surviving carpets, so combining social studies with carpet studies. For if we neglect the memories of those who designed, wove and commissioned what must be tens of thousands of Jewish carpets, and if their where, their when and their why is to be lost, surely we have failed in our respect for the truth.

Years ago I was much taken with an article written by Ita Aber, an international textile expert.[1] She asked whether any of a group of about a dozen extraordinary and brilliant carpets woven in fifteenth-century Spain and today scattered among the great museums and private collections of the world might not be Judaic. These carpets are all called 'Admiral' or 'Armorial' because some of them display the coats of arms of don Alfonso Enriquez (1354–1429), of his son, don Fadrique Enriquez (1390–1473) – both holders of the ancient office of Admiral of the Kingdom of Castile and of the Order of Banda – in addition to the escutcheon of don Fadrique's first wife, Marina de Ayala (d. 1431). Others bear the coats of arms of Alfonso's daughter Maria and her husband Juan de Rojas (d. 1454), and of Maria of Castile, Queen of Aragon (d. 1458). Ten years passed by before I could try to answer Ita Aber's question by asking myself the following questions:

1. What were the religious, social, economic and political circumstances of the nobles who commissioned these carpets?
2. What were the religious, social, economic and political circumstances of the weavers who wove them?
3. What different meanings might be attributed by Jews, Christians and Muslims to the symbols on these carpets?

It was not going to be enough to ferret out the facts – for they by themselves are inert; only the meanings behind them would explain what happened. As Americo Castro, the great Spanish historian of the period, put it, 'A fact is like a sack. It won't stand up if empty. For it to stand up it must be filled with the reasons and the feelings which caused it to exist.'[2] To understand a culture, one best be of that culture, or near to it, for only then will one intuitively recognize its unique convolutions, its strengths and its weaknesses. Finally, having answered (so far as possible) the above three questions, I then would have to study the convergences of those answers, each to the other.

One of the Admiral carpets is in the Vizcaya Museum in Miami, Florida. It intrigued me; there were no hidden Hebrew letters to be discovered in this beautiful and typical Hispanic–Moresque carpet, but some of the symbols were familiar to me, for I had seen them often enough in Jewish Bibles of the period. I wondered if I had not seen some of those Islamic symbols in the famous Spanish synagogue carpet housed in the Islamic Museum in Berlin. I returned to London worrying about the migration of symbols and of their altered meanings in different cultures.

Detective stories demand both motive and evidence. So my next step was to investigate the Enriquez family in the fourteenth and fifteenth centuries. Most historians agreed they were *conversos* – that is, Jews who in an increasingly hostile society had, in public at least, converted to Christianity. So far, so good. But clearly not good enough. For all I knew, the Enriquez's stance as Christians was totally authentic. I could understand the historic reasons why Christian Spanish aristocrats might commission a grand carpet displaying Islamic symbols but were there, I wondered, historic reasons for those symbols to have different meanings for them. Further, given the pattern of many New Christians who, at least for a generation or two, continued, but now in total secrecy, to practice the faith of their fathers, and given the dire penalties payable were their apostasy to be discovered, the possibility of unearthing such secrets was remote indeed. The diversity of the views of the numerous authorities on the history of medieval Spain and on the history of medieval Jewry, allied to the paucity of information on the carpets of the time, made researching this work a complicated but ultimately rewarding task.

Many days were spent in the ever-helpful British Library and then in the Murcia and Albacete regions of Spain learning something of the life and times of the Enriquez, the weavers, the Jews and *conversos*, and of their relationships with the dominant cultures. As with much discovery, gathering together a large number of small bits of information creates patterns and pictures and probabilities – the peripheral falls away as the essential emerges. Dates, of course, are as critical in conveying the progression of events, as is the technical data about the wool, the loom, the dyes and the knots, but at least as important are the beliefs, thoughts and the feelings, the zeitgeist, that lead to those events, for disregarding the basis on which people act and interact is to rob oneself of a framework of understanding.

I have had to look closely at a very wide range of background material, criss-crossing in time and space and then weaving the separate threads together into one coherent whole. Studying and selecting the poetry, the prose, the pictures and the personal and public accounts of the time took me closer to the lives of the Jews and *conversos*. For it was only through analyzing and resolving the histories and dispositions of the Enriquez, of the Jewish weavers, of the symbols and of the circumstances that converged in fifteenth-century Spain to create the Vizcaya carpet, that Ita Aber's question might be answered.

In responding to that question I viewed the Vizcaya carpet as if it were a lens through which, by looking at the world that created it, I saw it again – but this time more richly and clearly than before, for seeing it in its context, it was as if I was seeing it for the first time. It is, for me, this concern that counts, for, as a cultural chronicle, the Vizcaya carpet recaptures something of the memory of how the mighty and the humble lived, giving purpose and meaning to their lives amid the darkening realities of those times, times both alien and yet familiar to us, too, as the tolerance of each of the three great Abrahamic religions is being tested today, just as it had been in fifteenth-century Spain.

Anton Felton, 2012

NOTES

1. Ita Aber, 'Are the Spanish Carpets Jewish?' *Jewish Art*, 18 (1992), pp.87–99. See also Roderick Taylor, 'Spanish Rugs at Vizcaya', *Hali*, 52 (August 1990), pp.101–10.
2. Americo Castro, *The Structure of Spanish History*, trans. Edmund King (Princeton, NJ: Princeton University Press, 1954), p.vii.

PART 1

BACKGROUND HISTORIES

Weaving in Spain and Murcia

Weavers and carpet makers have been at work in southern Spain for at least the last 5,000 years.¹ Since the late Neolithic Age, esparto weaving has been a major industry. The region is good sheep country with excellent alum (the mordant needed to fix the dye into the wool), and varied flora and fauna (including the saffron flower for a rich yellow dye, and the expensive Kermes beetle and the more commonly used madder root for various reds), as well as the adjacent markets in North Africa providing the other dyes and chemistry for the subtlest of colours. Two thousand years ago, as a province of the Roman Empire, Spain was renowned for the superior quality of its wools (particularly in natural black and reddish colours) and for its linens and skilful weavers.

By the eighth century, Islam had conquered most of the Iberian Peninsula, usually ridding it of its chaotic and barbaric Visigoth rulers. Murcia, underpopulated and unimportant, was an exception to this, its Muslim conqueror, 'Abd al-'Aziz, making a pact with Count Theodemer permitting him to remain in power in return for a substantial annual payment. Oleg Grabar, the eminent authority on Islamic art, affirms that 'The craftsmen of Arabia itself were generally non-Arab, mostly Jews, and the practice of crafts was not honoured',² and that what usually happened was that Muslim conquerors would take up the art, craft and the craftsmen of the peoples they conquered. There seem to be very few original words in Arabic referring to artisan or artistic work. Under the Umayyads (755–976) extensive irrigation systems were constructed, sericulture introduced, the quality and quantity of the sheep improved, and weavers moved from Baghdad to set up more workshops, all massively to increase the production of carpets in Spain.³ The wool, silk, cotton, flax and allied industries and general economy flourished, for commerce was basic to Islam. Muhammad himself had been a merchant and in Islamic (but not Jewish) tradition, Ishmael, oldest son of Abraham and the founding father of Islam, was also a textile merchant. The ancient tradition of textiles in Spain prior to its conquest by Islam probably led to its rug industry being one of the earliest in the Muslim world and possibly quite independent of the development of carpet production in Persia and Asia Minor. The emirate of Murcia, right from the beginning, was the major centre of Islamic rug manufacture and, by the tenth century, Almeria, the coastal town just to the south of Murcia, had become the most important Spanish port, shipping Spanish textiles and fine goods to North Africa and the East.[4] It is probably here in the eleventh and early twelfth centuries that the exquisite Almoravid silk lampas textiles were woven with such fine details that they were more like painted miniatures than textiles.

Probably the earliest mention of Spanish weavings in the Islamic period is in a tenth-century work, *The Chronicle of Rassis, the Moor*; the next reference is in an eleventh-century Latin poem. Often enough we do not know the exact nature of the fabric or the use to which it was put, but fragments of these early Spanish textiles, dated to the twelfth century, have been recovered in Egypt,[5] possibly traded there through the Jewish merchants who were the major textile merchants in the Mediterranean.[6] There is, however, no doubt that these weavings were being made in Spain well before the tenth century.

In the Middle Ages textiles and agriculture were the major industries of the Mediterranean area and involved the great majority of the working population. Functionally essential, textiles were part of a family's wealth, often consisting of many types of carpet.[7] And in feudal Europe, albeit a rigid hierarchical world dominated by soldiers who held sway over your body, and by churchmen who wielded authority over your mind, the weavers' importance was evidenced by their power. Their first recorded strike took place in Douai in Flanders in 1245 and they went on strike again in the 1320s. In 1379 the weavers of Ghent and Bruges rose against their feudal lord. In 1345 ten woolworkers were put to death for agitating for the right to organize; the church declared that spinners wasting wool would be excommunicated. In 1378 the wool carders of Florence rioted and actually held the city for some months.[8]

Sheep farming, requiring less labour and being less reliant on good weather, was far more profitable than agriculture. Spain's central plateau provided excellent grazing for numerous flocks of sheep. So great was the profit to be made from sheep's wool, hide and meat that in the late thirteenth century the king of Castile and his nobles granted themselves a monopoly, known as *La Mesta Real* (the Royal Guild), which controlled the movement of sheep in the winter down from the northern midlands to the warmer south. The shepherds would drive their flocks as many as 500 miles along the *Cañadas*, broad strictly regulated tracks to the provinces of Murcia (where the Vizcaya carpet was woven) and to other depots in Castile and Valencia. There the sheep would graze on land that had been harvested, enrich the soil with their dung and then, before the sowing of the spring crops, be shepherded back north. Over the twelfth to the fifteenth centuries a superior breed was introduced and cross-bred with the natural Spanish sheep. Called the Merino, probably after the Marinids who ruled Morocco and the Atlas, it became known for its luxurious wool and robust qualities. Soon the wool of Spain was of such high quality that it was sometimes exported even to sheep-rearing, wool-exporting England[9] as well as to the major manufacturers in Italy and the Low Countries (Holland). Its price, too, improved as much as its quality – for the repeated debasing of the Castilian currency through the fifteenth century, and the heavy export taxes imposed by the English government on its wool exports, gave Castile an increasing share in the international wool market and a healthy balance of payment surplus.

The new horizontal loom and silk thread had appeared in Spain and southern France as early as the ninth century, two or three centuries before they were used on any scale in the rest of Europe. These two advances rapidly enhanced the quality and the output of Spain's weaving industry.[10] This loom had been in use in China ever since the first century and was probably brought to Europe by the Radhanites. They were Spanish (or possibly Provençal) Jewish merchants who, in the ninth century, in a journey lasting a year or two, would travel to China, trade there and return home. Rashi (Rabbi Solomon ben Itshaki) (c.1040–1105), the great Jewish scholar who lived in Troyes, France (and a renowned weaver himself), described the horizontal loom as one by which men weave with their feet.[11] Worked by foot treadles, it greatly speeded up the production of linens and facilitated new inventions for carding and spinning sheep's wool, goats' hair and flax.[12] The Vizcaya carpet, however, was most probably woven on the classical vertical loom used for making rugs, tent fabric, sacks and coarse clothes; it was sometimes known as *naul shacr*, the 'goats' hair loom', that probably being the main material employed. It was in use by the Sephardi weavers in and around Safed in Israel until recently.

Carpets, the supreme artefact of Islam, occupied generation after generation of gifted Muslim, Jewish and Christian craftsmen working to satisfy a critically important cultural and commercial need. Carpets were valued and valuable statements of power. So, for example, the list of gifts given to the caliph by one of his viziers in 929 includes no fewer than 100 prayer rugs.[13] Usually made of wool, occasionally of silk, carpets were placed on the floors of mosques, before the altar in churches, and by the Ark and on the walls of synagogues. Outside of a religious context, they were laid on or next to beds, on tables, desks and chairs and draped over windows, balustrades and balconies, and on cupboards, chests and window seats.[14] The variety of uses for the same textile seemed limitless.

Under Islam, the economy of Spain in general – and the textile industry in particular – boomed. The tenth-century chronicler Ibn Hauqal writes about the export of Spanish weavings to Egypt, Persia and many other countries[15] and a surviving ship's manifest of goods shipped from Spain to Egypt in the twelfth century includes ten carpets.[16] Spanish carpets are described in English inventories of the fourteenth century and we have a record of one Spanish carpet trader, Antonio Ferandez, who exported three particularly grand carpets, valued at £6.13.4 (then an enormous sum of money), to England. Landing at Southampton in 1428, they must have sold well, for the following year Ferandez brought more weavings to England.[17]

But what do we know of the carpets of Murcia under Islam? As noted, from Islamic times and at least as early as the tenth century, carpets were being woven there,[18] and by the twelfth century the numerous accounts of its carpet weaving industry were extremely complimentary. The geographer Muhammad ibn Muhammad al-Idrisi, writing in the first half of the twelfth century about the carpets of Chincilla, one of the towns in Murcia, attributes their fine qualities to the region's exceptional air and water.[19] He notes too that many of these rugs were exported to Egypt. We get a sense of the level of production from his report that in Almeria alone there were 800 silk weaving looms.[20] In the next century al-Himyari reports: 'They used to make fine and valuable carpets in Murcia. The people of Murcia have unequalled skill in manufacturing and decorating carpets.'[21] His comments are echoed by yet another chronicler, 'Ali ibn Musa ibn Sa'id (1214–86), who remarks on the high prices obtained in the east for the carpets of Murcia.[22] Ibn al-Walid Isma'il ibn Muhammad al-Shakundi (d.1231 or 1232) again confirms that the carpets of Tantalya in Murcia must have been particularly fine, for they were 'exported to all the countries of the East and the West'.[23] Writing about Alsh, a town in Murcia, another Muslim writer eulogizes: 'Splendid carpets which have no parallel in the world for beauty are manufactured there.'[24] They were also valued in Spain, for we know the Bishop of Cuenca (a major centre of carpet production) bought some Murcian carpets in 1273. Later, the inventory of the estate of the great collector Jean Duc de Berri of France included thirteen carpets from Murcia, two of them displaying the six-pointed star.

In London in 1255, when 16-year-old Prince Edward, heir to the throne of England, celebrating his marriage the previous year in Spain to Eleanor, Princess of Castile, brought many of the sumptuous Spanish textiles included in her dowry to London, they were displayed in her apartment and in the streets.[25]

In 1260s, as the Christian knights and their ragtag armies of mercenaries, outcasts, adventurers, fanatics and killers all advanced deep into Murcia, its Muslim population was promised that if they surrendered without a fight they would keep their land and their homes, their lives and their freedoms. However, in view of the usual rewards given to, or just taken by, the mercenaries – rape, pillage and murder – most Muslims who could fled south to the security of Muslim-held Granada. Skilled weavers were especially welcomed there[26] and the Muslim weavers of Murcia migrated en masse.[27]

How wise they were! For once in power, the Christian armies so oppressed those Muslims – who, relying on the knights' promises, had remained – that a series of armed rebellions soon erupted, threatening King Alfonso's still fragile hold on Murcia. King James I of Aragon came to his aid and in the revolt of 1264, in village after village, the remaining Muslims who were not slaughtered were expelled, until but a few Muslim communities of any importance remained.[28] And the fines, the floggings and the confiscations continued. Ten years later, another great Muslim revolt, supported by promises of help from Africa, erupted. But the aid never arrived, the revolt was suppressed and the reprisals against the Muslims exceeded anything that they had previously experienced. Granada was once more overwhelmed by the Muslim refugees from Castile, to the extent that the population density in Granada exceeded five persons per square kilometre – an extraordinary figure for medieval Spain.[29]

Skilled carpet designers and weavers were honoured in Judaism and Islam – we know of a Muslim weaver in the eleventh century who became the chief advisor to Muhammad III and Hisham III[30] – but the attitude of the Christian knights was quite different. Unlike the Jews, who revered creative labour (for had not the Almighty Himself laboured to create the world?), while coveting the craft they despised the craftsman. So they claimed the weavings of their Jewish and their remaining Muslim subjects as payment towards the new taxes they imposed on all the textiles and carpets manufactured in their domains.

It is extraordinary really. Through much of the Middle Ages, Castile was racked by frontier and internal wars, ransacked by rapacious mercenaries, ruined by crippling inflation and financial anarchy, ravaged by recurrent plagues and racial and religious and power conflicts – yet, despite all, it thrived. Records of catastrophic times can sometimes make it seem as if disasters were constant and overwhelming, but often, awful as they were, they were limited in both time and space. By 1480 the total stock of sheep had grown to the staggering figure of some five million. The production of carpets in Spain, and particularly in Murcia, continued to expand, and by the fifteenth century it seems to have overtaken that of any other place in the Mediterranean.[31]

Let us now turn to place the Jews of Spain into this context. How did they get there? What were their roles and relationships in Muslim and then Christian host cultures? What were their numbers and significance?

NOTES

1. Mary Schoeser, *World Textiles: A Concise History* (London: Thames & Hudson, 2003), p.43.
2. Oleg Grabar, *The Formation of Islamic Art* (Newhaven, CT and London: Yale University Press, 1987), p.77.
3. A. Morena (ed.), *La España Gotica* (Madrid: Ediciones Encuentro, 1997), Vol. 12, pp.127–220. When 'Abd al-Rahman III (912–961) was due to receive a Christian emissary in his palace, some four miles distant from Cordoba, not only did he have a double column of his soldiers at the side of the road, but the road itself was overlaid with mats and weavings.
4. Bernard F. Reilly, *The Medieval Spains* (Cambridge: Cambridge University Press, 2001), p.66.
5. S. Sherrill, *Carpets and Rugs of Europe and America* (New York: Abbeville Press, 1996), p.30.
6. Florence Lewis May, *Silk Textiles of Spain* (New York: Hispanic Society of America, 1957), pp.4, 87.
7. S.D. Goitein, *A Mediterranean Society: An Abridgement in One Volume*, revised and edited by J. Lassner (London: University of California Press, 1999), p.233.
8. Norman Davis, *Europe* (London: Pimlico, 1997), p.413.
9. That was despite the trade war in much of the fifteenth century between Spain and England over wool. In 1436 the *Libelle of Englysshe Polycye* boasted that Spanish wools were no good for cloth making unless mixed with English wools, and in the 1440s the magistrates in one

town in the Low Countries required all drapers to 'swear an oath annually upon the holy cross to use none but English wools'. David Jenkins, *The Cambridge History of Western Textiles* (Cambridge: Cambridge University Press, 2003), p.289.
10. V. Mann, T. Glick and J. Dodds (eds), *'Convivencia', Jews, Muslims and Christians in Medieval Spain* (New York: George Braziller in conjunction with the Jewish Museum, 1992). Juan Zozaya, 'Material Cultures in Medieval Spain', in *'Convivencia'*, p.159, citing Manuel Returece, 'El templén: ¿Primer testimonio del telar horizontal en Europa?', *Boletín de Arqueología Medieval*, 1 (1987), pp.71–7.
11. Jenkins, *Cambridge History of Western Textiles*, p.194. This is the first description we have of the new semi-mechanized horizontal loom. Horizontal looms had been used in China since at least the first century BCE. How they travelled to Europe is not known but by far the most significant merchants travelling between Europe and China were the Radhanites. Ibn Khurdadhbih (c.846), in his *Book of Routes*, records that having started out from Spain, 'on their return from China they carry musk, cloves, camphor, cinnamon and other products ... Some made sail for Constantinople to sell their goods to the Romans; others go to the palace of the king of the Franks [Charlemagne].' They also learned and brought back the process required to make paper. The first paper mill in the Middle East was opened in Baghdad by Jews in the eighth century and, as late as the twelfth century, Peter the Venerable (1092–1158), Abbot of Cluny, recorded 'his objection to paper as a Jewish production on which unbelievers copied the Talmud and other obnoxious literature'. Cecil Roth, *The Jewish Contribution to Civilization* (Cincinnati, OH: Union of American Hebrew Congregations, 1940; London: East and West Library, 1956), p.50. Regarding Rashi as a weaver, see *Encyclopaedia Judaica* (Jerusalem: Keter Publishing, 1971), Vol. 13, p.1558.
12. Jenkins, *Cambridge History of Western Textiles*, p.194.
13. Richard Fletcher, *Moorish Spain* (London: Phoenix, 2004), pp.68–9.
14. Jenkins, *Cambridge History of Western Textiles*, p.365.
15. Eliyahu Ashtor, *The Jews of Moslem Spain*, Vol. 1 (Jerusalem: Jewish Publication Society, 1973), p.272, citing Ibn Haukal, 'Surát al-Ard', *BGA* (Leiden), l (1938–39), pp.110, 114. See also R.B. Serjeant, *Islamic Textiles: Material for a History up to the Mongol Conquest* (Beirut: Librarie du Liban, 1972), p.175, citing Makkari.
16. S.D. Goitein, *A Mediterranean Society* (London: University of California Press, 1999), Vol. 1, p.210.
17. Robert Pinner's Introduction, in Robert Pinner and Walter Denny (eds), *Oriental Carpet & Textile Studies, 2: Carpets of the Mediterranean Countries 1400–1600* (London: Hali Publications, 1986), p.8, citing W.R. Child, *Anglo-Castilian Trade in the Later Middle Ages* (Manchester; Totowa, NJ: Manchester University Press; Rowan and Littlefield, 1978), p.140.
18. *Chronicle of Rassis the Moor*, cited by W.G. Thompson, 'Hispano-Moresque Carpets', *Burlington Magazine*, 18 November 1910, p.100; E. Kühnel and L. Bellinger, *Catalogue of Spanish Rugs, 12th Century to 19th Century* (Washington, DC: The Textile Museum, 1953), pp.2, 7; see also Plate 3 for another fragment of a carpet woven in Murcia in the thirteenth or fourteenth entury.
19. Sherrill, *Carpets and Rugs of Europe and America*, pp.239–40, citing Muhammad ibn Muhammad al-Idrisi, *Description de l'Afrique et de l'Espagne*, trans. R. Dozy and M.J. de Goeje (Leiden, 1866), text p.195, trans. p.237. Al-Idrisi was probably born in Ceuta and studied in Cordoba.

20. Arthur Dilley, *Oriental Rugs and Carpets*, revised by M.S. Dimand (Philadelphia, PA: Lippincott & Co., 1959), pp.231, 232; M. Dimand and J. Mailey, *Oriental Rugs in the Metropolitan Museum of Art* (New York: Metropolitan Museum of Art, 1973), p.252.
21. Serjeant, *Islamic Textiles*, citing Ibn 'Abd al-Munin al-Himyari, *Kitab al-Rawd al-Mitar La Peninsule Iberique au Moyen-Age*, edited and translated by E. Levi-Provencal (Leyden, 1938), text p.184, trans. p.222.
22. Abi ibn Musa ibn Sa'id (1214–86). Quoted by Ahmad ibn Muhammad al-Makkari (d. 1632), *Analects sur l'histoire et la literature des Arabs en Espagne*, edited by R. Dozy and M.J. de Goeje, Vol. 50 (Leiden, 1855–61), p.123; Serjeant, *Islamic Textiles*, Chapter 17, p.38.
23. Sherrill, *Carpets and Rugs of Europe and America*, p.30.
24. Serjeant, *Islamic Textiles*, p.175, citing Yaqut, *Mu'jam al-Buldan: Geographisches Wörterbuch*, edited by F. Wüstenfeld (Leipzig, 1866–73), 4, 517 (2, 961).
25. Kühnel and Bellinger, *Catalogue of Spanish Rugs*, p.1.
26. May, *Silk Textiles of Spain*, p.134.
27. Thomas F. Glick, *Islamic and Christian Spain in the Early Middle Ages* (Princeton, NJ: Princeton University Press, 1979), p.223.
28. A. MacKay, *Spain in the Middle Ages* (Basingstoke: Macmillan, 1977), p.68.
29. Reilly, *Medieval Spains*, p.190.
30. May, *Silk Textiles of Spain*, p.9.
31. Murray Eiland III, *Starting to Collect Antique Oriental Rugs* (Woodbridge: Antique Collectors Club, 2003), p.168.

The Jews of Spain

Tradition has it that Tartessus, an ancient Phoenician seaport on the Mediterranean coast of Spain, was the biblical Tarshish towards which Jonah fled in his struggle to escape the command of the Almighty. Another tradition and some Bibles[1] hold that King Solomon's ships (Figure 1) crossing the Mediterranean and anchoring off Tarshish, traded for silver,[2] iron, lead and tin,[3] the metals needed to build the Temple in Jerusalem; tin was also wanted as a mordant to fix dyes into thread. Some of Solomon's mariners and traders may well have settled in Tartessus and possibly in Sagunto in Valencia, for there is an engaging legend about a tombstone found there with the Hebrew inscription 'Adoniram, treasurer of King Solomon, who came to collect the tax tribute and died'. Murcia is located beside and below Valencia; its seaport of Cartagena was established late in the third century BCE by the Carthaginians – descendants of the Canaanites and Phoenicians, and biblical neighbours and allies of Israel.[4]

We know there were substantial Jewish settlements in North African Carthage and in all probability there were similar settlements in Carthaginian Spain, for textile weaving and dyeing was a major Carthaginian industry. The murex sea snail – crushed, each one provides a single drop of the dye for Phoenician red or Tyrian purple – was fished to extinction off the Atlantic coast of Spain by the Phoenicians. Homer, writing perhaps in the eighth century BCE, remarks on the colourful Carthaginian weaves, and Hermippos, in the fourth to third century BCE, notes that a significant level of Carthage's business was exporting (and so presumably manufacturing) cushions.[5]

In the Middle Ages it was commonly held by both Christian and Jewish scholars that Jews had settled in Toledo after the destruction by Nebuchadnezzar of the First Temple in 586 BCE. One thousand years later the Jews of Toledo, now charged as Christ-killers, sought in vain to understand how they could possibly have any responsibility for the crucifixion – for their ancestors had left Palestine and settled in Toledo 600 years prior to the crucifixion. The Bible itself refers to 'The Exiles of Jerusalem who are in Sepharad',[6] where the word 'Sepharad' is thought by some (probably incorrectly) to refer to Spain. To this day, the Spanish Jews and their descendants are known as Sephardim.

There is, however, no firm archaeological evidence of any significant Jewish settlement in Spain until Rome, in its wars with Carthage, conquered and colonized much of the Iberian Peninsula in 200 BCE. In the first century CE St Paul, in his letter to the Romans, writes that he intends to take the gospels to Spain and, according to Clement (c.95 CE), he did. Spanish tradition tells us St James the Greater was warmly welcomed there and that the apostles and evangelists would usually go first to the synagogues to preach and gain many converts. This points to the existence of substantial Jewish communities in Spain, but the first solid evidence of the presence of Jews in Spain is provided by their tombstones (those links between the living and the dead), the earliest dating from the third century CE. For hundreds of years the Jews, Muslims and Christians of Spain coexisted in a rich and complex society – sometimes fruitfully, sometimes less so, until the expulsion of the Jews in 1492 and of the Muslims shortly thereafter.

In 63 BCE the Roman general Pompey the Great conquered Judea and incorporated it into the Roman Empire. Many Jews, resisting foreign domination, fought wars of independence in the Land of Israel in 66–72 CE and again in 132–5 CE as well as in other parts of the Roman Empire. All of these revolts were put down with utmost ferocity. Many exiles and refugees, including captives sold into slavery, settled in Spain and other parts of the empire and there is little doubt that they were employed in or set up textile workshops, for weaving and dyeing had been second only to agriculture in the skills and economy of the Jews. This movement of highly skilled weavers from Judea to Spain is highlighted in a letter written in 70 CE to the Roman general Titus, the son of and successor to the emperor Vespasian. Having finally put down the major revolt in Israel, Titus is busy exiling, enslaving or crucifying, when a letter arrives from the Roman governor of Spain begging that he send him Baruch Albali, a Jewish master weaver.[7] There was probably quite a demand for skilled weavers in Spain, certainly from the first century, with really sophisticated twenty-three-carat gold thread used in their fabrics. In Pompeii, a textile workshop preserved in the debris of the volcanic eruption of 79 CE reveals the names of the spinners and weavers, two of whom, Vebius Tamudianus and Maria, were probably

Jewish. They may well have been slaves who had been sold to the weaving master following the collapse of the revolt of 66–72 CE. In addition to at least one Hebrew inscription and references to the Hebrew Bible, a large pottery jar has been found, its painted label stating its contents to be kosher fish sauce – it was guaranteeing that favoured Roman delicacy contained no shellfish.

So much of what little we know of those times comes from secondary or tertiary evidence, but the two insurrections inside Israel have armed us with primary and material evidence of the sophistication of the Jewish weavers and dyers of the time. As the Roman legions advanced, mopping up all resistance and laying waste to the land, some surviving Jewish units fled south to the arid mountainous region at the edge of the Dead Sea. There, in 70 CE, nearly 1,000 of them made their last stand in King Herod's mountain-top fortress at Masada. Besieged by the Roman Tenth legion, they held out until 73 CE when, rather than surrender to Rome, all save a few committed suicide. Again, in the revolt of 132–5 CE, one of the last Jewish units sought refuge in a remote cave halfway up the face of a sheer mountain, also near the Dead Sea, now called the Cave of Letters. There they starved to death. Nearly 2,000 years later, archaeologists retrieved balls of wool and yarn and remnants of some textiles and rugs from both Masada and the Cave of Letters.[8] The fragments found at Masada included a sophisticated two-sided woollen rug with knotted cut pile in red, blue and yellow.[9]

Carthage had for centuries dominated the textile trade in the western Mediterranean[10] but in 146 BCE it was conquered by Rome. While no record of any Jewish settlement prior to 146 BCE has come down to us, some scholars maintain that the expansion of the Phoenicians from Tyre and Sidon would have owed something to the collaboration of the Hebrews from Palestine. Subsequent to 146 BCE, traces of rugs have been found, and from the major Jewish cemetery at Gamart and other sites in Carthage, numerous oil lamps, decorated with the menorah and the rosette, of the second to fifth centuries CE, have been excavated. The Punic rugs, according to the Roman historian Silius Italicus (late first century CE) in his epic poem *Punica*, were as famous and celebrated as those of Corinth and Syracuse.[11] We may conjecture that some refugees in 146 BCE fled to Spain, possibly to the Cartagena district. As happened later with the captives from the two failed revolts in Israel, those young men and women who were not crucified, and particularly those with valuable skills such as weaving, were sold into slavery and, like the Baruch Albali, dispersed over the Roman Empire, where their craft was in demand. Throughout much of the Roman world and beyond, Jews were renowned for the fine quality of their weavings.[12] Then, early in the fifth century, in the twilight of the Roman Empire, we hear St Jerome complaining in the most bitter terms at the extent of the productivity of its Jewish artisans and craftsmen.[13]

Time erodes and the host culture erases most traces of Jewish settlement but sometimes the odd tombstone survives to give witness to that experience. The earliest known Jewish tombstone in Roman Spain dates back to the third century.[14] It commemorates Annia Salomonula who was one year, four months and one day old when she died.[15] Engraved on another Spanish Roman tombstone is a picture of a weaver working on a warp-weighted vertical loom (Figure 2). A number of Roman tombstones of the third century CE have been found with epitaphs to Jewish women weavers with images of spindles and distaffs but this tomb has that – and more. Above Atta Altica's name is an intriguing six-pointed rosette – held by Erwin Goodenough, the pioneering authority on Greco-Roman symbols, to be the antecedent of the Star of David. Other authorities note that rosette and the spiral patterns were not that common in Roman art so it is not impossible that this third-century tombstone may be that of a Spanish Jewish weaver.

In the next century, in 313 CE to be precise, the Emperor Constantine made his momentous decision to change from being a persecutor to becoming a protector of the Christians. Two years later he made it illegal for Jews to proselytize. Following the subsequent adoption of Christianity as the official religion of the Roman Empire, Constantine's successors passed laws that effectively turned the Jewish Romans into second-class citizens. Then, early in the fifth century, Germanic tribes conquered and colonized much of the Iberian Peninsula and by the end of that century the Visigoths, infamous for their sack of Rome in 410 CE, became the dominant group. They were converts to Arianism, a form of Christianity that did not believe Jesus to be co-eternal and consubstantial with the Father but to be His instrument for the salvation of the world. They restored Jewish religious freedom.

Another Jewish Iberian tombstone, this time from Tortosa and dated to the fifth or sixth century, has survived. Engraved on the stone are a five-branched menorah and a five-pointed star. The inscription in Hebrew, Latin and Greek tells us of Rabbi Jehudah and his wife, the lady Miriam, mourning the loss of Melissa, their daughter. In the same period, the same three languages appear on what was perhaps a stone sarcophagus for a child. It is from Palleros in Tarragona and carved alongside a menorah is a Tree of Life and two facing peacocks – ancient Jewish symbols which we shall see time and time again

(Figure 3). Carved into the corner, that timeless prayer in Hebrew reads: 'Peace in Israel, on us and on our children.'

The Arian Visigoths, under attack from the Church of Rome, persecuted the Catholics, many of whom, to save their lives, continued in public to worship according to the Arian rites while privately and secretly practising the creed of Rome. In a further foretaste of the future, marriage between Arians and Catholics was often forbidden. However, once the Visigoth King Reccared (586–601) converted to Catholicism, the roles were reversed as he turned on the Arians. Now it was their turn, for at least a generation or two, publicly to convert to Catholicism, while privately continuing to follow the Arian creed. As for the Jews, kings Reccared, Sisebut, Dagobert, Ervig and most of their various replacements successively banned Jews from any religious life, flogged them, embargoed their trade, enforced penal taxation, brought in mandatory conversion and finally expelled any who remained.[16] In 602 in the reign of Sisebut, some 90,000 Jews are thought to have become what in later ages were known as *conversos*.[17] Pope Gregory the Great (590–604), albeit implacably hostile to Judaism, condemned conversion under pressure on the wholly logical grounds that it could not possibly produce true believers. But the Visigoths ignored this condemnation – a decision to be followed by many of the successive rulers of Spain.

Early in the seventh century, in the depths of the Arabian Desert, Islam was born. With its clarion call of monotheism, justice and morality, it swept like a hurricane through Arabia, Persia and Egypt, conquering them all within 100 years of its birth. On what became known as the Barbary Coast, between Carthage and Tangiers, the Jews and the Berbers under their Jewish Queen Kahana resisted the onslaught for as long as they could. The Arab historian Ibn Nuwairi records that they fought like furies and only by the will of Allah did the Muslims triumph. Many of the defeated Jews and Berbers converted to Islam. Indeed, Tariq ibn Zaid, the commander of the small Berber army that from the rock of Gibraltar invaded Spain in 711 and so triggered off the Islamic conquest of much of the peninsula, was himself believed to be a descendant of *conversos*. The rock was named in his honour 'Jabal-al-Tariq', and the name stuck, being transcribed into 'Gibraltar'. There had been no openly Jewish communities left in Spain, for Egica, the last Visigoth king, in 693 forbade the Jews from following any trade, and having thus made sure they had no means of paying their taxes – increased them! He then banned them from his kingdom, and those who had not fled converted publicly to Christianity. Little wonder that they welcomed their new Muslim rulers as deliverers from oppression, and many who had sought sanctuary in North Africa returned home to Spain. Many Christians also welcomed their new rulers, some freely converting to Islam and others even faking an Arabic lineage.

By the ninth century the country was prospering, exporting its manufactured goods and importing its grain. Under Islamic Umayyad rule, Jewish life and culture in Spain flourished, giving rise to generations of gifted philosophers, poets, politicians and weavers,[18] and great international travellers, diplomats, courtiers and merchants too. In 797 Charlemagne the Great sent a diplomatic mission, including Isaac the Jew, to Harun al-Rashid, Caliph of Baghdad. Isaac alone survived the journey, returning to Charlemagne's court accompanied by an elephant. It would have been a long and dangerous journey, but was as nothing to those of some of the Jewish merchants of Spain who, as noted, quite regularly travelled as far as India and China.

Early in the twelfth century, liberal tolerance fell victim to the fervour of fanatical Islamic sects who, seizing power, outlawed all who did not submit to their fundamentalist beliefs. Many Jews migrated to the Christian-held parts of Spain; others, in an echo of what had happened to the Jews under Roman rule,[19] then under Visigoth rule, now, in an ominous portent of what was to happen to them yet again, saved their lives by outwardly embracing Islam but secretly continuing to hold fast to the faith of their fathers. The confusion and the pain of the Jewish condition is expressed in the poetry of the time. One of the greatest of the poets, Abraham ibn Ezra (c.1055 to after 1135) writes as a Jew in relation to Christianity:

> Lord, I have heard of your Unity's mystery
> Although I could not fathom it in my iniquity:
> I've longed for the One, besides which is none
> And despised all thought and talk of the Trinity.
> Bear with a broken heart's transgression;
> It longs for your mercy, though I still sin.
> Pardon my falseness, then send me word;
> As you have asked, I have forgiven.[20]

But the predicament of the Jew in an alien land did not go away and it was his own son, Isaac ibn Ezra, who, mainly for social conformity, converted to Islam. In one of his poems Isaac reveals the price he and others paid for conversions of convenience:

> But if I begin each prayer ...

> I do so with my lips alone, my heart responding
> 'You are a liar and your testimony is invalid'.

Later, Isaac converted back to Judaism, but until the day he died he lived with grief and pain for his irresponsible conversion.[21] In one of his last poems, he wrote:

> I have returned to the shadow of Your way
> I ask you, God, for Your forgiveness.

In the enigmatic history of Judaism, the famous lines of Judah Halevi, the twelfth-century Spanish poet and philosopher,[22] constitute one of the most lyrical statements of the Jewish dilemma:

> My heart is the East, and I am in the West
> As far in the West as West can be!
> How can I enjoy my food?
> What flavour can it have for me?
> How can I fulfil my vows
> And do the things I've sworn to do,
> While Zion is in Christian hands
> And I am trapped in Arab lands?
> Easily, I could leave behind
> This Spain and all its luxuries! –
> As easy to leave, as dear the sight
> Of the Temple's rubble would be to me.

From the middle of the thirteenth century and over the next 200 years, bit by bit the Christian knights conquered Moorish Spain. As was not uncommon in the conflict between the Crescent and the Cross, Jews sometimes fought on both sides. In one instance the opposing Christian and Muslim generals are said to have declared a truce on the Sabbath, for their Jewish soldiers would not fight on that day.[23] For some of the Jews of Spain, but by no means all, much of the thirteenth and early fourteenth centuries was a second golden age and, in relation to what was happening to Jews in the rest of Europe, it was indeed a happy time. Spain, especially Leon and Navarre, opened their doors to refugees following the expulsions of the Jews from England, France and Aquitaine in 1290, 1306, 1324 and 1394.[24] The Spanish Jews were literate, powerful and productive; some even owned castles and villages and exercised feudal rights.[25] In the 300 years to 1376, there was never a time when the ruler of Castile did not have a Jewish official holding one of the highest offices in his administration, and for the next 100-odd years, right up to their expulsion in 1492, Jews frequently held similar cabinet rank as royal favourites.

To gain context, to appreciate the extent of the Jewish population of Castile, the accounts of taxation paid by the Jews are revealing. The records of 1284 reported a Castilian Jewish population of some 850,000,[26] and the tax returns for 1294 showed that a significant proportion, some 22 per cent, of the total local revenue was provided by the Jews. In that year the Jewish community of Murcia petitioned Sancho IV, king of Castile, to renew certain privileges and exemptions which had originally been granted to them to persuade them to go and live there.

As for Murcia, it was not enough for the Christian knights to conquer it in the thirteenth century; the imperative was to colonize it – and quickly, too, for it was a frontier region abutting Islamic lands. Demographically overstretched and close to collapse, the kings of Aragon and Castile did everything to encourage Jews to settle there, typically by giving them generous tracts of real estate on condition that they lived there and cultivated the land. Other conditions often included the duty to provide military aid and materiel. But not only did the kings want the Jews in their new lands, they often wanted the Muslims out. A deed has come down to us, between the king of Castile and Abraham Albanna, a Jew of Tortosa: Abraham is granted a licence to transport Saracens out of Castile, paying the king two *besants* a head.

The kings saw Jewish communities as invaluable elements providing economic and administrative stability, so extending and enforcing their royal authority over their new territories. At a time when Jews in much of Europe and, under the Almohads, in Islamic lands were suffering exploitation, persecution and expulsion, Murcia offered them freedom to follow their religion and their trades and professions. For example, so important were the Jewish bankers of Murcia by the end of the thirteenth century that two brothers, Moses Juceff and Albolazar, were specifically granted the exact same rights and protection as were enjoyed by all Christians.

A further example of these inducements, which brought many Jews from southern France, northern Spain and North Africa to Murcia, were the major land grants made to Çag Alconqui – his name suggests he played some part in the reconquest of Murcia. He is described in the Land Grant document as *caballero mayor*, the title of one of the highest social rank, putting him – and other wealthy Jews settling in Murcia – on a par with Christian nobles.

At the end of the thirteenth century Murcia was part of the Kingdom of Aragon, and its king, Jaime II, urged Jews to settle there, even those with criminal records. Then, after Castile finally gained control of Murcia and tackled the question of what penalties should be payable by Jews for attacking Christians, Alfonso XI could not have spoken more clearly: 'it is our wish that Christians and Jews be equal in this point as in other matters'.[27]

This inclusiveness of Castilian society is clear from the inscriptions on the tombs of Ferdinand III (d. 1252), the great Castilian conqueror, and of his son Alfonso X, which were carved in Arabic, Latin, Castilian and Hebrew. Alfonso, known as the Wise, had both the Qur'an and the Talmud translated into Latin. For Jews, this inclusive society, this *Convivencia*, partly came about through those unique elements (mulled over in Chapter 8) which have enabled them to survive millennia of persecution.

Linguistic confusion was perhaps another contributing factor, as this was a society in which the rulers and the ruled were often unable to speak to each other. The Christian knights and their brutish mercenaries, moving down from the north, spoke a variety of European languages, but in the main many of their subject people still spoke Arabic. Few Christians and Muslims could actually read or write, very few Christians spoke any of the languages of the Islamic conquerors and even fewer Muslims spoke any of the European languages.

Into this breach stepped the literate and multilingual Jews as civil servants, doctors, translators, traders and diplomats,[28] many conversant in Arabic, Hebrew and Castillian or Aragonese. The Jews, through their devotion to the Bible and Talmud and known in Islam as the People of the Book, were also people who, in the main, could read a book. Their literacy enabled them to learn, to retain and to expand knowledge. Never before, despite anti-Jewish tensions and outrages, had there been such relative harmony between the Jews and their Christian host culture. This uneasy pluralistic society had blossomed into a brilliant age, again producing generations of philosophers, poets, politicians and an exponential explosion of culture and of knowledge in so many disciplines including astrology, armoury, cartography, medicine, metallurgy, mathematics, manufacturing, maritime activity, painting, silversmithing and the all-important textile industry that provided much of the economic base to pay for it all. We see this in the estimates that 35–60 per cent of the income of each Iberian kingdom was provided by the Jews,[29] and later that the Jews of Murcia paid the highest amount of tax of all the regions where we have the records of taxes they paid.[30] The significance of these two points cannot be overstated and we will return to them later. Taxation lies at the heart of government and it was the Jews, predominant in the civil service and taxing agencies, who provided not only much of the intermediate technology and the mercantile base to generate income, but also most of the machinery to tax it — revenue avidly needed by the kings to pay for their courts and their courtiers, their courtesans and their conflicts.

By the fourteenth century the Jews of Spain constituted a significant segment of the population of every major city and many minor ones, their ratio to the general population often being as high as one third.[31] The involvement and contribution of the Jewish artisans of Spain to its textile industry was considerable.[32] We get a further sense of the integration and spread of their widespread participation in the crafts of Spain by what they were later banned from doing. For example, in 1415, Pope Benedict XIII banned Jewish craftsman from making crucifixes and ritual goblets, and in 1480 they were forbidden to paint images of Jesus and Mary.

To see the Vizcaya carpet as it would have been seen by the Jews of medieval Spain, we need to know the significance of carpets in Jewish culture — which leads us to the next section. After that, we will look at the synergy of the Jewish weavers of Spain and North Africa around the time the Vizcaya carpet was woven.

NOTES

1. R. Patai, *The Children of Noah* (Princeton, NJ: Princeton University Press, 1998), p.18. Another Jewish tradition has it that Nebuchadnezzar, having conquered Jerusalem in 597 BCE, sent many Israelites as slaves to Spain, which was then governed by Hispanus who gave his name to Spain. This legend conflates with a non-Jewish tradition that Hispanus, who was one of Hercules's men, had, following the Trojan war, gone on to conquer Spain.
2. Jeremiah 10:9.
3. Ezekiel 27:12, 25.
4. 1 Kings 5:15ff; 2 Chronicles 2:13. Punic, the language of the Carthaginians, was closely related to Hebrew.
5. G. Markoe, *The Phoenicians* (London: British Museum Press, 2000), pp.163, 213.
6. Obadiah 1:20.
7. L. Freehof and B. King, *Embroideries and Fabrics of Synagogues and Home* (New York: Heathside Press, 1966), p.19. Also see Franz Landsberger, *Development of Jewish Art* (Cincinnati, OH: Union of American Jewish Congregations, 1944).
8. Yigael Yadin, *The Finds from the Bar Kokhba Period in the Cave of Letters* (Jerusalem: Israel Exploration Society, 1963), Plate 60 et seq.
9. Hero Granger Taylor, 'Legacy of Masada', *Hali*, 82 (August/September 1995), p.77.
10. Mary Schoeser, *World Textiles: A Concise History* (London: Thames & Hudson, 2003), p.60.

11. Arthur Dilley, *Oriental Rugs and Carpets*, revised by M.S. Dimand (Philadelphia, PA: Lippincott & Co., 1959), p.4.
12. A Jewish testator in the second to third century BCE made a bequest to the Guild of Carpet Weavers and Purple Dyers of Hierapolis in Phrygia (North Syria) to decorate his tomb every Passover and Shavuot (J. Ungerleider-Mayerson, *Jewish Folk Art from Biblical Days to Modern Times* [New York: Summit Books, 1986], p.38). Many funerary portraits (not necessarily Jewish) of women holding weaving equipment have been found in Phrygia and Palmyra, and Jews had been settled in many of its major wool and weaving regions (including Gordium, where legends say Alexander the Great cut the Gordian knot) since at least the third century BCE. A leading expert has suggested that the provenance of the famous third- or fourth-century-BCE Pazyryk carpet – with its floral star patterns and rosettes – is neither Scythian nor Persian but was made by Phrygian weavers (Jacques Anquetel, *Carpets, Techniques, Traditions and History* [Paris: Octopus, 2003], citing Volkmar Gantzhorn, *The Christian Oriental Carpet* [Cologne: Benedikt Taschen, 1991]). Subsequently, in novel form, Bevis Longstreth proposed resolution of many of the numerous questions as to the provenance of this truly remarkable carpet with an innovative and imaginative leap by suggesting the designer/weaver might possibly have been a Jewish master weaver from Sardis, an important Jewish and carpet weaving centre at the time (Bevis Longstreth, 'The Riddle of the Pazyryk', *Hali*, 137 [November–December 2004], pp.49–51).
13. St Jerome, *Comm in Ezekiel*, xxvii, in *Pat. Lat.* 25.313, 'Orbe, Romano Occupato'.
14. *Encyclopaedia Judaica*, Vol. 15, p.220.
15. Benjamin R. Gampel, 'Jews, Christians, and Muslims in Medieval Iberia: Convivencia Through the Eyes of Sephardic Jews', in V. Mann, T. Glick and J. Dodds, '*Convivencia*', *Jews, Muslims and Christians in Medieval Spain* (New York: George Braziller in conjunction with the Jewish Museum, 1992), p.11, citing L. Garcia Iglesias, *Los Judios en la España antigua* (Madrid, 1978), p.53.
16. Jane Gerber, *The Jews of Spain* (London: Free Press, 1994), pp.8–13.
17. Ibid., p.12.
18. One of the most interesting of the many interesting Jews who rose to power in the Iberian Peninsula under Islamic and Christian rule was Abu Yusuf Hasdai ibn Shaprut (c.915–c.970). Chief minister to Caliph Abd al-Rahman III (912–961), Hasdai negotiated treaties with Byzantium and with Rome, obtained protection for the Jews of southern Italy and wrote a famous letter to Joseph, King of the Khazars – a powerful Turkic tribe whose ruling classes had converted to Judaism. It was as a diplomat that he went to see Sancho the Fat, King of Leon and Navarre. Sancho's barons had expelled him from Leon and he had fled to Tota, his grandmother, in Pamplona, the capital of Navarre. Hasdai negotiated with Sancho and, in return for the rights to ten fortresses, the Muslim caliph and his army led the Christian king and his grandmother in triumph back to Leon. Hasdai as a physician also cured Sancho of his obesity, or at least sufficiently so as to enable him to ride his horse – an essential attribute of kings.
19. John Barclay, *Jews in the Mediterranean Diaspora* (London: University of California Press, 1996), p.77. Many Roman Jews under the Emperor Domitian (81–96CE), in an attempt to avoid penal and discriminatory taxation, would publicly disavow Judaism but privately and secretly continue to follow the faith of their fathers ('Judaicus fiscus acerbissime actus est') Suetonius, 'Domitian', 12:2. In the event, so brutal were Domitian's trials to determine who was or was not a Jew, and so corrupting were the activities of numerous informers, that the Emperor Nerva, his successor, put a stop to this inquisitorial system, even minting a coin with the leg-

end 'The End of False Accusations arising from the Tax on the Jews'. See also H. Mattingley, *Coins of the Roman Empire in the British Museum* (London: British Museum, 1936), Vol. 3, nos. 15, 17, 19. See also Benjamin Isaac, *The Invention of Racism in Classical Antiquity* (Oxford: Princeton University Press, 2004), p.460. But anti-Jewish feelings, as expressed in the writings of Cicero, Tacitus and Apuleius, were endemic in classical Rome; even great Seneca described them as the 'most wicked of peoples'. To this list we may add Philostratus, Apion, Lysimachus and Manetho.
20. P. Cole, *The Dream of the Poem* (Princeton, NJ: Princeton University Press, 2007).pp.182–3.
21. Daniel Frank (ed.), *The Jews of Medieval Islam: Proceedings of an International Conference held by the Institute of Jewish Studies, University College, London, 1992* (Leiden: Brill, 1995), p.189.
22. Maria Rosa Menocal, *The Ornament of the World* (New York: Little, Brown & Co., 2002), pp.160–1.
23. Lewis Browne, *The Story of the Jews* (London: Jonathan Cape, 1926), p.175. The same phenomenon is to be seen in the seventh-century wars between the Persian and the Byzantine empires. The Jews of Persia enjoyed an important role, owing both to their large numbers and their part in Persia's international trade. So successful were they that the Persian commander would call a halt to fighting on Jewish holidays. Gil Moshe, *A History of Palestine* (Cambridge: Cambridge University Press, 1997), p.6.
24. Abraham Neuman, *The Jews in Spain* (Philadelphia, PA: Jewish Publication Society, 1948), Vol. 1, p.165.
25. Beatrice Leroy, *The Jews of Navarrae in the Late Middle Ages*, Hispania Judaica Vol. 4 (Jerusalem: Magnes Press, 1985), p.17.
26. Benzion Netanyahu, *The Origins of the Inquisition in Fifteenth Century Spain*, 2nd edn (New York: New York Review of Books, 2001), p.1097; p.1314, n.20, n.22, citing (i) Jose Amador de los Rios, 'Historia de los Judios en Espana y Portugal', *Historia II*, 1–111 (1875–1876), pp.531–52; (ii) L. Suarez Fernandez, *Documentos Acerca de la Expulsion de los Judios* (1964), pp.67–72; (iii) H. Graetz, *History of the Jews, 1894–1945* (Jerusalem: Jewish Publication Society, 1956), pp.462–3, n.10 (800,000 in Castile in 1290); (iv) N. Roth, *Conversos, Inquisition, and the Expulsion of the Jews from Spain* (Madison, WI: University of Wisconsin Press, 2002), p.376, c.1,000,000 in 1400; (v) H.C. Lea, *A History of the Inquisition of Spain*, Vol. 1 (New York: Macmillan, 1906), p.86, citing Amador de los Rios, 'Historia de los Judios en Espana y Portugal', I, pp.28–9.
27. Juan Torres Fontes (ed.), *Coleción de Documentos*, Vol. 6, p.136, no. 121.
28. Anne Wolff, *How Many Miles to Babylon* (Liverpool: Liverpool University Press, 2003), p.11.
29. Gerber, *Jews of Spain*, p.95. This compares with England where not more than a few thousand Jews provided one twelfth of the Royal revenues. Israel Abrahams, *Jewish Life in the Middle Ages* (Jerusalem: Jewish Publication Society, 1930), p.42, n.3, citing Zunz, *Zur Geschichte*, p.497; and J. Jacobs, *The Jews of Angevin England* (London: David Nutt Publisher, 1893), p.328. John A. Crow, *Spain, the Root and the Flower* (Berkeley, CA: University of California Press, 2005), p.110.
30. J. Valdéon Baruque, *Los Judios de Castilla y las Revolucion Trastamara* (Valladolid: Gráficas Andrés Martín, 1968), p.55.
31. Neuman, *The Jews in Spain*, Vol. 1.
32. See Benjamin Braude, 'The Rise and Fall of Salonika Woollens, 1500–1650: Technology Transfer and Western Competition', in Alisa Meyuhas Ginio (ed.), *Jews, Christians and Muslims in the Mediterranean World after 1492* (London: Frank Cass, 1992), p.227, n.29.

The Role of Carpets in Jewish Culture

And after tools came twine ... for the earliest findings of animal and vegetable twining are at least 40,000 years old. Wall paintings of 9,000 years ago in Anatolia point to the weaving in coloured wools of covers and wall hangings. Today in the Israel Museum in Jerusalem we may see a pre-Judaic weaving found in the Judean desert, just to the south-west of the Dead Sea, and carbon dated to the seventh millennium BCE. In addition, a herringbone-patterned, twill plaited straw mat dated to the fourth millennium BCE has recently been recovered from the Cave of the Warrior in the same region.

But let us start some 3,800 years ago, in Akkad in Iraq: Abraham, the founding father of Jewish people, is preparing to leave Ur, a city whose economy is substantially based upon the wool industry. It is a city where a loom is to be found in almost every home, and its language has many words for different parts of the loom and different types of wool. So important was the production of textiles around the time of Abraham that Hammurabi, king of Akkad, had legislated to regulate the trade. Classifying the workers into fullers, spinners, dyers and weavers, he subdivided those groups into apprentices, craftsmen and masters. Then, distinguishing between slaves and freemen, he laid down laws providing protection for the slaves and the minimum wages to be paid to the freemen. Archaeology reveals that piled (knotted) textiles were woven there from at least the fifth millennium BCE.[1]

Eve, the first woman, is seen by some as the first spinner[2] but in Jewish tradition it is Naamah, the daughter of Lamech and sister of Tubal-Cain, to whom all the secrets of spinning and weaving were revealed. Right from the beginning, textiles of all sorts were a significant component in Jewish culture.[3] Indeed, they could not possibly have had a more auspicious start than at some time between the fifteenth and the thirteenth century BCE, when the Divinity issued very specific and detailed instructions as to how the framework and the flat kelim-type rugs and tent cloths for the Tabernacle were to be made: 'You shall make a curtain of blue, purple and crimson yarns, and fine twisted linen; it shall have a design of cherubim worked into it. You shall make a screen for the entrance of the Tent, of blue, purple and crimson yarns, and fine twisted linen, done in embroidery.' Exodus 26:31–3 and 36–7.[4] (See below, note 13.)

It was Aholiab, son of Ahisamach of the tribe of Dan[5] (we can see how he was seen in Spain in the Middle Ages in Figure 4), who with the Israelite women wove the walls, floor and inner hangings of the Tabernacle – the mobile shrine to house the Tablets of the Law during the Israelites' wanderings in the desert.[6] Later exegesis describes this Holy Tent as having being placed in an open court bordered by fencing over which costly rugs were hung.[7]

The introduction into ancient Egypt of the vertical two-beamed loom with the domed spindle wheel and of other weaving techniques advanced greatly under the Hyksos, a partly Semitic tribe identified by many scholars with the patriarchal Israelites, so linking them to the biblical account of Joseph and of the Exodus. The Hyksos ruled from 1655 until 1570 BCE, when they were expelled towards Palestine, where archaeologists have discovered the frames of the new weighted loom dated to the 1450s. Fourteenth-century-BCE business papers from Syria mention textiles from Ashdod, a coastal town in the Land of Israel, and papyri from the Egyptian countryside in the Ptolemaic period (c.230–30 BCE) record Jews as weavers.

Self-evidently, weaving has been an almost universal craft since the earliest times, but often enough we do not know the exact nature of the textile that the weavers wove, be they clothes, kelims, pile carpets et al. – the list is almost endless. Egyptian influence, however, during the years of exile was probably a key factor in the importance of the rugs, but it was also the practical realities of Israelite life in the Middle East that made weavings such critically fundamental functional and cultural artefacts. What else might more cheaply and effectively shade you from the sun during a wedding ceremony than the Chuppah – the bridal canopy? And help shade you, too, when celebrating the ingathering of the harvest, in the Sukkot booth?[8] And what else might better protect you from the cold ground at night than a rug to sleep on? Even today, apart from a simple frame, almost the entirety of the nomad's tent is made up of weavings; fittingly, an Arabic term for tent is *Beit al-shaʻr* – literally 'house of hair'. Inside the tent, rugs have ever served as doorways, room dividers, wall and floor covers, sleeping bags, cushions, sacks and bags. Outside the tent, rugs have been used for saddlebags and ground covers. In life these critically functional weavings were media of exchange and stores of future value; in death, they would be funerary coverings. The weaving of fibrous material was fundamental to almost every civilization, with the very processes of spinning and weaving providing the setting in which oral tradition and folk memory might be nurtured and nourished, where concepts and customs were in turn memorialized in the wool and the silk textiles produced. Socrates himself affirmed that of the four skills essential to the Greek city state, the most important was the skill of the weaver.[9]

In the tenth century BCE, after the Israelites had settled in Israel, King Solomon built the First Temple in Jerusalem (c. 961–586). Echoing the textiles of the Tabernacle, the hanging in the Temple protecting the Holy of Holies was also coloured blue, purple, crimson and white and, according to subsequent exegesis, gold.[10] Textiles and agriculture were the major industries of the Israelites. The significance of sheep and wool in the ninth century BCE is clear from both biblical and non-biblical sources. The Moabite Stone, dated to around 850 BCE, is the most valuable extant monument of Israelite history in its explicit, albeit incorrect, statement that Mesha, king of Moab, had destroyed Israel – the actual line translates as 'And Israel perished with an everlasting destruction.' The inscription goes on to record that Mesha's spoils of victory were Israel's sheep and shepherds. Just prior to the war it had been Mesha who was paying tribute to Israel, for 2 Kings 3:4 tells us: 'Now Mesha, king of Moab, was a sheep breeder; and he had to deliver annually to the king of Israel a hundred thousand lambs and the wool of a hundred thousand rams.' Recent archaeology reveals that the eighth- to seventh-century-BCE town Beit Mirsim was almost wholly devoted to weaving and dyeing, and findings from an eighth-century-BCE shipwreck discovered off the coast of Haifa included remnants of mats and other coverings. The first-century-CE hanging in the Second Temple (520 BCE–70 CE) was seen and described by the contemporary Jewish historian and soldier Flavius Josephus (c. 38 to after 100 CE) as being 'blue and white and scarlet and purple and of a truly wonderful texture'.[11] Later descriptions also tell us this proto-*parokhet* was embroidered with flowers, plants and, interestingly, with stars (see Chapter 12);

it was the women weavers who kept the Temple hangings in repair, and in Christian apocrypha[12] the Virgin Mary herself was chosen for this work. We are told what happened to it, for St Mark in his gospel (15:38) records that at the crucifixion, 'the curtain of the temple was torn in two, from top to bottom'. In Jewish tradition, according to II Baruch (early second century CE), when Jerusalem finally fell to the Romans in 70 CE, as the Temple was being consumed in one vast conflagration, an angel appeared and rescued the *parokhet*.

In the early biblical period recorded in the five books of Moses, people may not have sat on chairs at all, for not once is one mentioned. Significantly, however, there are numerous references to carpets.[13] The panegyric detailing the attributes of the ideal wife includes her skills in collecting and spinning wool and flax, making and selling fine textiles and the weaving of kelims, for 'she maketh herself a rug'.[14] This is not an economic exhortation, it is a religious duty, carrying with it social purpose, for the working in wool was a yardstick of a woman's worth and respectability. Again we see the critical centrality of weaving in the lives of the ancient Israelites in the dire warnings of Jeremiah: 'Their tents and flocks shall be taken, their tent cloths and all their goods.'[15] The contribution of weaving to Israelite and other cultures cannot be overestimated, for it was in the reflection and the rhythms of such daily work that the tales were told, retold and retained. It was in this spinning of the yarns that weaving became a natural metaphor in daily life, and still today, echoing down to us through the ages, we hear Job's lament (7:6): 'My days are swifter than a weaver's shuttle.'

In the later biblical period, weaving may have become the speciality of a particular sub-clan, the house of Ashbea.[16] Weaving craft guilds, often patrilineal, occur throughout the history of Jewish weaving. In the second century BCE, Ben Sirach in the Apocrypha stresses the importance of weaving among all the crafts,[17] and in the book of Tobit, it is his wife, Anna, who during his four years of blindness keeps the family alive by selling her weavings. Non-biblical sources of the same century tell us of a Jewish weaver at work not in Israel but in Upper Egypt. Later the Talmud could not have more clearly spelled out the primacy of textiles, reinforcing the injunction of the biblical panegyric cited above, for it decreed that even if a wife has brought her husband 100 maidservants, yet still should she work with wool.[18]

It is no surprise that there is hardly an archaeological site in Israel today (and indeed throughout the eastern Mediterranean) that has not yielded up numerous loom weights. In Oxyrhynchus roughly half of the working population was engaged in the textile trade. As Israelite society expanded and developed, with all its ups and downs, so did the importance of the weaver. In 70 CE when the Romans vanquished Judea, the numbers and economic importance of the weavers was clear. For example, in Jerusalem, in life they gathered together in their own synagogue and in death were buried in their own weavers' cemetery, and in other major towns, including Lydda, Sepphoris and Tiberias, the weavers' guilds also maintained their own synagogues.[19] The master weavers who formed these guilds were called Tarsim, after Tarsus, the great rug and tent weaving centre in what is now Turkey, but the socio-economic status of the everyday commercial weaver, varying in time and place, was usually less elevated. In the Middle Ages some communities in France did not accept their testimony in legal proceedings.

Under Roman rule the most important centre was probably Beth Shean, where Jews also dominated the interrelated crafts of weaving and dyeing. In Figure 5 we can see an example of their work. There, depicted in the mosaic floor of the Beth Shean Synagogue, is a *parokhet* hanging before the Ark. We shall examine it in more detail shortly. The Talmud noted the 'fine linen vestments that come from Beth Shean',[20] as did the Roman emperor Diocletian in his 'Edict of Maximum Prices'.[21] In the first century in Hierapolis in Phrygia we learn of the guild of purple dyers and carpet weavers whose members were either mainly or entirely Jewish.[22] Even under Roman and then Hellenistic rule, textile production was, after agriculture, the major industry in Palestine and, right up to the time of the Arab conquest in 634, Sepphoris and Tiberias continued to be famous for their mats and other weavings.[23] Some historians report that Jewish carpet weavers were active throughout the entire 1,000 years of the Roman Empire (third century BCE to seventh century CE).[24] Apart from the wealth of evidence provided by secondary sources, we may see today significant surviving fragments from 70 CE and 135 CE (Chapter 2) and from the third-century findings at Dura Europos.[25] Special textiles woven with pictures of fabulous beasts were, according to the fourth-century Roman poet Claudius Claudianus, known as 'Jewish veils'.[26] In Chapter 4 we continue the story of Jewish carpets in Spain and North Africa.

Weaving, one of the most mundane and repetitive events in everyday life, is embedded in Judaism. It is the fate of most artisans and craftsmen to live, to create and to die, leaving barely a trace behind, and carpet weavers and designers are no exception. From the second century onwards, tombs displaying spindles and whorls have been found in major weaving centres such as Beit Shean and Beit Shearim, although it seems this practice was not approved by the rabbis. So it is that the ageless and enormous contribution of the Jews to textile and carpet weaving has also largely faded from history, for there is so little information available and such information as we have crops up by chance – being tangential to biblical or Talmudic writing, historical, geographic and military reports, the rabbinic *Responsa* (the written replies of prominent Rabbis to questions put to them, usually on matters of interpretation of Jewish law) or through the work of archaeologists. So, for example, we see the importance of textiles from the thirty-nine different types of work that may not be done on the Sabbath: no less than twelve are associated with the production of textiles.[27] It is only by plucking out and bringing together these diverse and peripheral pieces of information that we may glean any sense of the extent of the involvement in and contribution of Jews to textile and carpet weaving over the millennia.

Occasionally we do learn of the names of Jewish weavers through their significance in other contexts. Flavius Josephus records the activities of a weaver named Jonathan who, in the aftermath of the destruction of the Temple, had fled to the Jewish community in Cyrenaica, probably in 73 CE. He must have been a charismatic figure, for he raised a large army among the local Jews directed to destroy the Roman regime and inaugurate the messianic era. Josephus also tells us of two Jewish brothers, Asinaeus and Anilaeus. Apprenticed by their widowed mother to a carpet weaver in the major Jewish centre of Nehardea in Babylon, they abandoned weaving to become leaders of a powerful band waging war against the Parthian King Artabanus III[28] and for some fifteen years they actually ruled their own independent Jewish state. Then in 351, led by Patricius, the great weaving regions of Sepphoris and Tiberius rose in revolt against Rome – but to no avail.

In Persia, the Babylonian Talmud, noting the extent of carpet weaving under Sasanian rule,[29] records a dispute between the weavers of Pumbedita and the wool merchants, which was settled by Rabbi Kahana.[30] In another dispute in Persia, the chanting of the weavers in their workshop was banned by Rav Huna but, rather mysteriously, the work songs of the boat hauliers and the ploughmen were not so interdicted.[31] So much has disappeared, but the mosaic floor of the sixth-century synagogue at Beit Alpha is considered by some to have been worked directly by local craftsman from pattern books intended for textiles or mosaics. The style and design of the floor may be all that has survived of the lost Jewish art of weaving which flourished in Scythopolis – an art form that may have been created by the descendants of the Jewish weavers who had fled Scythopolis during a crisis in the state-controlled weaving factories in the fourth century.[32]

Occasionally we are privileged to see a Jewish carpet of the Byzantine era – or at least its image painted on the walls or set in mosaic on the floors of the synagogues of the time. My favourite Byzantine Jewish carpet is the finely detailed hanging before the Ark portrayed in the mosaic floor of the sixth-century synagogue at Beth Shean. Suspended by seven rings on a rail, its triangular forms on the upper border are echoed at random on the central field, and eight fringes hang from a wide band at the lower end of the carpet (Figure 5). By their very nature, and by the nature of Jewish history, few Jewish carpets and textiles have survived, yet from the secondary sources it is clear that they formed a vibrant thread running through the rich tapestry of Jewish history. They are manifestations, indeed cultural chronicles, of the historic processes of both change and continuity that the Jews have undergone over the past 2,000 years in Roman, Greek, Persian, Christian, Islamic and Communist societies. Aholiab, that first known weaver, has been followed ever since by numerous honoured Jewish weavers and designers, including St Paul,[33] Rashi (1040–1105) (the great Talmudic commentator) and, in our time, Marc Chagall (who designed the carpets replete with biblical iconography which grace the parliament of the State of Israel).[34]

Today at the Passover table, the festival recalling the Israelites' escape from bondage in the land of Egypt, Jews do not sit upright but lean to one side, possibly also recalling the time when nomadic Israelites, at ease on their carpets, would also have been lounging to one side. In Figure 6, a rare picture, drawn and painted in fifteenth-century Spain, we see a Jewish family leaning to one side as they celebrate the Passover.

With these potted histories of the Jews of Spain and of the role of the carpet as a significant cultural artefact in Judaism we are now able to place the Jewish weavers and traders of Spain into the context of their times. In the next chapter I shall review the strength and the organic unity of their weaving communities throughout the Mediterranean under Islam,[35] the Jewish weavers of Alexandria, the Sephardic craft guilds, the relevant findings in the Cairo Genizah, and the implications for the Jewish weavers of Murcia of the flight of the Muslim weavers in the face of the Christian conquest of the region. I conclude with some thoughts about the Mamluk carpets and the enormous expansion of the weaving and carpet industry under the Ottoman Empire created by the Jewish weavers who had sought refuge there in the years leading up to and following their expulsion from Spain in 1492.

NOTES

1. See Udo Hirsch, 'The Fabric of Deities and Kings' commentary on Leonard Woolley's discovery in Ur of a piled textile some 4,500 years old, *Hali*, 58 (August 1991), pp.104–14. The Code of King Hammurabi, drawn up around the time of Abraham in 1800 BCE, listed wool as one of the three main products of Babylon. 'Domestic Animals of Mesopotamia, Part 1', *Bulletin of Sumarian Agriculture*, Vol. 7, ed. J. Postgate and M. Powers (Cambridge, 1993), p.14. This contribution to the Bulletin cites an article by E.L. Ochsenschlager, 'Village Weavers: Ethnoarcheology at Al Hiba', recording two women carpet and wool traders.
2. See the Savajero Haggadah, written and illuminated in medieval Spain, where Eve is portrayed after the expulsion from the Garden of Eden as spinning. Franz Landsberger, *Development of Jewish Art* (Cincinnati, OH: Union of American Jewish Congregations, 1944), p.210. It calls to mind that timeless questioning couplet of early English social dissent:

    When Adam delved and Eve span,
    Who was then the gentleman?'

3. I would not include the two carpets of Pharaoh Akhenaten's (1379–62 BCE) that we know of, one being a pile carpet that is seen to be a wall painting (R. Izady Mehrdad, *The Kurds: A Concise Handbook* [London: Taylor & Francis, 1992], p.250), the other being a sack woven in a carpet weaving technique excavated at his capital city of el-Amarna (E. Barber, *Prehistoric Textiles* [Princeton, NJ: Princeton University Press, 1991], p.49, n.6), as in this category of the earliest Jewish carpet. Current scholarship does not give much weight to Sigmund Freud's suggestion that Moses may have been an Egyptian high priest who kept Akhenaten's near monotheism alive by fleeing Egypt. The similarity, however, between Akhenaton's hymn to his all-powerful god Aton and Psalm 104 is remarkable.
4. Exodus 26:31–3, 36–7; 2 Chronicles 3:14.
5. Exodus 26; 31:1–6.
6. Archaeological and historical studies confirm that similar portable tents of worship were in use among the Bedouin even in pre-Islamic times. M. Buber, *Moses, the Revelation and the Covenant* (New York: Harper Torchbooks, 1936), pp.148–9; William Albright, *From the Stone Age to Christianity: Monotheism and the Historical Process* (New York: Doubleday Anchor Books, 1957), p.266.
7. Landsberger, *Development of Jewish Art*, p.89.
8. The use of carpets in the coverings of the Succah booth is stated in Oholuth 8:1, Babylonian Talmud, Seder Tohoroth, ed. I. Epstein (London: Soncino Press, 1938), p.179. And Seder Mo'ed: 'Surely it was taught: if one covered it [the festival booth] according to law and decorated it with hand-made carpets and tapestries ...'
9. Plato, *The Republic*, 369B–371E, cited in Aristotle, *The Politics*, ed. Betty Radice (Harmondsworth: Penguin Books, 1958), p.247.

10. Jules Harlow, 'Jewish Textiles in Light of Biblical and Post-Biblical Literature', in Barbara Kirshenblatt-Gimblett, *Fabric of Jewish Life* (New York: The Jewish Museum, 1977), p.31.
11. Josephus, *Jewish Wars* (London: W. Whiston, 1737), 5.5:4. Late in the second century, Eleazar ben Yosi I, on a diplomatic mission to Rome, is shown the treasures sacked from the Temple, including the blood-splattered *parokhet* (Tosef, Yoma 3, end).
12. 'Proto-Evangelium Jacobi' (Proto-Evangelium of James), in *New Testament Aprocrypha*, ed. W. Schneemelcher (Louisville, KY: John Knox Press, 1963–66), 10.1.
13. Even today, the few hundred remaining Samaritans in their synagogue near the top of Mount Gerizim still sit on rugs and not on pews.
14. Proverbs 31:22. *The Revised Standard Bible* (London: Wm Collins, 1971) translates the Hebrew word *Yeriah* as 'coverings'. Other English-language Bibles translate *Yeriah* as 'screen' or 'curtain'. A more accurate translation, depending upon the context, according to *The Jewish Encyclopaedia*, edited by I. Singer (London: Funk & Wagnalls, 1916), p.390, is 'rug' or 'tent cloth'.
15. Jeremiah 49:29.
16. 1 Chronicles 4:21.
17. Ben Sirach 38:27–8.
18. Mishnah Ketuboth V: 5.
19. M. Wischnitzer, *A History of Jewish Crafts and Guilds* (New York: Jonathan David, 1965), p.16. Bab. Tal., Megillah 26a and Nazir 52a.
20. Kiddushim II, 5–62c.
21. Avi Yonah, citing Th. Mommsen (ed.), *Der Maxamaltarif des Diocletian* (1893), cap. 26–8, in *Israel Exploration Journal*, 12, 2 (2007), pp.128–9.
22. Landsberger, *Development of Jewish Art*, p.166, citing Humann, Cichorius, Judeich, Winter, *Altertuemer von Hierapolis* (1898), pp.46, 174. A number of the tombs depict weavers' spindles and distaffs. M. Peskowitz, *Spinning Fantasies* (Berkeley, CA: University of California Press, 1997), p.167; p.199, n.20. Peskowitz also notes that the Talmud uses different words to distinguish the wool used for the light woof threads from the heavier yarn used for the horizontal warp.
23. Wischnitzer, *History of Jewish Crafts and Guilds*, p.20. And probably much later too. A beautiful floor mat, loom-woven of reeds and hemp, of the tenth century is to be seen in the Benaki Museum. Its Kufic inscription, a blessing on the owners who had commissioned the carpet from a workshop in Tiberas, does not indicate whether the workshop was run by a Christian, a Muslim or a Jew.
24. J. Juster, *Les Juifs dans l'Empire Roman*, 2 vols (Paris: Geuthner, 1914), p.306, cited by Wischnitzer, *History of Jewish Crafts and Guilds*, p.52. See also J. Ungerleider-Mayerson, *Jewish Folk Art from Biblical Days to Modern Times* (New York: Summit Books, 1986), p.38.
25. R. Pfister and L. Bellinger, *The Excavations at Dura-Europos: Final Report 4: Part 2 – The Textiles* (New Haven, CT: Yale University Press, 1945), pp.46, 58. Among the numerous textiles saved by archaeology from this third-century synagogue were piled fabrics, in particular a red, green and purple pile rug woven in Sehna knots, as well as other wool and goats' hair textiles.
26. Landsberger, *Development of Jewish Art*, p.166.

27. Shabbat 7.2; 13.1–4.
28. Wischnitzer, *History of Jewish Crafts and Guilds*, p.42, citing Josephus, *Jewish Antiquities*, 18, 9, 16.
29. Wischnitzer, *History of Jewish Crafts and Guilds*, p.43.
30. Ibid., pp.42–3.
31. Babylonian Talmud, Sotah 48A.
32. Marilyn Chiat, 'Synogogues and Churches in Byzantine Beit Shean', *Journal of Jewish Art*, 7, p.17, citing Goldman, *Sacred Portals*, p.144.
33. C.J. Jung, *Man and his Symbols* (London: Aldus Books, 1972), p.89. As least as late as the 1930s, if not later, tent cloth from the fine hair of the Cilician mountain goats was still being woven in Tarsus. In addition, the Acts of the Apostles tell us of Aquila, one of St Paul's earlier followers. Aquila, born a Jew in Pontus, lived in Cornith and like Paul was a weaver of the large kelim-type textiles that formed the fabric for tents.
34. Carpets, as cultural chronicles reflecting aspects of the history of the Jewish people, continues to our times. I cannot help but also mention Kitaj's huge tapestry that daily greeted me in the lobby of the British Library. In the lower half, in a stagnant pool, we see the upper body of a man, perhaps a soldier. He may be still alive. To the left a naked Eve-like figure seems to be attacking a mild-looking man who (just like me) wears spectacles and has a hearing aid. To the right a woman seems to be trying to escape from some horror. A broken statue, other ruined things and a sheep (that symbol of sacrifice) in their isolation evoke alienation and disgust. Then, as we look to the upper half, a hellish sky overlooking what is below, we see the gateway to Auschwitz.

    I hope in my next book to illustrate and discuss another powerful and poignant Jewish carpet. It was woven in the ghetto in Lodz during the Nazi era, where the Jews were offered a few more weeks or months of life in return for mass-producing uniforms for the Luftwaffe. Out of the scraps of wool and cotton this extraordinary chronicle was woven. Under a Hebrew inscription in the central field we see a father and son at work on the loom, making uniforms for their masters.
35. One of the oldest of their communities lived in the mountains of the desert in the south of the Maghreb; their homes were often caves or high rock forts.

The Jewish Weavers of Spain and North Africa

Following the eighth-century Arab conquest of most of the Iberian Peninsula, the whole focus of Spain's religious, political, economic and cultural alignment moved south as it was integrated into the Islamic hegemonies of the Middle East, and became particularly closely aligned with its next-door neighbours on the coast of North Africa. The world of Islam was reconfigured with the Mediterranean at its centre, and the Jews' near monopoly of dye manufacture and their active and widespread participation in the design, manufacture and marketing of carpets and textiles[1] contributed greatly to the ensuing economic boom throughout the new Islamic empire of Spain and North Africa (see Chapter 1).[2] Of course, there were many Jewish and Christian craftsmen in the newly conquered territories; indeed, they had to provide their new masters with so many carpets a year, and it is worth repeating Oleg Grabar: 'The craftsmen of Arabia itself were generally non-Arab, mostly Jews, and the practice of crafts was not honoured.'[3]

Given the common religious and political culture of Spain and North Africa, much of what was happening in one region was happening in the other. Between Spain and Egypt lay the Maghreb, comprising Morocco, Algeria and Tunisia (and Libya). The word *Maghreb* derives from the Arabic for 'west' and the territory, according to the Arab geographers, included Spain. From as early as the eighth century, Tunisia, with its substantial and ancient Jewish population, had prospered, becoming a major centre for the manufacture of carpets, fine glass and pottery.[4] By the eleventh century, and probably earlier, Jews were trading in prayer rugs throughout the Mediterranean. And by the twelfth to fourteenth centuries the Maghreb was producing countless carpets, its best-known centre being Tlemcen, as famous for the rich and beautiful carpets in its palaces[5] as for its learned rabbis. Until the collapse of the Marinid kingdom (1286–1465),[6] Tlemcen and Fez, protecting its Jewish communities, had flourished; one great source of its wealth was trans-Saharan trade, the other was its manufacture of important carpets. In 1492 Tlemcen alone gave refuge to some 9,000 Jews and *conversos* who had fled from Spain. As to Fez, its economic strength and social priorities in the thirteenth century may be gauged by its thirty-seven soap factories, its ninety-three public baths and its 3,064 loom sites.[7] To the west, on the Atlantic seaboard, Azemmour was also a significant carpet trading centre with a fifteenth-century document recording that as many as one in eight of its inhabitants were Jews;[8] other sources indicate that it welcomed in a particularly large number of *converso* craftsmen. Turning to the east of Tlemcen, further along the coastal plain, carpets were a major export at the great trading centre of Kairouan – which was also home to a famous Jewish seminary.[9] Then further east, just off what is now Tunisia, is the island of Jerba, noted in documents of 1315 and 1365 as a depot for carpets,[10] which was also home to an ancient Jewish community famous for its remarkable embroidery with the identifying Stars of David, which would customarily be displayed on their clothing.[11]

Now what can we conclude from this? These five major carpet centres – Tlemcen, Fez, Azemmour, Kairouan and Jerba, all located in a common cultural (and for four of them, geographic) zone between Spain and Egypt – were also home to five significant Jewish communities. This is surely no coincidence. The fact is that in this region, wherever there was a substantial and successful Jewish community, there was a major carpet centre, and it surely follows that they were reciprocal, each part of the other. To suggest that the Jewish and the carpet communities had no profound involvement with each other is simply perverse: clearly, for much of the time each contributed greatly to the richly productive culture and economies of the other. Beyond the Maghreb we see the selfsame synergies of a Jewish community and of a major carpet-trading or manufacturing community in Syria, Ragusa (Dubrovnik), Chios and Rhodes.

This concurrence of Jewish and weaving communities was not confined to the major towns of the Maghreb, for there were also many smaller carpet weaving and textile centres with their own important Jewish communities in Marrakesh, Sefran, Algiers, Bône, Tunis and Tripoli.[12] Many of these communities produced Cairene carpets, in addition to the high-quality carpets woven in Cairo itself[13] which, with its own substantial Jewish community, also welcomed and prized the carpets of Murcia.[14] After the pogroms of 1391 and throughout the fifteenth century, the major expansion in the trading of carpets in Egypt and their manufacture in the Maghreb was propelled by the Jewish weavers and traders of Spain and Italy. They faced three choices: they could stay and try to endure the pressures and persecution of being Jews; they could convert to Christianity; or they could seek refuge in Islamic lands where, joining their co-religionists in a weaving and rug making society, they might continue both to follow their faith and to earn a living as weavers.

Information about medieval centres of carpet manufacture, their carpets and their weavers often comes to us indirectly. If the mob had not ransacked the Cairo home of a wealthy emir in 1341, we would never have known from the reports that he had sixteen pairs of noble Cairene (or Egyptian) carpets, each pair worth an astonishing 12,000 silver dirhams.[15] Then, from the documents pieced together from Cairo Genizah, we learn of young Joseph being apprenticed to a master weaver,[16] and of the permanent presence in the carpet market of the caliph's civil servants, probably Jews, whose office was sited there.[17] At the heart of their duties was the probity of weights and measures and the inspection of artisan manufacture. The Genizah also throws light on the lives of women, very many of whom were engaged independently in the textile industry – spinning, weaving, dyeing and embroidering – and often keeping the profit themselves.

The Cairo Genizah is the attic storeroom in the Ben Ezra Synagogue in Fustat, now a suburb of Cairo. Jews believe that any object bearing any one of God's names on it should be preserved and never destroyed. So material stored in the Genizah, from the seventh century and over the next 1,000 years, grew into the most extraordinary treasure trove, uniquely illuminating mainly Jewish but also Christian and Muslim life in the Mediterranean basin and beyond. The documents (actually disintegrating fragments of paper and parchment which are lovingly and skilfully still being pieced together, mainly in the Taylor-Schechter Collection, Cambridge) also tell us of the enormous cultural and commercial importance of carpets to the Jewish communities throughout the region.

For example, we read a letter from a weaver who, having been forced to work in the royal factory in Damascus, complains that 'The artisans of this profession are Jews but I am the only Karaite among them.' Then the *Ketuba* (the pre-nuptial contract) of a poor bride (she had been married in Tyre in the Lebanon in 1054) reveals that she had but one pile carpet which also had to serve as her bed. Another document tells us that a Spanish rug costing thirty-three quarter dinars was sent to Egypt in 1050. We find references to wall-to-wall carpeting as well as to the classic placement of carpets – one large central rug framed by two long runners either side and a smaller door mat to the front. Another setting would be to hang a carpet on the wall opposite the main entrance so that it would be the first thing to strike a visitor; alternatively, it might be laid on the floor in the front of that wall. In a letter sent from Aden to India (how it ended up in Cairo is a mystery) we read of another pile carpet with the signs of the zodiac woven into it. Abraham ben Yiju, writing in the 1140s from Mangalore, a port on the south coast of India, sends away to the Horn of Africa for his mats and buys at least one velvet-like carpet made in Gujarat. We read also of complaints against wives stealing their husbands' carpets and of husbands pawning their wives' carpets. A court order of 3 September 1159 determines a partnership dispute over a carpet factory and a later document refers to the 'carpet house' in old Cairo. We glean from another letter that the *Gaon* (head) of the Jewish Academy of Baghdad had actually been a weaver. This is not as surprising as it may seem. Although biblical study was the most important activity for men, all were reminded to follow a trade or profession so that they would not be financially dependent on the community they served. Weaving, as with most other skills, was either learned within the family or through an apprenticeship. So, in a twelfth-century contract, we read of a father hiring out his son as an apprentice to a weaver at a minimal wage for four months, after which the boy was to be paid the full wage of a weaver. In the same century we learn that a Spanish manual instructing the market supervisors included ensuring that all the market staff pray regularly.

Donations to the synagogue would customarily include carpets and other textiles to decorate the walls, the columns, the floors, the threshold, the reader's desk and the Ark.[18] Few *Ketubot* or wills were complete without reference to fine clothing, wall hangings, tapestries and elaborate carpets – for both functionally and financially they were among the prime assets of the day. Hoarded by the wealthy and cherished by the poor, textiles were part of the pomp and pageant of most ritualized activities. Typical is the will of a Jewish doctor of 1172 bequeathing a number of assets in trust for his son, including a carpet twenty-two cubits long with a white centre and blue border, as well as a white sleeping carpet. At night, sleeping carpets were rolled out on the floor, and in the day, bundled up, would serve as containers of considerable size.[19]

Sometimes our information about the Jewish weavers and their carpets is direct, other times less so – but nonetheless as convincing. For example, in eleventh-century Cairo there were two major synagogues, the Palestinian and the Byzantine. They were (what indeed is ever new under the sun?) at odds with the other, each trying to persuade the other's members to defect to it. The inducements to new members offered by the Byzantine synagogue included various high-sounding titles and honours. The allurements of the Palestinian synagogue included its shorter services, precious Bible Codices, magnificent Torah scrolls and 'beautiful sitting carpets'.[20] As for the quality of those carpets, I am sure they were splendid, since the religious imperative is that ritual objects be made as beautifully as possible.[21] As to the quantity, an inventory of the Babylonian synagogue's carpets and fabrics of 1080 reveals 'one mixed carpet, three carpets for the Torah scrolls, golden smeared with black, one small one of their type for the book of the Haftarot [sic], red carpets mixed with gold, carpets of brocade and *siqlatun* for the walls, twenty; and a carpet for a "round" and nine of brocade; some early and others new, which are in need of partial cleaning'.[22] The periodic inventories between 1075 and 1186 list wall hangings of carpets made from rich fabrics often embroidered with silver and gold threads.

Alexandria, located in the delta of the Nile and so between the Occident and the Orient, had been founded by Alexander the Great in the fourth century BCE. By the next century, under the Ptolemies (who ruled from 232–30 BCE), and with the introduction of the Miletus sheep from Asia Minor, wool products – mats, rugs, and clothes – flourished. Alexandria was also home to a substantial Jewish community of merchants and artisans, and of learned Jews too, for Ptolemy II Philadelphus (285–244 BCE), on the advice of Eleazar, High Priest of Jerusalem, gave seventy rabbis (or seventy-two, according to another story, being six from each of the twelve tribes) the task of translating the five books of Moses (the Pentateuch) into Greek. Locked into seventy (or perhaps thirty-six) cells, all seventy (-two) rabbis rather miraculously produced identical translations. Hence the title of their Bible, the Septuagint – Greek for seventy. Clearly the weavers of Alexandria were busy, for the Roman playwright Plautus in 184 BCE refers to the purple carpets of Alexandria,[23] as later does Clement of Alexandria in describing a god of the Egyptians as a wild beast wallowing on a purple carpet. Clement goes on to describe the textile workshops of Alexandra as places filled with 'crafty women and effeminate men who blend their deceptive dyes with dainty fabric, [and] carry this insane desire beyond all bounds'. Philo (d. 50 CE), the great Jewish philosopher of Alexandria, tells us of its weavers' guilds,[24] and Pliny (62–133 CE) records the draw-loom fabrics of Alexandria.[25] In Figure 7, in a wall painting representing Jewish activities in Alexandria in the Hellenistic period, in the Beth Hatefutsoth Museum, we see Jewish weavers at work on a carpet. Then, in the sixth century CE, the Christian writer Cosmas Indicopleustes of Alexandria, in discussing weaving and many of the other crafts referred to in the Bible, significantly reports that 'even today we find most of these occupations followed by Jews'. An interesting man, Cosmas, after travelling the Near East and India, went into monastic retirement and, in writing of his experiences, described the Jews as a people 'Endowed by divine grace with special aptitude for handicrafts'.[26] Pictorial tapestries, as noted earlier, were so closely associated with Jewish textile workers, particularly in Egypt, that they were known as *Judaica Vela*.

Rudolph Berliner, of the Textile Museum in Washington, writing about weaving in the region of what was later Cairo in the late seventh century, affirmed that 'the Jews were of enduring importance in the production and distribution of textile goods'. He went on to note that 'We have almost positive documentary proof that Jewish weavers like Joseph and Zacharias at first worked the same stylistically for Arabs as for their other customers.'[27] Joseph's and Zacharias's fellow Jewish weavers in Islamic Spain would doubtless also be making similar adaptations.

One possible survivor of this vast output is a seventh- to ninth-century knotted carpet. Today, in the Fine Arts Museum in San Francisco, this Fustat rug is in tatters, its imagery unrecognizable. Its symmetrical knots raised above the ground weave point to it being woven in Egypt. Most scholars believe it to be the oldest extant Islamic carpet; another opinion is that it is a Christian carpet; finally, a third opinion is that it depicts a partially draped menorah – where some see the claws of a lion, others see Hebrew characters.[28] I think that like the well-known seventh–ninth century Eastern Mediterranean tapestry weave (currently in the Hermitage Museum) with its Stars of David, it is quite likely to be Judaic[29] as is the Coptic band of the same period, which is almost certainly Judaic, for along with its Star of David it displays the menorah (Figure 8).[30] To look more closely at these weaves, by analogy let us look at the contemporary Coptic weaves generally and the society that produced them. D.L. Carroll, in his authoritative work *Looms and Textiles of the Copts*, notes how very few Coptic weaves displayed any Christian themes and how those that did appear late in their history (say the early fourth to the eleventh century) feature stories derived from the Jewish ('Old') Testament. One reason why non-Christian themes — and therefore arguably their non-Christian customers and weavers — so hugely outweigh even those possibly Christian themes as are extant, is perhaps because the old gods of Egypt, Persia, Greece and Rome took half a millennia to die.

Alexandria fell to Islam in 639. The Arab general, in his triumphal report back to his caliph listing all the newly acquired assets, records 40,000 poll-tax-paying Alexandrian Jews. The weavers were clearly a very important, probably the most important, section of the Jewish community, for not only did they live in their own zone in the city but also a special part of the great synagogue was set aside for their exclusive use. They would also add value to their textiles by piling them high on top of Jeremiah's tomb in the Ben Ezra Synagogue in order that their manufacture might be blessed and sanctified.[31] Alexandria was one vast commercial centre and, in the twelfth century, Benjamin ben Jonah, a gem dealer of Tudela, Spain, in his account of his travels, lists the many countries ranging from Scotland to India whose ships docked and traded from Alexandria's capacious port.

In 1365, Christian knights besieged and then ransacked Alexandria but the city soon recovered. The sultan, celebrating its restoration, paid it a state visit and, so the story goes, his path for miles was strewn with silk carpets. The city's productive capacity is evidenced by a report of 1388, which tells us of 14,000 looms in Alexandria,[32] that number falling over the next fifty years due to excessive taxation and the shift of power from Alexandria to Cairo.

Let us rejoin Benjamin ben Jonah, to journey beyond Spain and the Maghreb to see the fuller extent of the economic and social significance of carpets in Jewish life during Middle Ages. In Thebes in Greece he sees Jewish silk weavers and purple dyers, 'who are the most skilful in all Greece'.[33] In 1147, Roger II, the Norman king of Sicily, busy building an empire, in a lightning raid kidnapped many of the Jewish weavers of Thebes and set them to work in his factories in Palermo.[34] For nearly 300 years, from the twelfth to the fifteenth century, there was a flourishing guild of Jewish silk weavers at work in Sicily. Perhaps there was more to the kidnapping than we know, for King Manuel I of Thebes then allowed those weavers who remained to form their own guild and radically improved their working conditions.[35] Benjamin ben Jonah reports (it is uncertain that he personally went far into Persia, which at that time was in a chaotic state) on the carpet weaving centres of Persia, of Hamadan, Isfahan, Shiraz and Fars and on the significance and the status of their Jewish communities,[36] and on his way back to his home in Spain he records the same high skills in weaving and dyeing among the Jewish communities in southern Italy.[37] Another twelfth-century commentator notes that the 15,000-strong community of Tustar actually controlled the carpet trade of the region![38] What is significant, of course, is that the concurrence of weaving centres and of Jewish communities in Spain and North Africa described earlier in this chapter also occurred in Islamic Iran and Christian Italy.

Rabbi Petachia, yet another great Jewish traveller of the Middle Ages, marvels in his journal at the rare and costly carpets decorating the Jewish academy in Baghdad.[39] Then, travelling on to pay his respects at the tombs of some of the Talmudic sages, he records one of the most inspired use of Jewish carpets I have ever known in all the years I have spent studying them. Perhaps it is apocryphal. Some of the graves had been desecrated, but each was now covered by a carpet under which – hidden, coiled and ready to strike at anyone who dared to disturb the dead – was a snake! Later, in the fifteenth century, a prominent Italian rabbi, Obadiah Jare of Bertinoro, describes how the Sabbath meal of the Jews in Arab lands would be served on a carpet upon which the family and guests would sit in a circle, with the food and wine placed on a cloth in the middle. Obadiah continued on to Jerusalem, where he met a rabbi whose equal for humility and fear of God he had never seen, for 'he weaves night and day when he is not occupied with his studies'.[40]

It was also worth noting that Benjamin of Tudela, Rabbi Petachia and the thirteenth-century Spanish-Jewish poet Judah al-Harizi tell us something of the life and times of the more isolated Jews of Kurdistan. Later studies report that weaving light rugs and spinning wool was common among the Kurdistani Jews, especially among the farm-workers in winter, and in the towns even some rabbis were part-time weavers. According to Benjamin II their woollen rugs were so fine as to be desirable exports.[41]

As discussed earlier in this chapter, it is clear that throughout the Mediterranean virtually every major centre engaged in the manufacture and marketing of carpets and weavings was also home for much of the time to a substantial, involved and often affluent Jewish community. The essential unity of Jewish life transcended the geographical, religious and political boundaries of the Mediterranean, and indeed went far beyond. For it seems that in other carpet weaving areas, Jewish motifs were being woven into their carpets. This may sometimes reflect the use of such motifs or Hebrew letters not only by Jewish but by Muslim weavers as well as talismanic symbols. Tyilo Khizghilov, writing about the Jewish weavers of Caucasia (where they had settled in the eighth century, if not earlier), observed: 'In Jewish art forms, particularly rug weaving, one may also find motifs to which magical powers were ascribed and which were handed down by weavers from one generation to the next.'[42]

But let us get back to the Jewish communities of Spain and the Maghreb. From the treasure trove of the Cairo Genizah, we learn how really closely knit together they were. United by family ties[43] (for marriage would often cement business relationships), commerce, the same religious schools and the same rabbinic authorities enforcing the same legal system,[44] their scholars and skilled craftsmen (the two were often the same) travelled extensively throughout and beyond the Islamic realms of Spain and North Africa.[45] It was not unusual for a merchant to make several journeys in his lifetime between Spain and India.[46]

The frequency and extent of inter-community travel is to be seen in the regulations made to protect the goods and belongings of travellers who died at sea. Legal documents from the eleventh century onwards make it clear that such property was to be handed over to the heads of the Jewish community of the next port of call, from where arrangements would be made with the community of the deceased traveller. For the same laws applied equally to the Jewish communities in Spain and in the Maghreb. So, for example, we know that a power of attorney executed in Spain was revalidated in Alexandria and legally binding in Cairo. And a Jewish villain (we do not know his crime), having been excommunicated from the community in Spain, fled to Alexandria only to have his case reviewed by the head of the community there. The merchants even ran their own postal service with a special formula written on the envelope warning the bearer that he was forbidden to open it. Under Islam, Spain boomed. Heavy taxation by the new rulers on all non-Muslim families led to many Jews leaving the land for the towns and villages to join those engaged in the booming craft industries such as weaving and dyeing. For 700 years, from the Arab conquest in the eighth century and right up to the expulsion of the Jews of Spain at the end of the fifteenth century, the Jews of Spain and North Africa were as one with their own strong culture spanning the two territories – which, at the shortest point by Gibraltar, are but twenty miles apart.

A letter preserved in the Cairo Genizah illustrates the closeness of the two communities of Spain and North Africa. The community of Najera in Castile writes to the community in Cairo asking for a contribution from them towards the ransom they had paid to free a woman and her two daughters who had been imprisoned following the murder of her husband. Then among the lists found in the Genizah of the Cairo community's charitable payments is an entry to 'the woman from Spain'.[47] Whilst we do not know if this was the same poor widow, these two findings from the Genizah are typical and indicative of the closeness of the communities. Each gave refuge to the other in time of need and the Maghreb communities, especially those of Morocco, welcomed the Jews of Spain during the pogroms of 1391 and up to and following the expulsion of 1492.

The Jewish communities of Spain and the Maghreb were part of a broad network of Jewish merchants and scholars linking various parts of the wider Mediterranean, Iraq, Persia[48] and the Indian Ocean.[49] We see the breadth of this network and of the wide geographic spread of its merchandise in another brief letter written in Alexandria about a journey in Spain which refers to a consignment of gold from Morocco, silk from Spain, ambergris from the Atlantic and musk from either Tibet or Malaya. In yet another letter, a Spanish trader in Fez writes to his father in Almeria about certain import taxes.[50] Travel was relatively easy, with direct shipping lines between Alexandria and the ports of Spain. A *responsum* of Maimonides tells us of some Jews who were actually regular passengers on ships commuting between Seville and Alexandria.[51] Indeed, so regular were the journeys of the merchants of Alexandria that many of them would buy second homes in Almeria.[52] As for transport along the coastline of the Maghreb, the Venetian merchant Emanuel Piloti,[53] who was resident in Egypt for much of the period 1396–1436, recorded that 'Every year between eight and ten ships arrived in Alexandria from Tunis and points further west.' Such points doubtless included Azemmour, Tlemcen, Kairouan, and Jerba – as we have seen, all major Jewish settlements – with cheap mats and other weavings amongst their cargoes.[54] Maimonides, attesting to the pride of the synagogues of Muslim Spain, North Africa and the land of Israel, noted that the synagogues in Muslim lands all supplied mats for sitting on the floor, whereas those in Christian countries provided seats. He himself had had an especially large carpet woven for his waiting room in Cairo in 1176–77. It was not that unusual for carpets to be made to specific size and design order, and we read of another letter in the Genizah from a notable in Cairo instructing agents to commission a particular weaver to make him some carpets.

In tenth-century Spain, the quality of the work and the status of the Jewish weavers, particularly those working in silk, is clear. Ibn Daud reports that among the many Jews engaged in that industry were two Jewish master weavers, the brothers Jacob and Joseph ibn Gan, personal weavers for al-Mansur (976–1002), the all-powerful military dictator of the time.[55] Jacob was supreme judge of the Jewish community of Cordoba and, in partnership with Joseph, had a major silk weaving business. They probably employed many skilled Jewish women as well as men,[56] for much of the weavers' work had been done by women[57] whose role in life had been spelled out by the Sephardi poet, Samuel ha-Nagid (993–1056):

> Walls and palaces were created for women
> Their glory consists in winding wool and weaving.[58]

Although not directly related to Spain and North Africa, we get a sense of the significance of carpets in Islam in the description of one of the Umayyad Caliph Hisham's carpet. It was an incredible 157 feet long, woven in silk and embroidered in gold.[59] The Umayyads were followed by the 'Abbasids (749–1258) and the scale of their carpet production was staggering. Caliph Harun al-Rashid's palace was said to be adorned with 38,000 carpets, 12,500 of which were made of silk and gold. Fragments may be seen today in the Cairo Museum.[60]

Starting from the end of the fourteenth century, we learn more about the Jewish weavers of Spain from the rabbinic *responsa*, from the poetic literature and from church and government records. The *responsa* bring us close to the times and the troubles of the ordinary Jewish weavers. For example, a judgement of Asher ben Yehiel, chief rabbi of Castile (1305–27), records a case of a weaver who, having accepted a commission, asserted that the client's material was not of the quality he had been given to understand it would be. Accordingly, he had asked to be released from the contract. His client, however, had persuaded him, in consideration of a higher fee, to continue with the work. Subsequently the client refused to pay anything more than the original fee, arguing that he had been forced, when he had no choice, to agree to pay the increased cost. I think there was more to it than the bare facts that have come down to us, for Asher ben Yehiel held that the weaver was bound by the original contract.[61]

Skills and their secrets were usually kept within a family for, as it is written in the Talmud, 'A father who fails to teach his son a trade virtually teaches him robbery.'[62] It seems each trade had its own badge: the wool carder displayed a woollen thread; the dyer a range of coloured threads – and the weaver goes out with a small whorl on his ear, proud of his occupation. (A whorl is this context is usually a weighted disc at the end of the rod around which thread is coiled.) There is an interesting and odd contract of 1406 between a Christian dyer who undertakes to teach a Jewish weaver the secrets of concocting certain dyes. It is interesting because other dyes are specifically excluded and odd because Jews were even more famous as dyers than as weavers. For example, the Jewish Dyers Guild of Barcelona was internationally famous, and its dyeing of such high quality that despite the costs and risks of shipping, merchants in other countries would send them their fabrics to be dyed.[63]

Another surviving contract, endorsed in 1440 by the local authority in Saragossa, is worth noting, for in revealing high levels of cooperation between Christian and Jewish craft guilds it demonstrates the strength of the Jewish craftsmen. The purpose of the contract was to maintain the quality of the products of both guilds and so protect both reputations and the value of their work. Basically, both parties agreed to permit access to and inspection of the other's workshops and to share all the fines levied for violations of the rules of workmanship.

The constitution of the Jewish shoemakers' guild of Saragossa, granted recognition by Pedro IV of Aragon, provides insight into the functions of the Jewish artisan guilds, for these cooperative societies provided a significant social and economic base. Their prime concern was the care of their sick, with guild wardens visiting sick members twice a week, on Monday and Thursday, and guild members visiting sick colleagues on Saturday. Destitute fellows received a stipend from the guild treasury and, in the case of death, the members would remain with the body until the religious services and burial had been completed. The guild was involved in all the family events of its members.

Spanish Jews participated in the whole cycle of making and selling carpets. A twelfth-century document reports that most transactions in silk and other textiles were handled by Jews of Spain. In southern Italy and Sicily, under Frederick II (1194–1250), Jews actually held a monopoly on dyeing, silk processing and weaving.[64] In that monopoly we see, too, something of the common culture and the unity of the Jewish weavers of the Mediterranean (whether in the Christian Norman Sicily or in Muslim Fatimid Egypt or in Spain, all three having their own long-established communities of Jews and weavers) in the similarity of the silk designs, many with their bands of confronting animals or of peacocks facing Tree of Life palmettes. The Christian conquest of much of Spain by the thirteenth century had little impact on the local Jewish merchants and their trade in carpets and other goods with Islamic lands. By the late fifteenth century, these exports would include the beautiful Mamluk carpets, some of which may well have been made by *converso* weavers in Spain as well as in Cairo and the Maghreb.[65] I will return to this point later in this chapter.

The level of carpet production in Spain and the Maghreb and Egypt was enormous. In addition to the major manufacture in Murcia there was an important Jewish workshop in Borja in Salamanca. The carpets made by the Jews in Tunis and Sfax (Gafsa) were particularly well known in the Middle Ages and much sought after. Fuelled by the political and economic expansion of the Islamic world, the Maghreb became the major trading centre between the Near East, Spain and Europe. To the south, caravans of camels bearing African gold, ivory and slaves would regularly cross sub-Sahara Africa, so further enriching the Maghreb. The demand for carpets was fed by this new wealth, and the central role of carpets within Islamic and Jewish culture was met by numerous carpet weaving centres which, for much of the time, as we have seen, were also home to their own actively participating Jewish communities.

At various times over the Middle Ages the popes banned all trade with infidels – an act which directed the substantial trade either to those merchants who purchased his special absolution (crown and church would share the proceeds), to those who ignored it or to the Jewish traders. The latter, living in both territories,[66] had a common language and commercial custom, a system of international credit (which by increasing the money supply expanded the volume of trade) and the same legal system with sophisticated contract, joint venture and partnership law enforceable in the rabbinic courts, all in addition to the close ties of commerce and marriage set in the culture of the extended family. They were primary producers too, for later we learn of a *converso*, Anton de Rio, selling 'fine white merino wool' from his flocks for the enormous sum of four-and-a-half million *marcos* to Genoese traders.[67] Some of these traders may well also have been *conversos*, for the productivity and the prosperity of fourteenth- and fifteenth-century Genoa was partly based upon a massive immigration of skilled artisans from Spain to that independent and (for so long as it was profitable) tolerant society. In sericulture, too, Jews were famed for their skill in breeding silkworms and producing silk in commercially viable quantities. The records show that even at the end of the fifteenth century there were still Jewish weavers in almost every small Iberian community. Indeed, in the Calatayud district (believed by some to be so named from the Arabic *qal'at al-yahud* or 'the Jewish quarter') the weavers were so numerous and successful that they worshipped in their own synagogue and studied in their own yeshiva.[68]

It is impossible to arrive at any considered estimate of the numbers of Jewish carpets in medieval Spain displaying overt Judaic iconography, since only the Spanish synagogue carpet (Chapter 6) has survived, having been discovered rotting in a Swiss church in the 1880s. Yet given the many hundreds of synagogues and the fact that carpets were one of the greatest media of cultural expression, almost every synagogue would have had its carpets – their quality and quantity being a function of the wealth and disposition of each congregation.[69] Let us recall Maimonides's comment, cited earlier, regarding the pride that the synagogues took in their fine carpets. In a domestic setting, it was common to hang a carpet or other marker adorned with Judaic symbols on an eastern wall of the home – facing Jerusalem – as a directional finder for prayer and reminder of the Divine omnipresence.

We do have a brief description of the hangings in an Egyptian synagogue in the Middle Ages. With their rich fabrics of light green and blue, often embroidered with stripes of gold or silver, they must have been magnificent.[70] In Jewish colour symbolism, gold represents Divine Light (Zechariah 6:11) and silver denotes innocence (Isaiah 1:22). But apart from the Spanish synagogue carpet, no other synagogue carpets of Spain have survived. Annexed by church and king, the carpets of the Jews, as with so many of their books and finally their bodies, were destroyed in the fires of the pogroms and of the auto-da-fé. In the ashes of the silk and wool, there for the taking by their new owners, were the gold and silver melted from the threads that had adorned the carpets.[71]

Turning now to Murcia, we are at the centre of Spain's carpet weaving industry, where the Vizcaya carpet was woven (this will be more fully discussed in Chapter 9).[72] When the Christian knights took control of the town of Murcia in 1266, high walls were built to separate its Jewish, Christian and remaining Muslim communities.[73] As discussed earlier, the Jews were offered many special inducements to replace the fleeing Muslim population, including grants of homes, shops and land, elective privileges and tax exemptions.[74] Some 2,000 settled there, earning their livelihoods in a variety of activities centred around the primary economy of textiles. The flight of the Muslims had left much productive land abandoned, and the subsequent collapse of a rental yield on agricultural land led to a corresponding exodus of their new Christian landowners; many areas remained depopulated.[75] But the weaving industry thrived and the production of cheap esparto mats was taken over from the Muslims by Christian artisans.[76] Two hundred years later, the town plan of Murcia of 1481 still shows a substantial Jewish quarter (Figure 9). In 2005 I tried to track its boundaries from this map but no trace of the Juderiá was left; the adjacent Palacio de la Inquisición was closed for business and the ladies in the tourist office did not know where the Juderiá had been – or even what it was. Many of the Jews of Murcia had found refuge in Debou, a town with no less than seventeen synagogues, in north-east Morocco, where they joined Jews of Seville who had settled there after the pogroms of 1391. Now known as the Murciano, they were able to continue their major economic activities, mainly weaving and sheep raising, and their women excelled in embroidery.

There had also been a number of other Jewish urban communities in the province of Murcia and in Valencia just to the north. The authoritative historian Luis Rubio Garcia reports that much of the commercial effort of the Jews of Murcia was devoted to the weaving and the marketing of textiles. Noting that both the quality and the actual trading in those weavings was regulated by the state (the Enriquez-governed Murcia), he records the 'strong relationships between the textile and the silk industry which had a strong tradition in Murcia and was practiced [sic] with a unique level of skills [by the Jewish community]'.[77] In an illustration for a book, drawn and painted in fifteenth-century Spain, we may actually see two Jewish weavers at work embroidering wall carpets (Figure 4). A fourteenth–fifteenth-century

Hebrew poet, Yitzhaq Alahdab, gives us a vivid, if caricatured, sense of the weaver in his poem of the trades:

> I'm skilful as skilful ever comes
> And so I've mastered many trades,
> I know about spinning and weaving on looms,
> And how, with warp, the weft is made.[78]

The substantial contribution of the Jews of Murcia to its prime commercial activity of carpet production is evidenced in the social legislation and the economic data. As to the former, so important was their contribution that early in the fifteenth century, in defiance of the rulings of the church, Jews were even permitted to trade on Sundays. As to the latter, I cited earlier the very significant statistic that 35 to 60 per cent of the income of every one of the Iberian kingdoms was contributed by Jewish farmers, artisans and merchants. Another study informs us that the Jews of Murcia paid the highest amount of taxes of all the Jewish communities in Spain.[79] Given the dominant position of the carpet weaving industry in Murcia and, as we see above, the magnitude of the taxation levied on the Jews, it would be perverse to think that the Jewish involvement in and their contribution to the carpets of Murcia was of anything but the highest order.

From perhaps the middle of the fourteenth century, many churchmen, the emerging middle classes and the mob united in turning against the Jews. The monarchs joined in later and on 31 March 1492, Ferdinand and Isabella, reigning monarchs of a now united Spain (apart from Navarre), banned all Jews from their kingdoms. Putting aside the church's demonizing of the Jews and the enormous wealth and power the church thereby acquired, its premise was that the remaining overt Jews were supporting and suborning the covert Jews among the *conversos* – and while it had authority over and could do something about the latter, it had no sufficient control over the former. Hence the need to expel the Jews – but not the New Christians, albeit so many of them had converted to Christianity, not because they believed in the divine nature of Jesus but simply to save their own and their families' lives and livelihoods. History seems to teach us that often individuals and nations act wisely only after they have exhausted all other options, and half a millennium was to pass before Spain in 1968 repealed Ferdinand and Isabella's Statute of Expulsion. What happened to those Jewish weavers who converted to Christianity is considered in Chapter 9. And what happened to those who fled abroad is also part of the story of the Jewish weavers of Spain. The estimates vary greatly but some commentators, working primarily from Ottoman tax records, suggest that well over 100,000 Jews found refuge in the Ottoman domains. As Eliyahu Capsali, the sixteenth-century Jewish historian, explains:

> So the Sultan Baylze [Bayazid II, 1481–1512], king of Turkey, heard of all the evils that the Spanish king had brought upon the Jews and heard they were seeking a refuge and a resting place. He took pity on them and wrote letters and sent emissaries to proclaim throughout his kingdom that none of his city rulers may be wicked enough to refuse entry to the Jews or expel them. Instead they were to be given a gracious welcome.[80]

As indeed they were. For as busy as Christianity was in supplanting Islam in the West, so was Islam busy supplanting Christianity in the East. Byzantine Christians fleeing the Ottoman advance caused the Serphardim, a people in need of a land, to find a land in need of a people. Among the many skills they brought with them, in addition to their major skills in the manufacture and marketing of textiles, the production of dyes, the breeding of silk worms and so of producing silk in viable quantities, was the manufacture of advanced ammunition and the invention of the first wheeled gun carriage, all of which contributed greatly to the military supremacy and the economy of the Ottoman Empire.[81]

But our topic is the weavers, who by the sixteenth century had raised the previously very modest Turkish carpet weaving craft into an internationally famous high-quality industry yielding major revenue for the sultan's treasury. The growth in the Jewish population of Salonica alone was phenomenal. According to an authority cited by Gerber,[82] by 1430 it numbered some 17,500 (the exodus of the Jews of Spain had begun after the pogroms of 1391 and 1411); by 1519 there were 28,000; by 1553 it numbered 56,500 and by 1663 the Jewish population of Salonica had grown to 77,000. There, they had joined 11,000 Christians, Muslims and a small group of Romaniot Jews (who had first settled there in the fifth century BCE, but most of whom had been moved to Istanbul after 1453), and they transformed Salonica into a major celebrated manufacturing and marketing textile entrepôt. In the fifteenth century there had been but seventy-six weavers in Salonica, but by the next century the town was swarming with Spanish and Portuguese, Italian and Sicilian Jewish designers, dyers and weavers who, aided by their advanced technology,[83] transformed the economy and the society of the region. The surveys of 1520–30 divide the total number of households in Salonica of 4,863 into 1,229 Muslim, 989 Christian and 2,645 Jewish households, by which time the workforce and the very language of the Salonica textile industry had become Spanish. That both the quality and the quantity of the carpets of Spain hugely declined, only to boom exponentially in the Muslim world, provides yet further proof of the substantial contribution of the Jews to the carpet weaving industry of Spain. The profusion of skilled Sephardi carpet weavers in sixteenth-century Salonica points to the correspondingly large numbers of skilled Sephardi carpet weavers in fifteenth-century Spain.[84] That they changed their weaving technique of the single warp knot to the Turkish knot was part of their adaptation into a new community with the demands of a new market. To get some idea of the level of those skills, do look at the copy of a superb surviving Sephardi Turkish carpet illustrated in Figure 10.

This carpet is a striking example of the adaptations made by the Jewish designers and weavers of Spain in their new homes and markets in Turkey, yet still linking them and identifying them to their lost lives in Spain. The format of this carpet is the same as that of any classical Islamic prayer rug of western Anatolia, with the same multiple borders of varying widths protecting the coupled columned prayer niche in the central field. But what makes this a carpet of the synagogue and not of the mosque are both the Hebrew inscriptions and the placement of the hands at the bottom centre, for the hands on a Muslim prayer rug are understood by many to be at each side, further up the field. The Hebrew inscription on the hands also identifies them as the blessing hand of the priest (kohen). The inscription at the top centre recites Psalm 118:20 'This is the Gateway of the Lord, through which the righteous shall enter.' And from the quotations woven in the borders we know that the designer and the weavers were Sephardim from Spain, for the carpet had been donated by Judah d'Avila, in memory of the soul of his daughter Garcia, to the Seville Synagogue – the town they had left many years ago, taking with them their talent and high traditions of Spanish Jewish carpet craft, and adapting them to their new homes in the Ottoman Empire.

It was not only in Salonica that the surviving Jewish weavers of Spain found refuge. Taking their skills with them, they also settled in other parts of the Muslim world, including the sultan's capital of Istanbul, whose population increased from 80,000 in 1453 to 700,000 over the next 100 years: in 1453 there were 1,647 houses in Istanbul inhabited by Jews; fifty years later there were five times the number. The Jews of Spain also found refuge in Syria and Egypt and beyond.[85] Many went to the Land of Israel, but those who settled in Jerusalem, according to Francesco Suriano, head of the local Franciscans, were treated like dogs 'and stepped upon, are beaten and tortured, as well they should be and God punishes them more than anywhere else in the world'. Perhaps he was exaggerating a bit, for Obadiah of Bertinoro, another of the great Jewish medieval travellers, and in Jerusalem in the 1490s, met with many *converso* weavers and other craftsmen who, renouncing the baptisms forced upon them, had settled in Jerusalem. Most, however, went on to settle in Nablus and Safed.[86] In Safed, the Kabbalists, settling in the old walled town, rapidly developed it into a thriving dyeing and weaving centre. Merino wool was shipped in from Istanbul and by day these pious men would weave; by night they would discuss the holy books. In the thirty-five years from 1525 to 1560, Safed expanded threefold, from an original 233 households to nearly 1,000.[87] At the average occupancy of eleven to one, Safed had become home to over 10,000[88] and by the sixteenth century its textile industry was second only to that of Salonica.[89] It was the same in Tiberias. The old ruined city was rebuilt, wool and merino sheep from Spain were imported and mulberry trees were planted for the silkworms.

Many found refuge in Syria where, as Jenny Housego suggests, some of the Maghreb Hispano-Moresque-style carpets may have been woven. Damascus alone at the end of the fifteenth century was home to 400 to 500 Jewish families, their numbers there being greatly increased both by the refugees from Spain after the expulsion of 1492 and the incorporation of Syria into the Ottoman Empire in 1517. Of all the photographs I have seen of the synagogues founded by the refugees in Syria and Turkey, not one was without its carpets hanging on the walls, draped over the balconies, placed on the floors and suspended either side of the Ark.

Another consequence of the flight of the Sephardi weavers may well be seen in the beautiful Mamluk rugs referred to earlier in this chapter. In the second half of the fifteenth century, two separate events occurred which I believe were linked. The first, as we have seen, was the large number of highly skilled Spanish Jewish weavers who, facing death unless they converted to Christianity, emigrated to the weaving centres along the North African coast – all those centres also being home to substantial Jewish communities. The second event was the sudden and surprising appearance in those Islamic lands of very large numbers of usually extremely well-crafted knotted pile carpets of sophisticated colour and designs that had not evolved from any pre-existing Islamic weaving tradition.[90] It was sudden and surprising, for the Islamic world was in disarray: to the east the Ottomans were beginning to battle with the Safavids, and to the west the Mamluk Empire in North Africa had stagnated, its earlier great textile industry in decline. From 14,000 silk looms in Alexandria alone in 1394, by 1434 only 800 were still in operation. Yet the Mamluk carpet appeared and thrived, its size, sophistication and its innovative artistic motifs and colours finding a ready market in the centres of wealth in the palaces and mosques of Islam and in the castles and churches of resurgent Christian Europe. Whilst it is in the nature of the history of the region, this surely could not have happened without a surge of new but skilled craftsmen coming to the North African coast and setting up their looms.

We do not know for certain the source of the different designs, of the lustrous wool of the Mamluk carpets, or of their weavers. There are no ready parallels in Islamic sources, objects or architecture, and in their palatial size, in some of their motifs, in their deep borders, in their vibrant cherry reds, powder blues and leaf greens, all enhanced with touches of yellow and white and the occasional blazon, the Mamluk rugs do have real empathy with the Admiral carpets. There are a number of different types of Mamluk rugs, but there are many examples of virtually identical ornaments appearing in both Mamluk and Spanish designs,[91] and little distinction can be made between Islamic and Judaic iconography in many of their typical borders and grounds with clusters of leaf forms and vines. Jon Thompson, in detailing a fifteenth-century Spanish carpet, notes: 'its main field is structurally related to the design in Mamluk carpets – and Turkish carpets'.[92] Murray Eiland III notes that after 1492 many Ottoman designs became 'more consonant with a European aesthetic'. As the eminent Kurt Erdmann pithily puts it, 'no other type of oriental carpet is so closely connected to Europe'.[93] Also, it is surely more than coincidental that the earlier and well-established motifs of the Sephardi weavers – such as the arch resting on two pillars evocative of a palm tree as well as the pomegranate – begin to appear in Turkish carpets from around the end of the fourteenth century, when persecution and pogrom drove many of them to seek refuge in Islamic North Africa.[94] The motifs of the cypress tree, of the rosette and of the palm tree are also typically ancient Jewish motifs, often appearing on the Mamluk carpets. In Ottoman arts and crafts, especially in their magnificent silk brocades, totally new patterns suddenly appear, revealing pomegranates (see Chapter 14) and other fruits and flowers.

The experts disagree as to the origin of the Mamluk carpets. I do not think that some of them, seeing as they do strong Turkmen and central Asian influences in some of these carpets, should exclude the possibility that the Sephardi weavers who fled to Islamic lands did not have a strong hand in their production, for two reasons. Firstly, the Turkic elements that do appear would be part of the process whereby these weavers adapted to the realities of the market place and to the host culture generally. We see this process of acculturation manifested among all the Sephardim; a clear example is the Sephardi folklore music which became greatly influenced by Turkish classical music and the music of the Balkans. Secondly, it depends upon your viewpoint, for it is culture that determines the style of the carpet. It is the ornamental themes and decorative compositions that give expression to and enable us to identify the culture of the carpet. So far as carpet studies are concerned, it matters not that any monocultural carpet is woven by a Muslim, a Christian or a Jew, for it is the patterning that defines the carpet. But in social studies it is the culture not only of the weave but also of the weaver that concerns us: we should not assume the two are the same, a distinction not always appreciated by carpet aficionados.

Sometimes the really discerning eye looking at the weave will tell us more about the weaver and his cultural influence. So it was that the pre-eminent expert Walter Denny solved the mystery of the enigmatic Bellini prayer rug, affirming that its design must also have originated in Spain, and for which there must have been a component of Jewish influence and/or artistic transmission around 1500 CE – only eight years after the expulsion of 1492.

For a major source of the wool for some of these carpets, we need perhaps look no further than the island of Jerba which, with its age-old Jewish community, had long been famed for the high quality of its lustrous wool. Some authorities have suggested that weavers were refugees from the wars in north-west Persia – but the timing does not really make sense. Given the high numbers and skills of the Jewish weavers of Spain, and the refuge given to them by the often prosperous Jewish communities situated and working within virtually every major carpet weaving centre along the Maghreb[95] and Egypt, and given the stylistic similarities noted above, to fail to consider the probability of a significant Jewish contribution to the creation and production of some of the Mamluk rugs would be an act of ignorance.

More speculatively, I wondered about the real origin and inspiration for Turkish 'Holbein' rugs which, imported into Spain in the mid-fifteenth century, so often appear in paintings of the time. Many scholars have noted their similarity to the Spanish carpets. Might they have been woven by Murcian weavers, who from the late fourteenth century had been finding refuge in the Ottoman Empire? And while current scholarship would not agree, I cannot but wonder if the Rabat rugs, albeit with Anatolian rather than Spanish characteristics, yet appearing in the major Jewish centres in the Maghreb, might not owe something to the Sephardi weavers.

In his beautiful book *Sovereign Carpets*, Edoardo Concaro discusses the Ushak rugs of western Anatolia which, by the fifteenth century, began to appear in large numbers in Europe.[96] In England, Cardinal Wolsey (c.1473–1530) ordered 100 of them! That western part of Turkey has a history of carpet making going back at least to the Byzantine period, and was also home to settled Jewish communities going back to Roman times. By the fifteenth century the Ottoman armies had conquered the whole country; many Greeks had fled, others – such as those of the great carpet weaving town of Bursa – were expelled. But carpet production flourished, for in the fifteen and sixteenth centuries, tens of thousands of Spanish and other Jews, fleeing from persecution, had found refuge in the Ottoman Empire, many settling in Smyrna, Izmir, Bursa and other carpet producing sites in the region. Given the significant increase in carpet production and given the number and skills of the Jewish weavers, I think we may safely surmise that some of the Anatolian rugs owe something to the Sephardim of Spain.

Finally, another possible consequence of the flight of the Sephardi weavers is worth mentioning, for there is a remarkable similarity between Moses de Cordovero's (1522–70) schematic design of the *Ten Sephirot* (the power of potencies of the Almighty as taught in the Kabbalah) and the designs in the Khotan carpets of east Turkestan. We know that Sephardi merchants – so often also Kabbalists and philosophical scholars – on the way east had settled in some oases in east Turkestan early in the eighteenth century. From that time too the Samarkand carpets portray the powerful Jewish symbol of the flower and the fruit of the pomegranate at various angles and at various stages in its development (we will consider this further in Chapter 14). It was for the Kabbalists an evocation of paradise lost.[97]

The seedbed of most creative development is to be found not in monocultural but in multicultural societies. Innovation is usually sparked off at the

The Jewish Weavers of Spain and North Africa 55

interface of two or more cultures, for it is surely diversity, not conformity, that engenders syllogistic creativity, and the Jewish experience of being a stranger in a strange land has through the ages repeatedly stimulated original and inventive thoughts. The structures, too, of Judaism facilitate such innovative activity, for without any all-powerful pantheon of priests, popes and saints presiding over the Jew, instructing him what he must and what he must not think, thoughts de novo are engendered. The rabbi is not an essential intermediary to the Hereafter; he is a teacher whose tools include dialogue and dialectic – for did not Abraham and Moses debate with (and sometimes even persuade), the Almighty? But perhaps I wander too far from my theme.

Such was the success of the Sephardi artisans and merchants that in the early sixteenth century the proud and powerful Venetians eventually appealed to the Egyptian Sultan Qansuh al-Ghawri, pleading that he suppress the stiff competition they faced from the Spanish Jews now living under his protection in the Ottoman Empire.[98] Later in that century we learn of the importance of the Jews in Venice in the carpet trade. In a rare document, the Sephardi Isac della Vida hired a number of Mamluk carpets to the prestigious Catholic school of San Rocco. But back to Salonica: writing in the seventeenth century, the geographer Mustafa ben Abdalla Hadshi Halfa said of the Salonican weavers, that 'they produce the world famous multicoloured carpets which nowhere are made so well'.[99] It is no surprise that the carpet weavers were called *Manteros*; from *manta*, the Spanish word for rug. As late as 1795, Felix Beaujour, the French consul in Salonica, reported the Castilian (textile) factories operated by skilled Spanish Jews to be renowned throughout Europe.[100] In Smyrna (Izmir) by far the largest Jewish guild was the carpet weavers' guild, with its own house of prayer, and under whose rabbi the members studied the holy books, including the Kabbalist Zohar. To become apprenticed to the guild a boy had to know the three daily prayers and benedictions.[101] Finally, there were many Sephardi weavers in Baghdad, and in Bursa, as late as the nineteenth century, there was a Sephardi carpet weavers' guild.[102]

In the first three chapters we have looked at the history of weaving in Spain, of the Jews in Spain and of the role of carpets in Jewish culture. This chapter then brought those background studies together to consider the history of the Jewish weavers of Spain and North Africa. Now that the context, the setting, in which the Vizcaya carpet was woven has been established, in the next chapter we look at the carpet itself.

NOTES

1. L. Mackie, *Weaving through Spanish History: Thirteenth–Seventeenth Centuries*, (Washington, DC: Textile Museum, 1972–73), p.2.
2. Richard Ettinghausen, 'The Early History, Use and Iconography of the Prayer Rug', in *Prayer Rugs*, exhibition catalogue (Washington, DC: Textile Museum, 1979), p.15. Jenny Housego, 'Literary References to Carpets in North Africa', in Robert Pinner and Walter Denny (eds), *Oriental Carpet and Textile Studies, 2: Carpets of the Mediterranean Countries 1400–1600* (London: Hali Publications, 1986), pp.103–7; and Robert Pinner's invaluable 'References to Carpet Production and Trade', also in Pinner and Denny (eds), *Oriental Carpet and Textile Studies, 2*, Appendix, pp.291–5.
3. Oleg Grabar, *The Formation of Islamic Art* (New Haven, CT and London: Yale University Press, 1987), p.77.
4. Bernard F. Reilly, *The Medieval Spains* (Cambridge: Cambridge University Press, 2001), p.65.
5. Housego, 'Literary References to Carpets in North Africa', pp.103–7. See also R.B. Serjeant, *Islamic Textiles: Material for a History up to the Mongol Conquest* (Beirut: Librarie du Liban, 1972), quoting Ibn Khaldun (1322–1406).
6. *Encyclopaedia Judaica* (Jerusalem: Keter Publishing, 1971), Vol. 6, p.1255. R. Le Tourneau, G. Vajda, A. Chouraqui, D. Corcos and Jenny Housego, 'Mamluk Carpets and North Africa', in Pinner and Denny (eds), *Oriental and Textile Studies, 2*, p.228.
7. R. Lopez and W. Raymond, *Medieval Trade in the Mediterranean World* (New York: W.W. Norton, no date), p.75
8. *Encyclopaedia Judaica*, Vol. 3, Azemmour, p.1003.
9. Haim Beinart, *Atlas of Medieval Jewish History* (New York: Simon & Schuster, 1992), pp.34–5. In a *responsa*, the chief rabbi of Tlemcen noted that the earlier Marranos always married among each other. See also Solomon Freehof, *The Responsa Literature* (Philadelphia, PA: Jewish Publication Society, 1955), p.217.
10. Housego, 'Literary References to Carpets in North Africa', pp.103–5. Jenny Housego also draws our attention to the profusion of carpets and (interestingly) of candelabra evident in the celebrations in Tlemcen in 1359. Leo Africanus also recorded the superior wool and substantial volumes of woollen textiles exported from Jerba: Leo Africanus, *Description l'Afrique tierce partie du monde*, edited by C. Schefer. *Recueil des voyages et documents* (Paris, 1896), XIII, III, p.177, cited in Serjeant, *Islamic Textiles*, p.180.
11. S.D. Goitein, *A Mediterranean Society* (London: University of California Press, 1999), Vol. 4, p.199.
12. Martin Gilbert, *The Jews of Arab Lands* (London: Board of Deputies of British Jews, 1976), Map 4. I cross-referenced from Martin Gilbert's book to Map 15, 'Muslim Textile Centres in North Africa and Sicily', in Serjeant's magnificent study, *Islamic Textiles*, as well as to the map on p.15, 'Major Jewish Centres', in Eli Barnavi's captivating book, *A Historical Atlas of the Jewish People* (London: Kuperard, 1998). See also Goitein's *Letters of Medieval Jewish Travellers* (Princeton, NJ: Princeton University Press, 1973), p.81, with reference to the medieval Jewish silk weavers.
13. Donald P. Little, 'Data from the Haram Documents on Rugs in Late Fourteenth Century

Jerusalem', in Pinner and Denny (eds), *Oriental and Textile Studies*, 2, p.91, n.2.
14. Robert Pinner, Appendix, in Pinner and Denny (eds), *Oriental and Textile Studies*, 2, pp.295, 296, citing F.R. Martin, *A History of Oriental Carpets Before 1800* (Vienna: Martin, 1908), citing Ibn Said.
15. Robert G. Irwin, 'Egypt, Syria and their Trading Partners 1450–1550', in Pinner and Denny (eds), *Oriental and Textile Studies*, 2, p.79.
16. Stefan Reif, *A Jewish Archive from Old Cairo* (London: Curzon, 2000), pp.196–7.
17. Goitein, *Mediterranean Society*, Vol. 2, p.474, n.7. Serjeant, *Islamic Textiles*, p.129, names al-Nahawandi as the Jew who drew up the custom tariff for the port of Aden.
18. Goitein, *Mediterranean Society*, Vol. 2, pp.53, 149, 150. See ibid., Vol. 4, pp.117–129, for full information regarding carpets, mats and textiles revealed in the Genizah.
19. Ibid., Vol. 4, pp.336, 462.
20. Ibid., Vol. 2, p.52.
21. Exodus 15:2, and as elaborated in the Talmud (Babylonian Talmud, Shabbat 133B) and specifically reinforced in fourteenth-century Spain in the writings of Profiat Duran. The point is that ritual objects may only be aesthetically pleasing to facilitate approaching the invisible but omnipresent God. In no way whatsoever are they manifestations of the Divine.
22. C. Le Quesne, 'The Synagogue', p.85, and M. Ben-Sasson, 'The Medieval Period', pp.214, 215 in P. Lambert (ed.), *Fortifications and the Synagogue* (Montreal: Canadian Centre for Architecture, 1944).
23. Arthur Dilley, *Oriental Rugs and Carpets*, revised by M.S. Dimand (Philadelphia, PA: Lippincott & Co., 1959), p.3.
24. Joseph Gutmann, *Beauty in Holiness* (Jerusalem: Ktav Publishing, 1970), p.22.
25. M. Dimand and J. Mailey, *Oriental Rugs in the Metropolitan Museum of Art* (New York: The Metropolitan Museum of Art, 1973), p.7.
26. Franz Landsberger, *Development of Jewish Art* (Cincinnati, OH: Union of American Jewish Congregations, 1944), p.190.
27. Rudolph Berliner, 'Remarks on Some Tapestries from Egypt', *Textile Museum Journal*, 1, 4 (December 1965), p.39.
28. Susan Edmison, *The Wall Street Journal*, 15 January 1987.
29. Editor of Hali's comments to a letter from Gabrielle Hold, *Hali*, 156 (Summer 2008), p.25.
30. The experts at the British Museum date it to the eighth or even ninth century.
31. Babylonian Talmud, Megillah 26a; Babylonian Talmud, Nazier 52a; Tosefta Sukkah 4:6.
32. Sean Gough, 'The Mamluk Sultanate', *Hali*, 4, 1 (1981), p.34
33. Lansberger, *Development of Jewish Art*, p.192. I have not been able to verify this quotation from the partial itinerary published by E. Adler in *Jewish Travellers in the Middle Ages* (New York: Dover Publications, 1946).
34. John Julius Norwich, *The Kingdom in the Sun* (London: Longmans, 1970), p.131, and Adler, *Jewish Travellers in the Middle Ages*, p.53.
35. M. Wischnitzer, *A History of Jewish Crafts and Guilds* (New York: Jonathan David, 1965), p.24, notes.
36. Adler, *Jewish Travellers in the Middle Ages*, p.53.
37. Mary Schoeser, *World Textiles: A Concise History* (London: Thames & Hudson, 2003), p.76, notes

that weaving, dyeing and silk processing in southern Italy and Sicily under Frederick II (1194–1250) was actually a Jewish monopoly.
38. Josephine Bacon, *The Illustrated Atlas of Jewish Civilisation*, consulting editor Martin Gilbert (London: Andre Deutsch, 1969), pp.31, 55. Also Lawrence D. Loeb, *Outcast: Jewish Life in Southern Iran* (New York: Gordon & Beach Science Publishers, 1977), p.280.
39. Adler, *Jewish Travellers in the Middle Ages*, p.70.
40. Ibid., pp.220, 237.
41. O. Schwartz-Be'eri, *The Jews of Kurdistan*, catalogue (Jerusalem: The Israel Museum, 2000), pp.26, 31.
42. Tyilo Khizghilov, 'Jewish Motifs in Caucasian Rug', in L. Mikdash-Shamailov (ed.), *Mountain Jews Customs and Daily Life in the Caucasus* (Jerusalem: The Israel Museum, 2002), p.152.
43. Goitein, *Mediterranean Society*, Vol. 1, p.48.
44. Ibid., Vol. 1, p.66.
45. Ibid., Vol. 1, pp.50, 51.
46. Jane Gerber, *The Jews of Spain* (London: Free Press, 1994), p.32.
47. Goitein, *Mediterranean Society*, Vol. 2, p.95.
48. Ibn al-Faqih wrote: 'It has been said that there were more Jews, weavers and adulterers in Isfahan than elsewhere.' Ibn al-Faqih, *Compendium Libri Kitab al-Buldan*, edited by M.J. Goeje (Leyden: BGA, 1885), pp.253, 254, quoted in Serjeant, *Islamic Textiles*, p.83. Was Ibn ad-Faqih referring to three separate sets of people or describing a single group?
49. Goitein, *Mediterranean Society* Vol. 1 – for examples of these close connections in the eleventh century, see pp.48–9, 55–6, 192, 212–13.
50. Chaim Raphael, *The Sephardi Story* (London: Vallentine Mitchell, 1991), p.91.
51. Goitein, *Mediterranean Society*, Vol. 1, p.213.
52. Florence Lewis May, *Silk Textiles of Spain* (New York: Hispanic Society of America, 1957), p.12.
53. Piloti, favoured by the Sultan, bought the warehouse next door to the customs house. Breaking through the common wall and extracting his goods free of tax, he became fabulously rich. Anne Wolff, *How Many Miles to Babylon?* (Liverpool: Liverpool University Press, 2003), p.85.
54. Irwin, 'Egypt, Syria and their Trading Partners 1450–1550', p.75.
55. Eliyahu Ashtor, *The Jews of Moslem Spain*, Vol. 1 (Jerusalem: Jewish Publication Society, 1973), pp.376–8, and Ibn Daud, *Sefer ha-Qabbalah*, edited by G.D. Cohen, pp.68–9, as quoted in Nachum Gross (ed.), *The Economic History of the Jews* (Jerusalem: Keter Publishing, 1975).
56. Wischnitzer, *History of Jewish Crafts and Guilds*, p.94.
57. Vivian Mann, *Jewish Texts on the Visual Arts* (Cambridge: Cambridge University Press, 2000), p.54 and generally.
58. *Remembering Sepharad* (Madrid: State Corporation for Spanish Cultural Action Abroad, 2003), p.90, quoting Tova Rosen's article, *Representaciones de mujeres en la poesía hispano-hebrea*, in Izquierdo Benito and Sáenz-Badillos (1998), pp.123–38.
59. Dilley, *Oriental Rugs and Carpets*, pp.8, 22. Hisham's carpet was not to be compared to Solomon's carpet which, in legend, was sixty miles long by sixty miles wide and of green

silk interwoven with pure gold.
60. Ibid., pp.23, 25.
61. Wischnitzer, *History of Jewish Crafts and Guilds* p.97.
62. B. Kiddushin, 29A.
63. Wischnitzer, *History of Jewish Crafts and Guilds*, p.111, citing D. Manuel de Bofarull de Sartoria, *Gremios y Cofradias de la Corona de Aragon*, Vol. 1 (Barcelona, 1876), pp.131–3.
64. May, *Silk Textiles of Spain*, p.4, and extended notes 7 and 8, pp.249, 250. Also Irwin, 'Egypt, Syria and their Trading Partners 1450–1550', p.75, citing Carlier de Pinon making a similar point for the sixteenth century. See also Schoeser, *World Textiles: A Concise History*, p.76.
65. Housego, 'Literary References to Carpets in North Africa', p.105, citing L. Golvin, *Les Arts Populaires en Algerie II* (Algiers, 1953), I, p.41 and Housego, 'Mamluk Carpets and North Africa', pp.230–40, citing Golvin, *Les Arts Populaires en Algerie II*, p.551 pre-eminently sensible suggestion, 'ne seraient – ils pas tout simplement espagnols?' See also Murray Eiland III, *Starting to Collect Antique Oriental Rugs* (Woodbridge: Antique Collectors Club, 2003), p.168.
66. A. MacKay, *Spain in the Middle Ages* (Basingstoke: Macmillan, 1977), p.165.
67. Alisa Meyuhas Ginio (ed.), *Jews, Christians and Muslims in the Mediterranean World after 1492* (London: Frank Cass, 1992), p.24.
68. Wischnitzer, *History of Jewish Crafts and Guilds*, p.111. Many Spanish place and other names may be traced back to their Hebrew origins, but an alternative and perhaps more accurate source of the place name Calatayud is from the Arabic Qal'at Ayyub (Ayyub's fortress).
69. Yom-Tov Assis, 'Synagogues in Medieval Spain', *Jewish Art*, 18 (1992), pp.7–29.
70. Goitein, *Mediterranean Society*, Vol. 2, pp.150–1.
71. Eleazer Gutwirth, 'Towards Expulsion 1391–1492: Spain and the Jews', in *The Sephardi Experience 1492 and After*, edited by Elie Kedourie (London: Thames & Hudson, 1992), p.72. I think burning Jewish textiles for the gold or silver in the thread was probably a common occurrence. We know from Jacob ha'Cohen (he was travelling in the Crusader kingdom shortly before it fell to Islam in the late twelfth century) that the tombs of ancient rabbis would be broken open, the bodies disturbed and their shrouds plundered for the gold or silver in the thread. Adler, *Jewish Travellers in the Middle Ages*, p.96.
72. E. Kühnel and L. Bellinger, *Catalogue of Spanish Rugs, 12th Century to 19th Century* (Washington, DC: The Textile Museum, 1953), p.2.
73. H.C. Lea, *A History of the Inquisition of Spain*, Vol. 1 (New York: Macmillan, 1906), p.64.
74. Gerber, *Jews of Spain*, p.93.
75. Thomas Glick, *Islamic and Christian Spain in the Early Middle Ages* (Princeton, NJ: Princeton University Press, 1979), p.102.
76. Ibid., p.223.
77. Luis Rubio Garcia, *Los Judíos de Murcia en la Beja Edad Media (1350–1500)* (Murcia: Universidad de Murcia, 1992), p.118.
78. P. Cole, *The Dream of the Poem* (Princeton, NJ: Princeton University Press, 2007), p.323.
79. J. Valdéon Baruque, *Los Judios de Castilla y las Revolucion Trastamara* (Valladolid: Gráficas Andrés Martín, 1968), p.55.

80. E. Capsali, *Seder Eliyahu Zuta*, eds. A. Schmuelevitz, S. Simonsohn and M. Benayahu (Israel: Ben-Zvi Institute, Tel Aviv University and Jerusalem University, 1976), Vol II, pp.218–19.
81. In his catalogue *The Classical Tradition in Anatolian Carpets*, Textile Museum, Washington (Washington, DC: Scala, 2002) Professor Denny, in his classically captivating and cogent style, looks at the contribution of the *converso* carpet designers and weavers to the carpets of Anatolia. See also de Nicolay who, accompanying the French Ambassador to Turkey in 1551, wrote: 'excellent workers in all crafts and manufactures among the recently arrived Spanish and Portuguese refugees, especially Marranos who, to the great detriment and damage of Christianity, have conveyed to the Turks many inventions, arts, and machines of war, namely, how to produce artillery, guns, gunpowder, cannon balls, and other weapons'.
82. *The Jewish Encyclopaedia*, ed. I. Singer (New York: Funk & Wagnalls, 1916). Vol. 14, p.699, gives an estimate of the population of Salonika in 1553 of 20,000 Jews. Gerber, *Jews of Spain* (p.153), writing some twenty-four years later, gives a figure of 20,000 male Jews, estimated, presumably from the tax rolls, by a German traveller of the time.
83. Esther Juhasz, 'Textiles for the Home and Synagogue', in E. Juhasz (ed.), *Sephardi Jews in the Ottoman Empire* (Jerusalem: The Israel Museum, 1990), p.65.
84. Benjamin Braude, 'The Rise and Fall of Salonica Woollens, 1500–1650: Technology Transfer and Western Competition', in Ginio (ed.), *Jews, Christians and Muslims in the Mediterranean World after 1492*, p.216–36.
85. They also took the secret methods of certain sophisticated types of embroidery, such as the famous *Point d'Espagne*, which, ironically, was much used for Catholic ecclesiastical garments. In Poland, not more than 100 years ago, the Yiddish phrase for a particularly high quality type of weaving was *Shpanyer Arbeit* – Spanish weaving/work.
86. Irwin, 'Egypt, Syria and their Trading Partners 1450–1550', p.78.
87. Abraham David, *To Come to the Land* (Tuscaloosa, AL: University of Alabama Press, 1999), p.99.
88. Dan Cohn-Sherbok, *Jewish Mysticism* (Oxford: Oneworld Publishers, 1995), p.32.
89. Wischnitzer, *History of Jewish Crafts and Guilds*, p.140.
90. Carol Bier of the Textile Museum, in the exhibition catalogue *Mamluk Rugs from Egypt* (March to September 2003), most lucidly and engagingly sets out the uncertainties of origin and early development. Edmund de Unger, 'An Ancestor of the Mamluk Carpets', *Hali*, 5, 1 (1982), pp.44–6, has no such doubts, seeing their genesis in the classical art retained by the Copts, which was much influenced by the numerous and sophisticated Jewish designers and merchants of Alexandria and the North African littoral. See also another of my favourite textile experts, the late Patricia Baker, in *Islamic Textiles* (London: British Museum Press, 1995), pp.78–80.
91. R. Pinner and M. Franses, 'The East Mediterranean Carpet Collection', in *Hali*, 4, 1 (1981), p.49, n.5; p.51, n.45. Robert Pinner, in his introduction (p.7), writes of their unique and splendid carpets, in attempts to attribute their sources, as going on 'a round trip of the Mediterranean, being in turn assigned to Damascus, Rhodes, Syracuse and Spain' – all places where they were substantial Jewish or *converso* communities. See also Carlo Marcia Suriana's analysis, 'A Mamluk Landscape', *Hali*, 34 (2004), pp.96–7.

92. John Thompson, in his book *Milestones in the History of Carpets* (Milan: Tabibnia, 2006), p.79. Sumiyo Okumura in *The Influence of Turkic Culture in Mamluk Carpets* (Istanbul: Centre for Islamic History, Art and Culture, 2007), authoritatively analyses the political and military crises of the time, leading to some migrations by Turkic peoples to the west. Were there to have been any significant Turkic symbols in any grouping of these rugs, I could see some strength in her view that the Mamluk carpets were designed and woven by Turkic refugees from the east. But no such conclusive patterning is to be found. Nor does Sumiyo Okumura make her case by asserting that there was some uniquely exclusive linkage between some of the dyes in the Mamluk carpets which came from Iran and Afghanistan and these Turkic refugees. The Jews of the Mediterranean were more famous both for their skills in the manufacture of dyes and in the extent of their international trading networks than they were as weavers.

93. K. Erdmann, *Seven Hundred Years of Oriental Carpet* (London: Faber & Faber, 1970), p.198. Of course the influence of the Jews of Spain on the Maghreb extended beyond carpets. See Caroline Stone in the British Museum's excellent book, *5000 Years of Textiles*, ed. J. Harris (London: British Museum Press, 1993). On page 287 she writes that the shapes of the Moroccan Jewish bridal and festival dresses are 'strongly reminiscent of the sixteenth century European dress'. Chechaouen produces veil ends 'reminiscent of carpet patterns'; Azemmour produces 'European stylised scrolls and amulets'. Again, on page 290, writing about the embroidery on men's shirts, she notes that those from the southern oases are 'again curiously reminiscent of those of southern Europe'. It would seem that whole areas of the later art of Morocco has its roots in medieval Spanish decorative art. Jenny Housego, surely one of the wisest experts today, seems to agree, for as earlier noted in 'Literary References to Carpets in North Africa', p.105, she cites L. Golvin, *Les Arts Populaires en Algérie*, II, p.41: 'he suggests that the so-called Egyptian or Mamluk carpets may be Spanish'.

94. E. Danon and R. Danon, *The Garden of Pomegranates* (Rome: Textilia, 2004), pp.22, 30. Techniques and motifs such as the pomegranate and the arch begin to appear in Turkish carpets after the expulsion of 1492. Examples of the pomegranate on some of the eastern Turkestan carpets illustrated in the Danons' quite beautiful book are very similar to the pomegranates on the Vizcaya carpet. See also note 3.

95. In some regions in the Maghreb, Jews were banned from owning land, so adding further thrust to the practice of crafts such as weaving.

96. Edoardo Concaro, *Sovereign Carpets* (Italy: Skira, 1999), p.17.

97. Danon and Danon, *Garden of Pomegranates*, p.30, and Nunzio Crisa, 'Secrets of the Pomegranates', *Hali*, 141 (2005), pp.42–3.

98. Irwin, 'Egypt, Syria and their Trading Partners 1450–1550', p.78–9.

99. Wischnitzer, *History of Jewish Crafts and Guilds* p.131, and I.S. Emmanuel, *Histoire de l'Industrie de Tissus de Israélites de Salonique* (Paris, 1935), p.18, n.250.

100. Wischnitzer, *History of Jewish Crafts and Guilds*, p.124, citing J. Hammer-Purgstall, *Geschichte des Osmanischen Reiches* (Pest, 1846), 3, p.213.

101. Wischnitzer, *History of Jewish Crafts and Guilds*, p.139, citing S. Asaf, *Mekorot l-toledot hahinnuk b'Israel* (Tel Aviv, 1936), 3, pp.82, 84.
102. Wischnitzer, *History of Jewish Crafts and Guilds*, pp.42, 141; S.A. Rosanes, *Dibre Yeme Yisrael be-Togarmah*, Vol. 2, p.131; L.A. Frankel, *Nach Jerusalem* (Leipzig, 1858), 1, p.24.

PART 2

THE CARPETS

The Vizcaya Carpet

In fifteenth-century Spain, in the twilight of what had for many in the peninsula been a golden age of tolerance and of culture, especially in the age of the Umayyads of Spain and some of their successors, as the lengthening shadows of bigotry inexorably extinguished enlightenment, the extraordinary Admiral carpets were woven. Their importance to us today rests in their rarity as cultural chronicles: they offer, if we care to look, salient insights into the lives of the mighty of the time. Five hundred years ago they were important statements of their owners' status, whose lineage and power was conveyed by their coats of arms and whose wealth was implicit in the costliness, quality and size of these brilliant carpets. The Vizcaya carpet has been reduced in length and today measures twenty-six feet and ten inches by seven feet and eight inches; but still this was unusual, for most Spanish carpets of the time were much smaller. Our carpet (Figure 11) is in the care of the Vizcaya Museum in Dade County, Miami, Florida.

It is worth carefully scrutinizing the Vizcaya carpet: a number of borders and guard stripes frame the central field; their colours are brilliant, their patterns are intricate. The outer borders bear Kufic-looking inscriptions and small panels containing Star of David designs, five-branched menorot (candelabra) or five-fingered hands; pomegranates, sheep; roosters, ducks; doves; Kabbalist demon birds; possibly Torah Arks; and other human, animal and floral motifs. Many of these symbols are also to be seen on an earlier Spanish synagogue carpet (see Chapter 6) and appear in numerous Jewish religious books and on other artefacts (see Chapters 12 to 18). The inner borders are mainly geometric and decorative. The large central field starts at one end with octagons and hexagons separated by diamonds before suddenly, surprisingly, switching to continuous Stars of David. The section with the octagons and hexagons is not part of the original carpet but is an inserted fragment from another carpet. We do not know why the repeat pattern in the central field was changed, for in the central field of the other Admiral carpets, which also have repairs, it is relatively consistent throughout. Within the central field are coats of arms and other ceremonial devices of the Enriquez – the noble and powerful family who commissioned and owned the carpet.

In addition to its unusual knot (the Spanish or single-warp knot), the layout of the Vizcaya carpet and of the other Admiral carpets is quite unlike that of any classical carpet of the Islamic cultural world.[1] At first sight, one wondered if the originating tradition might be Coptic, for in vain did one look for the forms of Islam, the arabesques, the alignment of the horizontal and vertical borders and the adjoining borders with consistent relationships to the other. Emblazoned on the central field are nine complete coats of arms, the arms and honours of Fadrique Enriquez, Lord of Medina de Rioseco, Castroverde and Aguilar, Count of Melgar and Ruenda, holder of the Order of Banda, Master of Santiago and Admiral of Castile; we see too, the heraldic device of his first wife, dona Marina de Ayala. The blazons are grand. Fadrique's shield is argent a lion purple mantled of gules and triple towered castles or, dona Marina's is also argent two wolves sable and a bordure gules with coupled saltires and the Shield of Banda is or with a cotice gule. Peeping out at the end of the carpet, quite unaccountably, are the tips of two more shields. We do not know what they were designed to display, but planned they were, for they are integral to the original carpet. Then, mysteriously, the weave of two of Fadrique's blazons is not continuous. We do not know if they were added subsequently and, if so, what it was that they replaced.[2] Finally, all the shields sit rather uneasily in the central field: being of equal size and located on the same axes, indicating a European rather than an Islamic tradition.

No one knows exactly when during the fifteenth century the Enriquez Admiral carpets were woven. The authoritative historian Americo Castro studied the Enriquez family thoroughly, and cautiously proposed that their carpets were woven sometime in the seventy years between 1405 and 1475.[3] The Vizcaya carpet, displaying the coat of arms of Fadrique's wife, dona Marina, would probably only have been woven after the couple were married on 10 August 1425. However, we cannot be certain that the wife's coat of arms was not added to the carpet after it was woven. Nor would her death on 17 December 1431 necessarily have prevented the subsequent introduction of her coat of arms on this carpet.

There are two other surviving Admiral carpets bearing the blazons of this branch of the Enriquez family. The one in the Philadelphia Museum of Art is stylistically and technically similar to our Vizcaya carpet and attributed to Alfonso Enriquez (Fadrique's father) – but there are problems in its dating. The wonderful Textile Museum in Washington has the other Enriquez carpet, which bears the coat of arms of Fadrique's younger sister, Maria. While both these carpets share many of the same iconographic elements, neither, it seems to me, has quite the same geometric layout or preponderance of powerful Jewish symbols displayed in the Vizcaya carpet, nor, significantly have they suffered anything like its subsequent alterations.

The Art Institute of Chicago has an Admiral carpet which is most like our Vizcaya carpet, differing mainly in its field design and blazons. A similar star-studded carpet, woven 100 years earlier, is to be seen in a fresco (Figure 12) by Matteo di Giovanetti da Viterbo in the Palace of the Popes in Avignon during the reign of Clement VI (r. 1342–52). A previous pope, John XXII (r. 1316–34), was said to have ordered carpets from Spain, so Matteo di Giovanetti's carpet may have been one of them[4] and it may well have been ordered through one of the Jewish merchants in Avignon, for out of its ninety-four textile merchants, eighty-seven were Jews. As to the hexagram star, see Chapter 12 for its history and symbolic meanings in Jewish iconography.

There are over thirty known fragments of Admiral carpets in various museums and private collections, and two such fragments are thought to be from the twin of the Vizcaya carpet. Such carpets were woven on huge looms and often in pairs. Many of these fragments were among the Fustat finds of Old Cairo, so linked to the ancient Ben Ezra Synagogue there with its Genizah, its attic filled with a treasure trove of documents ranging from the sixth to the nineteenth century. The two Admiral carpets most like the Vizcaya carpet may be seen in New York: one in the Metropolitan Museum of Art and the other in the collection held by the Hispanic Society of America. The Metropolitan Museum of Art also has another carpet which displays Fadrique Enriquez's coat of arms, but it has a single blazon set against a floral background and is quite unlike the Vizcaya carpet. There are other similar Admiral carpets, but none of them has either the very particular iconography or the specific circumstances applicable to the Vizcaya carpet and the Enriquez family. We do not know how many other such carpets were woven and, like tens of thousands of carpets of other types, wore out and disappeared. Following the increasing pressure on the *conversos* and, in 1492, the expulsion of the Jews from Spain, no more Admiral carpets, with one exception, were woven. They had all been made for a closely knit group of Spanish nobles and most probably by the same highly skilled weavers (see Chapter 9). While a comparative study of the iconography would be of value, along with an analysis of the material from which these carpets are woven and of the knots and dyes of all these fragments, in this study I have concentrated on the Vizcaya carpet.

Like the earlier Spanish synagogue carpet discussed in the next chapter, these Admiral pieces are woven from sheep's wool or goats' hair, with supplementary wrapping wefts forming cut pile through a single warp knot. Each carpet might have been copied by the weavers from an earlier Admiral carpet but there would have been an original design, probably drawn and painted on extended sets of graph-type paper, called cartoons – a practice well known from later periods. Each square on the paper represented one knot; the colour of each square was the colour of the wool to be used for that knot, and a little over 100 knots of differently coloured wool or goats' hair have been tied in every square inch of the carpet. Goats' hair is much coarser than wool and since the earliest times has been woven into mats, sacking, saddlebags and the like. A carpet like this would probably have been woven on the old Roman two-beamed vertical loom, the favoured mechanism for weaving carpets, rugs and tapestries. The warp is Z2S twist and the weft is 2ZX1. Most European carpets of this time were made of many tens of thousands of such knots, all tied onto a hemp frame, but not so the Admiral carpets. It may well be more than coincidental that just like some of the Mamluk carpets, they are made entirely of goats' hair and sheep's wool, so complying with the biblical prohibition against the joining together of different species (for example, hair and wool are both animal products but hemp is a vegetable product).[5] The rabbis were divided in their opinions as to whether the prohibition applied exclusively to clothing or whether it included carpets.

Whilst the patching of Spanish carpets in the Middle Ages was common, the Vizcaya carpet has undergone far more work than one would expect for normal repairs and maintenance. At least thirteen separate pieces of other carpets have been added and the insertions interwoven. We shall never know what these additions covered up, but that there was a need to alter the carpet is intriguing. What, I wonder, were the original decorative elements, and why was it imperative that they be obliterated?

Five hundred years ago the Enriquez put their carpet in the care of Santa Clara de Palencia,[6] a convent founded and funded by Alfonso Enriquez and his wife dona Juana and thereafter closely associated with the family. In the nineteenth century, when many Spanish monasteries and convents were being closed, it appears that the carpet was returned by the convent to an heir of the Enriquez family who sold it on. The Vizcaya Museum eventually acquired it, and there, for many years, it was referred to as 'The Jewish Carpet'.

This extraordinary carpet cannot be understood by anyone starting from modern presuppositions and I have endeavoured to see it as it would have been seen 500 years ago.[7] In the next chapter, we look back to a happier time in the twelfth to the early fourteenth century, when the pressure on the Jews to pretend to be Christians was less harsh, even often non-existent, and when the earlier Spanish synagogue carpet was woven. Sharing many of the same Judaic symbols as the Vizcaya carpet, it provides primary and direct evidence of the strength of the traditions and the quality of the Jewish carpets of Spain – and of the cultural affinity of both carpets.

NOTES

1. The Spanish knot is to be found in early some Chinese Turkestan carpets (second to sixth century CE) and in some German medieval carpets (1175–1225 CE). Whilst there is little direct evidence to support the connection, Jewish merchants are believed to have settled in Chinese Turkestan and China by the sixth century. As to Germany, substantial Jewish communities had lived there since Roman times.
2. May Beattie, 'The "Admiral" Rugs of Spain: An Analysis and Classification of their Field Designs', in Robert Pinner and Walter Denny (eds), *Oriental Carpet & Textile Studies, 2: Carpets of the Mediterranean Countries 1400–1600* (London: Hali Publications, 1986), p.283.
3. A. Castro, *El Real Monasterio de Santa Clara de Palencia y los Enriquez, Almirantes de Castilla* (Valladolid: Sever-Cuesta, 1982), pp.75–9.
4. John Mills, 'The Coming of the Carpet to the West', in D. King and D. Sylvester, *The Eastern Carpet in the Western World from the 15th to the 17th Century*, exhibition catalogue (London: Arts Council of Great Britain, 1983), p.11.
5. Leviticus 19:19, and Deuteronomy 22:9–11. See also Exodus 26:7, where God instructs the Israelites to 'make curtains of goats' hair for the Tabernacle'.
6. Palencia, in northern Spain, is not part of Murcia but was part of the Enriquez domain. Its textile industry was one of the most productive in the whole of Castile. Falah Hassan,

'"Abd al-Hussein", 'Las Ferias de Medina y el Commercio de la Lana: 1514–1575', in Lorenzo E. Medina de Campo (ed.), *Historia de Medina del Campo y su Tierra*, (Valladolid, 1986), Vol. 2, pp.13–42.

7. My thanks to the eminent expert, John Mills, for his valuable insights into the Admiral carpets given at the May Beattie lecture at the Ashmolean Museum, Oxford, 29 May 2002. Then his great kindness in reading an incomplete, inaccurate and immature draft of this book and making critically helpful comments and suggestions (all of which, save one, I acted upon) has more than multiplied my debt of gratitude to a wise and generous gentlemen.

The Spanish Synagogue Carpet

The oldest surviving Spanish carpet was most probably woven in Murcia,[1] but might possibly have been made in the Maghreb, in the coastal regions of North Africa. Woven not later than the fourteenth century – and possibly earlier – for one of the most important synagogues in Spain,[2] it is also one of the earliest surviving Jewish carpets,[3] and an important ethnographic document providing primary material evidence of the tradition and the quality of the Sephardi carpets. We can see it as it had been originally constituted in Figure 13 before and in Figure 14 after its restoration.[4] An earlier representation published in 1923 (Figure 15) more clearly reveals its ancient Jewish motifs, which prior to the 1920s were thought to be either stylized floral motifs or meaningless decorative devices.[5] But they are incontrovertibly Jewish, and for devout Jews, whose inner world is filled with biblical imagery, these symbols would ignite very specific thoughts and feelings. Let us try to look at this carpet not through today's secular spectacles, but through the eyes of the Jews of medieval Spain. Let us try to see, as they did, far more than the manifest form of the symbols, because to them each symbol sparked off its own powerful and poignant perception of the metaphysical, with each image attesting to the illusory nature of our material world and to the ineffable splendours of the world to come.

Firstly, and irreducibly Judaic, the little cabinet-shaped shrines branching out either side of the central vertical tree form are Torah Arks – cabinets to house the Scrolls of the Law – and, with their gabled roofs, their crockets (those curved and hooked protrusions) and double panelled doors, are part of a pictorial tradition originating in the destruction of the Temple in Jerusalem by the Romans in 70 CE. We see similar features on the Torah Ark of the fourteenth- to fifteenth-century Prague Synagogue in Figure 16. The impulse to embody thought in images was not to be denied, and the now exiled Jews replaced the visual focus of the Temple with imagery of the Scrolls of the Law, housed in their cabinets within a gabled shrine.

The upper section of these Torah Arks[6] (gabled isosceles triangles) can be seen here in the Spanish synagogue carpet.[7] The same Torah Arks are visible on clay oil lamps of the second and third centuries CE and on gold glass goblets of the third to fourth centuries.[8] They are also to be found embedded in the mosaic floors of the sixth-century Beth Alpha (Israel) and of other fourth- to sixth-century synagogues (Figures 17, 18 and 19),[9] only to reappear in an illuminated book from the tenth century and in the Ark of the synagogue in Ferrara in the late fifteenth century,[10] and yet again in the 1520s in the Torah Ark of a Roman synagogue, the Scuola Cataluna, founded, significantly, by Jewish refugees from Spain. The Torah Arks hinted at in the Vizcaya carpet are discussed in Chapter 17. Writing about the gabled doors on a Yemeni Hannukiah lamp of the fourteenth century, Erwin Goodenough, the pioneering authority on early Jewish symbols, pays tribute to 'the long persistence of their active symbolic value'.[11]

Each cabinet displayed in this carpet contains two central and vertical diamond shapes, which in turn contain another central form, so echoing the forms on a well-known group of glass jars of the sixth and seventh centuries made in Jerusalem for Jewish pilgrims; the identifying insignia for Christian pilgrims and Muslim travellers on such jars were quite different.[12] In addition to the concentric lozenge and double diamond forms, those Jewish glass jars also reveal stylized Tree of Life forms, menorot and shofar (ritual trumpets).[13] In a tenth-century Egyptian Hebrew Bible many scholars see a similar Torah Ark form with its pilasters ornamented with niches (Figure 19). Some scholars also note the Tree of Life form in the fine stucco reliefs of circa 1350 in the El Tránsito Synagogue at Toledo.[14]

But returning to the Spanish synagogue carpet: in the upper cabinet to the left in Figures 13 and 14, and to the right of its central double doors, we see three rams with curved horns thrust back. The upper two rams are white, the lower one is blue. They reappear again in Figure 13 on the fourth Ark form to the right. No creatures proclaim Judaism more than the ram and the ewe: the ram's horn is fashioned into the ritual trumpet, their fleece is woven into the prayer shawl, their shank bones displayed at the Seder (the first night of the Passover festival), their hide produces the parchment for the Torah scroll and even the image and essence of their offspring, the lamb, is offered up as a metaphor for the Jewish people. Sheep are by far the most important and the most frequently mentioned animal in the Bible, where a metaphor for God is that of the caring shepherd; that Christianity later took up the symbol of the lamb in metaphors such as 'the Lamb of God' did not take away its value in Judaism (see Chapter 16).

At the left of the lower cabinet, three Ark forms down, again to the right of the central double doors, we see three geese or possibly ducks – fairly familiar figures both on gravestones[15] and on the mosaic floors of a number of early synagogues. Particularly good examples are to be seen at the synagogues at Naarinx[16] and Beth Yerah.[17] They are the selfsame birds we see on the Vizcaya carpet (Figure 64), linking these two carpets yet again – not only to each other, but also through the repetition of the common forms to the wider Jewish inheritance. We have seen very similar birds hovering over the Torah Ark displayed in the mosaic floor of the sixth-century Beth Alpha Synagogue (Figure 17). The iconographic link between a carpet weaving and a mosaic floor is close, for carpets are often movable versions of immovable floors. One of the later examples of a rug design portraying a floor is to be seen in a Marbadiah carpet of the 1930s, which replicates a detail from the mosaic floor of the Beth Alpha Synagogue.[18] Geese (ducks) and the other birds displayed on the Vizcaya carpet are discussed in Chapter 15.

To the left of the geese (ducks), are three undeniable Stars of David. They are the same stars we see in a Spanish anthology of games, *Juegos de Axedrez: Dados y Tablas*, published in 1282–83. Alfonso X, known as the Wise, king of Castile and Leon from 1252 to 1285, was a patron of learning who attracted many Jews to his court; even his minister of finance was a noted Talmudic scholar. Producing many important books and often acting as translators, the Jews of Spain had an important role in bringing Muslim, and thereby Greek, Roman, Persian and Babylonian civilization to Europe. In Alfonso's 'Book of Games', not all the decorative elements are in artistic harmony with Muslim art,[19] and the section on chess is particularly interesting, for the Jewish identity of the writers and artists is revealed through two distinct Jewish symbols – each authenticating the other. The chess problem (chess buffs please refer to note[20]) in Figure 20 incorporates a Star of David on a tassel, the latter representing one of the four fringes of the prayer shawl worn by Jews throughout the ages in accordance with the biblical instruction of Numbers 15:37–41. It was the practice of medieval scribes and illustrators to leave their marks, and these Stars of David inset in the tassels and other Stars of David scattered throughout the 'Book of Games' are unambiguous statements of Jewish identity.[21] We see the Star of David twice on the blue band placed over the centre of the table in the fifteenth-century picture of a family celebrating the Passover in Figure 6. The three Aramaic words in the picture are the introductory instruction to pour the wine into the cup before making kiddush (the prayer of sanctification over wine recited on Sabbaths and festivals).

The message can overwhelm the medium, and a devout Jew, in responding to the symbols, might not actually notice the carpet. For it is culture that determines perception: so, for example, while a Confucian will define a bowl by its sides, a Taoist will do so by the space inside, for without that space there would be no bowl. The symbols of the Torah Arks, the sheep, the birds and the Stars of David, would spark off in a devout Jew a sense of transcending his own petty physical existence, of being a little nearer to that state of beatitude in the intimate union of the soul and its divine source.

The combination of these Jewish motifs, the contemporary presence of a substantial number of skilled Jewish designers and weavers (see Chapter 4) and of a large, devout and relatively affluent Jewish population make it likely this carpet was designed and woven by Jews – although the identity of the weaver of a Jewish carpet is not as important as its iconography, the uses to which it is put and its significance to Jews; for it is those three aspects that characterize it as Jewish.

The splendid Textile Museum in Washington has a Coptic hanging with similar images of panelled doors, birds and geometric motifs.[22] Should one therefore question the validity of the uniquely Judaic motifs on our Spanish synagogue carpet? I think not, for the custom of employing hangings in Christian architecture originated in the textiles of the Tabernacle and of the First and Second Temples. We see the same hangings in the frescos of the third-century Dura Europos Synagogue (Syria) and in the mosaics of the fourth-century el-Khirbeh Synagogue and the sixth-century Beit Shean Synagogue (Israel). Given that from at least as early as the third century CE such hangings were used in the synagogues of Egypt, and given the antiquity of panelled doors in the Jewish tradition, and the very large numbers of Egyptian Jews who converted to Christianity from the second to third centuries, we may assume the Judaic origin of the symbols on – and the possibility of the Judaic user of – the Coptic hanging in the Textile Museum.[23]

and on similar Coptic hangings. As Louise Mackie, discussing weavers in the early Islamic period put it, 'we have pieces that unless there is an inscription, are absolutely interchangeable and could have been found in mosques, synagogues or churches'.

It is not only the symbols on the carpets that have values beyond the obvious; carpets themselves may become endowed with symbolic meanings as a consequence of their functions. Numerous paintings of men of power in the late Middle Ages and Renaissance show their carpets to dramatize their secular strengths, and spiritual meanings are also surely to be implied from the glorious pictures of places of worship in Christianity, so often overflowing with carpets on the floors, on the steps of the altar and on the lectern. And so was it too, with carpets such as this synagogue carpet and other hangings before the Ark.

I also wondered about the effect of the Second Commandment, which forbids the creation of human or animal forms (graven images), yet here we see sheep, geese, ducks and other birds. But the prohibition had always been more honoured in the breach than in the observance and Maimonides, the most authoritative Jewish thinker of the Middle Ages, had specifically ruled that the prohibition did not apply to two-dimensional forms like paintings or carpets.[24]

Blending into the style of the Islamic host culture with its generous use of carpets in the mosque, carpets were also essential elements in the medieval synagogue, often used as *parokhets* – that is, hangings in front of or either side of the Ark – or simply as floor coverings. Our carpet here, due to its length and narrowness, would more likely have been placed in a gangway perhaps leading to the Ark, or just possibly for seating. As we know from a *responsum* of a Spanish rabbi, Asher ben Yehiel (d. 1327), the images on the carpet used in the synagogue were matters of deep concern and debate. His advice was sought as to the suitability in the synagogue of a prayer rug decorated with the Ka'aba, the sacred shrine of Islam – the great mosque, housing the Black Stone, sited in the central square in Mecca. His response could not have been clearer; he forbade the use of such carpets not only for decoration but also for seating. But the issue did not go away, for his son Rabbi Judah ben Asher (1270–1349) was asked a similar question about the use of prayer rugs in a synagogue.[25] No such problems, however, surrounded the Kufic letters in the border of our carpet, for Kufic writing on carpets had changed from being a statement specific to Islamic power to a pleasing meander border with honorific associations duly enhancing the desirability and authority of many a carpet. The script itself was a common decorative variation of the Islam affirmation of faith, probably reading 'There is no God but Allah.' We see the same Kufic script in Christian art, for example on the edge of a carpet in a fifteenth-century painting by an unknown Castilian artist of St Anne Enthroned with the Virgin and Child.[26] That the lettering on our Spanish synagogue carpet — designed and woven under Muslim rule — is not readily decipherable suggests that the designers and weavers saw it as a decorative device. Maimonides appears to have approved the use of carpets in synagogues as helpful in inspiring people in their devotions, but he also let it be known that he would close his eyes while at prayer in order to avoid distractions.[27]

The single warp knot that forms this carpet is unusual but not unique to Spain. The earliest known examples, excavated in Central Asia early in the last century by the great explorer, Sir Aurel Stein, are dated between the third and the sixth centuries, and three surviving carpet fragments with the same knot, woven in twelfth- or thirteenth-century Germany, have also been found. A similar but not identical knot had been used by both Coptic[28] and probably Jewish weavers in Egypt since the fourth century.[29] Finally, in the tenth century, the single warp or Spanish knot first appeared in Spain.[30] Because the knots were staggered, fewer materials were used than in denser carpets and yet complex designs could still be created.

We began by looking at the particular historical backgrounds of the Jews and of weaving in Spain and North Africa, and then in the last two chapters we inspected the Vizcaya carpet in detail. The next step is to examine the turn of events. Why would the people who ordered the Vizcaya carpet and the people who wove it for them have any interest in a sophisticated carpet filled with discrete Jewish symbols, and was this interest a pattern of behaviour and of production?

NOTES

1. S. Sherrill, *Carpets and Rugs of Europe and America* (New York: Abbeville Press, 1996), p.30.
2. Friedrich Sarre, 'A Fourteenth Century Spanish Synagogue Carpet', *Burlington Magazine*, 56 (1930), pp.88–95.
3. But see Chapter 3.
4. I am grateful to Frau Kienaptel of the Museum of Islamic Art, Berlin, for this information

and for her courtesy when I inspected this extraordinary carpet on 26 August 2003.
5. Sherrill, *Carpets and Rugs of Europe and America*, p.31.
6. V. Gervers, 'An Early Christian Curtain in the Royal Ontario Museum', in V. Gervers (ed.), *Studies in Textile History in Memory of Harold B. Burnham* (Toronto: Hali, 1977), cited in Linda Woolley, 'Pagan Classical Christian–Egyptian Hangings of the 4th to 7th Centuries', *Hali*, 48 (December 1989), p.31.
7. Sherrill, *Carpets and Rugs of Europe and America*, p.31. Indeed, Sherrill remarks on the similarity of the imagery on the mosaic pavement of the Beth Alpha Synagogue to that of the Spanish synagogue carpet.
8. The Jerusalem Mishnah Torah, c.1400, Jewish National and University Library, Ms. Heb. 411193, fol. 33v. G. Sed-Rajna, *Ancient Jewish Art* (New Jersey: Chartwell Books, n.d.), p.53.
9. Yaffa Levy, 'Ezekiel's Plan in an Early Karaite Bible', *Jewish Art*, 19–20 (1994), p.68–85.
10. E. Adler, *Jewish Travellers in the Middle Ages* (New York: Dover Publications, 1946), p.ii, Plate 1. From a prayer book in the collection of Me.E. Bicart-Sée.
11. E. Goodenough, *Jewish Symbols in the Greco-Roman Period* (London: Pantheon Books, 1953), Vol. 1, p.149. See also the Arc flanked by menorot in the fourth-century synagogue of Khirbet Susiya, and Francis Spalding's interesting book, *Mudejar Ornament in Manuscripts* (New York: Hispanic Society of America, 1953).
12. Julian Raby, 'In Vitro Veritas: Glass Pilgrim Vessels from 7th Century Jerusalem', in Jeremy Johns (ed.), *Bayt Al-Maqdis: Jerusalem and Early Islam*, Oxford Studies in Islamic Art (Oxford: Oxford University Press, 1999), Vol. 9, Part 2, p.182.
13. D. Harden, *Glass of the Caesars* (Milan: Olivetti, 1987), p.177.
14. D. King and D. Sylvester, *The Eastern Carpet in the Western World from the 15th to the 17th Century*, exhibition catalogue (London: Arts Council of Great Britain, 1983), p.50. Sed-Rajna, *Jewish Art*, Fig. 86.
15. Goodenough, *Jewish Symbols in the Greco-Roman Period*, Vol. 5, p.57.
16. Ibid., Vol. 2, p.255.
17. Ibid., Vol. 2, p.263.
18. A. Felton, *Jewish Carpets* (Woodbridge: Antique Collectors Club, 1997), p.115.
19. See again Spalding, *Mudejar Ornament in Manuscripts*.
20. The chessboard in the illustration poses a problem in an earlier form of Islamic chess called *Shatraji*, which differed from classical chess in that the bishop may jump over other pieces or check through another piece. Secondly, what seems to be the queen can in fact only move one square diagonally at a time, so here it is not checking the white king. This quite well-known problem, probably dating back to the tenth century, is for white to checkmate in five moves.
21. Victor Keats, *Chess, Jews and History* (Oxford: Oxford Academic Publishers, 1994), pp.140, 141, 179–181, 187.
22. V. Mann, T. Glick and J. Dodds (eds), *'Convivencia', Jews, Muslims and Christians in Medieval Spain* (New York: George Braziller in conjunction with the Jewish Museum, 1992), p.247.
23. Alberto Boralevi, in a lecture in June 1983: 'I think that it could have been used as an Ark curtain, a late Roman Parokhet.' Boralevi also cited A.J.B. Wace, *Preliminary Historical Study: A Late Roman Tapestry from Egypt*, Textile Workshop Notes, Paper No. 9 (1954), Plate 2. See

also Goodenough, *Jewish Symbols in the Greco-Roman Period*, Vol. 2, p.119, and Pau Figueras, *Decorative Jewish Ossuaries* (Leiden: Brill, 1983), p.40.
24. Mishnah Torah, *Avodat Kokhavim ve Hakkoteihem*, 3:10–11; Joseph Caro, author of the *Shulhan Arukh*, the definitive compilation of Jewish laws, concurred, the point being that only objects that cast a shadow are capable of embodying reality – so that in representing them, man's motive would be the insensate desire to compete with the Almighty.
25. Mann, Glick and Dodds (eds), *Convivencia*, p.247, citing R. Asher ben Yehiel, *Responsa*, Section 5, no. 2.2; and R. Judah ben Asher, Zikhron Yehuda, No. 21.3.
26. John Mills, 'The Coming of the Carpet to the West', in King and Sylvester, *The Eastern Carpet in the Western World*, p.20. The picture is in the Metropolitan Museum of Art, New York. See also *The Last Supper*, School of Burgos, Spain, late 15th century, illustrated in the *Textile Museum Journal* (1977), p.24.
27. Maimonides, Mishnah Torah, Hilchot Avoda-Zarah 3:6.
28. Sherrill, *Carpets and Rugs of Europe and America*, p.398, n.16.
29. M. Dimand, 'An Early Cut-Pile Rug from Egypt', *Metropolitan Museum Studies* (Metropolitan Museum of Art) 4, 2 (March 1933), pp.151–61.
30. M. Dimand and J. Mailey, *Oriental Rugs in the Metropolitan Museum of Art* (New York: Metropolitan Museum of Art, 1973), p.253.

1. Israelite ship on a seal, eighth century BCE.

2. A Spanish, possibly Jewish, weaver's tombstone, Roman era.

3. Hebrew, Latin and Greek inscriptions on a Spanish sarcophagus, fifth–sixth century.

4. Spanish Jewish weavers at work, Bezalel and Aholiab, fifteenth century.

5. *Parokhet* hanging before the Ark, detail from the mosaic floor of the Beth Shean Synagogue, sixth century.

6. Stars of David decorating the Passover table, the Barcelona Haggadah, fourteenth century.

7. Jewish weavers in Hellenist Alexandria.

8. Jewish Egyptian weave with Star of David and menorah, eighth–ninth century.

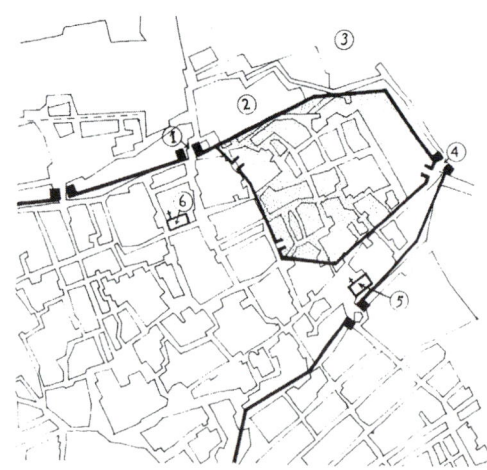

9. The Jewish Quarter, Murcia, 1481.

10. Copy of a Sephardi carpet, early seventeenth century.

11. The Vizcaya carpet.

12. Star-studded carpet in a fresco by Matteo di Giovanetti da Viterbo (c.1300–68) in the Palace of the Popes, Avignon.

13. The Spanish synagogue carpet (thirteenth–fourteenth century) as originally presented.

14. The Spanish synagogue carpet (thirteenth–fourteenth century) as restored, post-Second World War.

...lem uns ein vergleichsweise gut erhaltenes Fragment überkommen ist. Es befindet sich im Kaiser Friedrich-Museum zu Berlin, ... hinsichtlich der Mannigfaltigkeit der vertretenen Typen eine ... instruktive Sammlung alter Teppiche besitzt.

Abb. ... Altertümlicher Teppich des XIII. Jahrh. im Kunstgewerbe-Museum zu Berlin.

...er es spricht aus diesem letzterwähnten merkwürdigen ... (Abbildung 2) doch auch ein anderer formaler Sinn ... aus den persischen Stücken des XVI. und XVII. Jahrhunderts. Wir sehen eckige, starre Formen, hakenförmige Ansätze

15. Synagogue carpet (thirteenth–fourteenth century) as published in 1923.

16. Stars of David on the Ark, fourteenth–fifteenth century.

17. Geese or ducks guarding the Ark. Detail from the mosaic floor of the Beth Alpha Synagogue, sixth century.

18. Draped hanging before the Ark. Detail from the mosaic floor of the Beth Hammath Synagogue, fourth century.

19. Ark form in an Egyptian Hebrew Bible, tenth century.

20. Star of David on a tallit, identifying the designer or possibly the player, in the 'Book of Games', Castile, thirteenth century.

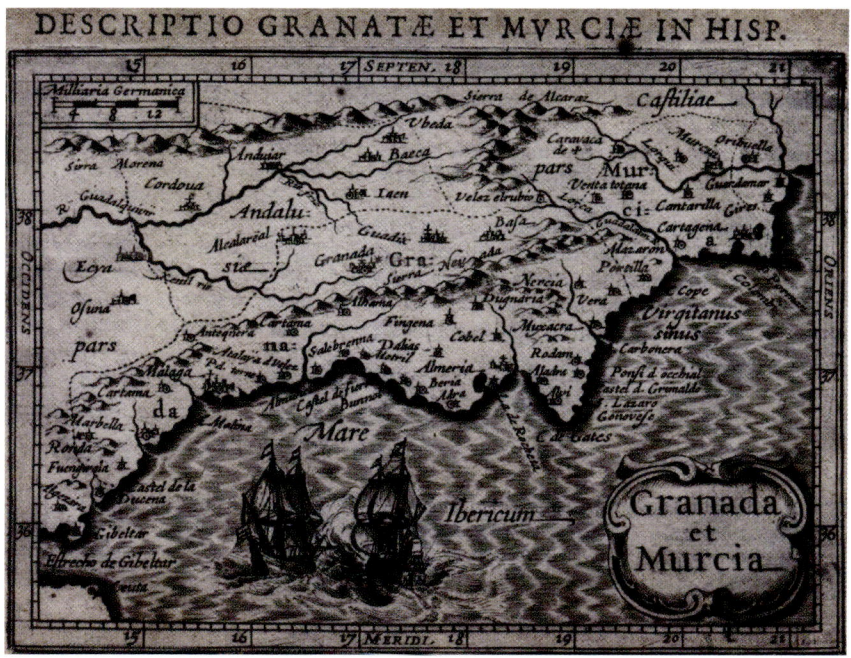

21. Map of Granada and Murcia, sixteenth century.

22. Dragged down to Hell, French School, fifteenth century.

23. In Hell, from *De Civitate Dei* by St Augustine, French School, fifteenth century.

24. St Dominic presiding over the Burning of Heretics, Pedro Berruguete (c.1450–1504).

25. A *converso* Hannukiah, Spain, fifteenth century.

26. The Menorah on the Triumphal Arch of the Emperor Titus, first century.

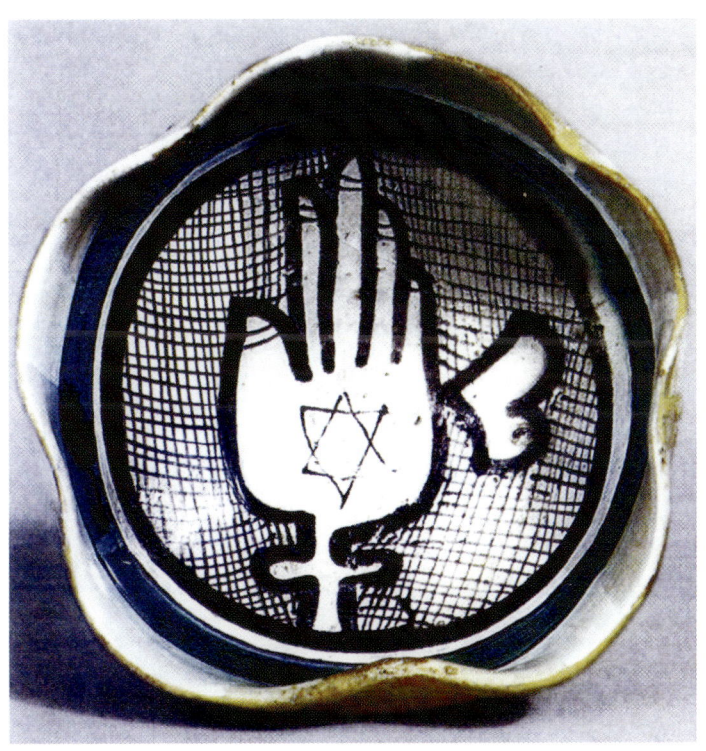

27. The Star and the Hand on a Spanish salt dish, fourteenth–fifteenth century.

28. The private chapel in Buckingham Palace.

29. Star of David, the Capernaum Synagogue, third–fourth century.

PART 3

THE TURN OF EVENTS

The Enriquez

Woven into the frame of this ancient carpet are numerous symbols which, to those in the know, convey powerful Judaic and Kabbalistic messages. One possible explanation for this enigmatic iconography is that in the fifteenth century the Enriquez, one of the most noble and powerful families in the land, were *conversos*: that is, in this context, Christians in their public lives, but Jews in their private lives – whether still profoundly religious or simply confused. To explore this possibility let us look to the known facts.

The story begins in the middle of the fourteenth century – a time of civil war and social chaos. In the Kingdom of Castile and Leon, in the reigns of Alfonso XI (r. 1312–50) and of his son Pedro (r. 1350–69), the conditions for Jews, compared to the rest of Europe, were remarkable. In 1348 Europe was decimated by the Black Death – and the Jews were blamed. In other parts of Spain the mob would riot, looting, burning and murdering, whereas in Castile the Jews were protected and productive.[1] But following Alfonso's death, Enrique de Trastamara (r. 1369–79), the oldest of Alfonso's ten illegitimate sons, supported by his twin brother Fadrique, claimed the throne from Pedro (who, with the help of his mother, the queen, had had Enrique's and Fadrique's mother, one of the king's mistress, executed). The Jews supported Pedro, the king's legitimate heir. In the ensuing nearly twenty years of civil war, in the words of Professor Netanyahu, 'Enrique was the first nobleman in Spain to use anti-Semitism as an instrument of propaganda and a means of attaining political control.'[2] An example of this black propaganda was the rumour that Alfonso's queen had taken a Jewish lover, so that Pedro was not only not of the royal bloodline but also, as son of a Jew and a crypto-Jew himself, could have no right to the throne of Castile.³ Enrique could not have made his position clearer. Calling Pedro 'King of the Jews', he and his faction declared themselves to be enemies of the Jewish race⁴ – a significant moment which pointed to the time that anti-Semitism extended from the religious to the racial. His vow that on gaining the throne all debts due to Jews would be cancelled guaranteed him mass support and aided his ultimate success. Those Jewish communities that survived his army's massacres were taxed mercilessly, many people selling themselves into slavery to pay their debts. In Toledo alone, 8,000 Jewish men, women and children were butchered. In the words of a contemporary chronicler, 'Few escaped death and the king (Enrique II) forced them to pay such a tax that not as much as a scrap of bread remained for its inhabitants.'⁵

Treachery had triggered the war of succession and treachery ended it. Pedro, besieged in a castle by Bertrand du Guesclin, the great Breton commander, came to an agreement that in return for six fiefs and 200,000 gold dobles, Pedro would be allowed to escape. Pedro left the castle, whereupon du Guesclin promptly seized him and presented him to Enrique. Enrique had won the war. Crowning himself Enrique II, with his own dagger he killed Pedro and poisoned Tello, another half-brother. Geoffrey Chaucer, poet, diplomat and spy (his patron, the Black Prince of England, supported Pedro [Peter]), was frequently in Spain and expressed his horror at Enrique's murder of his own brother in *The Monk's Tale*:

> O noble, worthy Peter, glory of Spain,
> Whom Fortune held so high in majesty,
> How bitterly should we lament thy pain,
> Who, by thy brother driven forth to flee,
> After a siege wert caught by treachery,
> And thus betrayed wert taken to his tent,
> Where with his own bare hands he murdered thee,
> And gained succession to thy throne and rent!⁶

As king of Castile and Leon, Enrique set about annexing vast estates for himself. His twin brother Fadrique had been captured and killed by Pedro in 1358 and his (Fadrique's) son, Alfonso, among other grants, secured the eastern coastal province, which included the major carpet weaving region of Murcia (Figure 21). Then, suddenly and astonishingly, breaking his undertakings to his followers, contrary to all his past practices and to the outrage of so many of his supporters, Enrique rapidly did a complete about-turn. He changed from being the prime persecutor to being the prime protector of the Jews. He forbade both his own troops and the dangerously independent French mercenary units from reaping the fruits of victory, which they had been promised and had hitherto so greatly enjoyed – that is, inter alia, raping, murdering, looting and destroying Jewish communities. His army demanded that he turn over to them all fortresses held by or protecting Jews. He refused to do so.[7] Breaking his solemn oath that all debts owing to Jews would be cancelled if he gained the throne, he reinstated those debts as binding legal obligations. When his subjects complained, asking at least for more time to pay, he rejected most requests, stating that 'the Jews had suffered enough already'.[8] Eventually, however, he did agree to reduce these debts by one third, payable over two years.[9] Numerous petitions presented to Enrique expressed the anti-Jewish feelings of the time. Refusing the substantive pleas, he accepted the less significant ones, but then actually did little about them. When Ferrant Mártinez, the anti-Semitic archdeacon of Ecija whose fiery harangues ensured him a huge peasant following ever ready to compete with the troops in pillaging and murdering, protested, Enrique's response could not have been more forceful: 'Do not dare to interfere in judging any dispute which involves any Jew in any manner.'[10]

Now, some see Enrique's about-turn in casting off those who had brought him to power as sound political practice. Others see it as economic wisdom, for he and his ravaged kingdom would gain from the activities of Jews, primarily as civil servants (especially tax collectors), financiers, physicians, traders, and artisans. In fact almost all the financial systems during his reign were dominated by Jews.[11] But at the time when they were being persecuted and expelled from so many parts of Christian Europe (despite their value to those societies) it was rare for any monarch to protect them. It was particularly unexpected in Castile because they had supported Pedro, and he, Enrique, had butchered so many of them and impoverished the survivors.

While political and economic factors doubtless played their part in Enrique's volte-face, perhaps as important – and this was an age when the personality and the predilections of the ruler were critical in determining state policy – Enrique's twin brother Fadrique had married dona Juana.[12] She was Jewish and, like so many tens of thousands of Jews seeking to escape humiliation and persecution had, at least in public, moved over to the Church of Rome. Such conversions fell very far short of Damascene revelation, being most often acts of social, political or financial convenience, if not of simple survival. It is not clear that dona Juana had married Fadrique to the entire satisfaction of the church, as some reports refer to her as Fadrique's Jewish concubine.[13] It may perhaps be, as was customary among the *conversos*, that prior to going to church and in the presence of two Jewish witnesses,[14] she and Fadrique had been discreetly married according to Jewish law. This custom of discreet Jewish marriage legitimizing descent was later endorsed in a key *responsum* of Rabbi Simon ben Zemah Duran (1400–67), who ruled that the descendants of a *converso* lady married to a non-Jewish man remained Jewish.[15] This precept conforms with general Jewish law which defines descent through the mother, not the father, and that the children of such unions be raised in the Jewish religion.

Murcia under the Enriquez became a haven for the Jews. One of the best authorities on Murcia in the Middle Ages is Luis Rubio Garcia. He writes: 'an important group of citizens in Murcia was made up of the Hebrew community ... Enrique II quickly changes his position as a persecutor of the Jews to a protector of the Jews, because these people were excellent economic contributors. In Murcia we find the Jews fully integrated into municipal life'.[16] Later, many Jews who in other parts of Spain had been forced under the threat of ruin or death to convert to Christianity and who could flee had found safety in Murcia. There, in the synagogue, they would publicly renounce their forced conversion and openly revert to Judaism.[17] Murcia was very much Alfonso's domain, and as the king's nephew and master of the powerful military order of Santiago, was not a man lightly to be crossed.

Enrique II's son, Enrique III, had continued his father's policy of protecting the Jews and had tried, unsuccessfully, to stop the pogroms of 1391. In a public letter of 1392 he decreed: 'our law neither orders nor consents that any should turn to the Catholic faith by force and against his wishes'.[18] As to his cousin Alfonso, according to one account, while it was certain that Alfonso was the son of Fadrique, the identity of his mother was less certain. Extraordinary, really (surely paternity may be far more reasonably and factually questioned than maternity?), but from the fifteenth to the eighteenth and even nineteenth century, many in Spain sought to obscure any trace of any Jewish ancestry. What had happened was that in 1449 the Purity of the Blood law decreed that potentially anyone with Jewish ancestry was a second-class and suspect citizen. Most significantly, the king prohibited any enquiry into Alfonso's descendants (who were partly of the royal bloodline) as being 'unnecessary'.[19] But as early as 1384 a chronicler had already described Alfonso as, 'the son of a Jew'.[20]

Was it not extraordinary and therefore questionable that one of the noblest Christian Castilian families had intermarried with Jews and *conversos*? On the contrary, it was actually extremely common. By the middle of the fifteenth century, the royal secretary, Fernán Diaz de Toledo (himself of *converso* descent), had analysed the degree of such intermarriage among the nobility and clearly established that there was hardly a single noble Castilian family that did *not* have *converso* relatives or ancestors.[21] And later in the sixteenth century, Cardinal Francisco Mendoza y Bobadilla, Archbishop of Burgos, declared that almost all the aristocracy of Spain had Jewish ancestors.[22] His genealogical analyses were totally thorough and have never been contradicted. Indeed, neither Ferdinand or Isabella would have passed their own Purity of the Blood laws, for both had Jewish forebears, as did Isabella's chief minister, Enrique de Guzman, Duke of Medina Sidonia and Viceroy of southern Castile. A man of his times, in the 1470s he protected the persecuted *conversos* of Seville but by the 1480s had ceased to do so.

Alfonso had held some of the highest offices in the land, including that of Admiral of Castile and governor of Murcia. His duties as governor of Murcia included both issuing instructions on behalf of the king and reporting back to him 'everything that happened, with special attention to clarity and without omitting even the tiniest detail'.[23] In 1388 or 1389 he married the fabulously wealthy Juana de Mendoza, heiress to another politically powerful *converso* family. The Mendozas and the Ayalas had been stigmatized by Lope de Barrientos (1395–1469), the Dominican Master and Bishop of Segovia, as all being descendents of a certain Rabbi Solomon and his son, don Isaque de Valladolid. De Barrientos, expert on the Jewish ancestry of the great Christian families, provided a veritable 'Who's Who' of Spanish nobility, and his statement that Alfonso was partly of royal and partly of Jewish descent could not have been clearer.[24]

In 1390, Alfonso's and dona Juana's first child was born. They named him Fadrique after his grandfather, and went on to have ten more children together, while Alfonso separately had at least a further three children. Interestingly, they named their first-born son after his (deceased) paternal grandfather, for that was the custom of the Jews of Spain, an ancient and deeply entrenched tradition going back to Hellenistic times and often an indication of Jewish origin.[25]

Alfonso has been described as 'very good to those who were good to him. He was of noble lineage and not arrogant, one could always count on him for help.' This description continues with the sort of coded phrases we meet time and again in connection with *conversos* and which I discuss in Chapter 10: 'His household ... always understood more than what had been said.'[26]

Alfonso's son Fadrique also had a full life. He was probably brought up like any other *converso* boy of noble family: christened at birth, in public known by his baptismal name, dutifully performing in public all the formalities of the church, attending Mass, being shriven and taking the sacrament as occasion demanded. But this was all a masquerade and he would probably repeat some private formula to himself, as did so many Marranos, to atone for their outward observances. In 1425, like his father and grandfather before him and in accordance with the custom of the aristocratic *conversos*, he too married the heiress to a wealthy and powerful *converso* family. Accounts vary, but it seems that his wife, dona Marina Diez de Cordova Ayala – whose coat of arms also appears on the Vizcaya carpet – had no children. Let the Jewish historian Eliyahu Capsali of Crete, in his memoir written in 1523, take up the story:

> There was a Jewish lady called Paloma.[27] She was very beautiful and of noble birth. One day she went out wearing sumptuous clothing and precious jewellery, escorted by her slaves, servants and followers. She met the admiral of Castile, Fadrique Enriquez. He was the most powerful man in the kingdom after the king. Immediately he fell in love with the young lady. But she was married. Ignoring that obstacle, our admiral kidnapped Paloma. She became pregnant and was rejected by her husband. She gave birth to a wonderful boy. The admiral's servants who saw the boy and knowing the secret of his birth advised the admiral to admit the boy into the palace. Fadrique Enriquez sent his men to take the boy from his mother. He educated him and brought him up like a prince. The child accepted this for he was gifted with great intelligence. Later on he married a princess of the most aristocratic Spanish family. After Fadrique Enriquez died his son inherited all his possessions and became his father's successor and Admiral of Castile.[28]

Dona Marina died in 1431. From the 1440s the fragile economy collapsed and confusing and chaotic civil war erupted again, with much of the violence directed against Jews and *conversos*,[29] who were blamed for everything, including being responsible for a special tax imposed by the king.[30] The Toledo revolt of 1449 marked the critical point in the plight of the *conversos*.[31] As noted earlier, in that year the strictures of the *Limpieza de Sangre* ('the Purity of the Blood') came into force, defining who was an Old Christian – that is, one whose blood had not been infected through having a traceable Jewish ancestor. This legislation marked the first major official attempt to exclude *conversos* from public office. As we have seen, most significantly by royal decree, the Enriquez were exempted from any such enquiry. Whilst our interest is focussed on Murcia, it is significant that the support shown by the Enriquez to the Jews was not confined to Murcia, for the Palencia region in northern Spain, another part of the Enriquez domains from the 1450s, was also a major textile centre and home to one of the wealthiest and largest Jewish communities. The principal Christian families there, against the national trend, had stood by the *conversos* in the anti-*converso* troubles of 1465[32] and, as late as 1490, Palencia remained home to a substantial Jewish as well as a *converso* population.

The year 1449 marked the beginning of the end of the amazing, creative, pluralistic and heterodox Spanish society. The emergence in the fifteenth century of the endangered caste of the *converso* did not present itself at the time as inevitable or progressively cumulative or as a universal phenomenon. For the individual *converso* and his family – whatever their belief, whether devout or ambivalent Catholic or crypto-Jewish – so much depended upon who and where you were.

It had not always been so. With all its ups and downs, *Convivencia* – living at peace with your neighbours – had been real for many. Early in the thirteenth century, the Sufi poet ibn Arabi (b. in Murcia, d. 1240 in Damascus) wrote of the diversity of religious forms:

> My heart can take in
> Any form:
> Gazelles in a meadow,
> A cloister for monks
> For the idols, sacred ground
> Kaaba for the circling pilgrim
> The tablets of the Torah
> The scrolls of the Qur'an
> I profess the religion of love;
> Wherever its caravan turns
> Along the way, that is the belief
> The faith I keep.[33]

As late as 1465 or 1467, two Czech noblemen, in describing the estates of their host, a Castilian nobleman, noted that 'On his lands there are Christians, Jews and Muslims. They say the Count is a Christian but one cannot tell what religion he professes. He lets everyone live in peace with their own beliefs.'[34] But *Convivencia* finally died with the birth in the 1480s of a ferocious and specifically Spanish Inquisition. In 1492, with the expulsion of the Jews, Spain finally changed from the most tolerant to the most intolerant nation in Europe. Over the next 350 years the New Christians (the *conversos*) were ever suspected of continuing to practise Judaism in secret, while their church and their king remained ever dedicated both to saving the souls of the New Christians and to confiscating their property. The fear of being accused of having a Jewish ancestry paralyzed intellectual activity, and it is said that by the mid-sixteenth century one sign of noble (pure) lineage was not to know how to write one's name.

The Enriquez played a leading role in the struggle for power between the king of Castile and his ambitious and powerful nobles. In 1420 King Juan's younger brother attempted to seize the throne but, finally, with Alfonso Enriquez's support and Alfonso's rescue of Juan at Villalva, the revolt collapsed. Interestingly, the rebels were protesting against the influence of Juan's Jewish courtiers, especially his controller of revenue, and to support their anti-Semitic propaganda they had tortured a leading Jewish court physician into confessing he had poisoned Juan's father. Powerful nobles make for weak kings and some twenty years later Fadrique Enriquez headed a revolt designed to replace Juan II by Juan's son. Accounts vary but it seems at the battle of Olmeda, Fadrique escaped capture and went into exile. In 1448, negotiating with the kings of Aragon and Navarre, Fadrique was offered joint command of a major Aragon military force, and the funds to pay for its upkeep, to invade Castile. Nothing came of it and in 1464 Fadrique was pardoned and an uneasy peace treaty was signed at Medina del Campo.

Five years later, Fadrique, along with don Abraham Seneor, last chief rabbi and supreme judge of the Jews of Castile, was the key figure in organizing, against the king's wishes, Isabella's marriage to Ferdinand; the two would go on to be king and queen of a united Spain and to expel the Jews of Spain. Fadrique died in 1473 aged 83. Now, in his last will and testament, he required that he be buried in the family church of Santa Clara de Palencia. A near-contemporary chronicle notably failed to laud him as a luminary of the church but in yet another of the *conversos*' coded phrases (discussed in Chapter

10), he is described as 'a brave gentleman, a stout hearted man who boldly would put himself and his family out on a limb to protect his relatives'.³⁵ The distinction made between 'his family' and 'his relatives' is unusual, but makes sense if 'his relatives' is read as code for his fellow *conversos* whom he had protected and given sanctuary.

The public lives of these generations of the Enriquez were, within the context of the times, extraordinarily ordinary. The Enriquez were typical Castilian grandees whose lives were dedicated to the pursuit of power through whatever political, dynastic, commercial and military means were available. They were great admirals too. In their time the navy of Castile had overrun the Isle of Wight, wrecked the major English coastal towns from St Ives to Southampton, destroyed the fleet of the Hanseatic League, kept their own coasts clean of corsairs and pirates and established their supremacy over the Bay of Biscay. Fadrique wrote a sophisticated military manual containing thirty-nine chapters with detailed instructions on maritime navigation and docking. His Castilian galleons, often propelled by more than 100 oarsmen – freemen, not chained criminals – were the most advanced and manoeuvrable ships of the age. It is, however the private lives of the Enriquez that concern us here.

Death is the time of truth, a time when a person highlights the strength of his values, his hierarchies and his cultural patterns. And sometimes in death we say more than ever we chose, or dared, to say in life. Death in melancholy medieval Spain was far more ritualized and important than it is to many today – for to them then, it was the inevitable doorway to the Hereafter. The gospel accounts of the Day of Judgement, all amplified and embellished in sermons, art and literature, emphasized the doom-laden despairing zeitgeist of the Middle Ages. The Spanish were obsessed with death and the circumstances and rituals surrounding it, and the subsequent funeral and burial would, they believed, often decide whether they were to partake of the delights of Paradise, wait uncomfortably in Purgatory or burn in Hell until the End of Time.

As to the *conversos*, their classic pattern, as described in an anti-*converso* Catholic tract of 1449, was that as they drew near the end of their days here on earth, their faith in Judaism (whether original, suppressed, confused or actively maintained) revived. The quest for eternal salvation dominated medieval life, and while Christians generally shared with Jews a strong belief in a virtuous life, including the imperative of performing charitable deeds, it was the fundamental difference between the Catholic and the Jewish anticipations of the afterlife that engendered so many *converso* deathbed reconciliations to Judaism. For those differences could not have been greater; in Judaism one best finds favour with the Almighty through doing the good deeds laid down in the law. For St Paul, however, good deeds alone were not enough, declaring: 'For if a person could achieve through good works (the law), then Christ would have died in vain' (Galatians 2:21 and 3:10; Romans 3:28). Paul's critical central point is that only through an absolute and total faith in Christ might one escape the fires of hell. Unsurprisingly, such an absolute and total faith was rare in the *conversos*.[36] Now the Catholic afterlife was fearsome, for few doubted that the vast majority would be eternally damned. 'Salvandorum paucitas, damnandorum multitudo' (few saved, many damned) was the stern principle maintained by all the church leaders from Augustine to Aquinas. The proportion saved was usually estimated at one in 1,000 or even one in 10,000. So it was that deathbed reaffirmations in Judaism (for critically Judaism has hardly anything akin to the Catholic concept of an ever-punishing, painful, vengeful hell) became common among the *conversos* and was accompanied by an increasing rejection of Christianity with all its rituals to which they had had to submit all their lives. I think it likely Alfonso and dona Juana, by their wills, were following this well-established pattern. And it is in the critical differences between the Christian and the Jewish funerary rituals that Alfonso's and dona Juana's true beliefs are made manifest. By their wills, if they were Christians, they would be condemning themselves to an eternity of hellfire.

Turning first to the Christian funerary requirements, we note that their primary purpose was to ensure salvation of the soul. The church fabricated its image of heaven through the display of its own powerful religious symbols on the tombs and in the internal and external decor and architecture of its buildings. The idea was to express a posthumous ascent to heaven as concretely as possible. The mortal remains of kings, nobles and their ladies, often richly attired, would be laid to rest inside an ornate stone sepulchre. Their arms would be crossed in prayer and sometimes their legs too (a medieval convention designed to convey dignity) and occasionally the corpse would be boiled and boned; crosiers, bibles and other symbols of the church would be placed by their remains. Their effigies, usually portrayed enjoying everlasting beatitude, were cast or sculpted on top of the tomb and often surrounded by images of monks and nuns praying for the welfare of their souls, as permanent examples to stimulate the prayers of others for that purpose. The sides of the sepulchres, the surrounding architecture and every available surface of the church, in the true gothic style of the Middle Ages, would be covered with graven images, monograms of Christ and other sculpted representations. Often there would be a canopy adorned with angels, and on the walls and pillars complicated tracery with lavish and elaborate filigree work would surround a superabundance of iconographic expression. Chalices, monstrances, reliquaries and crucifixes would abound, as would effigies of Christ on the cross, statues and carvings of the apostles and of great saints and evangelists as well as specific scenes in the life of Christ, of which Christ on the road to Calvary was the most common.[36]

The Jewish funerary requirement was very different. Following the ordinance of Rabbi Gamliel in the second century, Jewish burials were simple, indeed rather austere, for in death are we not all equal?[37] The Second Commandment could not have more clearly and strongly prohibited all graven images, particularly representations of human beings. Whether they be the embalmed mummies of ancient Egypt, the cast or sculpted bodies of Rome and the Middle Ages or the portraits of the Renaissance, lifelike effigies would not be countenanced. Any image of the deceased atop his tomb would be condemned instantly as idolatry. Jewish law requires that the eyes and mouth be closed, the arms and hands extended alongside the body, which must be thoroughly washed in salt and warm water, the hair and beard combed and the toenails and fingernails cleaned and trimmed. This ritualistic washing of the corpse, carrying with it a sense of the washing away of sin, was particularly repugnant to the church. By the Middle Ages, the body, usually dressed in a simple shroud of white linen, muslin or cotton without any pockets, buttons, knots or seams, was laid to rest in the earth, for 'you are dust and to dust you shall return' (Genesis 3:19). In the twelfth century, Maimonides advised that dressing the dead, even though they be princes, in costly garments of gold or silver, was forbidden. Sometimes the hand would be clenched into a fist or the fingers would be bent in such a way as to form one of the names of God – a folk practice designed to drive any evil spirits and one frowned upon by the rabbis. Other times the same effect was thought to be achieved by placing metal or salt by the body. Even though the wealthier Jews of Spain, tending to assimilate, would sometimes be buried in coffins with their personal jewellery and accessories, the general rules were applied. The bodies would usually be buried with the head towards the west and their feet facing east, awaiting the advent of the Messiah. Although not material for these purposes, the timing of the funeral was different, for in Judaism the burial should take place on the day following death, but in Christianity it is usually within a week.

Dona Juana had worked to ensure that the building of the family church of Santa Clara de Palencia be completed while she was alive so that she might control its final appearance and imagery. In the last year of her life, in an addition to the family's normal subvention, she donated the huge sum of 100,000 maravedis to speed up its construction. We get a sense of the importance of the family's carpets, for among the many treasures she bequeathed to the Convent at Santa Clara de Palencia were 'two more large carpets with the shields of my husband the Admiral, and mine'.[38] We do not know if one of these was the Vizcaya carpet but we do know she left a surprisingly large number of carpets to different people and places. I wondered if she had been a major, if not the major, commissioning customer of her fellow conversos carpet weavers (see Chapter 9, and note 41 of Chapter 9 where the scholar Lavado Paradinas reports that the weavers of the Admiral carpets most interestingly moved to be closer to dona Juana and the Admiral).

Researching into possibilities of 500 years ago, possibilities that the people involved would have had every reason to conceal, is a chancy business. But dona Juana's last will and testament could not have been clearer; a will in medieval Spain was more than the means of settling one's estate on one's beneficiaries – it was a religious document designed to settle one's soul. So important was a will as evidence of one's true faith that the synod of Saragossa, as early as 1359, had forbidden a Christian burial to all who died intestate. What is extraordinary, what takes dona Juana and, as we will see, Alfonso Enriquez right out of the Christian and right into the Jewish tradition, is that in her will she decreed that apart from the family coats of arms, there must not be any kind of funeral iconography whatsoever on her sepulchre; in other words, it must not display any kind of Christian imagery. Some conversos, caught in the conflicting cross-currents of religious duties in their private life, became cynics and agnostics,[39] but not so Alfonso and dona Juana, for if such had been their beliefs, surely they would not have cared, and therefore would not have left such detailed and specific instructions about the nature of their tombs. Their old private faith was clearly spelled out, for dona Juana would not otherwise have very exactly, very specifically, stipulated that there should be no *Yaciente*, or sculpted (graven) image of the deceased, atop the tomb. These statues, being quite the grossest form of graven images, had been prohibited by the Second Commandment:

> Thou shalt not make into thee a graven image,
> Nor any manner of likeness of anything that is in the heaven above,
> Or in the earth beneath, or that is in the water under the earth.[40]

The enormity of their decision can only be properly understood in the context of the religious fervour and spirit of the time – of the sure and certain knowledge of the ever-tempting omnipresent Satan and all his minions waiting to drag one down to the everlasting torments of hell, all so graphically described in every gory detail in the sermons, in the literature and in the art of the church. One picture saves a thousand words, and these pictures of hell left nothing to the imagination. Vivid representations of death and punishment abounded, with dancing skeletons and corrupted corpses beckoning one on to the gates of hell. In Figure 22 we see what they saw then – there are the sinners tumbling down into hell's fire and Figure 23, another contemporary picture, depicts what awaits the fallen when they arrive.

By far the most exact and exacting description of Christian medieval hell was set down in the fourteenth century by Dante Alighieri (1265–1321) in his *Divine Comedy*. With awesome seriousness, Dante describes his journey through hell, purgatory and heaven, and in painful graphic detail depicts the unending agonies of the damned. Alfonso and dona Juana, in their rejection of Christian ritual and tradition, were condemning themselves to that part of Dante's hell dedicated to those whose pride had resisted all earthly efforts to cleanse them of erroneous beliefs. There, such sinners would spend eternity in agony on a plain of white-hot sand, screaming as a slow fire descending like rain would add to their pain and their just punishment. Alternatively, they might anticipate being consigned to the ninth pit of hell, a special place dedicated to those who, not being properly supportive of the church, must suffer again and again and yet again, until the final Day of Judgement, to be split apart by a demon with a sword.[41] There would be no escape from the burnings, the beatings and the endless torture awaiting all who did not follow the teachings of mother church, for life here on earth was but a preparation, a testing time for the hereafter. As awful as were the ending of most people's lives in the death-obsessed Middle Ages, none could compare to the eternal torments of those who died without conforming fully and exactly to the rituals of Rome.

The profound and passionate importance to Jews of their symbols was equalled by the profound and passionate importance to Christians of their infinitely more extensive and explicit icons and images. Many Christians believed that Christ existed in potential or in actuality in his image in the same way that he was present in the wine and the wafer of the Eucharist. This was more than a matter of belief. It was a matter of heartfelt and sure and certain knowledge that was not to be denied. To reject his image, to refuse sculptures of the crucifixion or murals of Christ and the disciples or saints was to reject the saviour Himself. Few wills would be complete without the words 'ut evadam portas inferni' or 'pro extinguenda incendia gehenne ignis'. It was impossible for Christians to see death as the end of their individual life; it was for them but a brief phase, and a testing one at that, in their progress to life everlasting. There can be no greater proof of Alfonso's and dona Juana's real religious beliefs, for by rejecting the Catholic canon and its funerary requirements, were they to have been of the Catholic faith they would have been voluntarily condemning themselves to an eternity of hellfire.[42] Given the manifest depth of their beliefs and given that both their son's wife and his lover (who was the mother of his heir) were *converso* ladies, one may reasonably assume that their son Fadrique and his wife dona Marina (both of whose coats of arms are inscribed on the Vizcaya carpet) were also *conversos*, continuing, like so many, in their private lives to follow in the customs of the family. Such endogamous marriages over many generations were of course the norm for people struggling to maintain to their faith as a private matter.

The nature of the final resting-place was more important to dona Juana than to her husband. For while Alfonso Enriquez's will indicated that he wished to be buried in the family cathedral in Santa Clara de Palencia, he gave dona Juana the last word as to where his remains were to be interred. The choice was hers.[43] It seems that, typically, Alfonso (the son of one *converso* lady and the husband of another) was dominant in their public lives, and dona Juana (the daughter and wife of *conversos*) was dominant in their private lives. I think the role of these three generations of *conversa* Enriquez ladies, the wives and the mother, was critical and customary in maintaining the family culture and faith.

The synagogue, the cultural epicentre of Judaism and a male-dominated one at that, was clearly no place for crypto-Jews. And so the focus of the religious lives of the *conversos* moved from the public arena to the privacy of their homes where, fitting comfortably into the classical pattern in medieval society, the woman, through her control of the household, usually had the key role in preserving her family's traditions and beliefs. In fifteenth-century Germany, Victor von Karben, a Jewish convert to Christianity, attributed much of the Jews' religious devotion to the women. Such, too, was the position in Spain where the home and the family became the last bastion of cultural resistance, with the Inquisition records revealing that frequently the husband's crime was passively to have permitted his wife to continue running a Jewish home. The Inquisition was aware of the strong role of women in Jewish culture[44] and it was no accident that Queen Esther (the heroine of the biblical story who, as a crypto-Jew, saves the Jews of Persia from extermination), became a major figure in the secret *converso* festivals.[45]

Even their requirements as to the placement of Alfonso's sepulchre in their chapel were in conflict with the hallowed practices of Christian entombment. For his white alabaster tomb, shaped like a huge ship (he was Admiral of Castile), decorated only with his coat of arms and without any Christian imagery, was so placed in the middle of the chapel as to block some of the view of the critical centrepiece of the chapel – the altar.[46] Dona Juana's tomb was slightly smaller.

The symbols throughout the mainly gothic architectural tracing and vegetal motifs on the walls and the ceiling of the chapel[47] were, just like those on the Vizcaya carpet, capable of interpretation either as merely decorative or as Judaic. There were grape leaves and grapevines (ancient symbols of the Jewish people – Psalm 80:9), clusters of grapes (peace and messianic Redemption – Micah 4:4), nuts (new life–Song of Songs 6:11) and pomegranates – one of the most popular Jewish symbols signifying fertility, love and remembrance (see Chapter 14). It was surely no coincidence that all the forms – architectural, vegetal and geometric – were not only similar to those in the medieval synagogue of Santa Maria La Blanca in Toledo but also rather dissimilar to those in contemporary Spanish churches. There were also some fantastic half-human images in the Enriquez chapel which seem to echo those portrayed in Jewish manuscripts of the time. Finally, the internal decor of their church, apart from some formal statuettes, was in far greater accord with Jewish than with Christian custom. The items were simple – mainly family shields and flowers – and all quite at odds with the usual extremes of Gothic style.

These tombs tell us that the Enriquez' support for Jews and *conversos* was motivated by far more than economic self-interest. A major Talmudic tenet held that a life of good deeds (mitzvot) would ensure salvation of the soul and ultimately bring about the salvation of the Jewish people. Their tombs point to the probability that like so many New Christians they continued for a few generations privately, discreetly, to practise Judaism. But it was not to last. By the next century no longer was power unevenly and often anarchically split between the regions, the king, the barons, the church, the new middle classes, Muslims and the Jews. Now all power rested in a partnership of the monarchs of a united Spain (Navarra had been taken over in 1516) with its own Spanish Inquisition – a partnership dedicated to extirpating any groupings, let alone any ideas, other than its own. By the 1550s, no one of known Jewish descent could with total ease hold any position of authority in the church, the army, the university or the government. It was the activities of the Inquisitor General, Tomás de Torquemada (1420–95), that had set the scene for the next 300 years. Few, however powerful, dared to confront him, and Torquemada's attack on two very senior and respected fellow churchmen who happened to have some Jewish ancestors was a clear lesson to all: one was the bishop of Calahorra and President of the Council of Castile; the other, Juan Arias Dávila, the bishop of Segovia, had more than proven his family's newfound faith through the ferocity of his attacks on the *conversos* in his diocese. The most interesting charge against Dávila (at least from our point of view) was that he had had the remains of his own forebears exhumed in order to destroy the evidence that they had been buried in accordance with Jewish rites.[48]

The example of Juan Arias Dávila could not have been more convincing, and Fadrique Enriquez de Cabrera (1485–1538), heir to the Enriquez wealth and titles, tried to erase all traces of his *converso* inheritance. By now, any deviant ancestral sepulchre had become a danger. Riding roughshod over the express terms of Alfonso's and dona Juana's wills, desecrating their tombs, he had their mortal remains removed to the Convent of Nuestra Senora de las Esperanza in Valdescopezo.[49] I think he must have had their remarkable sepulchres, which had clearly been so important to them, destroyed, for they were never seen again. Interestingly (possibly significantly), he gave really most generously to the very small churches of Letur and Liétor (I shall discuss these villages in Chapter 9, for it was there or nearby that the Vizcaya carpet was most probably woven); his prodigious gifts included velvet, gold and silver. I reported in Chapter 5 that one very odd feature of the Vizcaya carpet is that it has undergone far more subsequent work than one would expect, for whole sections of other carpets have been added to it and insertions interwoven. I wondered if it was at this time, when the Enriquez heir was busy suppressing anything that might throw any doubt as to the purity of his faith and his blood, that the changes to the carpet were made and any overtly Judaic icons were removed. I wondered, too, if his lavish gifts to the two churches nearest to the weavers of his family's great carpets had been made in consideration of those changes.

In an ironic aside to this story, we may note that Fadrique's son married and had four daughters, whom he married off to kings and nobles. The youngest daughter married Juan II of Aragon – whom, as we saw, also had Jewish forebears. It was their part-Jewish son Ferdinand who, with his queen Isabella, in 1492 expelled the Jews from Spain.

Given that we now have both circumstantial and substantial evidence that the Enriquez were very likely to have been crypto-Jewish *conversos*, the next step in this enquiry is to look closely at what was happening to the *conversos* in the period in which the Vizcaya carpet was woven.

NOTES

1. H. Graetz, *History of the Jews, 1894–1945* (Jerusalem: Jewish Publication Society, 1956), Vol. 4, p.75.
2. Benzion Netanyahu, *The Origins of the Inquisition in Fifteenth Century Spain*, 2nd edn (New York: New York Review of Books, 2001), p.104.
3. Ibid., p.102.
4. H.C. Lea, *A History of the Inquisition of Spain*, Vol. 1 (New York: Macmillan, 1906), pp.101–3.
5. *Remembering Sepharad* (Madrid: State Corporation for Spanish Cultural Action Abroad, 2003), p.146, citing Chapter 50 of R. Yosef ben Saddiq, *Compendio Memoria del Justo* (Moreno Koch, 1992), pp.58–9.
6. Geoffrey Chaucer, *The Canterbury Tales*, trans. Nevill Coghill (London: Penguin Books, 2003), p.201. Need I add that Pedro, known by his enemies as 'the Cruel' was also a man of his time. Having saved the Jewish community of Miranda del Ebro from a mob intent on its destruction, Pedro, *pour encourager les autres*, boiled one of the mob's leaders and roasted another. Lea, *History of the Inquisition of Spain*, Vol. 1, p.102.
A contemporary ballad entitled 'At the Feet of Don Enrique' writes of Pedro:

> Some say that he was just
> Others that he has done evil
> That the King is not cruel, if he was born
> In a time which made it necessary to be so.

D. Baraz, *Medieval Cruelty* (Ithaca, NY: Cornell University Press, 2003), p.135.

Pedro's links to England were strong; he gave Edward, the Black Prince, a huge ruby which Elizabeth I described as the size of a tennis ball. It can be seen today in the Tower of London, sparkling in the crown of England. Chaucer's brother-in-law, John of Gaunt, Duke of Lancaster, having married Pedro's daughter, unsuccessfully claimed the throne of Castile from Enrique. Typical of the time, Chaucer, while expressing hatred of the Jews (pp.170–5) coveted their work (p.182).

7. Americo Castro, *The Spaniards* (Berkeley, CA: University of California Press, 1971), p.536.
8. J. Valdeón Baruque, *Los Judios de Castilla y las Revolucion Trastamara* (Valladolid: Gráficas Andrés Martín, 1968), pp.58, 59.
9. Netanyahu, *Origins of the Inquisition in Fifteenth Century Spain*, 2nd edn, p.115.
10. Ibid., pp.131, 1 199, notes 4 and 6, citing the order of Enrique II, dated 25 August 1378.
11. Valdéon Baruque, *Los Judios de Castilla y las Revolucion Trastamara*, pp.63–4.
12. The Jews of Castile believed that it was dona Juana who was successful in persuading the king of Castile to change from a persecutor to a protector of the Jews, and compared her to Esther in the biblical Purim story of Esther and the king of Persia.
13. Luis Marco Idachs, *Los Judíos de Cataluña* (Barcelona: Ediciones Destino, 1985), p.219.
14. Luis Rubio Garcia, *Los Judios de Murcia en la Beja Edad Media (1350–1500)* (Murcia: Universidad de Murcia, 1992), pp.xxxi, 113, 200, 224, 227, 250.
15. Solomon Freehof, *The Responsa Literature* (Philadelphia, PA: Jewish Publication Society, 1955), p.116.
16. Ibid., pp.88–92 (Responsum 89).
17. *Encylopaedia Judaica* (Jerusalem: Keter Publishing, 1971), Vol.12, p.530.
18. N. Roth, *Conversos, Inquisition and the Expulsion of the Jew from Spain* (Madison, WI: University of Wisconsin Press, 2002), p.34.
19. A. Castro, *El Real Monasterio de Santa Clara de Palencia y los Enriquez, Almirantes de Castilla* (Valladolid: Sever-Cuesta, 1982), p.34.
20. Ibid., p.34.
21. A. MacKay, *Spain in the Middle Ages* (Basingstoke: Macmillan, 1977), pp.85–6.
22. *El Tizón de la Nobleza de España*, cited in Americo Castro, *The Structure of Spanish History*, trans. Edmund King (Princeton, NJ: Princeton University Press, 1954), p.523.
23. Alonso Enrique, *Honras y Obsequios que hizo al Catolico, y Christianismo Rey Don Felipe Tercero Mestro Señor fue muy noble y muy leal Cuidad de Murcia* (Murcia: Luys Beros, 1622–32), p.19.
24. Roth, *Conversos, Inquisition and the Expulsion of the Jew from Spain*, pp.93, 94, 377.
25. Edgar Samuel, *At the End of the Earth* (London: Jewish Historical Society of England, 2004), pp.4–5, 82. Samuel, in this fine study, notes that the custom was referred to twice in the writings of Nahmanides (1194–1235).
26. Castro, *El Real Monasterio de Santa Clara de Palencia y los Enriquez, Almirantes de Castilla*, p.74.
27. Paloma was Paloma bat Gedaliah, daughter of Gedaliah ben Shlomo, apparently of the Davidic line – that is, a direct descendant of King David.
28. E. Capsali, *Sedeh Eliyahu Zuta*, edited by Aryeh Schmuelevitz, Shlomo Simonsohn and Meyer Benayahu, 3 vols (Israel: Ben-Zvi Institute, Tel Aviv and Jerusalem Universities, 1975, 1977, 1983), Vol.1, pp.182–4. King Ferdinand's half-brother Alfonso married a Jewish lady with

the delightful name of Amiator Conejo, but on adopting Christianity she changed her name to Maria. Roth, *Conversos, Inquisition and the Expulsion of the Jews from Spain*, pp.150–1.
29. Angus MacKay, 'Popular Movements and Pogroms in Fifteenth Century Castile', *Past and Present*, 55 (1972), pp.34, 35, Table 1.
30. Roth, *Conversos, Inquisition and the Expulsion of the Jew from Spain*, p.89.
31. Gregory B. Kaplan, *The Evolution of Converso Literature* (London: University Press of Florida, 2002), p.24.
32. Henry Kamen, *The Spanish Inquisition* (London: Phoenix, 2003), p.29.
33. Ibn Arabi, trans. Michael Sells, cited in Jerrilynn Dodds, Maria Menocal and Abigail Balbale, *The Arts of Intimacy* (New Haven, CT: Yale University Press, 2008), pp.128–9.
34. Castro, *The Spaniards*, p.559.
35. Castro, *El Real Monasterio de Santa Clara de Palencia y los Enriquez, Almirantes de Castilla*, p.171.
36. A fine example of a Spanish medieval tomb is that of Juan II of Castile and Isabel of Portugal near Burgos.
37. Judaism teaches that life is a divine gift to be cherished in itself; it is not simply a testing ground for the world to come. There are no 'last rites' in Judaism, nor is there anointing of the dead as in Christianity. The shrouds should be simple: a headdress, trousers and shirt for a man or an overdress for a woman – both covered with a wrapping sheet. Mishnah Kilaim 9. 41; Maasey Sheni 5. 12; Tosefta Nedarim 2. 7. Sometimes fragrant leaves were placed on the clothes; at other times lime was put on the body to hasten decomposition. Since Talmudic times, it had been customary to bury a man in his tallit (prayer shawl) after the fringes had been rendered ritually unfit.
38. J. Mañueco, *Jornadas Sobre el Arte de las Ordenes Religiousas en Palencia* (Palencia: Gráficas Iglesias, 1990), p.158.
39. Y. Baer, *A History of the Jews in Christian Spain*, Vol. 2 (Philadelphia, PA: Jewish Publication Society, 1992), p.274. I think that for the mindset of most people of the time, to doubt the existence of the supernatural was for most as impossible as doubting their own existence; they lacked the vocabulary, the argumentation and the science.
40. Exodus 20:4. The prohibition is not absolute, being qualified in Exodus 20:5 and Deuteronomy 5:9: 'Thou shall not bow down to them nor serve them.' Later, the Talmudic sages, clarifying any lingering doubts, stated: 'What is treated as a deity is prohibited, what is not treated as a deity is permitted' (Mishnah Avodah Zarah 3:5); and 'The idol of an idolater is prohibited forthwith, but if it belonged to an Israelite it is not prohibited until it is worshipped' (Avodah Zarah 4:4). Many, however, adhered to the strict prohibition of Exodus 20:4.
41. Dante Alighieri (1265–1321), *The Divine Comedy*, trans. Peter Dale (London: Anvil Press Poetry, 1996); Andrew McCall, *The Medieval Underworld* (Stroud: Sutton Publishing, 2004), pp.286, 287. Interestingly (albeit irrelevant to our topic), in the course of his journey through hell, Dante failed to encounter any Jews among the heretics and usurers in whose sinful ranks Jews were believed to dwell.
42. The Jewish view was more complex. Maimonides and his Aristotelian-inclined followers, not believing in the immortality of the individual soul, held that nothing remained of a man after death save his intellect, which was stripped of any individual identity. There was

no general agreement about the nature of the surviving intellect or even about the physical body.

The Kabbalists believed in the immortality of the soul for, being part of the divine emanation, its spiritual essence guaranteed its survival after death but generally Judaism is far more concerned with fulfilling the commandments of God in this world than with any rewards in the World to come. There was, however, no general agreement as to the details of reward and of punishment after death. Judah Halevi (before 1075–1141), the great Spanish Jewish poet and philosopher, in his book *Kuzari* has the king of the Khazars say of Judaism: 'The anticipations of other religions are grosser and more sensuous than yours.' Scripture does not fully and clearly express the notion of the immortality of the soul and the Talmud exhorts one not to speculate over much on 'what is above, what is beneath, what was before time and what will be hereafter' (Mishnah Hagigah 2:1).

43. Mañueco, *Jornadas Sobre el Arte de las Ordenes Religiousas en Palencia*, p.157.
44. Renée Levine Melammed, *Heretics or Daughters of Israel* (Oxford: Oxford University Press, 1999), p.12.
45. Jane Gerber, *The Jews of Spain* (London: Free Press, 1994), p.122.
46. Mañueco, *Jornadas Sobre el Arte de las Ordenes Religiousas en Palencia* p.156. J. Gonzalez makes a similar point in his *Historia de Palencia*, Edades Antigua y Media, Vol. 1 (Madrid: J. Soto Impressor, 1948), p.318.
47. Mañueco, *Jornadas Sobre el Arte de las Ordenes Religiousas en Palencia*, p.157.
48. Castro, *El Real Monasterio de Santa Clara de Palencia y los Enriquez, Almirantes de Castilla*, p.170.
49. Roth, *Conversos, Inquisition and the Expulsion of the Jews from Spain*, p.151.

1391–1492: Action and Reaction

The hellish pogroms that spread across Spain in 1391, the butchering of thousands of Jewish men, women and children, drove many thousands more to the baptismal font. One hundred years later, in 1492, the Jews were expelled from Spain. It is in the period sometime between 1405 and 1475, according to the Spanish historian Americo Castro, that the Admiral carpets were woven. In the preceding chapters we have gone back in time to understand the three major factors (the Enriquez, the Jews and carpets) that came together to produce this carpet. But now further understandings may be gained by looking at both contemporary and subsequent events. One must, of course, bear in mind that while profound social and political change often appear in hindsight to have been inevitable, for many – if not most – people at the time, they were not only *not* inevitable – they were unthinkable.

The fourteenth and fifteenth centuries in Spain were a time of exceptional violence and lawlessness, etched with the extremes of privilege and poverty, of bigotry and brutality. It was an age of conflict between Christians, Muslims, kings, barons, the emerging middle classes and above all the church, which now militant, sought control over the hearts, minds, bodies and souls of every last person. To this end, the popes promoted the devil and all his hosts of hell; hitherto they had been relatively minor characters – Satan had been demoted and had almost disappeared from Judaism by the Middle Ages – but in Christianity the devil and his demons were now elevated to the highest ranks. The mid-fourteenth century saw the beginning of the age of witch persecution – a delusion that was to consume Western Europe for the next

300 or so years. The church, having greatly increased the strength of the powers of darkness, demanded greater powers to fight them. As early as the thirteenth century, the pope had sharpened the teeth of his armoury of condemnation, anathema, excommunication and ritual curses by establishing a system of Inquisitions. Following the devastating Black Death in 1348, the church, through torture, tore confessions out of its victims, purporting to evidence a worldwide conspiracy organized by the Jews of Spain to poison all the wells and to dominate the world.[1] The church ever needed accessible and vulnerable scapegoats and it is highly significant that over the course of 150 years some 30,000 witches were burnt alive in a Europe from which the Jews had been expelled – but few witches were to be found in Spain, where, over the course of 300 years, tens of thousands of Jews were burnt alive.

So it was that the Jews were demonized. St Augustine had attributed to blindness the refusal of the Jews to recognize the truth of Christianity, but now they were to be seen as intentionally wilful instruments of the Evil One. For the devil was the supreme liege lord and master of a multitude of evil creatures, all incorporated into one unspeakably foul entity under him. In the same way that the good Christian was a part of Christ's mystical body, so the Jews were part of Satan's mystical body, at one with him in all his works.[2] The role of the Jews as servants of the Antichrist was hammered home in the sermons, tracts and books of many a churchman, with perhaps the most influential book being *The Dagger of Faith*, by the Dominican, Raymond Martin (1210–85). The increasing representation of cruelty in the plastic arts points to this change, for we now see that the cruelty and suffering inflicted on Christ so depicted in ever more agonizing detail becomes a means to an end. The accusations against the Jews of the ritual murder of young children was, at a certain level, a re-enactment of Christ's passion. By so assigning such cruelty to the Jews, alienating and demonizing them, so violence against them was legitimized and encouraged.

From 1391 onwards the bishops of Castile would convene their own Inquisitions, a system of enquiries designed to detect and root out Christians who did not, heart and soul, believe in and follow the church's conclusive revealed truth. Christianity could not separate itself from its Jewish foundations, and indeed it defined itself in its rejection of Judaism. Having forced so many Jews to save their lives by pretending to become Christians, the church was alarmed to recognize that such conversions could not possibly be sincere, and a Spain full of private heretics was even worse than one full of public

1391–1492: Action and Reaction

Jews. In 1478 the Spanish Inquisition, a partnership between church and state, was established, for now to the church the mere presence of Jews had become hateful; to the kings they were a supply of money, and to the emerging mercantile middle classes and the murderous rampaging mob they were both hateful and a source of loot.

The turning points had been in 1378, 1391 and again in 1411–12, when riots erupted, spewing out a suppurating sickness of hatred over Castile, Leon and Aragon. The pogroms of 1391, enflamed by food shortages, corruption and a return of the Black Death, were by far the worst, breaking out on Ash Wednesday and raging like wildfire throughout that summer; the homes of the Jews, their livelihoods, liberties and lives were forfeit. Theft, rape, arson and murder became respectable, even sacramental, their evil clothed in Christian rhetoric. A pogrom, of course, is a highly profitable business. Christianity at that time forbade most forms of financing, be it a loan to help the farmer fund his next year's crop (failure of the annual crop often meant famine and death) or to the noble to arm and dress himself to the fashion. Many Jews, often banned from other occupations, became the major source of such funding, so a pogrom offered considerable profit: if the creditor and his family fled or were killed, not only might the debtor never have to pay his debt but the Jew's house, chattels, land and stock might well also be there for the taking. In the twenty-five years between 1391 and 1416 approximately one third of the Jews of Spain were murdered and one third to a half converted to Christianity. The lament of Yehuda ben David, written shortly after the pogroms of 1391, tells us of the trauma:

> Hear, O Earth and Heaven
> And I will weep many tears
> For the destruction of thousands
> From the day I left Jerusalem.
> There will be an especially great wail
> For the year 1391 of the destruction
> For the community of Seville was destroyed
> And many communities in Castile.
> And the communities of the people of Andalusia and Provincia
> Were struck by evil
> Catalonia was disgraced
> Together with Aragon.
> Judah and the people of Israel

> Depart from evil
> Perhaps the Almighty will have compassion
> And send the Redeemer to you.[3]

The dead were piled up in great heaps in the streets and many of the living sold as slaves to Muslims,[4] no matter that in its formal theology the church had no jurisdiction over the Jews. As the fourteenth and fifteenth centuries advanced in Spain, the reality on the ground was that so often churchmen and mob came together to see Jews as devils to be dragged to the baptismal font, ever citing Jesus's address to the Jews in John 8:43–4, which with all its power of gospel truth was not to be denied: 'You are of your father the devil and your will is to do your father's desires.' The sentence had been spoken, the sentence has been passed, and by such careful selection and emphasis of untypical statements the church reshaped its sacred writings, leaving behind the full meanings of its original testament of love. One of the church's great saints, St John Chrysostom (c.350–407) had condemned all Jews, living, dead and *yet to be born*, as Christ-killers. Another of the great saints, St Jerome (c.340–420), then endorsed this cardinal principal as canon law.

There was a paradox at the heart of the church's attitude to the Jews. The position of most popes and senior churchmen was well set out in Pope Innocent III's preamble to the reissuing in 1199 of *Constitutio pro Judeis*, in which violence against Jews was forbidden: 'Although Jewish perfidy is in every way worthy of condemnation, nevertheless because through them the truth of our own faith is proved, they are not to be SEVERELY oppressed by the faithful' (my caps).[5] But the deeds of some senior and many lesser clerics belied that doctrine, despite efforts to enforce it by many popes. The eminent authority Joseph Trachtenberg best sums it up:

> Herein lies the paradox of Christian policy toward the Jew. Bitterly condemned and excoriated, they (the Jews) were yet to be tolerated on humanitarian grounds, and indeed preserved on theological grounds, as living testimony to the truth of Christian teaching.
>
> Yet the impulse to punish the hated and to convert by all means the unregenerate constantly warred against the moral and dogmatic scruples which, at best, animated only a small minority of the more highly placed and responsible clergy.[6]

Whether the inquisitors were saintly holy men, fanatical psychopaths or simply soulless bureaucrats mattered not, for while Catholicism gives primacy to the intention (and it was the Jews who were at the receiving end of these intentions), Judaism gives primacy to the deed. In any case, while it is of academic interest to study the intent, that is the stated policy, of an organization as expounded by its leaders, it is what is actually happening to the people on the ground that more truly defines the terms of the relationship. It is of those people, whether protected grandees or common weavers, that I write.

In the Spanish pogroms of 1378, 1391 and 1411–12 some Jews chose martyrdom, believing that to be martyred in God's name was the highest privilege; their supreme act of faith echoed, with all its urgency and dignity, the Wisdom of Solomon:

> But the souls of the righteous are in the Hand of God,
> And there no torment shall touch them.
> In the eyes of the foolish they seemed to have died;
> And their departure was taken to be their hurt,
> And their going away from us to be their ruin:
> But they are in peace.[7]

Most, however, converted to become New Christians, a hybrid caste simultaneously Christian and Jewish, composed of three distinct categories of survivors: firstly, those who remained devout but discrete Jews; secondly, those confused and torn between the two, and lastly, newly devout Christians. This diversity to be found among the *conversos* then is as nothing to that of the scholars who study them today. At one end of the spectrum are those who hold that the life of Jews and *conversos* in fifteenth-century Spain was an unending series of pressure and persecution. At the other extreme are the scholars who assert that it was not church doctrine to harm Jews and force them to convert, adding that in any case such pressures and persecution were intermittent. There were many instances of churchmen seeking to protect Jews: indeed, as late as 1449 it was the *converso* Cardinal Juan de Torquemada, uncle of the Inquisitor General-to-be, who helped influence Pope Nicholas V's bull, *Humani Generis Inimicus*, which forbids any discrimination between old and new Christians. But the broad sweep of what was actually happening to the people is only too clear.

Jewish law provides that under overwhelming pressure it is no sin to convert to another religion, for it is fundamental that a man may be held responsible only for what he does or does not do of his own free will. Even the great Maimonides himself (who had fled from Spain as a child) had advised that Jews, to save their lives, might publicly adopt Islam whilst privately holding fast to their own ancient faith.[8] After all, they would doubtless say to each other, long before the advent of Christianity or of Islam, our forefathers lived in Spain. Persecuted first by Christian Visigoths and later by Muslim Arabs, they had survived by undergoing the formality of conversion. Was there not ample precedent? Is not the past but part of the present? The pattern of persecution, to be followed by the restoration of earlier rights played out in Egypt and Palestine in the early eleventh century, in Spain under the Almoravids later that century and again under the Almohads in the twelfth century, was well established and so would doubtless apply again. Had there not been crypto-Jews even at times in the Roman Empire?[9] And further back, in biblical times, had not our ancestors emerged intact in the Exodus from Egypt – by preserving their names, their language, their family life and sexual morality and, most importantly, by not informing on each other?[10] Has discretion in public not always been part of Jewish life? Is it not customary – although in defiance of Jewish law (Deuteronomy 12:5) – for our women to dress as men to avoid being molested when travelling, and for our men to dress as Christians, even as clerics? The answer, they would have told themselves a thousand times, was surely to convert, to lie low, and to hope and pray for better times.

Estimates vary greatly but by 1391 perhaps as many as 100,000 had fled Spain for Muslim lands, 100,000 had converted to Christianity and 100,000 had been murdered – and all in the name of gentle Jesus.[11] In the thirty years following the massacres of 1391, perhaps another 50,000 Jews converted – hoping that the storm would blow over, that their torment might cease and that soon they might again lead their own quiet lives following their faith within their communities.[12] Through the second half of the fourteenth century and the whole of the fifteenth century, the numbers and the strength of the Jews continually fell, while the number of *conversos*, for a time freed of the restrictions placed upon them as Jews, and now able to maintain their lives and lifestyles in Spain, increased. Today, as noted, nearly one in five of the occupants of Spain and Portugal had a Jewish ancestor. And, of course, the more who converted to Christianity, the easier it was for yet more to join them. But then some, having tried wholeheartedly to embrace Christianity, became disenchanted by the inhospitality and suspicion of some of their fellow Christians.

Alonso Cohen's story is typical. He had been a pharmacist in Murcia but gave up this profession in early 1391 to go and live in nearby Orihuela in Valencia. That summer, when the news of the pogroms reached the city, Alonso fled straight back to the safety of the Enriquez-controlled Murcia, leaving all his possessions behind. The priests and the mob got to Orihuela and, faced with the option of conversion or death, most of the Jews converted; only a minority managed to escape and, like Alonso, flee to safety in Enriquez' Murcia. Indeed, so protected were the Jews in Enriquez' Murcia that they were able to send help to the *conversos* of Orihuela. But there the authorities had confiscated such of Alonso's possessions that had survived plunder and refused to return them, despite the best efforts of the Murcian authorities on his behalf. In Enriquez' Murcia the Jews remained relatively safe and when the Dominican priests raised a mob to attack them, the town officials were sharply ordered to stop all such violence, and instructions were posted throughout the city banning attacks on the Jews. Twenty years later, in the anti-Jewish riots of 1411–12, Alonso Cohen converted to Christianity.[13]

Let us pause here to put the plight of the Jews into the broader context of the Middle Ages, for it was a fearful and violent time, a time of endless insecurity, a time of despoliation, disease and death; of plagues – bubonic, septicaemic and pneumonic; of leprosy and lawlessness; of hobgoblins and devils. Few could distinguish between the natural and the supernatural, and the horrors of hell awaiting them in their next lives were as true to them as were the harsh realities of their daily lives. Their world was one where benign or malign messages were everywhere, whether in the shape of the clouds or the stranger that stared at you as he passed by or the howling of a dog that told you the Angel of Death was stalking your shadow. Without the aid of the laws of science that today explain and treat so many of those many ills to which our flesh is heir, they found in the supernatural seemingly rational explanations for the chaos and cruelty of life. The Church of Rome knew itself to be the Almighty's sole and exclusive representative on earth, ordained by Him with the monopoly of saving souls. Its theology incorporated a multitude of residual pre-Christian folk beliefs and, as suggested earlier in this chapter, it was no accident that the development of anti-Semitism in the Middle Ages was paralleled by the rise to power and prominence of the devil and all his minions – for both were tools of social control created by the religious and economic elite. The creative genius of the church was undeniable. With this dualism, it not only fabricated the new, quintessentially evil, interventionist devil, it also invented the theoretical Jew, who had everything to do with the church's identity – and nothing to do with the identity, character and life of the real Jews. This theological Jew was needed both to authenticate the Bible and its revelation and to demonstrate his base and inferior nature through ample and endless humiliation. He must, however, be permitted to survive, for his conversion to Christianity at the End of Days was an essential precursor to the Second Coming. But the problem in Castile was that the Jews would not willingly conform to this model. As a group they were just too vibrant, too successful and, for a time, too useful.

As mentioned earlier, scholars are split in their understanding of the complex Christian–Jewish relationship in medieval Spain. Beyond the fundamental difference as to the perceived failure of the Jews to recognize the divinity of Jesus, neither Jews nor Christians seemed to hold one all-embracing view as to how they might treat with the other. Each within their own group often held huge disagreements as to principles, precepts and practices – all shifting and adapting in those times of monumental socio-economic and political change. My concern here, albeit at the risk of oversimplification, is to highlight and exemplify only the key doctrinal and behavioural elements that would have impacted on the Jews and *conversos* at that time. The problem was that the Jews, by not accepting that the only path to the world above was through belief in the divinity of Christ and in the Trinity, cast doubt upon those beliefs fundamental to Christianity. Their worldviews were so often worlds apart. The Catholic belief in the Middle Ages that life on earth for most was but a vile and painful testing ground leading to excruciating torments of the flesh in the afterlife – all endlessly detailed in the sermons, stained glass, sculptures, tapestry, poetry, paintings, dramas, illuminated manuscripts and religious tracts, all designed to frighten people into church and keep them there – was simply unbelievable to the Jews. Their belief that each one of us has a personal relationship with the Deity, and that (albeit within certain limits) tolerance and learning were to be valued, was heresy and anathema to the Catholic Church. And rightly so. For Judaism, with the authority of its venerable parental role in Christianity, by questioning both the nature and the very existence of the Christian hell threatened the most powerful tool in the church's armoury, as did the Jews' belief that the body, presenting no danger to the soul, was without need of pre-emptive punishment, such as flagellation. Their broadly held belief that it was no mortal sin within marriage to delight in the acts and arts of love was an affront to the ascetic Christian tradition which in the Middle Ages increasingly saw the flesh and the body as diabolical, as something akin to a place of debauch. The church increasingly objectified their belief in the sins of the flesh, making them subject to an ever more elaborate system of definitions, taboos, and sanctions. It was almost as sinful for a rabbi not to be married as it was for a priest to be married or certainly not celibate. That Origen (c.185–254), one of the most distinguished and influential of the founding theologians of Christianity, should take his belief in the mortification of the flesh to the point of having himself castrated was, to the Jews, a gross and incomprehensible offence against God.

Machiavelli, the arch realist who saw things for what they were, observed that 'the closer people are to the Roman church, which is the head of our religion, the less religion they have'.[14] Anyone who wavered from the church's belief in its own conclusive revealed truth, of a truth that could brook no others, had to be destroyed. The victims of the Church Militant in this war included tens of millions of Christians, Cathars, Waldensians, *Moriscos* (Christianized Muslims), *conversos* (Christianized Jews), Fraticelli, Wycliffites, Hussites, Paterini, Adamites, Manichaeans, Beguines, Beghards, Bogomils, Durangos, Knights Templar, Lollards and Erasmians in addition to numberless Muslims, Jews, homosexuals, witches, sorcerers, bigamists, pantheists, agnostics and atheists.[15] Whilst in law Jews and Muslims were outside of the church's jurisdiction, they would often be brought inside with charges of sorcery.

Of all these heresies, the church's response to the Cathars of Languedoc in southern France in the twelfth and thirteenth centuries is the most significant, for it presaged and shaped the fate of the Jews of Spain in the fourteenth and fifteenth centuries. The real sin of the Cathars was to see the Catholic priesthood as superfluous, for they believed that feeding the hungry and clothing the naked were more important than gilding statues and painting walls. Like the Kabbalists who lived among them and influenced them[16] they believed in the prime importance of direct and personal contact with and knowledge of the Almighty and, like the Kabbalists, found comfort and courage in their belief in the transmigration of souls. They believed that as all human beings, in which category they included women, Jews and Muslims, shared the same ancestors in Adam and Eve, no one could have any claim to any greater or lesser lineage. As equals in the sight of God it seemed to them that a rather beastly cabal in Rome had hijacked the original pure message of universal love and truth. But to see Jesus as a major prophet and a mortal being who, on behalf of the principle of love, had died on the cross, threatened the church to its core. Just as menacing, too, to the Church of Rome was the devout, simple and egalitarian life of the Cathar leaders; it was all far too close to the original message of Christ for their comfort.

Popes chose the names by which they wish to be known. Pope Innocent III (1160–1216) (as pope, he described himself thus: 'Less than God, but more than man') responded to the Cathars by summoning the fourth Lateran Council in 1215 CE. Described even in today's *Catholic Encyclopaedia* as 'the culminating point in the [Innocent's] glorious reign', it was the largest assembly of churchmen for 1,000 years: sixty-one archbishops, forty-two bishops, 800 abbots and priests, as well as delegates from every country in Christendom – 2,283 dignitaries in all. It was a critical moment in Christian history. The stage had actually been set in the previous century when Pope Gregory proclaimed that 'the Roman church has never erred, nor will it err in all eternity'. Up to 1215, the church had arguably used its power mainly in self-defence. But by now most of Europe had been converted to Christianity and the church moved onto the offensive. From this time forward, or so it seemed to many, Christians were licensed to oppress any and all who publicly disagreed with, or even peacefully doubted, the creed of Rome. After lengthy deliberation the Council resolved, inter alia, that the first duty of a physician was to care for the soul of his patient in priority to his body, that monks and nuns should really refrain from taking lovers, and that the Cathars were to be extirpated. Accordingly they were, with a ferocity and thoroughness that beggars description. Perhaps over one million Cathars were wiped out and their property taken, for heresy hunting was a supremely profitable business, and when packaged with the total remission of every single one of one's sins – including those yet to be committed – why, who but a heretic would not join in? The Inquisition was set up to root out anyone who by thought, word or deed faltered in following the ritual and the dogma of a church that, in many respects, had become so corrupt and degenerate that even one of its own popes in the thirteenth century, in a rare descriptive moment of truth, spoke of his own priests as 'worse than beasts wallowing in their dung'.[17]

The Lateran Council, in a measure carried into canon law, resolved that all adult Jews must wear identifying (and so separating and excluding) clothing. In 1271 this order was enforced in Castile but it was suspended two years later, the king informing the pope that as the greater part of his revenue was derived from the Jews he could not oppress them: he needed the money. In much of Europe, however, the wearing of a badge as a sort of distinguishing mark of Cain spread, and in 1371 Castile implemented the decree. In 1405, Enriquez III, yielding to the demands of the Cortes, required Jewish courtiers to wear a badge. Is it any surprise, some 200 years later, that Shakespeare has Shylock cry out: 'Sufferance is the badge of all our tribe'?[18]

And why the auto-da-fé, the burning alive of another human being? It means 'act of faith' – presumably referring more to the faith of the church than that of its victims? What was it that impelled the church to prefer that particularly vile form of death to any other? It seems that in 1252 the pope had formally approved the use of torture, but only so long as the victim did not die. As the Christian pacifist tradition did not approve of the shedding of blood, the church turned for what it called its Chastisement of Love to implements that should not normally draw blood, such as the mace, the rack, the thumbscrew, the strappado, water torture and, above all, fire. One speciality was to chain the suspect over a slow fire, baste his feet with fat and wait, while they cooked, for his confession. I would like to repeat, it was not the official policy of the Church to persecute Jews who, whether under dire threat to their lives, had converted to Christianity or not. The fact is that the Church did not physically (whatever it did psychologically, socially and commercially) torture Jews –it had no need to! For after their inquisitors had duly reached their verdict, the victim was handed over for torture to the civil authorities, where a clergyman would always be present to record the almost inevitable confession.

So it was that the Church of Rome took up the cult of death and now, with full ceremony and duly incorporated into ecclesiastic law, resurrected the ancient pagan practice of ritual human sacrifice. So it was that the message of the Abraham and Isaac story, which to many had heralded the end of the custom of abandoning unwanted children and of sacrificing human beings to the gods, was shorn of meaning. Not that there had never been instances of the Church of Rome torturing and executing Christians who expressed any doubt about the creed. One of the very earliest of such questioners included the Spanish bishop Priscillian and five of his disciples in 385.[19] But such acts appear to be isolated and sporadic rather than formal church policy at that stage. St Augustine, in his great work *The City of God*, had originally denounced the use of torture as a means of establishing guilt but later changed his mind, sanctioning its use in assessing the crime of heresy. It was in the thirteenth century that the church engendered one of its most successful – and totally false – stories. It was an accusation that took root in its traditions and flourished in its rituals, altarpieces, sculpture, paintings, art and legend, passing into the minds and folk memories of their flocks. It was this: that Jews desecrate the Eucharist and they kill little Christian boys to use their blood to bake matzah (unleavened bread). The church's accusations, evidenced often enough through torture, that Jews profaned the manifestation of Christ in the communion service, was sheer genius, for it was presented as proof positive that the sacramental elements in the bread and wine, when consecrated in the Mass, were changed into the body and blood of the risen Christ. There could be no reason, the argument went, for the Jews to desecrate the host if it had not, in fact, so metamorphosed. It was not only the Jews who fell victim to this Christian tradition; it would also be applied to non-compliant Christians. So, for example, a similar charge of murdering little boys for their blood was successfully levied against Marshal Gilles de Rais, Joan of Arc's comrade-in-arms who, accordingly, was roasted alive.

By the end of the fourteenth century the church in Spain and its Inquisition, predominant institutions in that brutal, insensitive and ignorant age, started turning upon its most poignant victims – primarily the *conversos*, ultimately the Jews.[20] But Murcia under the Enriquez was a haven. The pogrom of 1391 had very little impact on Murcia, and many Spanish and even Portuguese Jews fled there for sanctuary.[21] Once there, many who had been forcibly converted would go to the synagogue, publicly renounce their conversion and rejoin the faith of their fathers. Probably with the tacit support of the Enriquez, the Jews of Murcia would travel to other parts of Spain to help the surviving *conversos* and pay the ransom monies demanded to save the lives of their co-religionists.[22] Eventually the riots died out, but 1391 was a turning point in the history of the Jews of Spain. There was no knowing where and when they might not be attacked again. And they were.

What in the whole wide world could possibly be more pleasing than plunder masquerading as piety? For, as described earlier, not only could one liquidate one's debts by liquidating creditors but also, for one's pains, Mother Church guaranteed that all the delights of paradise awaited one in the next life. The Jews, now demonized by increasing sections of the church in its sermons, paintings, tracts and books (a good example is the Dominican Bernard Gui's (1240–1331) book, *The Inquisitor's Guide*), step by step, their position worsened. King Enrique II's (r. 1366–79) policy of protecting them from the church, the barons and the mob was maintained, albeit less powerfully, by his son Juan I (r. 1379–90)[23] and then by his grandson Enrique III (r. 1390–1406). As Graetz, the eminent historian of the period, puts it: 'Throughout the reign of Henry III [Enrique III of Castile] the life of the Jews was tolerable.'[24] In the riots of 1391, Enrique III had not only ordered that some attacks on the Jews cease, he sent detachments of his archers to make sure they did cease. But he died in 1406, and in 1408 an edict of his widow, Catherine of Lancaster, ruling in the name of the young Juan II (r. 1406–54), revived much of the old anti-Jewish legislation. Then, in 1411–12, the mass meetings of Vincent Ferrer (1350–1419), an anti-Semitic priest (later to be beatified as St Vincent), often led to more pogroms. Preaching in cemeteries, mainly as night was falling, surrounded by penitents and flagellants, his skill in inflaming a crowd was incomparable. Although seemingly to be against forced conversions, he forced Jews to attend his rallies and neither said nor did anything about the inevitable violence that followed his fiery sermons.

But in Murcia in 1411, when the Jews in the city complained that the Dominican preachers were inciting the mob to rob and kill them, the king ordered that all the Jews were to be protected and to have freedom of movement. To ensure none could claim ignorance of this order, he commanded it be posted in public places. In 1412 the Jews of Castile were widely banned from practising most artisan occupations, an act which condemned many tens of thousands of people to choose between starving or becoming New Christians. The ordinances of 1412 marked a milestone in the legislation imposed on the Jews of Castile. The disputation of Tortosa in 1413–14, a sort of show trial of Judaism, only added to their pain and danger. In 1420–21 a bull of Pope Martin V and some decrees of the now adult King Juan II relaxed some of these restrictions and penalties, and in 1443 King Juan issued an ordinance designed to protect many Jewish artisans, including the weavers[25] – but it was not to last.

The civil wars of the 1440s and 1450s marked the beginning of the end for the Jews of Spain; even the Jewish quarter in the town of Murcia was plundered. The fall of Constantinople to Islam in 1453 was claimed by churchmen to be part of the international conspiracy of the Jews and of the *conversos* to infiltrate and destroy Christianity. In 1464 the bishops were given the right to investigate the sincerity of the beliefs of all *conversos*, and we see the changing position of the Jews played out in a plot mounted by two of the king's generals. Their plan was to capture and ransom the Jews of Murcia and seize their homes and goods, such being the standard treatment meted out to enemies of the state – into which category the Jews, once valued citizens, were now consigned. The plot was foiled that time – only to become virtually state policy after 1492.[26] Throughout the Middle Ages, as bit by bit Islam retreated from Spain, its new Christian kings had followed a broadly pro-Jewish course which was both quite contrary to the practices and principles of the rest of the Christian world (of which their kingdoms were an integral part), and which was also against the increasingly powerful opinion of their own people. They had supported the Jews, but eventually ceased to do so, and consolidated their position as monarchs in an alliance with the Inquisition.

Faced with appalling injustice, racial hatred and religious persecution, how did the Jews respond? Many fled to Islamic lands. Others, equally demoralized and fearful, found the pressures of penal taxation, exclusion from public office, from commerce and agriculture, and of other innumerable civil disabilities, just too much to bear and they sought refuge in converting to the Church of Rome – seeing it as but a temporary expedient while waiting for the storm to pass over. Still others, reacting to the destruction of the lives, as they swung between hope and despair, sought and found distraction, refuge, solace, and, most importantly, purpose in the mystical world of symbol and imagination of the Kabbalah. What is sometimes thought to be the Aristotelian rationalism of Maimonides,[27] attempting to conjoin faith and reason, gave way before Kabbalah's esoteric and ancient speculations. Wearied by the waiting, exhausted by the endless delay in the coming of the Messiah, the Jews sought ways and means to reach out to the Infinite. Religious experiences were revitalized, messianic certainties were revived and symbolic charms and amulets multiplied. It is a time-honoured pattern in Jewish history that persecution results in movements into the metaphysical, whether it be the occult of the elite or the mysticism of the masses.[28]

With regard to the occult of the elite, behind the orthodoxy of ritual compliance supported by its rather specific rewards, there has always been a hunger for more profound spiritual experiences and understandings. These ancient mysteries are an undeniable part of Judaism and deeply rooted in it. And as for the mysticism of the masses, there has ever been tension between the morality and the monotheism of the rabbis on the one hand, and the folklore and the popular piety of the people on the other. Despite being officially denigrated or denied, charms and amulets, with their profoundly meaningful symbols, have in fact been cherished, certainly since the destruction of the First Temple in the sixth century BCE. From the Middle Ages onward, Practical or Magical Kabbalah emerged, its primary concern the winning of energies from the spiritual world for religious purposes. We see the same phenomenon in Christianity, in the tension between the refined thought and practices of the upper classes and the homespun traditions and lore of ordinary folk. These are dynamic processes, and in Judaism, when a particular custom had grown into a sufficiently widely held tradition, the rabbis, no longer ignoring or fighting it, would adapt and incorporate it into their tradition.[29] The relationship and division between magic and religion, between superstition and Judaism, is (thankfully) beyond the scope of this work. But the superstitions and the magical practices of the medieval Jews were significantly different from those of the host culture, for although the symbols and the purposes might be similar, Jewish magic was expressed in and confined to the Ur-text and culture of Judaism.

Knowing themselves to be at the mercy of events and knowing those events to hold but little mercy, many Jews turned in on themselves to the mystical theosophical system of Kabbalah, which many believed to be the key to the doorway of cosmic spirituality and immortality. Kabbalah became the epicentre of their lives. Earlier, under Islam, many had become sophisticated philosophers, politicians, men of science and of letters, profound and refined poets. But from the thirteenth century onwards the Bible, the Talmud and Kabbalah increasingly became the decisive force in their lives, spreading not only among the elite but also among the artisans and small traders, transmuting the base metal of their daily lives into the pure gold of mystic ecstasy. No longer thrusting after intellectual achievement or social and economic advancement, their dedication was now directed to the highest realms of spiritual insight, taking heart in the belief that every detail in our human world has a parallel on a spiritual plane. Today, as in fifteenth-century Spain, the symbols and formulations of Kabbalah may be seen as expressing a spiritual unity beyond the natural diversity of life. But then it was also their theurgic qualities, their power to influence the world and to control evil forces, that gave added comfort and hope to the Kabbalists. For now many Jews awaited and anticipated the Apocalypse. The End of Time was near, and the greater were their sorrows, the more fervent was their expectation of the imminent coming of the Messiah.

What had happened was that many earlier philosophical and mystical trends, particularly Gnostic and Neoplatonic, had coalesced in southern

France around Rabbi Abraham ben David of Posquières (d. 1198) and his son, Isaac the Blind (c.1160–1235). Numerological, alchemical and grammatological speculations multiplied. Then the church and its crusaders, in the course of extirpating the Cathars, turned on the Jews, and in 1242 the books of the Talmud were solemnly tried, found guilty and condemned to death by burning.[30] Many of Isaac's disciples fled to Gerona in Spain to set up schools and continue to teach their esoteric theosophy.[31] Moving radically from the position of defining God only in negatives, they reasserted the presence of the biblical God about whom assertions may be made, attributions ascribed and whose emanations reveal the Divine Unity. Attacking the limitations of reason, they sought through profound contemplation and devotion to communicate with the world of Divine Attributes. Nahmanides (1194–1270), the towering biblical and Talmudic scholar and supporter of Kabbalist thought, established a famous religious academy in Barcelona and his authority helped Kabbalah gain wide acceptance.

Kabbalah continued to spread, acquiring more structure and permanence through numerous books, of which Moses ben Shemtov de Leon's (1250–1305), the Zohar, was the most sacred, the most influential. It is an extraordinary book, of profound beauty and art, a powerful compendium of Jewish metaphysical writing and oral traditions over the ages dealing with esoteric doctrines about God, Creation, the soul and evil; it is still being studied today. De Leon, in keeping with prophetic tradition, presents the book as a lost and now rediscovered text, composed a millennium earlier by Rabbi Shimon bar Yonai while he was hiding in a cave from the Romans for thirteen years. Scholars track many influences, including the Gnostics, the German Hasids, the Cathars of Languedoc, the Sufis of Islam and the medieval interest in astronomy, astrology and Neoplatonic philosophy. Be that as it may, many schools of mystical thought developed in Spain at that time, all striving for beatitude in intimate union between the soul and its Divine source.

For 175 years, from 1325 to 1500, Jativa, a town in Valencia province, was the nearest and most important of the Kabbalah centres to Murcia. Whilst its greatest influence was within the elite religious academies, it is possible that some aspects of Kabbalah were also spread among ordinary folk by itinerant craftsmen such as weavers, who, moving from community to community and setting up their workshops, would be welcomed for their news and new ideas. So successful had been the activities of itinerant Cathar weavers in spreading their message that the Cathars had originally been called *Tisserands*, or weavers.

This flight into mysticism enabled many of the Jews of Spain to make sense of their inner selves, living more now in a remembered and nourishing past and in an anticipated glorious future than in the existential present. But in their outer lives considerable numbers could not withstand the humiliation and the persecution, least of all the wealthy grandees, most of whom converted. Take the case of one Solomon Halevi, rabbi of Burgos and scion of a distinguished family of Talmudists. In 1390, in a smart career move, he and his family converted to Christianity. As we see from his name he was a Levite, as was the Virgin Mary, and so he changed his name to Pablo de Santa Maria. Having deserted his flock and his synagogue for the church, so convincing was he in his newfound faith that having been appointed bishop of Burgos, with his special knowledge, he led the pack in ruthlessness in rooting out other *conversos*.[32] In Castile alone there were at one time at least four bishops who were *conversos*.[33]

Some conversions would have been sincere, but given the increasingly dire consequences of not converting, they would have been in the minority, for it is blindingly self-evident that conversion by force can never be sincere. The majority of those *conversos* became Christian in form but remained, for at least for a generation or two, Jewish in substance.

Some had foreseen the future. Rabbi Yehuda ibn Verga had warned the *conversos* that they were like three pairs of turtle doves (ancient symbols of the Jewish people – see Chapter 15). The first would stay in Spain and be fully plucked – that is, they would lose their property and be slaughtered or burned; the second pair of doves would also be plucked, and would lose their properties, but by fleeing would save their lives. The third pair, being the first to flee, would save both their bodies and their possessions.[34]

Numbers help give context and perspective. By the 1420s, the number of *conversos* approached perhaps one third of the entire Jewish population.[35] Whilst the Inquisition in Spain sought out all Christians who did not conform to their particular ritual and dogma, their major target was the *conversos*. So, for example, of all those tried by the Inquisition in Barcelona between 1488 and 1505, 99.3 per cent were *conversos*, and in Valencia between 1484 and 1503 the equivalent number was 91.6 per cent.

Let us for a moment look to 1492, when Columbus sets sail on his historic voyage.[36] Even the start of his journey from Genoa had meaning, for in setting out he had straight away to alter course because the sea ahead of him was crowded with Turkish ships bringing Jewish refugees to safety.

Typically, the *conversos* in his crew include his ships' doctors, his apothecary and Luis de Torres – his interpreter from Murcia, who only just managed to get himself baptized either the morning of or the day before the fleet set sail.[37] Church and king would soon be busy sending their men to Africa, Asia and the Americas. European civilization would go with them, along with all that it meant in terms of power, exploitation, wealth and misery to other peoples. On 31 March of that year the effect of the Edict of Expulsion was that the Jews (who had lived in Spain longer than they had lived in any other country, including even the land of Israel) must either convert to Catholicism or they must leave the Kingdom of Castile and Aragon – never to return.

The estimates of the numbers of Jews who abandoned their homes and their livelihoods rather than their faith vary enormously. First the upper estimates: writing 100 years later, the Jesuit Juan de Mariana stated that 'the number of Jews who left Castile and Aragon is unknown; most authors say they were up to 170,000 families, certainly a great number'.[38] Other estimates are far lower, and I look more closely as these numbers in Chapter 9. Those who stayed – and they were the majority – converted nominally to Christianity. All that the church and state had done (apart, that is, from destroying hundreds of thousands of lives and in effect expropriating much of their wealth) was to exchange a large number of non-believers outside the church for a lesser number of non-believers inside it. But conversion for most *conversos* was no salvation and many lived, or died, according to Rabbi Isaac ben Moses Arama's (c.1420–94) contemporary description: 'And now, in our times, in all the kingdoms of Spain and in the islands of the oceans, one third burned by fire, a third fleeing hither to hide and those who remain living in deadly fear and timidity out of fear for their lives and at the sights their eyes behold.'[39]

For most, but by no means all, over the succeeding generations the practice and the memory of their Jewish heritage faded away. I think the New Christians ranged in their beliefs from that of authentic Christianity through to crypto-Judaism, with perhaps most in the middle between those extremes, content to live as Christians, desiring to be accepted as Christians but maintaining certain patterns of living and of attitude which they had learned from their parents and grandparents – but which did not of itself entail an inner visceral identification with Judaism. Most became devout Catholics, but still suspect, still segregated, and categorized in law as a separate sub-species called *conversos*. But to the informers for the Spanish Inquisition and to the mob, they were better known as Marranos – Spanish for 'swine'.

Many fled to those parts of Italy where secretly they continued to live Jewish lives. Some joined old established communities in the Brescia region (where, by the fifteenth century, hidden Stars of David are to be found).[40] Others fled to the city of Ferrara, which by the 1550s housed no less than ten synagogues where a *converso* could, without any penalty, cast off his cloak of Christianity and, ceasing to have to pretend to be what he was not, reaffirm his Judaism. Others fled to the welcoming Ottoman Empire. A third group went off to the New World to escape the horrors of the Old, where, located in remote areas far away from the Inquisition, they might continue privately to live as Jews. A few even got to England and lived fairly openly in London as Jews – with the passive consent of Henry VII and to the dissatisfaction of Ferdinand and Isabella. Many *conversos* also stayed in Spain, often rising to prominent positions in society, conforming outwardly to its demands and rituals whilst over many generations and at great risk maintaining secretly their private lives as Jews. Finally, some, having left Spain, returned with assumed Old Christian identities to conceal their *converso* heritage.

The affidavits of the *converso* victims and of their informers, meticulously recorded in the archives of the Spanish Inquisition, tell us of the confusion and the pain of the *conversos*. I have not tracked down the detailed Inquisition records for the district of Hellin, where the Vizcaya carpet was woven, but the following are typical examples from other areas:

1. Diego de la Pena, an inhabitant of Guadalajara used to say that 'It grieved him that he had turned Christian.'[41]
2. Pedro Garcia, an inhabitant of Soria, said in the presence of witnesses: 'I tell you, I am more deceived in this religion than I was before.'[42]
3. Gregorio Lainez, a resident of Almazan, 'Confessed and asked himself how was it possible to know, or who could know, which law was better, ours or that of the Moors or Jews'.[43]
4. Sometimes the informers were Jews or *conversos*. A Jew, Jaco Donates, testified his neighbour Ruy Garcia de Lucio would go 'to the cemetery of the Jews to pray over the grave of his mother'.[44]

Such were their crimes.

In the first fifty years after 1492, some 20,226 people, mainly *conversos*, were put to death by being burnt alive – many of them in all probability protesting to the end that they were faithful Christians. One of the church's terms for that process was 'being relaxed'. Extraordinary, really – the church, having forced them to convert under the threat of expulsion or death, then burnt them alive for insincerity.

To put the plight of the Jews and *conversos* into the context of the times, early in the sixteenth century, in an attempt to arrest the spread of Protestantism in the Spanish Netherlands, the Inquisition there would burn unrepentant heretics alive. Men who had repented were given an easier death being put to the sword, but women who repented were still roasted alive! In that time, between 50,000 and 100,000 human beings were burned, beheaded, strangled or burnt alive.[45] In Spain the last such fire was lit by the Inquisition as late as 1826, when a Quaker and a Jew were solemnly and ceremoniously burnt alive while their executioners sang their hymns to the glory of their God.

A painting by Pedro Berruguete, circa 1495 (Figure 24), puts us in the picture. At the top there is St Dominic, founder of the Dominican order which was dedicated to extirpating heresy. At the bottom we see two heretics wearing tall cone-shaped hats and monks' habits; to the left of the middle are two heretics who will shortly die. From the end of the fifteenth century right up to the early nineteenth century the Inquisition was probably the most dominant force in Spain.

The auto-da-fé was a dramatic and highly satisfying entertainment for kings, nobles, clergy and the people. Usually staged on Sundays or on Saints' feast days to ensure maximum audiences, grand processions, and sermons and masses would support that vital central experience of seeing the victims writhing in agony, of hearing their desperate cries and of smelling their burning flesh. As an expression of the power of the church's Inquisition and of the king it was unsurpassed.

It is extraordinary, really, that despite so much inhuman pressure over so many generations, so many *conversos* survived with elements of their faith intact. Those historians who have earlier presented us with very low estimates of the Jewish population of Spain and of the number who converted to Christianity would not have had the benefit of the recent findings published in the December 2008 *American Journal of Human Genetics*.[46] There, an analysis of the binary and Y-STR heliotypes indicates that no less than 19.8 per cent of the present population of the Iberian Peninsula have Jewish ancestry. This fascinating figure points towards the huge numbers of Spanish Jews who converted to Christianity in the Middle Ages. Indeed, we know of isolated and reserved families in Spain and Portugal, and in the United States in New

Mexico and Texas, in the late twentieth century still following in varying degrees the faith and the ritual of their forefathers. In 1992 in Belmonte in northern Portugal, a Marrano community of some 200 people openly returned to Judaism. For 500 years they had secretly retained vestiges of Jewish ritual and in their isolation developed new rituals, including going to the river every Passover to smite the waters with branches to evoke the parting of the Red Sea. In Mexico today there are no fewer than five *converso* congregations which, after 500 years, have finally come in from the cold.

In closing this chapter I asked myself how it was, given the various pressures put upon the Jews in the 600 years prior to the expulsion of 1492, that they had been able to make such a huge contribution to the culture and the economy of Spain. What seems to have happened is that the Reformation and the rise of capitalism gave widespread respectability to the concepts of conscience and work – both values of great importance in Jewish culture. Until then, most feudal societies were divided into three exclusive classes whose ideas and functions were cast in stone. The first grouping was the warrior class, the nobility, whose duties were to defend their territory and to keep order vis-à-vis the peasant underclass. These warriors were described in a private paper written by Fernando de la Torre to the king in 1455 as 'proud and slothful and not so ingenious or industrious'.[47] Next came the priestly caste, who sought political power, the better to promote their exclusive truth, and in the process often acquiring great wealth – and the corruption that so often comes with wealth and power. The third class were the peasants and slaves whose job it was to serve both the nobility and the priestly caste, to produce the food and to do the dirty work. Slipping easily into this inflexible feudal matrix of princes, priests and peasants were the Jews, forming a sort of fourth estate providing the core of the mercantile, professional, administrative and artisan class whose goods and services were, for a time, needed by the nobles. Jewish society was the counterpoint to Christian feudal society for, without a homeland, there had been no intrinsic need, and therefore no major cultural expectations or patterns, for either a military or a peasant class. And perhaps, too, the loss of a homeland, changing Judaism from a religion based on Temple ritual to one more centred on intellectual activity, impacted on the cogitative style and capability of the culture. Abraham ibn Ezra, the twelfth-century Sephardi poet, sees in their songs and poetry something of the different preoccupations of the Jews and of their various host cultures:

> The Arabs write of love in boasts
> And the Romans of vengeance and battles
> The Greeks of wisdom and cunning
> And the Persians of fables and riddles;
> But Israel sings – in psalms and hymns –
> Of God, the Lord of hosts. [48]

Perhaps it was Erasmus (1466–1536), one of the greatest scholars of the Renaissance, who best summed up the differences between the worldview of the Jews and of the Christians of Spain: 'And much more pleasantly the Jews expect to this day the coming of the Messiah, and so obstinately contend for their Law of Moses. The Spaniards give place to none in the reputation of soldiery.'[49]

The mindsets were different. Islam (the word literally means 'submission') and medieval Christianity suppressed most independent thought, but Judaism (the word 'Israel' means 'contender with God') and dialectics are inseparable. Right from the start, in biblical times when the great prophets would argue with God Himself, to the Babylonian and Talmudic eras and onwards, the culture of discussion and argument engendered and nourished imaginative and intellectual activity. The mindsets were different, for the singularity of the God of the First Commandment and the iconoclasm of the Second Commandment aided abstract thought, so helping the Jews adapt to a hostile world by means of abstraction, concepts, symbols and invention. The Jews, being literate and multilingual, were more able than their usually illiterate and monolingual fellow citizens both to gain and to retain knowledge and experience. Independent thinking (within limits) was encouraged, for there can be no intermediary between man and God. A rabbi is not a priest but a teacher. This (substantial) freedom from a collective control of one's thoughts could not but develop doubts, heresies, originality and individuality, and perhaps this is what some in the church most feared. It is this spirit of critical thought, found in Jewish culture and rediscovered in classical Greek culture that, sparking off the Renaissance, sounded the death knell of feudalism. And perhaps, too, sometimes the exigencies and the realities of life in a hostile environment may tend to shape one's sensibility and to sharpen one's wits.

So it was that the Jews had a place and a purpose in Spanish society – until the increasing demands by the church for exclusivity in religious affairs and by the emerging middle classes for exclusivity in mercantile, professional, administrative and artisan affairs led to the oppression, exclusion and finally expulsion of arguably the oldest and most religiously stalwart section of the population of Spain – the Jews.

The next chapter builds on the elements discussed in this chapter – namely, what was actually happening to the Jews and *conversos* in the period the Vizcaya carpet was woven – to consider the questions of where, and by whom, was it woven?

NOTES

1. 'Black Death', in *Encyclopedia Judaica* (Jerusalem: Keter Publishing, 1971), Vol. 4, pp.1063–4.
2. See Benzion Netanyahu, *The Origins of the Inquisition in Fifteenth Century Spain* (New York: Random House, 1995), p.985: 'The view of the Jew as described and disseminated by the Christian theologians of that time was of a creature whose mission in life was to serve the Devil and do his heinous work. In the last four centuries of the medieval era the outlines of this image were sharpened and deepened, while the crimes imputed to the Jews were multiplied and became steadily more appalling. They now included such ghastly atrocities as the murder of Christian children for religious rites, the torture of Hosts by piercing or boiling them, and the use of sorcery to inflict cruel death upon multitudes of Christians. To be sure, in a sense these crimes were "human" (for murder was after all a human crime), but essentially they were inhuman and demoniac, since they were committed at the Devil's behest and frequently by means of magic. They were also inhuman because the Jew performed them without seeking to derive from them any benefit for himself. His sole interest in perpetrating these crimes was to vent the Devil's wrath, which filled his soul, on Christ and His believers.'
3. Yehuda ben David, 'The Golden Age, Expulsion and Inquisition', in *The Sephardic Journey 1492–1992*, exhibition catalogue (New York: Yeshiva University Museum, 1992), p.191.
4. Renée Levine Melammed, *Heretics or Daughters of Israel* (Oxford: Oxford University Press, 1999), p.3.
5. Joshua Trachtenberg, *Jewish Magic and Superstition* (Philadelphia, PA: University of Pennsylvania Press, 2004), pp.159–69. The Christian view of sin, although compassionate, was basically militant. Sin must be eradicated. The Jewish view, seeing sin as exile from God, was to call for its redemption, not destruction. As to the extent of the sufferings inflicted by the Catholic Church on the Jews and *conversos*, the evaluation of most historians are metaphoric. Some seem to maximize, others to minimize the numbers effected. At the extremes some authorities seem almost voyeuristic in their endlessly agonizing, detailed descriptions of the ingenuity and the efficacy of the tools of torture. And others seem to suggest that the Jews and *conversos* really should not take their persecution too personally – after all, were not these cruel times for everybody? In any case, were not the acts of the church justified for, in its own terms, its intent was wholly good? In the scale of priorities, why did the heretics not understand that nothing could be more important than the salvation of their souls?

6. Trachtenberg, *Jewish Magic and Superstition*, p.164.
7. Wisdom of Solomon 3:1–3.
8. Moses Maimonides, 'Epistle on Martyrdom', in Abraham Halkin and David Hartman (eds), *Crisis and Leadership: Epistles of Maimonides* (Philadelphia, PA: Jewish Publication Society, 1985), pp.31–3. Judaism broadly holds that to save life every commandment may be broken, apart from the prohibition against murder, idolatry and adultery.
9. John Barclay, *Jews in the Mediterranean Diaspora* (London: University of California Press, 1996), p.460.
10. Edgar Samuel, *At the End of the Earth* (London: Jewish Historical Society of England, 2004), p.45, citing *Minor Tractates, Tractate Seferim* 317, Ch.XXI, Rule 1.
11. Jane Gerber, *The Jews of Spain* (London: Free Press, 1994), p.113.
12. Ibid., p.117.
13. N. Roth, *Conversos, Inquisition and the Expulsion of the Jews from Spain* (Madison, WI: University of Wisconsin Press, 2002), p.85.
14. Machiavelli, *Discourses on the First Ten Books of Titus Livius*, 1.12, cited in A. Castro, *El Real Monasterio de Santa Clara de Palencia y los Enriquez, Almirantes de Castilla* (Valladolid: Sever-Cuesta, 1982), p.12.
15. So many of these breakaway movements, both those that survived only as footnotes in our history books or as Protestantism that thrived, would seek and find authority for their disagreement with the church in the Jewish origins of Christianity. But always at a price, for there was continual purges against nonconformity from which few were exempt. Even the great English hero king Henry V had been cautioned on his coronation in 1413 that he had better toe the party line – or else:

> What mighten folk of good byleeve seye,
> if bent were our kynges affection
> to the wrong part, who sholde hem help purveye?
> A Kynge set in that wrong opinion
> mighte of our faith be the subversioun.

R.H. Robbins (ed.), *Historical Poems of the XIV and XV Centuries* (New York, 1959), pp.107–8, cited in Margaret Aston, *Faith and Fire* (London: Hambledon Press, 1993), p.79.
16. St Martin of Leon (c.1125–1202) had no doubt that the Jews had influenced the Cathars: see *Remembering Sepharad* (Madrid: State Corporation for Spanish Cultural Action Abroad, 2003), p.144. And I don't either, for it was a classic pattern for Christians in seeking to reform their church to look again to its Jewish roots. However, the Cathar belief in dualism, and so its insistence on the enormous powers of the devil, was incomprehensible to the Jews. They had been living in Languedoc since at least the fifth century. In one account, Charlemagne's close companion William, Count of Toulouse, Barcelona and Narbonne and a Jew (thought to be a descendant of King David), was virtually in control of his own princedom, a sort of buffer state between Christian Europe and Muslim Spain.
17. M. Baigent and R. Leigh, *The Inquisition* (London: Penguin Books, 2000), p.8, citing H.C. Lea, *A History of the Inquisition of the Middle Ages* (London: 1888), Vol. 1, p.53.
    Little wonder that the Cathars, the many other proto-Protestant movements and the Jews, with their focus on conscience, morality and industry, were suppressed. Ex-pirate Balt-

hazar Cossa (1362–1415) must have been a most puissant man, for he celebrated becoming Pope John XXII with, inter alia, 200 maids, matrons and widows, and quite a few nuns, all falling victim to his lust. Georgina Masson, *Courtesans of the Italian Renaissance* (London: St Martin's Press, 1975). John was later deposed on a number of charges including murder, rape, sodomy and incest. Gibbon, however, goes on to warn us that the more scandalous charges were suppressed!

18. William Shakespeare, *The Merchant of Venice*, Act 1, Scene III, in *The Works of Shakespeare*, The Nonesuch Press (New York: Random House, 1929), p.90. It has been suggested that in the early Middle Ages, as most groups (guilds, religious and social) distinguished themselves by their public dress, the Jewish badge was not essentially anti-Jewish. If indeed this was the case, it was no longer so after the Lateran Council of 1215 where the intention to segregate and to humiliate could not have been clearer.

19. Baigent and Leigh, Inquisition, p.26.

20. H.C. Lea, *A History of the Inquisition of Spain*, Vol. 1 (New York: Macmillan, 1906), pp.68–120; and Baigent and Leigh, Inquisition, pp.xv, 5, 8, 79.

21. Roth, *Conversos, Inquisition and the Expulsion of the Jews from Spain*, p.85.

22. It is the duty of a Jew to ransom any fellow Jews who have been enslaved or unjustly imprisoned. There is a hierarchy of practices. Women come first; then one may ransom oneself before a father or teacher if only to then ransom the teacher and then one's father; thirdly a scholar; next the court can force a husband to ransom his wife; and money set aside to build a synagogue or for other charities may be used to ransom captives. Finally anyone who delays ransoming a captive is regarded as if he has spilled the captive's blood. Dan Cohn-Sherbok, *The Blackwell Dictionary of Judaica* (Oxford: Blackwell, 1992), p.447. Yet there were limits, for the Talmud (Gittin 45) laid down that not too high a ransom should be paid lest it encourage an increase in the enslavement of Jews.

23. S. Dubnov, *History of the Jews* (New Brunswick, NJ: Thomas Yosseloff, 1967), Vol. 3, p.222.

24. H. Graetz, *History of the Jews, 1884–1945* (Jerusalem: Jewish Publication Society, 1956), Vol. 4, p.193.

25. M. Wischnitzer, *A History of Jewish Crafts and Guilds* (New York: Jonathan David, 1965), p.118.

26. J. Torres Fontes, *Los Judios Murcianos en el Reinado de Juan II* (Murcia: Academia Alfonso X El Sabio, Sucesores de Nogues, 1965), p.14.

27. Reconciling faith and reason is none too easy a task. Aristotle's view of God was mechanistic rather than moral, leaving little room for Jewish concepts such as Reward and Punishment, Justice and Mercy. It is too simple to say that Maimonides sought to reconcile the monotheistic revealed religion of Judaism with the intellectually formulated philosophies of the Greeks. He neither agreed with Aristotle's physics and metaphysics nor with their conjoining with Neoplatonic metaphysics and astronomy. Maimonides believed it was rational intuition and not rationalistic categories that lead towards knowledge of the Almighty. However his moral empiricism – his counsel that, seeing the world as being equally balanced between good and evil, one man's good deed will tip everything to the side of good (Mishnah Torah, Laws of Repentance 7:5) – increasingly may have seemed less relevant to the Jews of Spain.

28. Whether as occult of the elite or mysticism of the masses, movement into the metaphysical

with its spiritual renewal in reaction to persecution is a familiar pattern. Whilst there are vital forces other than persecution that give rise to such movements, this pattern may be tracked through Jewish history. It starts in the eighth century BCE in Isaiah's response to the advancing Assyrian hordes and continues on to the sixth century BCE where the Book of Daniel describes new forms of spiritual life emerging as a reaction to the cruelty of Israel's alien dictators. The pattern repeats itself in the second century BCE as groups of great piety and fervour emerged in response to the religious persecution of Antiochus Epiphanes. Yet again, in the first century CE, Josephus points to the eschatology and secret lore of the Essenes as step by step the Romans laid waste to ancient Israel.

No sooner had Christianity become the state religion of Roman Byzantium than it turned on its non-believers, its pagans, its non-conformists and its Jews. We learn too, from many accounts at that time, of persecutions and martyrdom of Jews under the Sasanids in Babylon. The classic reaction was to revive ancient mystical rhythms, and the Hasidism, an esoteric movement that took numbers and letters as the basic building blocks of the cosmos, flourished among the elite. For the ordinary Jews the folk stories and legends of the Aggadah gave authority to this non-legalistic side of Judaism.

In the eleventh century the knights of the First Crusade, en route to rescue Jerusalem from Islam, diverted to plunder and destroy the ancient Jewish communities of Germany. Hasidism flourished again with many of those who managed to escape joining up with the Kabbalists in France. Then, as the church in France turned on the Jews, they fled down to Spain. There the persecutions, culminating in the disaster of the Expulsion in 1492, fed into the apocalyptic elements in Judaism. The rationalist optimism of Maimonides had failed. Seemingly forsaken by God, their desperation was defeated by exulted belief; now it was the hope of messianic deliverance that held sway. Indeed, the greater their suffering, the greater was their piety and their prayers, and the earlier it seemed to them would be their deliverance.

Movements into mysticism as a reaction to oppression continued long after the Vizcaya carpet was woven. In 1648 the Thirty Years War ended, having destroyed much of the food-base of Poland and the Ukraine, and the peasants and the Cossacks rose and murdered perhaps as many as 100,000 Jews. The Swedish wars of the 1650s were catastrophic, leaving those Jewish communities that had survived totally overwhelmed and unable to cope with tens of thousands of refugees seeking their help. The greater that affliction, the more desperately was deliverance awaited. By the 1660s the Jewish world was in ferment. The Messiah had arrived! His name was Sabbatai Zvi. But rather than be martyred by the Ottoman Sultan he converted to Islam and he and his movement faded away.

In reconstructing the past in terms of the rational we distance ourselves from understanding the extremes of despair and of joy that surely has characterized so much of Jewish history.

29. Such traditions include the bar mitzvah, the wearing of a hat, the breaking of a glass to celebrate a wedding, the great prayer of the mourner of the Kaddish – all evolved in the Middle Ages. The lines between true piety, tradition and superstition sometimes seem metamorphic ...
30. Baigent and Leigh, Inquisition p.208; Encyclopaedia Judaica, vol. 15, p.769.
31. The fundamental difference between Kabbalistic and Orthodox Judaism is that the

1391–1492: Action and Reaction   127

former hold God to be everything and the latter hold God and man to exist separately in different realms. Some modern philosophers propose that the space between God and mankind is too vast to place Him into human history at all. For me, one of the most startling of the Kabbalist concepts is that it was not God who expelled man out of the Garden of Eden but man who expelled God. The boundaries of intellectual and spiritual experiences are far from finite. Incidentally it might be noted that Ibn al-'Arabi, perhaps the most influential of the Sufi thinkers, was born in Murcia in 1165.

32. There has even been a line of conversos and of their descendants whose hatred of the faith of their fathers is pathological. In the nineteenth century Karl Marx is a prime example, as in our century is Mahmoud Ahmadinejad, currently president of Iran (Daily Telegraph, 3 October 2009, p.3).
33. Baigent and Leigh, Inquisition, pp.75–6.
34. Haim Beinart, Conversos on Trial: The Inquisition in Cuidad Real (Jerusalem: Magnes Press, 1981), p.3, n.4. Also cited in Paul Johnson, A History of the Jews (London: Weidenfeld & Nicolson, 1987), p.224.
35. Howard Sacher, Farewell España, The World of the Sephardim Remembered (New York: Random House, 1995), p.59.
36. It is interesting to compare the evidence of the converso status of the Enriquez with that of the great Spanish and American hero Christopher Columbus, for a case has also been made that Columbus was a converso.

What are the facts? Columbus would never speak openly but always most cryptically about his own background and yet boasted of a connection to King David. Whilst ever making a great show of Christian piety he spent much of his time in the company of Jews and conversos. He showed a strong interest in Jewish matters and his letters are filled with references to the Hebrew Bible – these were not the characteristics of an Old Christian. Most of his nautical tables and navigational aids were perfected by Jews, and his key colleagues (his ships' doctors, Marco and Bernil, and the apothecary and the interpreter), were all conversos (see note 34), as were the people who financed his first great voyage – nor was there a priest on that voyage. And of course the church's sure and certain knowledge that the world was flat contrasted to the Jews' ancient belief that the world was round, a belief restated by Moses de Leon in the Zohar in thirteenth-century Spain. Born in Genoa, where many Jews had fled after the pogroms of 1391, yet speaking no Italian, and speaking and writing only poor Latin but fluent in Castilian, and having the name of Colon (his father might have been related to the Colons of Pontevedra, a well-known Jewish clan) – these all pointed to Columbus's parents being Jewish refugees from Spain. The name Colon means 'dove' in Spanish and is thought by some to be a transformation of the word Cohen; his mother's name, Suzanne, was a common name among the Jews of Spain. There were too a number of Jews in Genoa known as Columbo. I should add that, typical of such refugees, both his grandfather, father and his father-in-law were weavers!

His mysterious signature is capable of the Hebraic interpretation of 'In God's name' which was a cipher used by religious Jews to preface a document; his account of his voyage begins with a reference to the expulsion of the Jews from Spain. He would sometimes date his correspondence not from the birth of Christ but according to the then Jewish tradition, as from the date of the destruction of the second Temple. He refers to the second Temple by the Hebraic term 'Second House': see *Encyclopaedia Judaica* (Jerusalem: Keter Publishing, 1971), Vol. 5, pp.756–7, and N.A. Bell in *Medieval History*, 5 (2004), p.48. We can only conjecture as to why his heirs destroyed so many of his private papers, but if they had contained any evidence of any doubts their father might have had about the beliefs or the practices of the church, their own position and their inheritances would have been endangered. Yet other branches of his family, who controlled Jamaica prior to its conquest by Britain in 1655, provided there a haven for Jews. It was virtually the only place in the Spanish Empire where the Inquisition had no power. Columbus was a typical tyrant of the time, versed in the use of summary judgements and torture, and never more so than against any who enquired into his family background (Consuela Varela, 'La Caida de Cristobal Colon', *El Pais*, July 2006).

A good case, but perhaps lacking the conclusive elements applicable to the Enriquez, firstly in their marriages and alliances over three generations exclusively with *conversos*, and secondly in dona Juana Enriquez's outright rejection of Christian burial norms; she essentially ended up requiring and complying with Jewish burial norms. But perhaps Columbus's bequest in his will to a Portuguese Jew parallels the Enriquez' wills, for after the stresses of a lifetime of concealment such death bed statements of identity were often made by *Conversos*. Cecil Roth, *The Spanish Inquisition* (London: W.W. Norton, 1996), p.208. See also Gerber, *Jews of Spain*, pp.xvi–xx.

37. *The Journal of Christopher Columbus*, edited by L.A. Vigneras, trans. C. Jane (New York, 1960), pp.51, 206, cited in Tudor Parfitt's most readable book *The Lost Tribes of Israel* (New York: Orion Books, 2002), p.29. Luis de Torres's knowledge of Hebrew and Arabic would have been of little use among the natives of the Caribbean and America. He was, however, the first European to discover their use of tobacco.
38. Juan de Mariana, *Historia General de España*, Biblioteca de Autores Espanoles (Madrid: Adres Ramirez, 1780), Book 26, Chapter 1; Henry Kamen, *The Spanish Inquisition* (London: Phoenix, 2003), p.23.
39. Beinart, *Conversos on Trial*, p.3, n.4.
40. Francis Bontempi, *Il Ferro e la Stella* (Brescia: Circolo Cultural S. Alessandro, 1994), pp.159–60, 254–6, and personal communication. We also see the Star of David in the fifteenth-century coat of arms of the de Norsas, a well-known Jewish family living in Ferrana, Italy. I need not add meaningless decorative devices are not usually displayed in coats of arms.
41. Archives of the Diocese of Cuenca, Inquisition Section, cited in Alisa Meyuhas Ginio (ed.), *Jews, Christians and Muslims in the Mediterranean World after 1492* (London: Frank Cass, 1992), pp.29–33.
42. Ibid., Section 749/15.
43. Ibid. Section 749/14.
44. Ibid., Section 748/2.
45. John Motley, *The Rise of the Dutch Republic* (New York: Harper Bros, 1900), p.85.
46. *American Journal of Human Genetics*, 83 (12 December 2008), pp.725–35.
47. Americo Castro, *The Structure of Spanish History*, trans. Edmund King (Princeton, NJ: Princeton University Press, 1954), pp.16–17.
48. P. Cole, *The Dream of the Poem* (Princeton, NJ: Princeton University Press, 2007), p.176.
49. Desiderius Erasmus, *In Praise of Folly* (New York: Dover Thrift, 2003), p.35.

Where, and by whom, was the Vizcaya Carpet Woven?

The questions were simple: how to answer them was complex. It seemed to me that the solution lay in tackling the problem as one would a jigsaw puzzle, for by bringing together fragments of information, small connections might be made which, bit by bit, would fit together to shape a complete picture. Numerous snippets gleaned from the Inquisition, the census and tax records, from the royal ordinances, the inventories of noble families, Muslim writings and from rabbinic *responsa* have all contributed to an integrated depiction of what probably happened. Earlier studies on the Admiral carpets had suggested that the weavers were Mudejars – subject Muslims. It became clear that this was quite unlikely. In any case the term is perhaps better understood to describe an artistic and architectural style that developed under Muslim hegemony and was taken over under Christian rule.[1]

I started by looking at populations. In the 500 years of Islamic rule in Spain there had been few moves either to expel Christians and Jews or to settle Spain with a Muslim population. The major exception to this was during the rule of the fanatical Almoravids (1055–1149), who drove many Jews from the Muslim-held parts of Spain up to Castile, where they were welcomed by Alfonso VI. As the authority Oleg Grabar, discussing the effect of the Islamic conquest, noted: 'Spain in general and even Andalusia remained largely populated by Christians and by an active Jewish minority in the cities.'[2] One hundred years later it was the turn of the conquering Christian kings to get rid of the Muslims. So, for example, in Valencia in 1238 and in Seville in 1248, the entire Muslim population was expelled. Mosques were converted mainly into churches, occasionally into synagogues. The fourteenth century saw the population decimated by the classic horrors of the Middle Ages – inflation, plague, war and famine. We neither know how many died in the Black Death of 1348–50[3] nor how many died in the wars as the Christian knights, step by step, conquered Spain and Portugal. Ethnic cleansing of the Muslims was not part of their policy but pillage and slaughter was the price demanded by their dangerously independent mercenary troops and ravaging camp followers. In face of these advancing barbarians the Muslims fled south, finding a safe haven in the remaining Muslim-held parts of Spain. Generally it was the really unskilled, who could not afford to leave, who were the ones who stayed. And many who stayed, now prizes in the rewards of war, were sold by the victors into slavery. Those with highly valued skills such as weaving moved to Granada,[4] giving rise there to quite an arts, crafts and commercial renaissance. As silk manufacture in the Christian-held part of Spain declined, the silk industry of Granada boomed,[5] a pattern that would have been familiar throughout the allied carpet weaving industry.

The Kingdom of Castile, which by the end of the thirteenth century included Murcia, had never had a large Muslim population at all and by 1492 Muslims represented around half of one per cent of its total population. As the Spanish historian Miguel-Angel Quesada notes, 'The Mudéjars were the most numerous in the Kingdoms of Aragon and Valencia, but were few under the crown of Castile during the last centuries of the Middle Ages.'[6]

The Muslims had not easily accepted the Christian conquest of the rest of Castile of 1264–66. As noted earlier, fierce guerrilla operations, then open warfare, followed by their slaughter, expulsion or flight, was the Muslim response to their new masters.[7] Also undermining the initial efforts of the kings of Castile to retain Muslim artisans and peasants in their underpopulated lands was Islam itself, for Muslim religious teaching had been unanimous: the faithful had no choice but to emigrate to Muslim lands.[8] The fatwa of al-Wansharishi could not have been clearer. Citing the authoritative twelfth-century religious leader Abu'l-Walid ibn Rushd, it decreed that 'The obligation to emigrate from the lands of unbelief will continue right up to Judgement Day.'[9] Unlike the Jews, the Muslims of Spain always had somewhere welcoming to go to, and we get a taste of the times in an open letter of 1415 in which King Yusuf III of Granada called upon all Muslims to rally to Granada for a Jihad. 'By God, Oh Muslims', his letter proclaimed, 'Granada has no equal and there is nothing like service on the frontier during the Holy War.'[10]

I have discussed both the numbers of the weavers and the quality of the carpets of Murcia in Muslim times and seen that their importance, economically and culturally, was such that those talented and successful weavers fleeing to the Islamic stronghold of Granada found there an especially warm welcome and immediate employment.[11] Around 1335, Alfonso X secured Letur and Lietor, and the abandoned homes of the Muslims were taken over both by Old Christians[12] (being broadly the descendants of pagans, Arians, Muslims and Jews who had converted to Rome prior to the thirteenth and fourteenth centuries) and New Christians (subsequent converts). Those few Muslims who remained were forced into increasingly restricted roles, both economically and creatively.[13] By 1495, in the whole of Murcia province there were only seven places where more than twenty-five Muslim families lived.[14] As to Leitor and Letur (then part of Enriquez' Murcia), the authoritative Rodriquez Llopis, in his invaluable work *La Villa Santiaguista de Leitor en la Baya Edad Media*, confirms that none of the carpets there could have been produced by Muslims, for they had all either fled or been expelled.[15]

A similar situation obtained with sericulture. Some Muslim silk workers had stayed following Murcia's conquest by the Christian knights, but production declined again after the Muslim revolt of 1264. In the fifteenth century, the Enriquez introduced a tax regime designed to encourage silk workers to come to Murcia, thus providing many *conversos* with both work and refuge. It was typical Enriquez policy. One might argue that this was designed solely to increase their income from the increasing production of textiles, but the numbers involved suggest that any economic benefit for the Enriquez was debatable. I think this may well be yet one more example of the Enriquez' cautious but clear support for their fellow *conversos*.

Some still think of the Jews of Spain as the vicious moneylenders parodied in numerous plays, poems and songs, from the great Spanish epic, the *Song of the Cid*, to Shakespeare's *Merchant of Venice*. In fact, most were poor and pious artisans and we turn to an ordinance of King Juan II of 6 April 1443. Along with their names it records the occupations of many thousands of Jews as clothiers, milkmen, tailors, curriers, leather workers, cobblers, basket makers, rope makers, saddlers, armourers, iron and steel workers, braziers, cutlers, tinsmiths, coppersmiths, goldsmiths, silversmiths, potters, bridle makers, carpenters, sailors, dyers and weavers (Figure 4). To further counter the common opinion that the Jews of Spain were generally either merchants or moneylenders, it is perhaps worth providing here Dr Neuman's listing of their trades and professions, for it shows how extensively and integrated they were in Spanish society.[16] The list includes high government officials, diplomats, bailiffs, ministers of finance, farmers and collectors of taxes, concessionaires of royal mills, salt marshes and other revenues. They were physicians, lawyers, teachers and scribes, rabbis and judges, preachers and cantors, notaries, town clerks, courtiers and couriers. They were brokers and bullion merchants, moneylenders, money changers, and international traders. They operated mines, raised sheep, grew flax, made gloves and other leather products as well as soap and candles; they traded in skins, furs, leather, wool, cloth, silk, timber, spices and oil. They were butchers and bakers and candlestick-makers, dealers in carriages, cattle, horses, mules, and exporters and importers of corn, grain and wheat. They maintained general stores of merchandise. There are references to dressers of skins, crossbow archers, makers of anchors, miners, braziers, brothel keepers, slave traders, jewellers, and watchmakers; sailors and shipowners, locksmiths and blacksmiths. In addition to their trades of tinkers, tailors, soldiers and sailors, rich men, poor men, beggar men and thieves, we find among them vintners, specialist weavers, dyers, tanners; also gilders, parchment-makers, bookbinders, rope-makers, saddle-makers, upholsterers and clothiers. There were Jews to be seen in the ranks of the professional gamblers, troubadours, dancers, mimics, musicians, acrobats, bullfighters and even lion tamers. And finally in this economically diversified population there were professional mourners – Jewish women who would be paid to attend Christian burials, sing Christian funeral chants and demonstrate all proper grief at the death of the departed.

In Chapters 2 and 8 I discussed the volatile relationships between the Jews, Muslims and Christians of Spain. As to the relationships between the New Christians and the Jews, sometimes they were close, other times not so. The will of a widow of 1470 comes alive, crying out to us as she wishes that 'Margarita, my Christian daughter, and my Jewish son and heir, Vidal de Piera, shall deal with one another in seemly fashion and shall live in peace and unity and love.' For some *conversos*, Judaism and the community was ever ready to encourage and support their return to the faith of their forefathers – a practice that was one of the factors behind the expulsions of all Jews in 1492. For other *conversos*, simply giving material support to Jews was a crime. So it was that Juana Rodrig of Toledo was arraigned before the Inquisition for lending a rug for the Sukkot booth. We see the confusion and the plight of the *conversos* in her speech in her defence: 'all of which I did in honour of and in keeping with the laws of the Jews, thinking I would be saved by it'. Assimilation into the host culture is one part of the story of the Jews; another part is their role as the litmus paper of the world's ills. Already in the thirteenth century we hear Judah ben Barzilay ha Bargeloni's lament: 'some intermingle with Gentiles, eat their bread, and become like them'. The experience of two Jewish doctors in Murcia at the beginning of the fifteenth century also tells its own story, for they converted. Their Jewish patients no longer consulted them and insufficient Christian patients sought their services. Eventually the Murcia local authority agreed to pay them stipends to compensate for their loss of income.

As to the Jews themselves, they were divided into two socio-economic groups. There were the ordinary folk detailed above and there were the wealthy ones who formed a self-perpetuating oligarchy, making the most of their matrimonial and commercial alliances within their closed group. Producing the great scholars to guide and the great courtiers to protect the rest of the community, the grandees held sway over them all. These aristocratic Jewish clans, whether publicly Jewish or discreetly *converso*, were incredibly wealthy. The Enriquez, for example, made their money from their control of one of the great medieval fairs, from their monopoly of the production and distribution of the still-famous Knights Castile soap,[17] from taxation and rents arising in their domains, and from generations of male heirs all marrying the heiresses of similarly enormously wealthy and politically powerful *converso* dynasties.

The censuses of the time help build up the picture. The census of the 1370s reported the population of the town of Murcia – Old Christians, Muslims, Jews and *conversos* – to be 11,000. After the anti-Jewish riots of 1391, from which the province of Murcia under the Enriquez had been substantially exempted, there were some 2,000 Jews and an unknown number of *conversos* living in the town.[18] We do not know the number of *converso* weavers, and converting to Christianity did not of itself cause one to abandon one's employment or business or one's home, family and friends in the Jewish quarter. As late as 1481, the town plan of Murcia (Figure 9) shows that there was still a substantial Juderiá and a major report of the Inquisition in 1488 stated in all seriousness that there was hardly a believing Christian in the whole of the province – they were all *conversos*![19] That, of course, is ridiculous, but that is what was believed to be true. We can, however, get a more rational idea of the very large numbers and the high skills of the Jewish and *converso* weavers of the Murcian province by bringing together three sets of facts. Earlier I discussed and gave evidence for these, but the conclusion to be drawn is substantial, and so merits repeating here:

1. The wool, silk and textile industry, including the manufacture of carpets, was the predominant economic activity of Murcia. By the beginning of the fifteenth century, Leitor's economy was almost exclusively based upon the weaving of carpets.[20]
2. The huge amount of tax – some 35 to 60 per cent of the total revenue – that was paid by the Jews in every Iberian kingdom (see Chapter 2, n.26).
3. The Jews of Murcia paid the highest amount of tax paid by those communities.

The above three facts indicate the large numbers of Jewish and *converso* weavers and textile workers in Murcia in the Middle Ages. As late as 1484, after so many Jews had converted or emigrated, the town's records report 141 Jews paying their taxes and seven years later, on the eve of the expulsion, the Murcian community was among the ten largest contributors of the remaining 216 Jewish communities in Castile required to pay a special tax to finance the conquest of Granada.

So far we have looked at both the substantial number of skilled Jewish weavers and the very small Muslim population of Murcia, which in any case was being continually depleted by the flight of Muslim weavers to Muslim Granada. What then were the concerns of the Jewish weavers? What was happening to them over the fifteenth century?

The simple answer is that faced with the certainty of prejudice and the probability of violence they were under attack on all sides, from the mob which, raised to a frenzy by a new class of anti-Jewish priests, might loot and burn down their homes and murder them and their families, and from the emergent Christian artisan and mercantile class who were using their growing economic and political weight to reduce or eliminate Jewish competition. As we have seen, in Castile in 1411–12, a spate of anti-Jewish measures were passed which, by grossly confining the activities of Jewish artisans and confronting them with a choice between penury or Christianity, propelled a multitude to the baptismal font.

There are few totally reliable statistics as to the number of Castilian Jews in the hundred or so years prior to the expulsion of 1492, or of the numbers who converted or fled, but some solid information can often be sifted out from the tax records. The great historian of the Inquisition, H.C. Lea, records the enormous sum of 2,561,855 gold maravadis coming into the exchequer of Castile from the Jewish Poll Tax of 1284. At three maravadis a head we arrive at a total of 853,951 married or adult males.[21] This figure is supported by the Poll Tax returns six years later for 1290–91, which produced a total of 2,584,855 gold maravadis, so indicating a Jewish population of 861,618.[22]

Some 200 years later, don Isaac Abravanel (1437–1508), was one of the most important Spanish Jews (an ally of the Enriquez, he was also in charge of levying the tax on sheep), and as key advisor to Ferdinand and Isabella he helped organize the exodus of the Jews following the order of expulsion of 1492. Abravanel, unlike many of the other Jewish grandees, rather than abandon his faith, abandoned Spain to join and to assist the refugees. He writes of the number of Spanish Jews in 1492: 'As the fear of God and the Honour of His Divine Presence are my witnesses, the number of Jews in the lands of the king of Spain in the year in which Israel was stripped of its glory [i.e. the year of the expulsion] was three hundred thousand souls.'[23]

Few scholars, however, agree as to the numbers, either of those who stayed or the numbers of those who left. A book recently published by the State Corporation for Spanish Cultural Action Abroad states that a far greater number remained and converted to Christianity.[24] As noted in Chapter 7, this is born out in an admixture analysis based upon binary and Y-STR haplotypes published in the *American Journal of Human Genetics* indicating 19.8 per cent of the present population of the Iberian Peninsula is of Jewish ancestry.[25]

Most *conversos* continued discreetly in various ways to continue the customs and culture of the forefathers, hoping for better times. From the late thirteenth century onwards, hundreds of thousands of *conversos* had struggled to merge inconspicuously into the general population – no longer Jewish in name but not yet Catholic in fact. Some sought to relegate their Judaism to the realm of a private family tradition, others remained connected to their community, still bound to God by an everlasting covenant. They sought only peace and privacy. But it was not to be. Little did they know they were in at the birth of the modern totalitarian police state, which needed to destroy all thoughts, practices and truths other than its own.

By the middle of the fifteenth century, depending upon when people or their forebears had converted, two quite separate social and legal types of Christians had evolved. The logic of the church was as impeccable as it was inflexible and inexorable. The Jews, refusing to convert to Christianity, could not but in some minds cast doubt upon the legitimacy of the church, for if Judaism remained valid then how could Christianity, believing it to be the New Israel, be valid? The age-old belief of the Jews that accorded every human being a personal relationship with the One Almighty meant they found it incomprehensible that there could ever be either any subdivision or any intermediaries in that relationship; to them any law or gospel that bestowed divinity or divine rights on any mortal creature, be he pope, priest, emperor or prince, was sacrilegious idolatry. That personal, passionate and ceaseless conversation between the Jew and his God which defines Judaism (and which was later to be the lifeblood of the Reformation) could not have presented a more fundamental threat to the very existence of the Church of Rome. So it was that the Spanish Inquisition, as prosecutor, judge and jury – and usually staffed by able zealots – spent the next 300 years tracking down and condemning the *conversos* and anyone else who did not heart and soul subsume to their exclusive creed. Most of the major Christian heresies, in their initial stages at least, could not but be influenced by the rich Jewish tradition of biblical exegesis and were far more receptive to the moral messages of the Hebrew and the Christian Bibles than to the demands of a corrupted church in Rome.

As mentioned earlier, in 1488 one of the most senior inquisitors, a close colleague of Fray Tomás de Torquemada, the Inquisitor General,[26] reported that there was hardly a believing Christian in the whole of Murcia.[27] Accordingly the Inquisition established a major permanent office there, and for the *conversos*, betraying some members of one's family, friends or neighbours to save oneself and family from poverty, prison or the incredible pain of being burned alive became a strategy for survival. In pursuit of their deadly duties even death itself was no deterrent to the Inquisition. Take the case of old Doctor Feyjoso. Lying in his bed, surrounded by his nearest and dearest, he was preparing to meet his maker. But he said something (or, who knows, was said by one of those nearest and dearest to have said something) that was reported to the Inquisition. Dragged before the tribunal, mercifully he passed away. But that did not stop his trial. He was posthumously found guilty of being a relapsed *converso*, his corpse was ceremonially exhumed and was, along with his wife's, who had also passed away, ceremoniously burned at the stake.[28] The church exhumed bodies for two reasons. One was political, as we have seen, in order to provide vital evidence as to whether the deceased had had a Jewish or a Christian burial (see Chapter 7 and the Enriquez exhumations). The other was theological, for by ensuring there was nothing left of the corpse, there would be less possibility of redemption from the fires of hell, even on the final Day of Judgement.

The manner in which one wished one's body finally to be laid to rest, as we have seen with Alfonso and dona Juana, tells us much about that person's beliefs. Take the case of Alfonso Fernández Samuel. Baptized past the age of 40 and dying in his 60s, he bequeathed a pittance to the church and a fortune of 100 gold pieces to some Jews so that they might not have to work on the Sabbath. Wisely he left his hat to the beadle and his donkey, knapsack and silk bonnet to the gravediggers in the hope that, as was their practice with *conversos*, they would not maltreat his body, and he stipulated that when laid out in his coffin the cross should be laid at his feet, the Koran at his breast and the Torah, 'his light and life', at his head.[29] Judaism, unlike Islam and Christianity, does not claim to be the only true religion and Samuel's will, like dona Juana Enriquez's, exemplifies the concerns and the confusions of the *conversos*. Nevertheless Alfonso Samuel's bequest to some Jews was a common way whereby a *converso*'s fundamental belief in Judaism was asserted, for the giving of alms would help ensure the salvation of one's soul and in return those receiving the alms would pray for both the sick and for the souls of the departed.

It is helpful to our understanding of the forces that drove the Jewish and *converso* weavers to the Hellin district of Murcia to get a sense of the condemnation that increasingly confronted them from the middle of the fifteenth century. This may possibly post-date the weaving of the Vizcaya carpet (which would not have been woven after 1475) but the clarity and the force of those strictures give us an indication of the climate, the condition and the culture that preceded and built up to that condemnation. A typical Edict of Faith, issued in Valencia in 1519, gave examples of suspicious deeds or words, which, on pain of excommunication, the faithful must report to the Inquisition. Entitled 'Guide for the Informers', it included acts such as one's neighbour preparing the next day's meal or changing table linen and bedlinen on Fridays, putting on clean clothes or not working on Saturdays, eating celery or bitter herbs, not eating sheep[30] or pork, or washing the bodies of the dead. And of the living, too! For the changing times in Spanish history were marked by the changing standards of personal hygiene. The Visigoths had destroyed the Roman baths, seeing them as encouraging softness and effeminacy. The Muslims then reinstated them and built many more, for Islam and Judaism use water constantly in religious ablutions. But under Christianity washing acquired a heretical meaning, with Spanish monks experiencing physical dirt as a sort of test and demonstration of moral purity. Priests were instructed to ask their young female penitents about the frequency of their ablutions, and absolution, depending upon their answer, might be denied. Being physically clean was prima facie evidence of heresy, for one of the oft-repeated phrases in the Inquisitions indictments was that 'the accused was known to take baths'. Indeed, any attention to one's personal cleanliness and hygiene as laid down in Judaism was suspect, such as washing one's hands before eating and after going to the lavatory.

I would hesitate to suggest that many devoted inquisitors and informers did not do what they did out of the highest of motives, out of a burning desire to ensure that the souls of their fellow humans might be saved and brought out of their state of misery and grief into a state of grace.[31] However, reading through the cases it seems to me that often nothing more than being wealthy was sufficient to incite the Inquisition and mob to destroy someone. The profit to be made by informing on *conversos* and their descendants, whether they had in truth become devout Christians or continued privately to practise Judaism or just hovered in confusion between the two, was huge. In the middle of the sixteenth century the Venetian ambassador to Spain reported back to the Council of the Doges that the value of the property acquired by the Inquisition by burning twenty-nine *conversos* had amounted to no less than the staggering sum of four million ducats.[32]

But to return to the *conversos* of Murcia. It is clear, for all the reasons discussed above and in Chapter 7 (the predominance of the carpet weaving industry in Murcia, the large number of Jews and *conversos* living there and the huge amounts of tax that the Jews were able to pay), the majority of *conversos* were in one way or another associated with the carpet and textile industry. Given that from 1391 onwards their lives and liberty were likely to be at risk, they faced two fundamental problems.

The first was where to live, so that by changing their names and their family histories they might pass themselves off as Old rather than New Christians. This process of concealment was a dynamic and ongoing movement, starting in the fourteenth century and coming to a head in 1492 when the terms of the expulsion were absolute. After that, anybody openly stating, like Pedro Hernandez of Hellin, that they were Jewish had little to look forward to. Even were Pedro to survive the flogging of 200 lashes it was the short life of a galley slave that awaited him.[33] Those who could, the minority, paid the hefty emigration tax and left Spain. Others moved from their Judería to remote parts of the Spanish mainland. As had happened with the Cathars 200 to 300 years earlier[34] the activities of the church militant also drove the *conversos* from the urban locations and into the mountainous regions or other remote and underpopulated areas far from the centres of ecclesiastical power – and indeed far from the mob. For the world was changing and even the peasants, long seen along with the slaves as obedient beasts of burden, were becoming something of a force to consider. We get a sense of the growing power of the peasants in the widespread rejoicing following their assassination of their feudal overlord, the Master of the Order of Calatrava, in Cordoba in 1476. Often their anger at the corruption of the church and the brutality of the feudal overlords was manipulated by both church and overlord to scapegoat and blame the Jews.

The second problem the *converso* carpet weavers of Murcia needed to solve was that wherever they went in search of greater safety, in saving their lives they still had to earn a living, and the best way to do that was through the exercise of their skills.

In the summer the coastal plain of Murcia bakes and the cicadas sing. As you move north-west the land rises sharply and soon you are in an out-of-the-way and particularly beautiful part of Spain, with arid imposing mountains rising up from deep gorges and soaring up to jagged peaks. With spectacular views, good soil, fresh water, many natural caves and a history of mining for iron, this remote region has sustained small isolated communities since the earliest times. It has, too, an ancient history of weaving, for since the Neolithic and Bronze ages the people here have been making rugs and textiles.[35]

The medieval centre of Murcia town had changed little in the twenty-odd years since I was last there. It felt good to be back but after a couple of days I was anxious to get to Hellin and I drove along the main highway towards Madrid, passing the significantly named Rambla del Judio, and stopped over in Hellin – a journey today of less than two hours. A good-sized town,[36] it was built up in the thirteenth century under Muslim rule. Around the impressive Cerro del Castillo, until very recently, remnants of weavings were still to be found.[37] Two days later I drove to Leitor, some twenty miles to the north-west. It too has grown – and not that agreeably – over the years but it has kept some of its Arab architecture and has a lovely ancient water trough. I looked for the craft-shop where, twenty years ago, I went in with my own drawing and they wove me a beautiful rug, but it seemed to have closed down. Next day I drove some thirty-odd miles back to the south-east over particularly harsh and lonely mountains to Letur, also an old Arab village but smaller than Leitor and quite charming. Boasting a fine fifteenth-century Arab tower among its architectural treasures,[38] in the words of my travel guide, 'With its pretty whitewashed Jewish quarter, this is perhaps the most picturesque village in the area.'[39] Even today many of Letur's residents still weave.

As earlier described, when the Muslim weavers and villagers fled Hellin, Leitor and Letur to find safety in the Muslim stronghold of Granada, their homes were taken over and repopulated by Christians, Old and New. In the wars of the 1440s a Muslim army from Granada sought to avenge the expulsion of their co-religionists and attacked Hellin with deadly results for its defenders, devastating the region before retreating. The critical point I make is that by 1450 neither Muslims nor Muslim converts to Christianity remained there.[40] If, therefore, the Vizcaya carpet was woven sometime after 1450, given its nature and the skills of the *converso* weavers, it is most likely to have been made by them. Hellin, Leitor and Letur were ideal for the *converso* weavers and their families. Probably founded after the pogroms of 1391, all three locations had well-established Jewish communities and as a small and remote region far away from the informers and the urban mobs it was a place where they could make a living as weavers and, albeit discreetly, continue to follow in the faith of their fathers. It was also, at that time, in the relatively protected domain of the Enriquez. Indeed, most interestingly, Lavado Paradinas suggests the weavers of the Admiral carpets had moved to be closer to dona Juana and the Admiral.[41]

There were other centres of carpet weaving in the region. Alcarez and Cuenca also produced fine rugs but it is around Hellin and Letur and Leitor, sometime in the fifteenth century, that the Admiral carpets were most probably woven. The evidence for this comes from the furniture inventories of various noble families, the earliest being Duke don Alvaro de Zuniga's. Dated 1468, it refers to 'three small fine carpets from Litur' (sic). A 1504 listing of Queen Isabella's carpets refers to 'another carpet from Lietur's [sic] looms'.[42] These inventories eliminate the other places where the carpets might have been woven. Certainly Alcaraz was a major producer of carpets, but the style of those carpets was quite distinct. As for Cuenca, it too was a significant carpet manufactory and was also home to a sizeable Jewish and later *converso* community, but it is a long way away from Hellin.

The hope of the New Christian weavers of Murcia that by moving to this harsh, remote and sparsely populated region they might continue privately and discreetly to live a quiet Jewish life was not to be. The Inquisition was not far behind them and it is largely thanks to its diligent homicidal passion that we know what we do today about the *converso* weavers of Hellin, Leitor and Letur. As painful as they are to read, the Inquisition records merit study, for the numbers of *conversos* actually arraigned in relation to the total populations of these three weaving centres establish both the existence and the significance of *converso* weavers of the region. It is possible these figures do not record every adult male but only the heads of households; be that as it may, the proportion of those arraigned for heresy to the total population (in Murcia province at the end of the fifteenth century it was but 15,000) would not really differ. Further, although the Vizcaya carpet would not have been woven later than the 1470s and the population figures we have are from 1468 to 1503, I see no dissonance, for the *converso* populations of the region had almost certainly been increasing steadily since the 1390s.

In 1468 Leitor was home to some 250 people. By 1498 the number of inhabitants had dropped to 160, and by 1503 there were but 139 people left in Leitor. We do not know the cause of this decline in the population but one reason might well have been the permanent presence there of an Inquisitor; a second reason might well be that subsequently fifteen people – one in ten of the total population in 1503 – had been brought before the tribunal on charges of heresy.[43] A third explanation, following on from the first two, might be that anyone who could possibly move elsewhere did so.

It was the same in Letur, where the same census of 1468 recorded an even smaller community with a population of some seventy souls. By 1498 it had increased to seventy-two and by 1503 it numbered eighty.[44] It is unclear whether it even had its own church prior to 1528, that being the date its present and quite delightful church was consecrated. Albeit half the size of Leitor, Letur most significantly had two resident Inquisitors compared to Leitor's one.[45] The attention paid by the Spanish Inquisition to the tiny village could not have been more intense. Some ten inhabitants were duly arraigned – one in eight of the total population.[46]

The permanent, powerful and disproportionate presence of the Inquisition in both these small villages tells us of the correspondingly substantial *converso* presence there, for the Inquisition usually focused its attention on the more populous and commercially oriented wealthy towns. The large villages might be visited periodically and the remote and poorer areas were often ignored by the Inquisitor and his travelling band of clerks and Familiars. These Familiars were a mix of armed guards, enforcers and spies, and often exempted from criminal prosecution. It is little wonder, therefore, that their jobs became so lucrative that they could be auctioned for substantial sums of money.[47] Whenever the Inquisitor Torquemada travelled he was escorted by fifty Familiars on horseback and another 200 on foot. He and his crew would arrive at a town or village, where the local civil administration promptly provided accommodation lest they too be subject to investigation. The villagers would be summoned, the days of grace decreed and thereafter confessions taken. Generally people who confessed voluntarily in the days of grace might be reconciled to the church without having all their property confiscated and without suffering more than a penance and a large fine – which would be much reduced when the penitents gave the inquisitors the details of the beliefs and practices of their families and friends. Moshe Natan, a mid-fourteenth-century poet, catches the world of secrets in his poem 'Prison':

> Dig a grave in your heart for your secret.
> Tellers of secrets don't know what they do.
> Your secret's your hostage as long as it's kept –
> But once you reveal it – the prisoner is you.[48]

I was not able to track down the actual census results for the much larger town of Hellin, but the Inquisition records confirm it was home to a large number of *conversos*.[49] Whatever one thinks about the Inquisition, their zeal and habitual thoroughness were astonishing. The most telling of all the figures I tracked down was the price paid by the weavers of Hellin for an officially notarized document, the *Cristiano Lindo*, which certified the purchaser's blood to be pure and untainted by that of a Jewish ancestor. In Leitor the price of this certificate, on which your life and that of your family might depend, was a hefty 528 *ducados* but in Hellin it was a staggering 2,000 *ducados*[50] – pointing to both the commercial success and the numbers of the *conversos* carpet weavers and merchants in the region. The significance of these figures cannot be overstated.

The material to make carpets was readily available: goat hair and sheep wool was obtained directly from the farmers and the dyes were bought in from suppliers. A form of sales tax of 10 per cent was levied on the finished product and payable to the Enriquez, for this was their domain. I was particularly interested to learn that the weavers, by selling their carpets direct to the merchants in Leitor, could avoid paying tax on them.[51] It made me wonder whether the Admiral carpets were actually woven outside the villages of Leitor or Letur, for weaving these carpets was very much a cottage industry, as easily located in a village as in a small hamlet. Were these two villages simply where the merchants lived, accepted commissions and contracted out the work to weavers who lived elsewhere? The attributions of Letur in 1468 and of Leitor in 1504 in the inventories mentioned above would then describe where the carpets were purchased – and not necessarily where they were made.

Given the small populations of Letur and Leitor and the large population of Hellin, the number of people required to make such huge carpets on thirty-foot-plus vertical looms[52] and the number of people required to support those weavers, I think the furthest one can sensibly go is to propose that the Vizcaya carpet was woven in or around Hellin. Given, too, that it was commissioned by the *converso* Enriquez, and given its covert Judaic symbols and the considerable number of highly skilled *converso* weavers, and the ever diminishing presence and then the total disappearance of any Muslim weavers in the region, it is most likely that the Vizcaya carpet was woven by *conversos*. There are other possible answers – but this is by far the most logical.[53]

So far we have been looking mainly at the Vizcaya carpet, the Enriquez, the Jews and the weavers. But I wondered about examples of our central theme in other media. Was it not possible that *conversos*, as discreet Jews, hid their true beliefs and identities from some but revealed them to others not only in this carpet but also in other forms of art and artefacts? In the next chapter I look at the work of some of the greatest Spanish writers of the time and try to read between the lines.

NOTES

1. J. Dodds, 'Mudejar Tradition and the Synagogues of Medieval Spain: Cultural Identity and Cultural Hegemony', in V. Mann, T. Glick and J. Dodds, '*Convivencia*', *Jews, Muslims and Christians in Medieval Spain* (New York: George Braziller in conjunction with the Jewish Museum, 1992), pp. 113, 131, citing G.M. Borras Gualis, *Arte Mudejar Aragones* (Zaragoza, 1978), p.20.
2. Oleg Grabar, *The Formation of Islamic Art* (New Haven, CT and London: Yale University Press, 1987), p.21.
3. Of all the descriptions of the Black Death surely none exceeds that of Boccaccio's in *The Decameron*.
4. Heather Ecker, *Caliphs and Kings: The Art and Influence of Islamic Spain* (Washington, DC: Arthur M Sackler Gallery, Smithsonian Institution; New York: Hispanic Society of America, 2004), p.35.

5. Linda Woolley, 'Hispanic Synthesis', *Hali*, 81 (1995), p.71.
6. Miguel-Angel Quesada, 'Mudéjares and Repobladores in the Kingdom of Granada (1485–1501)', in Alisa Meyuhas Ginio (ed.), *Jews, Christians and Muslims in the Mediterranean World after 1492* (London: Frank Cass, 1992), pp.53, 55. See also Bernard F. Reilly, *The Medieval Spains* (Cambridge: Cambridge University Press, 2001), p.163.
7. A. MacKay, *Spain in the Middle Ages* (Basingstoke: Macmillan, 1977), pp.65–70.
8. Reilly, *Medieval Spains*, p.195.
9. L.P. Harvey, *Islamic Spain 1250–1500* (London: University of Chicago Press, 1990), p.56.
10. H. Thomas, *Rivers of Gold* (London: Phoenix, 2003), p.6.
11. Florence Lewis May, *Silk Textiles of Spain* (New York: Hispanic Society of America, 1957), p.171.
12. Rodriguez Llopis, *La Villa Santiaguista de Leitor en la Baya Edad Media* (Murcia: Pictographia, 1993), p.59.
13. Thomas Glick, *Islamic and Christian Spain in the Early Middle Ages* (Princeton, NJ: Princeton University Press, 1979), p.246. Unlike all the other authorities cited here, Sanchez Ferrer suggests that few Muslims fled or were expelled from the region of Hellin. However, he then goes on to note that in the second half of the fifteenth century Letur and two other towns were abandoned by the majority of their inhabitants and repopulated by Christians. This is the point I make. Those Christians must have been New Christians, otherwise the overwhelming interest of the church and the Inquisition in their lives would not make sense. And for all the reasons set out in the text, the New Christians were far more likely to have been converts from Judaism than from Islam.
14. Harvey, *Islamic Spain 1250–1500*, p.70; and Quesada, 'Mudéjares and Repobladores in the Kingdom of Granada (1485–1501)', p.56.
15. Llopis, *La Villa Santiaguista de Leitor en la Baya Edad Media*, p.59.
16. Abraham Neuman, *The Jews in Spain* (Philadelphia, PA: Jewish Publication Society, 1948), pp.185–190.
17. Even today one of the finest soaps is Knights Castile or white soap. First manufactured commercially in the thirteenth century in Castile from pure olive oil and lye (the ashes of a common Spanish plant), it was probably one of the first hard soaps, famous for its mildness and purity. In 1371 Crescias Davin (a Jewish merchant also known as Sabonarius) introduced Knights Castile soap to Marseilles and soon it was traded throughout the western world. Castile had also produced the traditional black soap. Described in the book of Jeremiah and used by the Jews since biblical times, soap was not significantly used in Europe until early in the Middle Ages.
18. *Encyclopaedia Judaica* (Jerusalem: Keter Publishing, 1971), Vol. 12, p.530.
19. Y. Baer, *A History of the Jews in Christian Spain* (Philadelphia, PA: Jewish Publication Society, 1992), Vol. 2, p.397.
20. Llopis, *La Villa Santiaguista de Leitor en la Baya Edad Media*, p.53.
21. H.C. Lea, *A History of the Inquisition of Spain*, Vol. 1 (New York: Macmillan, 1906), pp.86, 125; and Amador de los Rios, *Toledo: Monumentos Ariquetectonicos de España* (Impreta de Antonio Cr. Izquicerdo, 1905), I, pp.28–9; see also Neuman, *Jews in Spain*, p.66; see also Max Dimont, *Jews, God and History* (London: New American Library, 2003), p.229.
22. Neuman, *Jews in Spain*, p.66; and Dimont, *Jews, God and History*, p.229.

23. N. Roth, *Conversos, Inquisition and the Expulsion of the Jews from Spain* (Madison, WI: University of Wisconsin Press, 2002), p.376. All sorts of numbers as to the Jewish population of Castile have been banded around. The starting figures of some 850,000 in 1284 to 1290–91 are pretty certain, but what actually happened to those numbers over the next 200 years (putting aside the net increase through birth and the decrease through death, especially due to the Black Death) is far from clear. Out of a total population in Spain by the 1480s, estimated by some at some 10,000,000, some 7,000,000 to 8,000,000 were inhabitants of Castile. Esther Benbassa and Aron Rodrique, in *Sephardi Jewry* (Berkeley, CA: University of California Press, 2000), p.xxxvii, suggest as a guess that between 100,000 and 200,000 Jews left Spain.

Caro Baroja, in *Los Judios en la España Moderna y Contemporanea*, Vol. 1 (Madrid: Istmo), pp.198–205, estimates the Jewish population of Spain in 1492 to be some 400,000, of which some 160,000 left Spain and some 240,000 underwent conversion and stayed. Haim Beinart, a leading scholar, estimates some 200,000 were expelled. Most authorities agree the majority of Jews stayed in Spain and converted to Christianity. Professor Beinart (*The Expulsion of the Jews from Spain* [Oxford: The Littman Library of Jewish Civilization, 2005], p.290) concludes his detailed analysis with the lament of Rabbi Abraham Baqrat:

> And they all left, about two hundred thousand by foot, men and women and children, spread out over the mountains and the sea like a flock with no shepherd. And our enemy took pleasure in our grief, saying, these people have no Lord ... And at that time there fell from the nation three thousand people, bodies dying from great wrong.

Michael Alpert, in his very readable book *Secret Judaism and the Spanish Inquisition* (Nottingham: Five Leaves Publications, 2008), p.17, gives further context to the numbers with his estimate that 25,000 out of 250,000 *conversos* were punished by the Inquisition in its first forty-odd years. One can only surmise the thoughts and fears of the remaining 225,000 who converted to Christianity. Today 19.8 per cent of the population of the Iberian Peninsula has a Jewish ancestor (*American Journal of Genetics*, cited in text).

24. *Remembering Sepharad* (Madrid: State Corporation for Spanish Cultural Action Abroad, 2003), p.204. Abraham Senior, an enormously wealthy and powerful Jew, converting to Christianity stayed on in Spain in 1492; Ferdinand and Isabella served as patrons at this baptism. But he almost certainly remained true to the faith of his fathers for some two hundred years later some of his descendents left Spain to settle in England and convert back to Judaism. And in 2010 archaeologists revealed Abraham Senior's palace in Segovia had a secret synagogue with the walls of the womens' section decorated with Stars of David (Rivka Zimmerman, 'A Shul that Lay Hidden for 500 Years', *Jewish Chronicle* 13 August 2010).

25. *American Journal of Human Genetics*, 83 (12 December 2008), pp.725–36.

26. Torquemada's grandmother is believed by some to have been Jewish. Simon Whitechapel, *Flesh Inferno* (London: Creation Books, 2003), p.52.

27. This citation comes from *The Book of Alboraiques* in the text of I. Loeb, *Revue des Etudes Juives*, 18 (1889), p.241. Alboraiques were insincere converts, so named after Mohammed's horse, which was neither a horse nor a mule.

28. Miguel Blazquez, *La Inquisicion en Albacete* (Albacete: Gráficas Panadero, 1985), p.76.

29. Baer, *History of the Jews in Christian Spain*, Vol. 2, p.275. However, Norman Roth, *Conversos, Inquisition*

and the Expulsion of the Jews from Spain, p.167, tracks this account, with significant variations, back to an anti-converso satirical set of poems. Whether Baer or Roth is right for our purpose is immaterial, for the facts alone reflect the attitudes and concerns of the time.
30. The belief of the Inquisition of Valencia that Jews are forbidden to eat sheep was quite wrong – and interesting, for it points to ignorance and misunderstanding on the part of some Inquisitors of a significant aspect of Jewish culture: the laws of what food is and what is not kosher.
31. A major thread in medieval Catholicism gave primacy to motive – to the result that a good intention which led to a bad result was superior to a bad intention which lead to a good result. Judaism tends to ignore motive, looking mainly to the results.
32. Cecil Roth, *The Spanish Inquisition* (London: W.W. Norton, 1996), p.67.
33. Blazquez, *La Inquisicion en Albacete*, p.73.
34. Edward Burman, *Inquisition* (Stroud: Sutton Publishing, 2004), p.89.
35. J. Blanquez-Perez, *Arqueologia en Albacete* (Madrid: Artes Gráficas, 1993), p.189.
36. T. Echeandia, *Atlas grafico del Reino de Murcia* (Aguilar S.A. de Ediciones-Grupo Santillana, 1979). British Library, Maps 57. Bb42, and *Carta de Correos y Postas de las Provincias de Albacete, Alicante y Murcia, Trazada por la Direccion General de Correos*, British Library, Maps 18325.1.
37. A. Morena (ed.), *La España Gotica* (Madrid: Ediciones Encuentro, 1997), Vol. 12, pp.127–220.
38. *Diccionario Geográfico de España* (Madrid: Hvali, Ediciones Movimiento, 1959), Vol. 2, pp.505ff.
39. N. Inman (ed.), *Spain* (New York: Dorling Kindersley, 2002), p.379.
40. Llopis, *La Villa Santiaguista de Leitor en la Baya Edad Media*, p.59.
41. Lavado Paradinas was, it appears, talking about Mudejar craftsmen from Albacete (the province then adjacent to the Hellin district), but for all the reasons stated and all the authorities here cited that is really most unlikely. What, however, is pertinent is his report that the weavers moved in order to be closer to dona Juana and the Admiral: Jose Ferrer, *Alfrombas Antiguas de la Provincia de Albacete* (La Roda: Artes Gráficas Quintanilla, 1986), p.26, citing Lavado Paradinas, *El Arte Mudejar* ...(Actes del II Simposio International de Mudejarismo de Turuel, pp.32–3).
42. Llopis, *La Villa Santiaguista de Leitor en la Baya Edad Media*, p.59.
43. Blazquez, *La Inquisicion en Albacete*, p.116.
44. Llopis, *La Villa Santiaguista de Leitor en la Baya Edad Media*, p.24.
45. Blazquez, *La Inquisicion en Albacete*, p.32.
46. Ibid., p.116.
47. Colbert I. Nepaulsingh, *Apples of Gold in Filigrees of Silver* (New York: Holmes & Meier, 1995), p.17.
48. P. Cole, *The Dream of the Poem* (Princeton, NJ: Princeton University Press, 2007), p.297.
49. Blazquez, *La Inquisicion en Albacete*, pp.32, 77–81.
50. Ibid., p.12.
51. Llopis, *La Villa Santiaguista de Leitor en la Baya Edad Media*, p.59.
52. J. Ferrandis Torres, *Exposicion de Alfombras Antiguas Españolas* (Madrid: Espasa-Calpe, 1933), p.23.
53. Ockham's Razor – a methodological principle dictating a bias towards simplicity in theory construction.

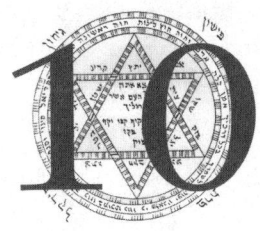

'For Things Are Never What They Seem'

The title of this chapter – it is a line from the prologue in de Rojas's *La Celestina* – encapsulates the genius, the magic, of the Vizcaya carpet. Almost every single one of the carpet's symbols, seen either individually or as part of a whole, conveyed uniquely important concepts to Jews and *conversos* – and to no one else. As the authority Colbert I. Nepaulsingh made clear, 'To blind the agents of the Inquisition, the authors of these acts of defiance used a technique of subtle concealment based upon Maimonides explicating Proverbs 25:11 in which figurative meanings of greater value than the obvious ones are hidden.'[1]

Censorship is the mother of metaphor, and this phenomenon is demonstrated in the literature of the *conversos*, where unorthodox ideas were there for those who were able to read between the lines, and the readership was well adapted to such exegesis, for much of Kabbalistic Judaism was devoted to revealing the hidden meanings in the Bible and the Talmud.[2] So, for example, there are four quite different ways of reading the Bible, each way offering different meaning. First there is the straightforward literal reading; the next reading is to seek out the allegorical meaning; the third reading is to make one sensitive to the Bible's homiletic values; and only then, finally, the last reading may connect you to its latent content. Judaism has a particular passion for hidden meanings. This proclivity is also to be seen in secular writing of the Jews of Spain. In his collection of fables, the popular writer Isaac ibn Sahula (b. 1244) used animals as metaphors for humans. In one prologue he writes:

> My cherished, golden treasures ye shall find
> Thereto appended, parables designed
> To mirror daily life, in which oblique
> Hints to develop understanding speak.

But it was Judah Alharizi (1165–1225) who was the past master of the secret text. In gate 8 of his *Book of Tahkemoni*, a collection of Jewish tales of Spain, he writes a letter that read straightforwardly is nothing but a standard paean of praise to a prince. But word for word it is totally and perfectly reversible! Read backwards and each glowing compliment becomes a bitter complaint. Later, a closer reading of one of his fables makes it reasonably clear that his figure of the lion is a description of King Alfonso X.[3] The words of the writer of the greatest Kabbalistic book, the Zohar, could not be clearer. 'I found myself constrained to write and to conceal and to ponder, in order to reveal it to all thinking men.'[4]

The fifteenth century begets the most beautiful of all the illuminated Bibles of medieval Spain. The Castilian Alba Bible (1430) had been commissioned by a leading churchman and completed by Rabbi Moses Arragel who supplemented the main text with a network of glosses in which, cautiously, he presented the Jewish view on a number of important doctrinal issues. But there is also a covert subtext presenting Arragel's fundamental beliefs. So, for example, the glossary, in defining the Antichrist, refers to the son of a demon clothed in human form and sent to persecute Israel. A Jew would recognize this as a coded reference to the church.

We can appreciate the *converso* perception, and therefore the way we should consider this carpet, through the works of one of the greatest Spanish writers, Fernando de Rojas, a *converso* who as a 12-year-old boy had witnessed his father being burnt to death by the Inquisition. As was typical among the *conversos* (we saw this pattern in the marriages of the Enriquez), he married a *converso* lady, only to witness her father suffering the same fate as had his own.[5] In the 1490s he wrote *La Celestina*, the earliest and one of the most important European novels. The hero of this tragicomedy is a young aristocrat who, following his falcon into a private garden, sees the captivating and alluring Melibea. Instantly desiring her, declaring his love he reaches for her skirts. She rejects him. He then hires a go-between to help him seduce Melibea, who is a beloved daughter with no idea that her parents may be *conversos*. The plot fails and they all meet untimely deaths. But to a *converso* there is a deeper meaning underlying the story. De Rojas gently and with irony

'For Things Are Never What They Seem'   149

reveals the superstitious and superficial faith of his characters. For on a deeper reading by some scholars the hero is a *converso* who through his weakness is seduced into idolatry, and in speaking of and revering Melibea as a goddess, and swearing she is 'his religion, his life, his God', he is, in allegorical terms, worshipping the Virgin Mary.[6] Other scholars see the same inter-cultural tension in a different interpretation – that it is Melibea, as well as her father, who is secretly continuing to practise Judaism. There is a certain lack of Christian language in her own and her father's speech, and his failure to invoke Jesus's or Mary's names at any time, and particularly on his daughter's death, is to the sensitive ear of the *converso* a significant omission.

The tragic life for a *converso* cries out in the final speech of Melibea's father:

> Where will I find refuge in my disconsolate old age? ... Oh life filled with turmoil and beset with misery! Oh world, Oh world! Fearlessly now, like one can lose nothing ... like a penniless traveller, who, without fear of highwaymen, goes singing in a loud voice (I shall cry out that) you seem to me a labyrinth of errors, a frightful desert, a place where wild beasts dwell, a game of men going around in a circle, a lake filled with slime, a region filled with thorns, a high mountain, a stony field, a meadow filled with serpents, an orchard that has bloomed and given no fruit ... your deceits, your nooses, your chains and snares ... Oh my shattered, broken daughter! ... Why have you left me sad and alone in this vale of tears?[7]

La Celestina is the greatest masterpiece of fifteenth-century Spanish literature and still today it is a standard textbook in Spanish schools. In the prologue de Rojas cautions:

> Anyone who seeks true meaning here,
> Must look beyond the plot, search for the essence,
> Pondering hints and questions,
> And hidden difficulties,
> FOR THINGS ARE NEVER WHAT THEY SEEM.[8] [My emphasis]

He might have been (and for all we know, he was!) writing about the Vizcaya carpet; it too (like much of the Spanish literature of the time) is a cultural chronicle to be read with care as we also ponder its hints and hidden difficulties in search of its essence – for it is the illusion of truth that conceals reality.

The text is there to be read in the textile. The messages written into the

Vizcaya carpet are the same messages written in the books of numerous other *converso* writers such as Francisco López Estrada, Alberto Blecua, Jorge de Montemayor and Alonso Núñez de Reinoso. Perhaps the majority of the important writers, poets and playwrights in fifteenth- and sixteenth-century Spain were either *conversos* or descended from *conversos*. After the massacres of 1391 the *conversos* found ways of conveying cultural coded messages that would be meaningful to Jews and *conversos* and to no one else. Writing about one of his own books, De Reinoso summed up the *converso* mentality: 'And so most of the things in that story have a secret ... because the truth is that I wrote no word without first thinking what it meant underneath.'[9] So in describing a beautiful woman with a lovely rosy Renaissance complexion, the metaphor he chooses for her colouring is of blood mixed with milk, a metaphor designed to shock a *converso*, for it strikes at the laws of kashrut forbidding the mixing of milk and meat: a Christian would be attracted to the woman but a *converso* would be repulsed. Yet another *converso*, Diego de San Pedro, in *Arnalte y Lucinda* directly asks his readers to read between the lines: 'but you, ladies, accept with service and not with roughness of expression I make public but what, by omission in its silencing, I cover up'.

Miguel de Cervantes, the greatest Spanish writer of the sixteenth century continued, in *Don Quixote de la Mancha*, to lay down the foundation of the modern novel established by de Rojas, addressing the pathos of latter-day life, where there is throughout a continuing questioning whether things could ever be what they appear to be, or what they claim to be, or what others need them to be.[10] Cervantes's ironic and lucid understanding of contemporary sophistry is outstanding. And as we relish that wonderful book-burning scene in Chapter 6, 'The Inquisition of the Books', we suddenly realise that Cervantes is telling us that books, which embody thoughts, had to be burnt along with the bodies, so killing off the lives, the languages and the cultural diversities that had made Spain the centre of the intellectual world. Fondly we smile at Don Quixote's foolish and inappropriate behaviour inspired by his idealized love for the beautiful Lady Dulcinea del Toboso – for Cervantes has told us in reality she is but a homely peasant woman. Then a little later he describes her as the 'best hand at salting pork of any woman in La Mancha'. Now suddenly we know, or at least the reader who seeks true meaning and has the skills to read between the lines will know – she is New Christian! For the public and ritualized curing and eating of ham was for the *conversos* a critically important display of Christian authenticity.[11] And what is

Sancho Panza, a kindly but illiterate and dim-witted yokel, if not a caricature of an old Christian peasant? And would Cervantes[12] have Don Quixote eat bacon and eggs in front of his Sancho Panza and on the Sabbath if not to hint at his hero's *converso* nature? Food, too, tells its own tale of the double life of the Marranos. Even today, the *Chorizo de Marrano* (Marrano sausage) recalls the time when Marranos would produce sausages that looked just like pork sausages and so demonstrated their Christian credentials – but that in fact contained no pork.

The clues in *converso* writings and artefacts are there – but like all symbols we only see them if we know them. So, for example, a casual mention of a group of ten men would have no special significance to anybody – apart from *conversos*, for that was the minimum number needed for a communal religious service. We see it in de Rojas's prologue where, revealing his secret authorship only through an acrostic with the first letter of each sentence spelling out his name, he explains: 'and this story will be no exception. No ten people [!] will be able to agree about the meaning, each one will interpret the facts the way he wishes, and argue about what it means.'

Listening carefully to the clichés and catchphrases of the Sephardim also reveals something of the realities of their double lives. One of the commonest phrases (one can almost hear a mother drumming it endlessly into her children's ears), is *Azerse del Mordehay* ('Act like Mordekai'), meaning: listen carefully, but pretend neither to hear nor understand.[13]

So few of the *conversos'* known dual-purpose artefacts have survived but we do know that what appeared at the time to be ordinary scarves or tablecloths were, in *conversos* eyes, prayer shawls; what appeared to be common decorative plaques on an eastern wall were directional finders for prayer facing Jerusalem. But there is a fifteenth-century Spanish lamp that has survived (Figure 25). It is a rare example of a *converso*-concealed ritual Jewish artefact. The crucifix at the head, with its elongated lower vertical, as the most powerful of all Christian symbols, would seem to define the lamp. But the rose window below, so popular in Christian medieval Spain, is also the rosette, so meaningful in Jewish symbolism (see Chapter 12). Below the rosette are three arched gates straight out of Islamic art and architecture, as are the crescents on which they rest. But to a *converso*, this lamp, with its eight cups, cannot be anything other than a Hannukiah menorah – the eight-day festival of light celebrating Judah Maccabee's defeat of the Greek overlord of Israel, and the cleansing and rededication of the Temple in Jerusalem in 168 BCE.

The custom of concealed messages in the books, the language, the practices and the artefacts followed through in the weavings of the Jews. We know this tradition was established in Meshhad (see note 14 below) and in Kashan a quite beautiful silk carpet of the nineteenth century has come down to us, inscribed with Hebrew letters so small as to be virtually invisible.[14]

Since ancient times discreet forms of communication have played a major part in the survival strategies of the oppressed. For example, in early sixteenth-century Holland the rapid growth of Protestantism led to a backlash of oppression by the Catholic Spanish overlords. In his great triptych, *The Garden of Earthly Delights* (c.1504–10), the Dutch painter Hieronymus Bosch (1450–1516), in the section devoted to hell, most tellingly portrays a nun whose face is partly concealed by her cowl. Look closely – and here is no pure and pious sister of divine love but a stinking, sullied sow.[15]

But back to fifteenth- and sixteenth-century totalitarian Spain. Envious neighbours, disgruntled servants, greedy relatives and fellow *conversos* desperate to prove the sincerity of their new-found faith all forced the *conversos* into 1,001 masquerades. I do not know how so many, leading double lives filled with fear, contradiction and conflict, survived for so many generations. And the usually meticulous records of the Inquisition tell us of some of those who did not survive. Let us look at some examples.

In one case a former servant of Juana Núñez reported that her mistress worked every night smoothing wool and wrapping it around a spindle – apart, that is, from Friday night, when she did no work at all. In another case Leonar Alvarez confessed that she kept her spinning wheel at hand so that if anybody came to her house on the Sabbath she might pretend to be spinning. In a third case (it is no accident that it also revolves around weaving, for such was the major activity in most such homes) Maria Gonzales would sometimes go to her mother's home on Saturday, taking with her wool and a wheel or spindle – but according to her servant, no work was ever done.[16]

Danger lay not only with domestic servants but also with neighbours, for maintaining a Jewish home in secret with its different rituals from its Christian neighbours was far from easy. For example, normally such homes would be specially cleaned for the Sabbath but anyone seeing dirt being swept from an open front door before the Sabbath might well assume it to be a crypto-Jewish home.[17] The phrase 'sweeping the dirt under the carpet' has its metaphoric as well as its literal meaning.

Sometimes in reading these accounts and trying to understand what was happening and why, the naivety of the *conversos* brings a rush of tears to one's eyes. Whenever the sign of the cross was to be made, Inez Lopez's hand would actually touch her forehead and one shoulder – but then it would near, but not actually touch, her breast and other shoulder. When it came to reciting, 'In the name of the Father, the Son and the Holy Ghost', gladly would she recite, 'In the name of the Father' – and then not another sound would she utter, as she mouthed but would not vocalize the rest of prayer.[18] Such was her crime.

Words matter. Praying only to the Father, critical to the quintessential 'Oneness' of the Jewish God, has no meeting point with the plurality of the Trinity in Christianity. The word 'God' in Spanish is *Dios*, but ending as it does in an 's', with the qualities and implication of plurality, the *conversos* actually created the unusual form, *Dio*, to express the singularity of their God.

Most things of any significance in a *converso*'s life had a double meaning, for they were leading double lives. Whether they were by now devout Catholics or had remained crypto-Jews, or just muddled between the two, indeed, whatever their beliefs actually were was less important than the impression or the declaration (be it true or false) of their families and neighbours, friends and enemies, regarding their beliefs.

Now that we have seen some of the ways in which *conversos* would both conceal their true belief to some and reveal it to others, it is time to turn to the symbols on the Vizcaya carpet and consider their meanings for Jews as compared to and contrasted with their meanings for Christians.

NOTES

1. Colbert I. Nepaulsingh, *Apples of Gold in Filigrees of Silver* (New York: Holmes & Meier, 1995), p.ix.
2. Leo Strauss, *Persecution and the Art of Writing* (Glencoe, IL: Free Press, 1952), p.25.
3. Isaac ibn Sahula, *Meshal Haqadmoni*, trans. R. Loewe (Oxford: Littman Library, 2004), Vol. 1, p.12.
4. Gershom Scholem, *Major Trends in Jewish Mysticism* (New York: Schocken Books, 1995), p.202, citing the Zohar.
5. Stephen Gilman, *The Spain of Fernando de Rojas* (Princeton, NJ: Princeton University Press, 1972), pp.28, 45. See also Cecil Roth, *The Jewish Contribution to Civilization* (Cincinnati, OH: Union of American Hebrew Congregations, 1940), pp.113, 114. The *Encylopaedia Judaica*, Vol. 15, p.1206, reports that it was de Rojas's father-in-law who was burnt at the stake. Fernando de Rojas's *La Celestina*, edited by Miguel Marciales, 2 vols (Urbana and Chicago, IL: University of Illinois Press, 1985).

6. Nepaulsingh, *Apples of Gold in Filigrees of Silver*, p.24.
7. Fernando de Rojas, *The Spanish Bawd*, trans. J.M. Cohen (London: Penguin Books, 1964), pp.13, 16.
8. Pamela Howard, *La Celestina*, quoted in the *Jewish Quarterly*, 186 (2002), p.42.
9. *Los Amores de Clareo y Florisea*, Atlas, Biblioteca de Autores Espanoles, 3 (Madrid, 1944), pp.432–68. Nepaulsingh, *Apples of Gold in Filigrees of Silver* pp.30–4, 141.
10. That no less than five of Cervantes's immediate family were doctors has been said by some to add to the possibility that he too was a *converso*, and indeed some authoritative historians assert that he was. A. Castro, *El Real Monasterio de Santa Clara de Palencia y los Enriquez, Almirantes de Castilla* (Valladolid: Sever-Cuesta, 1982), p.595.
11. Miguel de Cervantes, *The Adventures of Don Quixote*, trans. J.M. Cohen (London: Penguin Books, 1954), p.76. And do read Maria Rosa Menocal's marvellous book, *The Ornament of the World* (New York: Little, Brown & Co, 2002). Her insights into the *converso* subtext are on p.256–65.
12. H. Ecker, *Caliphs and Kings: The Art and Influence of Islamic Spain* (Washington, DC: Arthur M. Sackler Gallery, Smithsonian Institution; New York: Hispanic Society of America, 2004), p.12.
13. *The Sephardic Journey 1492–1992*, exhibition catalogue (New York: Yeshiva University Museum, 1992), p.166. On page 160 we read another of these profound and bittersweet catchphrases: 'En este mundo sufrimos porké somos Djidiós. En el otro sufriremos porké no fuemos Djidiós' (In this world we suffer because we are Jews. In the next we will suffer because we were not Jewish [enough]).
14. A. Felton, *Jewish Carpets* (Woodbridge: Antique Collectors Club, 1997), p.142. In 1839 the Jews of Mashhad, a prolific carpet weaving region in north-eastern Iran, faced with the choice between being torn to pieces by wild dogs or converting to Islam, duly converted. Called 'New Muslims', by the end of the nineteenth century many had fled from Mashhad. The remainder (excluding those who had intermarried with Muslims and abandoned practising Judaism in secret), immigrated mainly to Jerusalem in the 1950s. I have not traced any discreet Judaic symbols or Hebrew micro writing on any Mashadi carpet, but in the days of the Shah a London-based Mashhadi carpet dealer told me that such secret motifs would be concealed in *mizrach* and other ritual weavings.
15. Bosch is thought by some to have been a secret dualist heretic himself. Almost all the great artists of the Renaissance incorporated multiple meanings into their art. Lynda Harris, *The Secret Heresy of Hieronymus Bosch* (Edinburgh: Flons Books, 1995).
16. Renée Levine Melammed, *Heretics or Daughters of Israel* (Oxford: Oxford University Press, 1999), pp.79–80.
17. Ibid., p.73, citing Simha Asaf, 'The Marranos of Spain and Portugal in Responsa Literature', *Me'assef Zion*, 5 (1932–33), p.21, n.4 [Hebrew].
18. It puts me in mind of the scene in *Fiddler on the Roof* when the rabbi, asked if there was a proper benediction for the czar, in a loud sing-song voice chants 'May the Lord Bless and Keep the Czar', and then, after a pause, whispers 'far away from here.'

PART 4

THE SYMBOLS

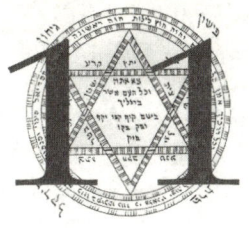

Symbols

Pictorial symbols – rather like words which also are symbols for things and thoughts, people and places – mean different things in different cultures. There is not a single culture without its own symbols, for the human mind needs its images. Pictorial symbols sort us out into cohesive groups, with shared non-verbal understandings, for words often fail to articulate the deep truths of consciousness and distort and corrupt what we are struggling to convey. Symbols, as simplified pictures, convey far more than the obvious meaning of the images they represent, and are the product of two separate elements: the concrete form and the abstract concept.[1] Moreover, as we see in the great Christian symbol of the cross, the abstraction may be the reverse of the concrete, for the very instrument of Christ's suffering and death is identified with a salvation and an eternal life previously unavailable to humanity. One symbol, saving a thousand words, offers us a non-intellectual language, somewhat akin to music and higher mathematics, in that it yields connections, insights and experiences that otherwise might well be beyond our understanding. In the mystical symbol, the infinite shines through the finite, for the Almighty lives outside the safety of speech. Take Ot, the Hebrew word for an alphabetical letter: it also means a sign, but more than that, it signifies – very specifically – a visible token of the mystical relationship between God and man, holding our memories, our values and our dreams, condensing knowledge and expanding awareness. Instantly we understand symbols – or not at all.

Whilst many of their origins are to be found in Babylonian, Canaanite, Greek and Roman cultures, most Jewish symbols evolved through profound historical experiences in response to real need, and over time, stretching from the biblical period to the present day. The loss of statehood and the destruction of the Temple in 70 CE changed the spiritual focus of Judaism. The surviving priesthood, with all their substantial liturgy and ritual, now no longer able to serve in the tangible Temple in Jerusalem, replaced it with abstractions, with visions flowing from Ezekiel 1, of heavenly palaces, of the throne of glory and of the divine chariot. Judaism moved from the natural to the spiritual and prophetic – elements best expressed in allegorical and symbolic terms. Now exiled from the Temple, the Jews exchanged its substance for its form, the real for the ideal. Old rituals were allegorized through the use of symbols into new meanings – religious, social, ethical – so giving hope and purpose amidst the degradation and dangers of life in exile.

Some of those symbols have survived to this day. The best example of this is the menorah (the seven-branched candelabra primarily symbolizing the light the Almighty shines on the world), which became the paramount and pre-eminent Jewish symbol only after the Roman army, having destroyed the Temple, carried its Golden Menorah in triumph to Rome (Figure 26). Prior to that time the menorah, being then a cultic vessel in the Temple, was not the symbol that it subsequently became.[2] But now, in the absence of the physical object, the Jews preserved and perpetuated the menorah's meaning and memory through its pictorial image, from then onwards to be seen carved, cast, sculpted, stamped, moulded, embossed, embroidered, printed, painted, woven and manifested in and on Jewish art, artefact and architecture everywhere.

Another example is the Tablets of the Law (the Ten Commandments). Initially depicted as two rectangular stones, then as scrolls, they first appeared in their present form – two connected oblong round-topped tablets – in the eleventh century. Strangely, they often serve at one and the same time both as sacred symbols in Christianity and as marks of Cain, to be worn as a discriminatory badge on the outer clothing of all adult Jews. In 1217 CE Henry III of England ordered that this badge be made of yellow material. Its purpose was to segregate and humiliate – but the Ten Commandments cannot thus be sullied. The stigmata of suffering became the badge of pride and appeared in synagogue decor, prayer books, Ark curtains and carpets. By the sixteenth century it had become a sacred Jewish symbol. This was a perfect example of inward assimilation – the adoption of an element from the host culture, which is then transformed for Jewish purposes. Another example of this process is to be seen in the Jewish hat. Basically it was a simple cone which Jews and Christians had to wear in Muslim lands as a sign of their inferiority and separateness. It had been introduced into Muslim Spain and, suitably amended, continued in Christian Spain. We can see this in Alfonso X of Castile's book, *Las Cantigas*. But soon we see Jewish illuminated manuscripts portraying Jews wearing those hats, now in the privacy of their homes and synagogues, and so freely incorporating them into Jewish culture.

Symbols have lives of their own. Few today seeing the Star of David and the crescent moon would have any doubt as to which of those two images meant what to whom. But go back awhile, not only to the Middle Ages but also to the Sasanian era, or even prior to the third century, when according to the eminent authority Daniel Friedenburg the device of the crescent moon and the star were identified as standing for Jews.[3] A good example of this use is to be seen on the seal of the Regensburg community of 1356. It is interesting to see a parallelism here. At the time that Jewish culture was focusing increasingly on the star so Islamic culture was focusing increasingly on the crescent as its prime symbol, with the five-pointed Seal of Solomon or the six-pointed emblem on David's shield as images of potent magic.

When the Vizcaya carpet with its complex imagery was woven in the fifteenth century, Jewish symbols were undergoing a profound change. The surging tide of anti-Semitism and the pogroms had triggered off two powerful and interrelated imperatives, impacting on the Jews and the use and meanings of their symbols.

The first imperative was the increasing need to give iconographic expression to the hope, the expectation, of messianic redemption. It is difficult, perhaps impossible, for us today to have any true understanding of the meaning and therefore the value and impact of these spiritual symbols for the Jews of Spain. For Here and Now can never be There and Then. Our thinking and our senses are so dominated by language and by the self-serving axioms of logic, we often fail to understand that another person's truth may to him be so profoundly self-evident that words and logic, as tools to reach out to truth, are not only irrelevant, but may also be positively unhelpful.[4] Clever-clever word play may scorn mysticism as sentiment that starts in a mist and ends with a schism, but there are intellectual, sensual and spiritual experiences neither founded in nor capable of articulation in language. It is hard for us today to see beyond the exoteric reality of our world and to sense the esoteric actuality as a gradation of emanations and vibrations.[5] Perhaps it is easier for us to think about what it must have been like for many in fifteenth-century Spain, with the very air heavy with the expectation of massacre and martyrdom, than it is for us to have the slightest understanding of the instant and profound certitude provided by these symbols. The more imminent the danger of exposure, the more vile, pitiful and savage became the reality of the *conversos*' existence, and consequently the more concrete and exact the meanings of their symbols. The more radiant their confidence in Divine deliverance, the greater grew their need for its symbolic representation.

Earlier magical traditions which featured the use of amulets with magical triangles, squares, rectangles, the Star of David, the menorah, birds and animals were revived and merged into Kabbalistic practices. New life was breathed into ancient symbols, striking the Kabbalist with that intimate vivacity of the instant and of that sense sublime, sometimes illumined through the metaphors of poetry, music and mathematics.

But with the greater need for the power and protection provided by the symbols came the reciprocal – and dire – need for those symbols to conceal the true beliefs of the *conversos*. Failure to do so ensured a constricted and lessened life or, by the fifteenth century, the possibility of dreadful torture relieved only by death. Surely cooking people alive over a deliberately slow fire must be the very worst death devised by man for his fellow creatures. So it was that the covert and cryptic nature of the imagery in the Vizcaya carpet, with its powerful Kabbalistic messages to the Jew, had to appear to others as nothing more than standard Christian symbols or bland decorative devices. By these means they communicated the esoteric through the exoteric, and the personal remained private – albeit paraded in public.

This paradoxical tension in the discreet symbols of persecuted minorities is common – and the more so where the majority and the minority group, sharing a common ancestor, also share many symbols. The migration of symbols, a process in which the same form is taken up by a different culture and endowed with a new meaning, is common. For example, many Christian symbols, which have their roots in Parthian and Syrian cosmologies, were taken up as Roman and Byzantine religious motifs and then in the fifth and sixth centuries converted to use in Christianity. So it was that ancient gods become saints, winged Victories become angels and magical powers become Divine Providence.[6] Even the cross itself, today the premier symbol of Christianity, only began to appear as such in the late fourth century and then with arms of equal length to the modern Roman cross, the subsequent sophistications finally superseding it from the seventh century. Prior to that time the early Christians, a persecuted minority, had used the outline of a fish as their major symbol. Fish in Greek is *ichthys*, which forms an acrostic: 'Jesus Christ, Son of God'. The symbol was simple to draw and would be used as a password or card of identity. So, if two strangers met, not knowing if the other was a Christian or not, one would draw an arc and the other would then draw the reverse arc – so forming the outline of *ichthys*.

In Judaism, where almost everything is an expression of an inner and ancient belief in the forces of the Infinite, symbols are profoundly meaningful representations of a connection to Him. In turn, Judaism's offspring, Christianity and Islam, inherited and reinterpreted both the Hebrew Bible and some Jewish symbols. But there is a major point to repeat here: in no way did that process of parturition deprive or debar the mother religion from continuing to use and to develop her own symbols, reflecting on and responding to them through her own eyes – and not through the varying viewpoints of her heretical offspring.

It is commonplace for discriminated minorities to assume the colouration of conformity with the culture of the majority, while holding on, in their private lives, to their own traditions and symbols. They develop discreet cards of identity, code words, handshakes, phrases, signs and symbols, all conveying one meaning to their own inner group and another meaning to the outer group. So it was that many *conversos* made covert their earlier overt religious and cultural practices such as keeping the Sabbath and the dietary laws. A common fifteenth-century catchphrase of the Jews of Spain, 'Djudio savi lo ke otros no tienin ni la idea' (Jews know things that others have no idea of), expressed the culture of secrecy and perhaps, too, something of intellectual elitism.

Biblical and Talmudic authority could not hold more strongly that the preservation of life is the primary imperative. There is not one law in Judaism (apart from the embargoes against idolatry, adultery and murder) that may not be broken to save a life. Maimonides, in his Epistle on Martyrdom, had ruled that to save a life one may, as a temporary expedient, overtly convert to Islam so long as one continued privately with the practices and the prayers of Judaism. The Jews of Spain maintained their symbols, the vital outer expressions of their inner lives, discreetly and in forms that would be meaningless to the outside world. As the great folklorist, Barbara Kirshenblatt-Gimblett made clear:

> although there are many similarities between the outward appearance of Jewish artefacts and that of the decorative traditions of the larger society, the cultural meaning and signifying power of forms differ. Whereas external similarities in form are testimony to the vigorous and creative interaction of Jews with their environment, the internal differences in meaning reveal the independence and vitality of Jewish tradition.[7]

We see the same use of covert Jewish symbols in fourteenth-century Germany. In his study of the white roosters (symbols of wisdom and redemption: Chapter 15) appearing on Jewish seals, L. Rahmani writes that they were 'to express thoughts, which were to remain hidden to the hostile Christians, but clear enough to fellow Jews ... It is perhaps in keeping with these concepts that the cock was again depicted on armorial devices by Italian Jews from the seventeenth century onwards.'[8]

We see the same phenomenon in Christianity where, in recording the adaptation of Christian craftsmen to the Muslim conquest of Egypt in 641 CE, Ludmila Kybalova reports: 'As a protection against persecution, Christian themes had to be disguised in symbolic and ornamental compositions in which pure form, colour, and composition overwhelmed all other values', adding later: 'the motif was popular among the Copts for several reasons ... It was also useful for concealing the Christian symbols, which the Copts had learned to camouflage, in terms of oppression in apparently abstract compositions.'[9]

We see similar endorsements in some of the Christian (Armenian) carpets where the Armenian letters S or E, or a particular cruciform, representing the Father or the Son, so conveys a sense of divine vision.

Earlier in Christianity, St Paul, a recent convert himself and under attack for accepting Christianity, eloquently advises his fellow converts in the art of such concealment:

> To the Jews I became as a Jew, in order to win Jews; to those under the Law I became as one under the Law – though not being myself under the Law – that I might win those under the Law. To those outside the Law I became as one outside the Law – not being without Law toward God but under the Law of Christ – that I might win those outside the

Law. To the weak I became weak, that I might win the weak. I became all things to all men that I might by all means save some. (1 Corinthians 9:20–3.)

A hundred or so years after the Vizcaya carpet was woven, the same phenomenon was to be found in England and much of north-western Europe where, following the Reformation and the Counter-Reformation, countless Catholics spent their lives pretending to be Protestants, and countless Protestants spent their lives pretending to be Catholics – each, too, with their own secret signs, symbols and phrases. There is a similar practice in the Islamic doctrine of *taqiyya* (more familiar among the Shi'a) which enables Muslims in the face of persecution to conceal their faith so long as its central private core is maintained. The critical point is that the same gesture, the same handshake, the same text and the same symbol may well all mean different things to different people.

But one must (as ever) be cautious. In the same way that artefacts initially taken for Christian or Muslim may in fact be Judaic, so items initially seen to be Jewish may possibly not be so. Take the fourteenth-century Spanish salt or spice dish in Figure 27. At first sight, displaying as it does the Star of David and Hand of God, surely it could not be anything other than Jewish? But we are told (for reasons that are not entirely clear to me) such is not the case. *Convivencia*, a splendid catalogue of the marvellous Jewish Museum of New York, in attributing a Muslim origin to this dish, makes the point fundamental to our theme: 'the *Convivencia* of different cultures led to different interpretations of the same symbols'.[10] It is with this in mind that we consider a thirteenth-century Hebrew Bible displaying the coat of arms of the united Kingdom of Castile and Leon, which incorporates two elegant hexagrams.[11] In that context, albeit inside a Hebrew Bible, the six-pointed stars are elements in the royal coat of arms and so are not Jewish symbols. Moreover when I saw the Stars of David carved on the pulpit in the old private chapel of the kings and queens of England in Buckingham Palace (the chapel was destroyed in the Blitz in 1940), albeit (I must confess) momentarily tempted, there was in truth no need to enquire further (Figure 28)! Clearly we look to the context. So, for example, the hexagram framing an elephant in the Duke of Suffolk's fourteen-century Pentateuch is a Star of David because it appears without any contraindications in a Jewish religious book.[12] But it is not always as simple as that. Sometimes the difference rests, as adjudged by Oleg Grabar, the eminent art historian, in 'the interplay between (visually perceptible) features and a feature that is less easy to comprehend, the mind of the beholder'.[13]

By the twentieth century, the emphasis of symbols had changed. As a result of the advances in medicine, a safer social environment, the iconoclasm of the Protestant Reformation and the general decline in the power of religion, many Jewish symbols – once instruments essential for communing with the Almighty – fell into desuetude, and others, losing much of their mystic, prophylactic and apotropaic strengths, evolved into secular or synagogue badges of identity. But as some symbols die, others are born. The Tower of David, the ancient structure guarding the entrance to Jerusalem, which emerged slowly as a symbol over the seventeenth and eighteenth centuries, is today widely recognized as a Jewish symbol of strength and independence, appearing on countless ceremonial and decorative objects, postage stamps, souvenirs and carpets.

Rarely does hindsight yield 20/20 vision – often enough we cannot see in the same way what was seen in times gone by, for our sight is distorted by the lenses of our own experiences and perceptions. But in the chapters that follow, let us try to take a fresh look at each of the significant symbols on the Vizcaya carpet, no longer in the context of today's Christian, Muslim or secular culture but as they would have been seen by, and as what they would have meant to, a family of New Christians, be they humble weavers or noble grandees, in those dire days some five hundred-odd years ago. Let us reach out and sense how these Jewish symbols would stir the hearts and minds of Jews pretending or trying to be Christians: how a glimpse of the symbols would inspire and connect them for a moment to that which is beyond us all.

NOTES

1. Roland Barthes, *Mythologies*, trans. A Lavers (New York: Hill & Wang, 1972), pp.112–13.
2. Victor Klagsbald, 'The Menorah as Symbols: Its Meaning and Origin in Early Jewish Art', *Jewish Art*, 12–13 (1986–87), pp.126–34. Klagsbald, comparing the only four known representations of the menorah prior to 70 CE to the hundreds of such representations in the late Roman and Byzantine eras, holds that while it was a significant symbol, it only became a universally accepted Jewish symbol after the destruction of the Temple. The

earliest of these four representations, appearing on a coin of Mattathias Antigonus (r. 40–37 BCE), suggests that its use as a symbol began only in the last period of the Second Temple.

3. Daniel Friedenberg, *Sasanian Jewry and its Culture* (Champaign, IL: University of Illinois Press, 2009), p.47, and in personal communications with Dr Friedenberg. On p.46 in his fascinating book a seal is illustrated. The Hebrew of the top reveals the owner's name, Jonah, and below the reclining lion in the middle we see the Star of David and the crescent moon. The star and the crescent appear together on many Ibero-Roman headstones, particularly in the Burgos and Leon regions: H.S. Jacob, *Idealism and Realism* (Leiden: Brill, 1954), p.167. Given that the conjunction of the star and crescent was recognized in the later Middle Ages as standing for Jews, and given that the Ibero-Roman period predated Islam and early Christianity, I wondered at the possibility that this use of the star – albeit in conjunction with the crescent – was an example of its very early use on those headstones as an Iberian Jewish symbol.

4. It's odd really. The opinion that no truth exists save those proven by the methodology of science is an assumption which cannot be proved by the very methodology which it claims is the only way to arrive at the truth. The beliefs of the atheist and the deist have much in common – both are acts of faith incapable ultimately either of proof or disproof within the quite limited terms of science and logic.

5. Albeit that science today joins in to tell us that nothing is what it seems to be. Now it is saying that our exoteric reality is just a chimera because virtually every single thing in our world – our solids, liquids and gases – are but billions upon billions of different types of ever-moving electro-magnetic waves. And we have no way of determining where or how they move. This 'indeterminacy' in respect of atomic and subatomic interactions surely puts an end to the deterministic classical conditions of proof, of experimental verification.

6. Anne Marie Stauffer, *Textiles of Late Antiquity* (New York: Metropolitan Museum of Art, 1995), p.11.

7. Barbara Kirshenblatt-Gimblett, *Fabric of Jewish Life* (New York: The Jewish Museum, 1977), p.37.

8. L.Y. Rahmani, 'Three Desk Seals in the Jewish Museum, London', *Jewish Art*, 19–20 (1993–94), p.160. Note A cites D. Friedenberg, *Medieval Jewish Seals from Europe* (Detroit, MI: Wayne State University, 1987), Nos. 82, 90, 91 and 100.

9. Ludmila Kybalova, *Coptic Textiles* (London: Paul Hamlyn, 1967), pp.14, 117.

10. V. Mann, T. Glick and J. Dodds (eds), *'Convivencia', Jews, Muslims and Christians in Medieval Spain* (New York: George Braziller in conjunction with the Jewish Museum, 1992), Mariá Paz Soler Ferrer, p.227.

11. *The Cervera Bible*, Biblioteca Nacional, Lisbon, MS IL.72, folio 7.

12. British Library, MS. Add. 15282.

13. Oleg Grabar, *The Formation of Islamic Art* (New Haven, CT and London: Yale University Press, 1987), p.5, and Kirshenblatt-Gimblett, *Fabric of Jewish Life*, p.37. Some say that a symbol or any object may somehow retain something of all the attention that has been focused on

it, an aura, a patina flowing from centuries of love and reverence by thousands of admirers surrounding the symbol or the object. This is surely a chimera; the only reality is in the heart and the mind of the viewer.

12

The Star of David

To understand the values of the star (as with any symbol) we turn to its history – which in this case is complex and contentious. We do not really know when the symbolic meanings attributed by a small number of people to a device had increased to the point that there was a sufficiently enlarged consensus as to the values of the sign to enable it to be called a cultural symbol. Symbols evolve out of need over time and not necessarily gradually and incrementally.

Jewish symbols were often influenced by changeable host cultures, and our knowledge of their origins, particularly of the star, is limited by the paucity of examples prior to the tenth century; for it is in the nature of Jewish history, with its massacres and migrations, that usually little trace of that history survives. This, in turn, leads on to another problem, for often enough we do not know whether a single surviving example of the hexagram is Jewish or not. The custom of only making such an attribution where it is linked to Hebrew writing or (but not invariably) another Jewish symbol may be academically correct – but it may also miss the whole picture. Then there is, too, a certain reluctance on the part of some scholars to agree a subject to be Judaic unless either it has abundantly clear biblical or Talmudic authority (which, given the danger of star worship among the early Israelites, is virtually non-existent) or is so accepted by such an overwhelming number of people that the extensive evidence of its prior use can no longer be ignored. It is this latter point I address in this chapter.

There is another problem, too, in that sometimes we cannot tell whether such an early surviving example of the star, albeit from a Judaic context, was an aberrant one-off decorative device or the sole survivor out of thousands of representatives of the symbol. Finally, there is a particular problem in taking a fresh look at the Stars of David in the Vizcaya carpet, due to a quite erroneous but common impression that having been taken up as a magical symbol or decorative device in Christianity and Islam meant it had been taken away from and had departed from Judaism.

Given that the Vizcaya carpet with its significant stars was woven in the fifteenth century and given that many scholars seem now to agree the star had become a recognized Jewish symbol by that time, arguably its history prior to that time is perhaps only of peripheral relevance to our theme. But the story of the star's epicene evolution from an ancient but relatively minor symbol was subtle, but consistent, and of interest because it demonstrates the endurance and power of the Jewish symbols.

Stars. Our world is governed by endless change and uncertainty as we are born, grow, reproduce, die and decay. For early man, living in an ephemeral, transient world, only the celestial bodies – as manifestations of cosmic order – offered timeless stability. The stars have seemed ever to hold all the answers to the mysteries of life and as instruments of divine revelation are deeply rooted in Judaism. That stars, essential directional guides for the nomad and the traveller, also appear in Celtic, Roman, Byzantine, Christian, Nabatean, Persian and Syrian cultures, does not detract from their role in Jewish culture since different cultures, while sharing the same symbols, will interpret them variously. Right from the beginning, Abraham enters into his covenant with God who tells him: 'I will multiply your descendants as the stars of heaven' (Genesis 22:17); Jacob blesses his twelve sons, who are linked in later exegesis to the twelve constellations of the zodiac. The Psalms and the Book of Job repeatedly refer to celestial phenomena and the astrological tradition continues in the later books of the Wisdom of Solomon, of Daniel, of Baruch and of Enoch. Amos (5:26) tells us that during the forty years in the wilderness the Israelites did not sacrifice to the Lord, but carried 'the star of your god, which you made yourselves'. Is it possible this was a five- or six-pointed star? In the fourth book of the Maccabees (a philosophical rather than a historical work owing far more to Graeco-Roman than to Jewish tradition), the martyrs of the persecution preceding the revolt of 168 BCE are promised that they will be transformed into astral bodies.

In the Second Temple period (515 BCE–70 CE), the heavenly bodies were seen as symbolic of the cosmos. The Greek Theophrastus (372–288 BCE) described the Jews as 'a race of philosophers, they converse with each other about the divinity, and during the night they view the stars, turning their eyes to them and invoking their God with prayers'.[1]

Then Tacitus, the anti-Jewish first-century-CE Roman historian, confusing his culture with that of the Jews, believed the planet Saturn to be the god of the Israelites.[2] For Saturn, as the seventh heavenly body, was allied to the seventh day of creation, and Saturday (originally Saturn's day) is still for Jews today the seventh day of the week, the day of rest.[3] Saturn also played its part in the cosmic creation of the celestial Star of David; according to some ancient philosophers and astrologers, one of the most important events in the universe occurs every twenty years when, in the cycle of the coordinates, Saturn and Jupiter are directly opposite each other – the hexagram, a sort of heavenly Star of David, is created.[4]

There are many views as to the origin of the six-pointed star – the number six has particular messianic significances. Some relate it to the Pythagorean tetractys;[5] others take it to be the ground plan for the campsite of the ancient Israelites during their wanderings in the wilderness – an interesting idea, for each of the six external equilateral triangles, if bisected, demarcate twelve locations, each equidistant from the centrally located tabernacle, a positioning that would have made it difficult for outsiders (or indeed for any of the tribes of Israel) to steal away with the Tablets of the Law. Still others, drawing a circle around the six external points and creating six inwardly facing triangles and six outwardly facing locations, also suggest the twelve separate locations were attributed to each of the twelve tribes. Then there are those who see the star's origin in nature, and it does look remarkably like the female flower of the date palm; there are yet others who see it as a schematic representation of the six-petalled fleur de lis. To support this last possibility, in a micrographic expression of Psalm 104 drawn in fifteenth-century Yemen, we see both symbols coming together with a fleur de lis placed over the Star of David.

Implicit in the six outer points is an external circle – a culturally universal symbol, its perfect form everlastingly turning and returning to its original point. The pure, abstract geometry of the Star of David makes it an amazingly good sign, with the two triangles encapsulating a coming together of opposites – male and female, fire and water, wet and dry, hot and cold. It is the power of all opposites, of thesis and of antithesis, subordinated to the principle of unity, which bring about a sense of transcendental synthesis underlying and overarching all things.

But the star's ascent as a Jewish symbol was far from straightforward. In

Deuteronomy 4:19 Moses had warned the Israelites against star worship: 'And beware lest you lift up your eyes to the heavens. And when you see the sun and the moon and the stars, all the hosts of heaven, you be drawn away and worship them and serve them.' In the seventh century BCE, Josiah vigorously suppressed star worship[6] and the Talmud laid down that Israel needs no guiding star, for God alone guides her.[7] Yet the ancient and medieval Jewish belief, that each and every one of us is accompanied by a star that governs our existence, survived.[8] Moreover, it thrived, for the second- or third-century mystical book the *Sefer Yetzirah* (The Book of Creation), recording astrology's strong role in Jewish cosmology, was a major influence on the medieval Kabbalists of Spain and on their Jewish astrologers who in the fourteenth and fifteenth centuries attended the courts of the kings of Castile and Aragon.

It is with timeless bittersweet humour that the poet/philosopher Abraham ibn Ezra (b. Spain 1089–d. 1164) highlighted the central dilemma of astrology:[9]

> The planets and spheres in their stations
> Changed their order when I first drew breath
> If I were a seller of lamps
> The sun would not set 'till after my death.
> The stars in my heaven have ruined my life
> I cannot succeed however I strive
> If I were to be a seller of shrouds,
> No one would die while I was alive.

The struggle against this common belief continued, for any reliance on astrological predetermination diminishes our freedom to choose between good and evil. This absolute difference between predestination and free will was seemingly resolved by rabbinical compromise. On the one hand, stars were held to be determinants in human affairs. But on the other hand, stars were also considered creations of the Almighty, and as such (see Judges 5:20), subject to His will – so a man's good deeds and piety might alter his original astrological destiny. Thus, it seemed, did free will triumph. And in the apocryphal Book of Jubilees, Abram (Abraham), who had been sitting out at night gazing up at the stars in an attempt to forecast the arrival of the critically important rainfall, finally says: 'All the signs of the stars and the signs of the moon and the sun are all in the hands of our Lord.'

And even today we still hear echoes of the belief that our fates are written in the stars in the congratulatory phrase *Mazal tov*, which literally means 'Good Constellation'. Stars have a part to play in Judaism, for only when three stars are to be seen in the sky has the Sabbath ended and a new week begun.

Perhaps the earliest origins of the Star of David (its hexagram shape formed by two triangles) may be seen in the use of triangles in the Israelite imaging of the Bronze Age. Incised in an unusual eighth-century-BCE sherd excavated in Jerusalem we see two humanoid deity figures formed by triangles; the male figure (essentially one inverted triangle) and the female figure (essentially one upright and one inverted triangle) are thought by some to represent Yahweh and Asherah. Given the widespread religious dualism of the time as expressed through opposing triangles, do we perhaps see in this coming together, the very first signs of the Star of David?

The symbols of the six-pointed hexagram and the five-pointed pentagram appeared quite commonly on seals, jars and pots found throughout the Near East. One particular jar embellished with pentagrams was used for holding oil and, dated to the fifth century BCE, may even have belonged to the treasury of the Temple in Jerusalem.[10] Indeed, the eminent folklorist Shalom Sabar of the Hebrew University of Jerusalem notes the possibility that the hexagram served as a symbol of the Temple at an early stage in its development.[11] Archaeology has revealed more stamped jar handles of the third century BCE with the pentagram – then probably the symbol of the high priest – with the letters for Jerusalem between its axes. Also Alexander Yannai (103–76 BCE), king of Judea and high priest, attempting to please both devout Pharisees and his more Hellenistically inclined subjects, issued a coin of choice. On one side, the inverted anchor reproduced the royal emblem of the Seleucids to emphasize the legitimacy of their Hasmonean successors, while on the other, Hebrew script surrounded the symbol of an eight-rayed star. During the Hasmonean period (167–37 BCE), strict adherence to the Second Commandment precluded the use of the ruler's portrait, but among the motifs and emblems used on coins, including wreaths, pomegranates (Chapter 14), the Temple façade and menorot (Chapter 13), stars are to be found. Herod the Great (73–4 BCE), in an effort to project himself as a heroic monarch, had a six-rayed star represented on his largest bronze coin. It also appears on lamps: for example, in the first-century-BCE lamp found in Jerash.[12]

In late Roman and Byzantine times, the hexagram was clearly associated with Judaism for it appears on lamps alongside the menorah,[13] on the wall of a catacomb and on bread stamps. In literature (according to Gershom Scholem), Flavius Josephus, the Roman Jewish historian of the first century CE, attested to the ancient Jewish legend about King Solomon's magic ring – known as the Seal of Solomon.[14] Originally it only bore the ineffable name of God but some time later, before the sixth century, it was inscribed with the hexagram or the pentagram. In the synagogues a particularly pleasing one was carved in a basalt stone arch of the third- or fourth-century synagogue at Khirbat Shura in the Galilee region. Sometimes the Jewish linkage is less certain, as with a beautiful Star of David on a fourth-century-CE fluted bowl found among the treasures of a Roman site at Mildenhall in England.[15] But what seems reasonably certain is that whatever the appearance or meaning of the star might have been in other cultures, it has appeared far too often in Jewish history, from early times to the Middle Ages, for it not to be considered an enduring and widespread, albeit minor, Jewish symbol. As a symbol without any biblical and little Talmudic authority its appearances have too often been written off either as superstitious or meaningless decorative devices. Too often yesterday's derided superstition is today's orthodoxy, and the incorporation of profoundly and widely held beliefs of the masses in supernatural powers and processes, and their accompanying symbolism, into orthodoxy points strongly to the prevalence and permanence of those beliefs prior to such incorporation.

The Hebrew word for the hexagram shape is Magen David, literally, 'Shield of David' or 'Defence' or 'Defender of David'. In a similar context, the Shield of Abraham is recited in a contemporary prayer (the *Amidah* prayer) which had first been written down in the second to fourth centuries CE. But the customary translation of Magen David is 'Star of David', and both words (shield and star) come together in the belief that the Star of David was indeed his star, for it was the symbol he had emblazoned on his shield. Its form took the first and last letters of his name, both Ds which, in tenth-century-BCE Hebrew (variously), in ninth-century-BCE Moabite (clearly) and later in the Greek alphabet are represented by equilateral triangles and which, placed inversely on top of each other, formed his star.

There is, too, a metaphoric meaning as an appellation of the Almighty in Genesis 15:1, where He is described as the *Magen* – for it is He who is our ultimate shield and protector and it is the protective purpose of the shield which propelled the sign forward. Then, in the Psalms, which are attributed to David (18:35), God is likened unto a shield. The same theme of the

Almighty as a shield is taken up by Ibn Gabirol (c.1021–c.1056), one of the greatest of the Sephardi philosopher poets:

> Thou, Lord, did shelter all my yesterdays,
> My morrows shelter – shelter me today:
> Thee, Thee alone against the world's forays
> I own my Shield – Lord, brook no more delay.[16]

Originally, Jewish seals, being mainly on signet rings (hence the name of such rings), were engraved with individual signs and used to identify and so protect the ownership of property. The seals then became invested with magical powers to safeguard what they identified – so that the protective imagery actually functioned as a protective shield. They each did the same job – the seal protected the property, the shield protected the person. From Roman times onwards purses would often be fastened tight with two seals. One would denote the sum of money it contained, the other the identity of the owners or of the official who had checked the contents. At the same time the supernatural aspect of the star was not to be denied and from the third to the eighth centuries it was to be seen in the central position of many of the mystical incantation bowls.

Judaism, then Christianity and later Islam, reinterpreted the biblical account of King Solomon and attributed and renamed these signs (whether five-, six- and eight-pointed forms, double-knots forms or seals or shield shapes) as the Seal of Solomon or the Shield of David. Solomon himself, a complex and deeply flawed character in Judaism, is mythologized in Christianity and Islam into a major figure, the perfect monarch, a king who would summon up magical forces to build great palaces where, sitting in judgement on an incredible throne, he dispensed perfect justice to all. This was quite an attractive idea for both ruler and ruled in the medieval world, bringing a sense of order and purpose to confront the chaos and cruelty of life. Shalom Sabar, with typical eloquence sums it up:

> The Muslims tied the authority of their rule to the image of Solomon: his seal became the symbol of wisdom, of mastery over the forces of nature and society, of the recreation of the cosmological order by means of correct administration, of the efficient use of natural resources, of ethical leadership and justice, of peace between all creatures and with the animals, and of the health of mind and body.[17]

By the Middle Ages, what had been for many an ancient amuletic talisman offering protection against evil spirits, as a result of its increasing attribution as the five-pointed Seal of Solomon or the six-pointed emblem on David's shield became major and most potent magic symbols in Islam and lesser symbols in Christianity.[18] The two host cultures' responses to the signs (albeit with a far greater emphasis on the magical component than in Judaism) were welcomed by many Jews, since stars harked back to their ancient traditions. And now, reinvigorated through their wide use in Islam and in the magical tradition in Christianity, stars regained their traditional strength for Jews as a symbol connecting them to the protective power of the Almighty. From the twelfth century onwards, astral magic appeared increasingly in Jewish thought as a means of harnessing the God-given force of the stars and other celestial elements for protection and healing. That Christians and Muslims for a while also saw the star as a protective talisman did not taint its significance for Jews because their perception of both the source and nature of that protection was quite different.

Circles and stars were also welcomed in part by church and king as marks of Cain to identify and so segregate and humiliate Jews. So it was that Alphonso, IV, king of Portugal (1325–57), decreed that all adult Jews must wear a badge attached to their hats or outer clothing.[19] By 1391, the year of the worst anti-Jewish riots in the Iberian Peninsula, the Portuguese Cortes complained to the king that Jews, no longer wearing their badges, could not be distinguished from Christians. Juan I's response was to decree that all adult Jews must wear the badge, but this time it was a six-pointed star made of red material. Sixty years later a painting by Nuno Goncalves, which features a portrait of the head of the Jewish community of Portugal, was placed above the altar in the church of St Vincent. On the rabbi's robe, just above his heart, we see the identifying Star of David. It is clear that for much of the time from the middle of the fourteenth century to at least the middle of the fifteenth century, all adult Jews in Portugal (the country closest to Spain) had to wear the circle or a star badge on their clothing to identify and segregate them from the rest of society.

The Star of David, albeit without any specific biblical and little Talmudic endorsement, has its part in the age-old history of the Jewish people.[20] But to demonstrate the stage to which the star had evolved when the Vizcaya carpet was woven in the fifteenth century, a more detailed review of some of the earlier and contemporary surviving examples of its use may be helpful. I

30. Two Stars of David, the menorah and the Eternal Light in a child's workbook, tenth century.

31. Stars of David and the menorah, on the Vizcaya carpet.

32. Star of David in an eleventh-century Bible.

33. Star of David in a fifteenth-century Bible from Yemen.

34. Star of David in a signature, Spain, thirteenth century.

35. Star of David in a signature, Barcelona, Middle Ages.

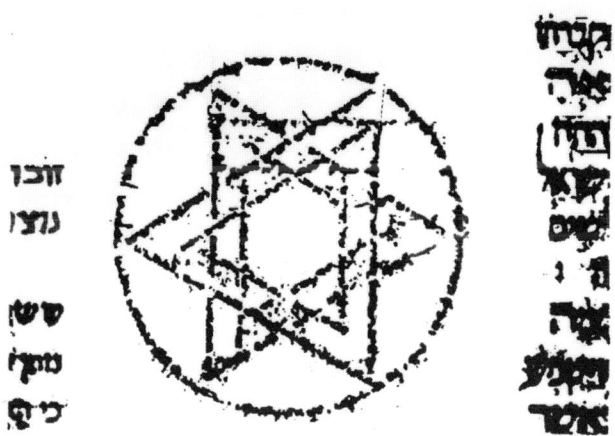

36. Star of David in a Bible, thirteenth–fourteenth century.

37. Star of David in the Golden Haggadah, 1320.

38. Stars of David identifying a Jew's room, thirteenth century.

39. Star of David protecting a rabbit, in a Haggadah, fourteenth century.

13th century London   14th century Switzerland

40. Stars of David on four seals, thirteenth–fourteenth century.

14th century Iraq/Palestine   14th century Germany/France

41 Star of David on a signet ring, early medieval.

42. Star of David in a synagogue window, thirteenth century.

43. Star of David on the flag in the Prague Synagogue, copy of the fifteenth-century flag.

44. Star of David on a mezuzah, fifteenth–sixteenth century.

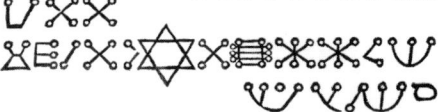

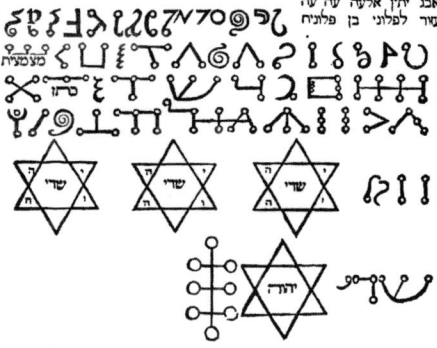

45. Two triangles in a Hebrew script, Spain, fourteenth century.

46. Stars of David in a book of medieval Jewish magic.

47. Star of David in a book of medieval Jewish magic.

48. Stars of David on the teacher's chair, Maimonides, *Guide to the Perplexed*, fourteenth century.

49. Hexagram in the Qur'an, twelfth century.

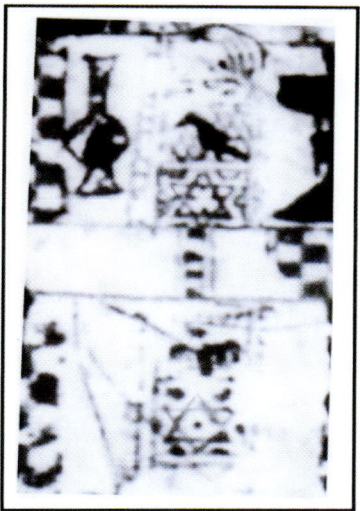

50. Four Stars of David.

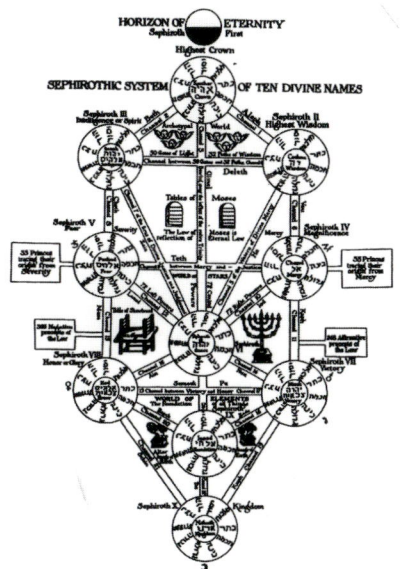

51. Sephirotic tree.

52. Menorot–*Hamsa* on the Vizcaya carpet.

53. The Hand of God in a Haggadah, Germany, thirteenth century.

54. The Hand of God, a ram and sheep in a Haggadah, Spain, fourteenth century.

55. The Hand of God delivering the Tablets of the Law to Moses, in a prayer book, Germany, fifteenth century.

56. A praying figure on the Vizcaya carpet.

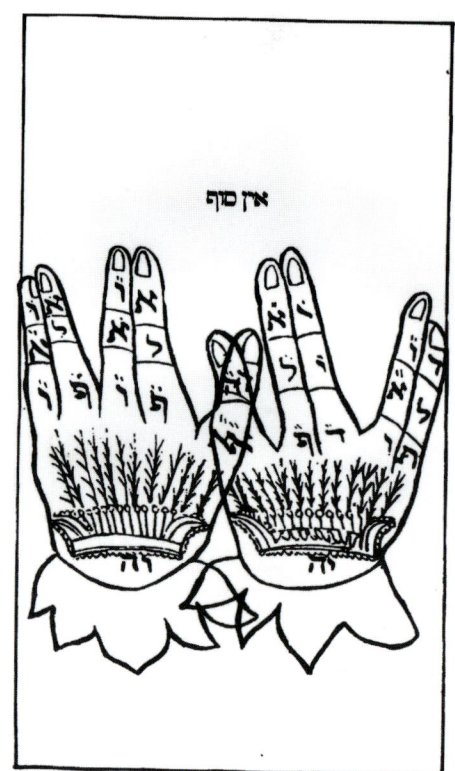

57. Kabbalist Hands.

58. Section of a pomegranate? The Vizcaya carpet.

59. Two peacocks on the Vizcaya carpet.

60. Peacocks, menorah and Temple façade on a magic mirror plaque, Byzantine period.

61. A dove on the Vizcaya carpet.

62. A rooster in a medieval Haggadah.

63. Roosters on the Vizcaya carpet.

64. A goose or duck on the Vizcaya carpet.

65. Demon birds on the Vizcaya carpet.

71. Ark and menorah on a Roman tomb, second–third century.

72. Menorot, Ark, temple instruments and lions in a gold glass base, fourth century.

73. Sephardi carpet, fifteenth–sixteenth century.

apologize for the somewhat repetitious nature of the summary that follows.[21] As a list it is far from exhaustive but exhausting it can be. *Les preuves fatiguent la vérité.*

So when did it all start? How far back do we go? Might it possibly be that the genesis of the star in Judaism echoes back to the Canaanites? It is arguable that the Israelites evolved in some measure not only from immigrants of Exodus but also from Israelites already living in Canaan. Either way one can consider the possibility that the star-focussed Canaanite culture influenced the evolving Israelite culture. For the influences were well-founded. The prophets who denounced the gods of the Canaanites came to claim for their own God the seasonal festivals and major elements of Canaanite culture. Gold four-rayed star medallions are to be found in many Canaanite excavations and in depictions by Egyptian artists on the necks of Canaanite captives.[22] Eight-rayed stars were also incorporated into their art; a good example of this is to be seen in a glass medallion of the late fifteenth to early fourteenth century BCE, recovered from Nuzi, near Kirkuk. Later, in seventh-century Lebanon, we see a Byzantine or neo-Persian seal, its Hebrew writing (naming Yosine Arcohen, Chief Priest) encircling eight rayed stars.

It is possible that we see the first use of the star as a form of identification in the eighth-century-BCE black obelisk at Nimrod. There is Jehu, king of Israel (c.842–814 BCE) (or if not Jehu himself, either one of his highest officials or possibly his predecessor Jehoram), humbling himself and paying tribute to his new overlord, Shalmaneser III, Lord of Assyria. Displayed above Shalmaneser is the winged symbol of the Assyrian god Assur on a bird-shaped plaque, and displayed above Jehu is a six-rayed star containing two central circles on a circular plaque.[23] Jehu's star is not the form that finally evolved into the two interlocking equilateral triangles, and the rayed star shape was also a common device of Assyrian power – and yet the positioning of the two forms, the bird-shaped plaque and the star, does seem to point to their use as identifying symbols. A little over 100 years later King Hezekiah (727–698), subdued by Sennachrib (705–681), also adopts the Assyrian symbol of the rosette. Again this might be seen as a sign of delegated authority and of submission – but it is not uncommon in Jewish history for signs of humiliation to be transformed into symbols of hope and redemption.

Back in the eighth century BCE, a limestone seal workshop in Judea was producing seals with star symbols, and in the seventh century BCE the star is clearly used as a specifically Jewish symbol on a seal belonging to Joshua ben

Asayahu found in Sidon. We have earlier mentioned the pentagram found on a jar, possibly belonging to the Second Temple,[24] and the stars and flowers which later exegesis suggests might have been displayed on the Temple *parokhet*.[25] In the late third and early second centuries BCE, pentagrams and hexagrams were carved on some of the tombs near Beit Jibrin at Marisa,[26] and in the next century in the ruins of the Herodian building at Beth-El, near Ramallah.[27] Throughout the late Hellenistic and early Roman periods, wheels and six-pointed rosettes are commonly found on ossuaries, sarcophagi, stone table tops and mosaics. We also see two rosettes purposefully flanking the menorah on the wall of the Yafa Synagogue[28] and on the tomb of Herod the Great (73–4 BCE) but perhaps the most famous rosettes are the 'three compass drawn circles containing six pointed stars [that] decorate the side of James' box'. Carved on the other side of this ossuary we read: 'James, son of Joseph, brother of Jesus'.[29] While it is uncertain whether all the inscription is authentic, what is certain is that those three six-pointed stars are genuine and typically Jewish symbols of 2,000 years ago. The authority on Jewish symbols of the Greco-Roman period, Erwin Goodenough, adjudged that 'Such wheels are beginning to impress us as a stated Jewish symbol, and will increasingly do so.' And they do, for he goes on to conclude that the six-pointed rosette was the antecedent of the Star of David.[30]

Symbols generally, being expressions of a culture, can change their form as that culture changes. One has only to consider the evolution of an early Christian symbol of the simple cross with its four uniformed arms of equal length into all the later sophisticated and varied crucifixes to accept the probability of the merging of rayed star figures and rosettes into the Star of David. Goodenough saw no inherent contradiction between symbols and decoration. In his monumental work *Jewish Symbols in the Greco-Roman Period*, in a statement of principle most germane to this work, he concluded that signs which may be decorative to some (and six-petalled rosettes were common to many cultures in the ancient Near East) were symbols to Jews if such was their purpose in mind when used. The centrality of this point cannot be overstated.

In the first century CE we get the first surviving reference to the Seal of Solomon on which, according to Josephus (c.38 CE to after 100), was carved the ineffable name of God. Early in the second century CE, a man known as Shimon bar Kokhba (Son of the Star), a mysterious figure about whom we know too little, led a disastrous revolt against Roman rule. His name 'Son of the Star' is an allusion to the biblical prophesy, 'A star shall arise from Jacob'

(Numbers 24:17). Some of the currency he struck has survived, including a tetradrachm dated 'Year Two of the Freedom of Israel' (or 133–34 CE), which displays a star form above a representation of the Temple.[31] A six-pointed rosette struck on a lead weight issued by bar Kokhba's administration has also come down to us. The Hebrew on a magic bowl found near the Sea of Galilee and dated to the second or third century CE reads: 'and with the Seal of Solomon and the [shield] of David'.[32] Later manuscripts refer to the symbol as a hexagram.[33] In the second to third centuries CE, the same symbol, along with six-pointed rosettes, appears in Israel on a frieze in the synagogue at Capernaum (Figure 29); in the third to fourth centuries on the mosaic floors of quite a few synagogues excavated in Galilee and then in the fourth century on a tombstone at Beit Shearim; on the lintel of the entrance to a Byzantine synagogue;[34] on late Roman silver vessels;[35] and on pottery lamps.[36] I think the star's appearance on Bar Kokhba's coins, on the Hebrew magic bowl, its incorporation into synagogue decor and on some of the other examples cited here, and reference to it in early post-Talmudic incantation[37] all demonstrate its early cultural and religious importance to Jews.

Gerban Oegema, one of the great authorities on the star, traces its use back to the Heikhalot mysticism of the second to the sixth centuries CE.[38] The hexagram, the pentagram, the names of the Seal of Solomon and the Shield of David all are part of Jewish culture, predating Christianity and Islam. That they became important major signs in Islam and, to a lesser extent, in Christianity does not detract from their role in Jewish magic. To the contrary, it supports it.

The story continues in sixth-century Spain where we see the star carved on architectural friezes both by itself and also alongside a five-branched menorah – we have met five-branched menorot before and will meet them again in the next chapter. In the same century the star was carved into the tombstone of the wife of Leon, son of David from Melos, in the Jewish cemetery in Taranto in southern Italy.[39] A few other surviving sixth-century tombstones in Italy and also in Spain display the star to denote the name David.[40] Around this time, too, it is mentioned in the Talmud[41] – significantly so, for the term 'Shield of David' is used as a metaphor to describe the Almighty's protection. A further Talmudic reference infers that the six-pointed star was engraved on the Seal of Solomon.[42]

It is from the seventh century onwards that the Star of David appears in great numbers as a magically protective sign on Jewish amulets and in associated literature.[43] In a tenth-century magical writing the star is described as representing the basic element of Fire and Water, and also representing Heaven and Earth.[44] Mystical linkages were revealed: for example, the words of Psalm 121, verse 7, 'The Lord shall preserve thee from all evil, He shall preserve thy soul', were inscribed on amulets in the form of the star and became a popular protection for women in childbirth. Gunter Plaut, another authority, suggests that the sign was itself a configuration of letters, for the saying 'God's seal is truth' alludes to the star, and the word 'truth', in old Hebrew script, could be shaped into two interlaced triangles.[45] But its use was not confined to its function as a protective symbol by Jews, for it was also employed intermittently as a symbol to identify Jews by quite a variety of host cultures. Some authorities have suggested that early in ninth-century Iraq, when the Jews were heavily taxed and residential restrictions were imposed, they were forced to wear the yellow star.[46]

I would like to pause for a moment. I am not suggesting that every one of these examples of the hexagram's use is incontrovertible evidence that it represented the Star of David. Conclusions are best drawn not by speculating about individual examples but by studying the entire phenomenon. Some examples carry neither Hebrew writing nor have any other Judaic connection. In other cases the respectable authorities I cite have not provided the reference for the source of the information, but the appearance of the Star of David at around that time and place turns otherwise unattributable (or wrongly attributed) items into objects of interest. Not to record these uncertainties would be less than frank, but to state only what is absolutely certain is to risk omitting what is material. One must ever look with sensitivity and knowledge to the associative context.[47] So, as mentioned earlier, the British Museum has a copy of a sixth-century amulet. One side shows two lions (ancient Jewish motifs) holding the star between them; the other side refers to the Seal of Solomon.[48] But, given that the amulet also displays some Christian images, it is unlikely to be Judaic – its interest to us lies in the linkage of the symbol to its name.

It is perhaps by the tenth century that the star really gets going on its long journey as it matures from a minor and intermittent to a major and constant Jewish symbol. Appearing again in Egypt either side of a menorah on the front page of a child's reader (Figure 30) are two Stars of David contained within an arch form from which a lamp, the Eternal Light, is suspended. Do compare this illustration with the two stars of David either side of a menorah on the Vizcaya carpet (Figure 31). This child's reader is an early example of the combination of the star and the menorah in Jewish art and is reflective of a long artistic tradition; an even earlier example is the Jewish Coptic band referred to earlier and illustrated in Figure 8.[49] This combination of the menorah with the motif of the Star in Egypt from the eighth or perhaps ninth century and then in the tenth is noteworthy for, as discussed below, it points to the probability that the star had become for many in Egypt as legitimate a symbolic representation of Judaism as the menorah.

Around this time the arched form of the mihrab was evolving. The word itself is pre-Islamic and probably means a columned area, often raised up, in a building. Owing its genesis to the Eternal Flame described in Leviticus 24:2–4, in all likelihood it originated in its Jewish prototype, since ancient synagogues were provided with a holy niche in the back and along the axis of the building. Indeed, although the mihrab was first to be seen in Islamic art and architecture from early in the eighth century, only as late as the fourteenth or fifteenth centuries is there extant evidence that the mihrab became an established design feature on Islamic carpets.[50]

In Chapter 4 I discussed the cultural closeness between the Jews of Spain and of the North African coast. Their structures, their strictures, their cultural and communal concerns were virtually the same, so what we know of the use of the Star of David in Egypt in the Middle Ages points clearly to that same use in Spain. A disc weight of perhaps the eleventh century, used to stamp an identifying impression of the star onto glass or other vessels, has been retrieved from Old Cairo, as has a cotton sampler also embroidered with the star.[51] And still in eleventh-century Egypt, we see a corrugated star and a six-branched menorah again among the jottings of a young Jewish child.[52]

The Ben Ezra Synagogue in Old Cairo is a treasure trove of information. Founded not later than the tenth century, it was reconstructed a hundred-odd years ago, 'with the same basilican design and interior elements' and retaining some of 'the earlier linear masonry pattern'.[53] I think it likely that the interior of the original building was as peppered with Stars of David as is the present one, for carved inscriptions on a surviving wooden fragment from the old synagogue reveal Stars of David[54] and, most significantly, a surviving fragment of carpet also reveals the Star of David![55] This is the earliest use of the star on a carpet in a Jewish context that I know of. Carpets with images were commonly hung on the walls of the homes of the Jews of Egypt. That the great synagogue of Aleppo in Syria (now partly destroyed), built around the same time as the original Ben Ezra Synagogue, displayed numerous hexagrams in a complex patterning adds to the probability that the Cairo Synagogue in the Middle Ages was adorned with the Star of David. The clincher is still to be seen today in the Rambam Synagogue in Cordoba where 'characteristically, the structure is embellished with plaster fretwork, with Stars of David and Hebrew lettering interwoven in the Arab manner'.[56]

The evidence of the early use of the hexagram by the Jews of the Near East multiplies. It appears in the form of the grille work of the lamps suspended from the ceilings of Egyptian synagogues[57] and the findings in the Genizah point to such lamps being used in the Palestinian synagogue in Old Cairo.[58] That this form was also much used in Islamic art and design does not detract from its particular position in Judaism. This conjunction of light and the star was also expressed in the marriage customs of the twelfth century, for the betrothal ring of the Jewish bride would often display the rosette and her dowry would include special oil lamps for her new home which would be fixed to a wooden device in the shape of the six-pointed star.[59] We see the same star-shaped copper-alloy Sabbath lamps from thirteenth-century England; hanging over the table they would be lit by the housewife on Friday evenings and on the eve of festivals. The same star-shaped lamp, the *Judenstern*, appears once more suspended from the ceiling of the homes of German Jews[60] and in their fourteenth- and fifteenth-century Haggadot.[61] We see numerous Stars of David in an Egyptian Bible dated to 1008 CE, now in the Russian National Library in St Petersburg (Figure 32);[62] on the fringes of a prayer shawl; and in Tunisia on a merchant's seal to identify his goods.[63] In addition, we see many Stars of David in a Pentateuch of 951 CE and on an Alexandrian Bible of 1122 CE, both also in the Russian National Library.[64] There is also a particularly dramatic example in the thirteenth-century Damascus Bible, produced in Islamic Spain by Menachem ben Avraham ibn Malek. The vertical diamond shape is formed of Hebrew script and four horizontal equilateral triangles of gold centred by a mystical circle.

To the north, in an eleventh- or twelfth-century Mesopotamian (or possibly Persian) Bible the star is to be seen between some particularly pretty borders, and to the south in fifteenth-century Yemen the star shines yet again in another bible (Figure 33). Then in mid twelfth-century Constantinople, Yehudah ben Elijah Hadassi, in his work *Eshkol Ha-Kofer*, uses the term 'Star of David' to describe the hexagram.[65] This is doubly significant, for the mention of the name David in any prayer or benediction is a messianic reference.

In the age-old Jewish community of Djerba, an island off Tunisia, we learn of the custom – although we do not know when it began – for Jewish women to weave the star along with the menorah and the Tree of Life symbols into their clothing.⁶⁶ Later, a nineteenth-century traveller recorded an old (again we do not know how old) tradition of the Jewish women of Djerba not only to wear the star on their clothing but also to form the shape with decorative nails hammered onto their cabinets, cupboards and tables.⁶⁷

From all the above examples it is clear that by the Middle Ages, in addition to its frequent appearance in Europe, the star was well on its way to being established as a self-identifying and a protective symbol in the Jewish communities of Egypt and along the North African littoral. Given that these communities all enjoyed extremely close cultural, familiar and commercial connections with the Jews of Spain, with the result that all their religious rituals, hierarchies, laws and symbols were all virtually identical, I think that the incremental use of the star in the Egyptian and North African Jewish communities points to its increasing use among the their co-religionists in the Iberian Peninsula. So let us look to the evidence.

In 1375, Abraham Cresques, the great Jewish cartographer, produced his finest map for the king of Portugal. What is odd about this marvellous map of the known world is that in contrast to the rather hazy flags Cresques painted on most countries, those placed on Morocco and central and southern Turkey show very clearly delineated Stars of David. Whether these three flags might have been his signature or some other statement it is very likely that Abraham Cresques himself knew that the star signified Jewish identity, for the king, delighted with the map, promptly exempted him and his son Judah from wearing the Jewish badge of identity.

The signatures of two Spanish Jews incorporating the star have survived. I wonder if this was a common practice and, if so, might it have indicated a general religious endorsement or a statement of identity, or was it possibly of relevance to documents required in legal proceedings? Perhaps for these two signatures its use was quite specific, either because both signatories were high state and community officials or because they both shared the name Solomon, and the star, of course, was also known as the Seal or the Shield of Solomon. The Bill of Sale of 1248 was witnessed by Vidal Solomon (Figure 34),⁶⁸ while the second signature was that of Solomon Bonafous (Figure 35).⁶⁹

In the twelfth century, one of the earliest Kabbalist works, *Sefer Gematriaot*, is peppered with hexagrams and pentagrams.⁷⁰ In the next century, Abraham ben Samuel Abulafia, a renowned Kabbalist and early exponent of practical Kabbalah, refers in his writings to the Seal of Solomon.[71] Also in the same century, the Spanish Kabbalist Joseph Gikatilla, in his book *The Gates of Righteousness*, describes the hexagram as the Star of David.[72] In the fourteenth century the great mystic, Abraham ben Isaac of Granada, is thought by some in his work on the names of God to point to the equilateral triangle structure of the star.[73] The star, albeit now in a modified form, for it was still evolving, is to be seen in an illuminated Hebrew Bible of 1299–1300, today in the National Library in Lisbon. Another remarkable Bible is the Rashba Bible which beautifully brings together two of the emblematic sources of the star, the rosette and the shield. Written and illuminated in Spain in 1383, it depicts a Shield of David incorporating, in burnished gold, a Star of David which in turn frames a six-sided rosette.

In 1307 the star is displayed in the first Bible of Joseph ben Yehuda ibn Merwas of Toledo (or perhaps Burgos) (Figure 36), and around 1320 the *Golden Haggadah* of Barcelona shows us a marvellously constructed Star of David (Figure 37) which most interestingly, exactly and very specifically replicates the special stars woven into the Spanish synagogue carpet (Figures 13, 14, 15). The same star reappears in the interlacing design of the exquisite fifteenth-century Kennicott Bible in the Bodleian Library in Oxford.[74] This Bible is of rare refinement and delicacy and must be the finest illuminated Hebrew manuscript to be seen today. There are also some beautifully constructed stars to be seen in the collection of the Hispanic Society of America,[75] and given the very many different representations and values of the star, to see that selfsame star replicated both in fourteenth- and fifteenth-century Jewish Bibles and on the Vizcaya carpet is not without significance.

In Chapter 6 we looked at the thirteenth-century anthology of games commissioned by Alfonso the Wise, king of Castile, with the stars and the prayer shawl identifying the Jewish scribes and illustrators. This was not an isolated event; the *Cantigas de Santa Maria* (Songs in Praise of the Virgin Mary), another book commissioned by Alfonso, tells the same story, for in a Christian depiction of a Jew's room, it is no surprise to see the curtains embroidered not with the more common badges of the wheel that Jews had commonly to wear but with Stars of David (Figure 38).[76]

The star is quite irrepressible. A fourteen-century Spanish illuminated manuscript displays a matzah stamped with the star,[77] and a bronze stamp for impressing the matzah with Hebrew script and the star has been found in

Catalonia. A particularly charming illuminated page from an Italian Bible of 1396 shows us a rabbit seeking sanctuary inside the sheltering symbol of the star, protected in turn by eleven birds including the symbolically powerful rooster, goose and dove (Figure 39), all of whom we shall meet again in Chapter 15. As late as 1472, the scribe Moshe ben Ya'akov completes his codex Bible in Seville with its stars of David created by micrographic (minute) lines of text.[78]

One can go on and on citing the star's use inside the religious books of the Spanish Jews in the fourteenth and fifteenth centuries – and indeed on the outside of these books, for the cover and binding of a biblical manuscript in Hebrew, dated to 1425 from Carcassonne, is replete with the Stars of David, as is the leather jacket of a beautiful Lisbon Bible of 1492. Examples of the star's appearance in these Sephardi manuscripts that may be seen today in England include:

(i) Castile: c.1300 CE in a Haggadah in the Department of Jewish Studies Library, University College, London.
(ii) Castile: fourteenth century in a Pentateuch and Hagiographa in Cambridge, Cambridge University Library, Add. 652 (three examples).
(iii) Barcelona: mid-fourteenth century in the Sister Haggadah in the British Library, London, Or 2884.
(iv) Barcelona: mid-fourteenth century in a Haggadah in the British Library, Add. 1476.
(v) Catalonia: 1396 CE in the Prophets/and Hagiographa in the British Library, Harley 5774–5775 (four examples).
(vi) Castile: mid-fifteenth century in the Second Castilian Bible in Cambridge University Library, Add. 3203.

Let us take another look at the use of the star in the Middle Ages by Jewish communities other than those of the Iberian Peninsula and North Africa. In thirteenth-century England (1222 CE, to be exact) laws were enacted forcing the English Jews to wear distinguishing signs possibly including the yellow star on their clothing.

In Venice, right at the edge of the ghetto, were two adjoining properties, one owned by a Christian, the other by a Jew. They could not agree as to where one property ended and the other began. What clearer statement about the meaning of the star in Christian eyes can there be than in the judgement of the Court of the Doges, for in settling the dispute it decreed the boundary posts should on their outer faces display the crucifix, and on their inner faces the Star of David.[79] What was particularly significant here was the use of the crucifix and not the coat of arms of Venice, for the two religious symbols so juxtaposed indicated overall and general categories and not purely local elements. And, still in Italy, there is a fifteenth-century Christian manuscript that clearly evidences the incremental use of the star as a symbol within Christian culture to identify Jews. For we see St Stephen, the first Christian martyr, being stoned to death. His attacker, stone in hand, is identified as a Jew by the Star of David.[80]

In twelfth-century Germany the pious Hasids were linking it into their mystical formulations.[81] It appeared in a window of the thirteenth-century synagogue in Hamelin,[82] as did the six-leafed rosette in the synagogue in Ratisbon.[83] The Star of David had a significant part to play in the marriage ceremony in many medieval German synagogues; at the conclusion of the ceremony, the groom would hurl a glass against a particular spot of the stone wall onto which was carved the protective six- or eight-pointed star.[84] Over twenty such wedding stones may still be seen today in what were German synagogues, and in the Middle Ages there would have been many more. Still in middle Europe, the star is found on some twelfth-century German coins,[85] in a German Hebrew Bible[86] and on some Polish coins which displayed both the star and Hebrew inscriptions.

The significance of the Star of David to the Jews of Western Europe is manifested in two caches of plates and jewellery discovered in the medieval Jewish sections of Colmar in France, and Erfurt and Weissenfels in Germany. The valuables date from the thirteenth and fourteenth centuries – but none are dated later than 1349 when the Jews, accused of causing the Black Death by poisoning the wells, were attacked. Many would hide their valuables and try to escape the pogroms – but most were massacred. The owners of both sets of treasure troves never returned to claim their property. The items emblazoned with the Star of David included a number of silver bowls, two with the star on the bases (reminding one of the plate of Burgos – see note 92); numerous rings – one of gold from Colmar and one of silver from Erfurt (on both rings the stars were juxtaposed to crescent moons – a motif associated with the Jewish communities of the Middle Ages); and a clasp with a cosmetic chain.[87]

The mystical meanings of the star multiplied, some seeing the three points of the triangle as representative of the three sons of Noah – the physical ancestors of mankind and archetypal emblems of the three aspects of human nature: spirit, feeling and intellect. Some interpreted the three points in the more philosophical light of thesis, antithesis and synthesis.[88] Still others viewed the two triangles as corresponding to the upper and lower worlds conjoined – for whatever is happening in this world relates to what is happening in the upper world[89] – and the form of the star reflected the balanced interplay of the forces that make up the existence and the continuation of the universe.

From the thirteenth century on, the star is increasingly commonly found on Spanish, French, German, Swiss and British seals (Figure 40).[90] The use of seals in Spain added authenticity but not actual legal authority – unless, that is, it was the seal of the king or a lord. Daniel Friedenberg writes: 'there was no question but that both Christians and Jews recognised the six-pointed star as a Jewish symbol. The pentagram and hexagram, common to Christians, Jews and Muslims alike (and shown on many Christian seals as well), had a mystical or cabbalistic religious connotation, with the hexagram being used far more than the pentagram on Jewish medieval seals.'[91]

Whether or not these seals are Jewish is usually determined either by a Hebrew inscription or by the nature of the owner's name. Two examples of fourteenth-century Spanish Jewish seals are those of Schlomo bar Gedaliyah and of Todros Halevi bar Shemuel Halevi.[92] The Hebrew inscription on Todros's seal is preceded by the hexagram. It is quite likely that Todros's father was Samuel ben Meir Halevi, prime minister to King Pedro II of Castile. Samuel, subsequently charged by his patron with conspiracy (he had perhaps loaned his king too much money for his own safety), died under torture – but not before he had built the fabulous El Transito Synagogue with its Star of David tiles. Today, the charming museum in the synagogue displays, among its other medieval Jewish exhibits, an embossed leather brooch and a belt buckle – both adorned with the Star of David. Stars were used not only by individuals but in public, too, for they decorate the seal of the Jewish communities of Seville, family badges (imitative of coats of arms) and, as we have seen, are on the seal for impressing stars onto the Passover matzah.

There is a particularly early Jewish seal illustrated in Figure 41. It is almost certainly part of a signet ring and was found in the papal enclave in Avignon. In the centre of the star is the Hebrew letter *shin*, standing for *Shaddai*, the Almighty, one of the biblical names for God which later appears frequently in Kabbalistic formulae. The seal is inscribed to Astruc, a common name in southern France and eastern Spain, and derives from the Latin *astra*, 'star'.

Apart from seals and manuscripts, few contemporary Jewish domestic artefacts have survived, but the archaeological finds in Burgos of Spanish medieval household silver did include a marvellous set of Passover plates. Inset in the centre of the plates are gilded Stars of David.[93] Another example of such artefacts is the fifteenth-century *converso* Hannukiah discussed in Chapter 10 (Figure 25).

We even get references to the star in the trial records of the Inquisition. One of the many charges raised against Elvira Ruiz, a *conversa*, was that because she studied the sky for the Star of Joseph (the reference was to Numbers 24:17, which with all its messianic implications refers to the star that rises from Jacob, but there is no such star as that of Joseph) she must have been waiting for the Messiah – and so was continuing to practise Judaism. Her trial began in 1500 and ended in 1517 with her acquittal.

What was happening in Prague in the centre of the Holy Roman Empire was particularly significant. In 1270, the star appears in the tracery of a window in the Altneu Synagogue (Figure 42), and later in the metalwork in front of the Ark (Figure 16). Then in 1354–55 the Emperor Charles IV clearly identified the star with the Jews, for he granted them a flag bearing a yellow Star of David surrounded in Hebrew by the great Unitary Declaration (the *Shema*) against a red background. It is called King David's Flag. The disintegrating flag was replaced 350 years later with a replica which can still be seen today (Figure 43). Back in fourteenth-century Bohemia the star appears in the synagogue at Budweis,[94] in the title pages of the early Hebrew books printed in Prague,[95] and on a coin, the groschen, minted there. In Budapest in 1476, when a delegation of the Jewish community marched out to welcome their king, Matthias Corvinus, on the occasion of his second marriage, they carried aloft their flag with its two identifying gold stars. The significance of this is that not only did the Jewish community see the star as their symbol, but that it was also seen as such by the civic authorities.

By the fifteenth century the frequency and the range of the star's appearance make it clear that it was gaining strength as a Jewish symbol. Despite all the above, its continuing use in both the magical formulations of Christianity and the decorative formulations of Islam ensured that it was nowhere near being *universally* recognized or used exclusively as a Jewish symbol.

From the tenth century the star was commonly added to the parchment citing Deuteronomy 6:4–9 and 11:13–21 which is placed inside the mezuzah, the small case fixed to the door posts of a house – an ancient inner tradition of Jewish magic had inspired this use as a prophylactic to warn off demonic powers. Maimonides, however, condemned all such decorative or symbolic alterations to the pure script and it is unlikely that he would have done so were this addition of the star to the script not widespread. But in vain, for by the fourteenth-century, with the rise of Jewish mysticism, the custom of portraying a five- or six-pointed star on the parchment had become well established,[96] to the extent that at this time the pentagram was also often called the Star of David.[97]

The form of the mezuzot (plural of mezuzah) may convey all sorts of contingent messages. Is it only my fancy, or does a fifteenth-century Italian mezuzah admit us to the birth of a star? Two stars, actually: in the lower form we see the embryo evolving from the ancient Jewish symbol of the six-pointed rosette and in the middle form we see the two equilateral triangles manoeuvring themselves into their birth position (Figure 44). It is one of the many treasures of the marvellous Jewish Museum in London.

Sometimes I wonder about this anticipating positioning. In Joseph ben Eliezer Bonfils's (b. Spain second half of the fourteenth century) manuscript (Figure 45), do those two triangles seem to hover, each ready to mount the other and beget the Star of David? Or does this hourglass being centred in the point where they meet, change into a form that may now spin on its pivot? More prosaically, while tapering triangles are a device common to the art of many cultures, in Kabbalah they often signify the removal of evil spirits. What happens is that starting from the broad base, the demon is pushed further and further along the ever-narrowing form, until right at the end it can no longer remain in the form and is expelled.

Echoing the sixth-century architectural frieze, the eighth- or ninth-century Coptic weave and the tenth-century child's reader (and our Vizcaya carpet), an Italian Haggadah of the fifteenth century displays both the star and the menorah with the latter symbol endorsing the Judaic values of the former. Gershom Scholem, the pre-eminent authority on Jewish mysticism, referring to this coming together of the star and the menorah in the late Middle Ages as the beginning of a new tradition, asserts: 'one gets the feeling here that the Shield of David must have become as legitimate a symbolic representation of Judaism as the Menorah'.[98]

Early in fourteenth-century Spain the star is to be seen again in Kabbalistic writings. There can be no greater demonstration of the star's connection to the inner magical tradition of Judaism than that found in *The Book of the Boundary* by David ben Judah, the Pious (a grandson of the great Kabbalist Nahmanides, who had taught in Barcelona).⁹⁹ Here are two hexagrams, both named as Stars of David, and within each are certain ancient magical names. In 1506 the *Shushan Sodot*, a Kabbalistic compilation of earlier works, refers to a magic ring bearing the Shield of David in a way that indicates that readers would be very familiar with the shape itself. And in the *Sefer Raziel*, an early-seventeenth-century compendium of Jewish magic ascribed to the eleventh-century sage, Eliezer ben Isaac of Worms, we see the star yet again (Figures 46 and 47).¹⁰⁰ Its function was therapeutic; problems today seen as psychological were in the Middle Ages attributed to evil spirits, and the Star of David, along with other symbols and breathing and meditative exercises, was used in practical Kabbalah to effect profound changes in consciousness.

In 1348 in Barcelona a copy of Maimonides's extraordinary work, *Guide to the Perplexed*, appears and in an astrological illustration we see the teacher holding up an astrolabe to a standard starry sky – but the throne on which he sits is peppered with Stars of David (Figure 48).¹⁰¹ A few years later, as earlier mentioned, Samuel ben Meir Halevi, the king's prime minister, builds the great El Transito Synagogue in Toledo with its ceramic tiles displaying three Stars of David¹⁰² and its ceiling replete with stars and rosettes. Two of its windows are intriguing, possibly hinting at something of the Kabbalistic Sefirot, the schematic representation of the attributes of the Divine.

A fourteenth-century Catalan manuscript portrays a figure holding a flag adorned with the star.¹⁰³ At the end of the fifteenth century (or possibly in the first five years of the sixteenth century) David ben Judah Messer Leon (c.1470–c.1535), a leading Italian Kabbalist, entitled one of his major books *Magen David* (the Shield/Star of David). He would not have done so were the meaning and significance of the hexagram not well established. Later, Joseph Caro (1488–1575), the illustrious Spanish Talmudic codifier, most interestingly adjudges images of stars to be forbidden in the villages lest they be used as idols, but their use in the towns is sanctioned for reasons of beauty,¹⁰⁴ an interesting distinction indicative, perhaps, of the very different worlds of the elite and the masses, and perhaps reflective of a wider spread of superstition in the countryside than in the towns? Nevertheless, a critical distinction for the worship of anything other than the Almighty Himself is absolutely prohibited. It is a distinction that demonstrates, as we have seen, the very different meanings and qualities attributed to the star by different peoples and now we see different values attaching to the star as between Jews.[105] The view parroted by too many today, who assert that because the star for a time was a Christian and a Muslim symbol it could not have been a Jewish symbol, is tediously untenable.

The sixteenth-century writings of the great Kabbalist Isaac ben Solomon Luria (1534–72) had the effect of encouraging the placing of the Star of David on a multitude of household objects, on tombstones and in synagogues. That the star by this time was well on its way to wide acceptance as a Jewish magical symbol is evident in the writings of the Christian philosopher, Paracelsus (1493–1541). In *De Occulta Philosophia* he describes how, with the five- and six-pointed stars, 'The Israelites and the necromantic Jews have done much and brought about much.' He then expressively notes: 'They [the stars] are still kept highly secret by a number of them.'[106] That the star was accepted by the Jewish authorities as a major symbol is implicit in a work of the influential Isaac ben Moses Arama (c.1420–94), for he writes that Psalm 67 ('May the Lord be gracious to us and bless us, and make His face to shine upon us') was engraved in the form of the menorah on King David's Shield.

The frequency, the extent and the nature of the star's appearances by the thirteenth and fourteenth centuries suggest for many, but not yet for all, that the hexagram was no mere ornamental device. While the increasing use of the star after the sixteenth century is outside the scope of this work, it is worth noting the 1969 *responsa* of Rabbi Feinstein (1895–1990), a leading Talmudist and head of many Orthodox organizations in America and Israel: 'As is known, Stars of David have drawn on Torah curtains, mantels and binders for hundreds of years.'[107] Again in our time, the Lubavitcher Rebbe, a spiritual leader and seer of the most extraordinary inspiration, erudition, generosity and thoroughgoing precision in all his *responsa*, when asked about the history of the star would say nothing more than that it had Kabbalistic significance.[108]

Shalom Sabar was recently quoted as declaring that 'It was not until the Middle Ages that symbols alone, like the Magen David, began to increase in popularity.'[109] It is clear that by the sixteenth century the Star of David was now well on the way to becoming as legitimate a representation of Judaism as any other symbol. From the seventeenth century onwards the use of the Star of David steadily and substantially grew to take up its role today alongside the menorah as the universally accepted Jewish symbol. I think it likely that most of the seventy-odd examples of the uses of the star collated here are but a tiny proportion of the potential and actual uses of the star by Jews,

Christians and Muslims in *a Jewish context* up to the sixteenth century.[110] The confiscations and fires, the migrations and massacres that make up so much of Jewish history have left us with but few surviving examples of that use, but it is witless to believe that what we do not know does not, could not and never did, exist. From the foregoing it is evident that by the eleventh and twelfth centuries the star was there, in parts of the Jewish world, through a crystallization of a long, complex but undeniable history.

It seems to me that some experts can get quite pernickety about attributing a Jewish provenance or even accepting the possibility thereof. Perhaps pernickety is the wrong word. But I find it puzzling that the small number of surviving Jewish artefacts would seem to be viewed with more stringent criteria than the artefacts of other cultures. Why is it that exclusively Jewish ethnic, thematic, functional or formal elements are required for a carpet or other artefact to be considered Jewish, when many carpets or other artefacts of different cultures could not satisfy such stringent criteria? I wonder if perhaps this is because it is just safer or simply customary to assume and attribute provenance to the majority culture than it is to say that one does not really know. Be that as it may, in fifteenth-century Spain the star as a symbol, rooted in an ancient inner tradition of Jewish mysticism, boosted by its use in Christian magic, used by Jews and significantly by Christians and Muslims to identify Jews, was maturing. To the world at large, however, the star was not yet considered an exclusively Jewish symbol – so making it a treasured symbol for the *conversos*. We see this clearly in the Stars of David decorated on the walls of the women's section in the secret synagogue, recently discovered, in Abraham Senior's palace in Segovia. An enormously wealthy and powerful man, rather than leave Spain in the expulsion of 1492 Senior converted to Christianity. But do see Chapter 9, note 24.

The best place to get lost is in a crowd. Displayed in earlier Roman mosaic floors, sculpted on Byzantine churches, printed on twelfth-century Fatimid amulets, sculpted on the outer wall of a thirteenth-century Turkish hospital, baked onto tiles throughout the Middle East, struck on Islamic coins (on thirteenth-century Ayyubid fils, Mongol dirhams and Mamluk fils) and inscribed in the Qur'an itself (Figure 49) – the star was omnipresent and therefore, to the outside world in the fifteenth century, still not *exclusively* a Jewish symbol. Indeed, in Spain it was a religiously righteous sign, displayed at the very entrances of the cathedrals and churches of Valencia, Burgos and Lerida.[111] The tracery in the great rose windows of the Burgos and Valencia cathedrals dating from the fourteenth century form large and beautiful hexagrams. Equally called the Seal of Solomon or the Star of David, it mattered not whether it had five, six or eight points.[112] That a star-studded carpet could be no smoking gun pointing at *conversos* was clear, for the 1410 inventory of King Martin I of Aragon described two of his carpets as bearing the six-pointed Seal of Solomon.[113] And did not the coat of arms of the Kingdom of Castile and Leon place the images of the castle and the lion within two golden six-pointed stars? The point that the star was not inevitably or exclusively a Jewish symbol to the non-Jewish world could not more conclusively be made than by looking at a fresco by Matteo di Giovanetti in 1344–46, painter-in-residence at the Palace of the Popes in Avignon (Figure 12). As described earlier, it was commissioned by Clement VI and shows St Martial reviving two pagan priests who had collapsed on the carpet – a carpet with the same six-pointed stars and general layout as the Admiral carpets.[114] Di Giovanetti also displays the star on the walls, arches, the frame and, in the lower section, in the upper window of a church. We know from an inventory of 1416 that Jean, Duc de Berri, had a Spanish carpet bearing the arms of Castile and, finally, in Holbein's *Madonna and Child with two Saints* of 1522 we again see a Spanish Admiral carpet with the same borders.[115]

To Jews either learned in the symbols of theosophical Kabbalah, animated by the magic charts and charms of practical Kabbalah or simply receptive to an archetypal pattern,[116] it was an ancient, powerful, redemptive and protective symbol. And when you look upon a star, it makes a difference who you are.[117] To Muslims it was a classic feature in Islamic ornamentation, perhaps originating in stylized flowers[118] while for Christians the triangle with its three equal sides was a symbol of the Trinity. Only slowly did the star grow in both Islam and Christianity into a *universally* understood badge of Jewish identity.

I find it thrilling to follow (that is, when I can) the workings of high scholarship, and the greatest of the textile scholars have always had a sense that the stars on some of the Spanish carpets may be more than common Islamic decorative devices. But if you do not speak the cultural language that engendered the symbol at that time you will not be able to eavesdrop into what it is saying to those who do. Nevertheless, May Beattie, the eminent carpet scholar, gently reproached some of her colleagues for the scant attention paid to the stars in the Admiral carpet. She discerned a difference, noting that alone among the other decorative motifs, these stars are systematically organized.[119] The same point of particularity is made by another eminent scholar, Louise W. Mackie: 'The second and primary field pattern is formed by continuous six-pointed stars, arranged in a scheme *unusual* for the Iberian Peninsula.'[120] I have stressed the word 'unusual' because it is highly significant that Beattie and Mackie, two of the most distinguished textile experts of the twentieth century, each independently reported strange elements in the composition of these carpets. Professor Walter Denny, the pre-eminent academic in the field today, followed suit, drawing our attention to the extraordinary colour system of another of the Admiral carpets.[121] That the key stars on the Vizcaya carpet are white and set against blue – the most important colour in the colour system of Kabbalah – would also convey symbolic meaning to many Jews in fifteenth-century Spain.

Yet another leading textile expert joins in noting the particularity of the star. Kjeld von Folsach, describing the perfect hexagrams on a quite beautiful silk which has been carbon dated to 1035–1255, most interestingly wrote: 'Geometric patterns of this type are rarely seen on textiles outside the Spanish–Muslim or Egyptian–Syrian area, and even there, these patterns have a different character.'[122] Earlier I have described the high skills of the Jewish weavers of Spain who were both influencing and influenced by the Jewish designers, dyers and weavers of Egypt.[123] By marriage, culture and commerce the Jews of Spain, Egypt and North Africa were all intimately connected to each other,[124] all observing the same Jewish law, all bound by the same Jewish authorities. The implications of Von Folsach's point, in which the geographic limits of the use of the hexagram are defined, are fascinating. Can it be that the reason the hexagram was rarely seen on textiles beyond the Spanish–Muslim and Egyptian–Syrian regions is precisely because those were the selfsame regions where, as discussed in Chapter 4, the Jewish settlements with their weavers and dealers were situated?

Finally, it is evident that quite apart from the constellation of stars flooding the central field, the Stars of David in the penultimate border of the Vizcaya carpet (Figure 31) are of the same very particular lineage as those nestling inside two of the Torah Arks in the Spanish synagogue carpet Figures 13, 14, 15) and in the contemporaneous 'Book of Games' (Figure 20). The Vizcaya carpet's stars differ from those in the earlier Spanish synagogue carpet only in that, reflecting the movement into Kabbalah, the centres of the stars now display mystical double six-sided or circular figures.

In Figure 50 we look again at the stars in the border of the Vizcaya carpet juxtaposed with three illustrations of the use of the star in settings that cannot be anything but Judaic. There is the eighth- to ninth-century Egyptian weaving (Figure 8) and the tenth-century child's workbook (Figure 30) – both authenticated by their accompanying menorot. Then from the fourteenth-century Barcelona Haggadah, here is a family sitting down to celebrate the Passover (Figure 6). The homogeneity, the sameness, of all four stars in all four pictures, is too significant to be ignored. They are surely the same stars with the same meanings to Jews and *conversos*.

NOTES

1. Theodore Feder, 'Solomon, Socrates and Aristotle', *Biblical Archaeology Review*, 34, 5, p.36, citing Poryphey, third century CE, in 'On Abstinence', 2.26. Louis Feldman and Meyer Reinhold, *Jewish Life and Thought Among Greeks and Romans: Primary Readings* (Minneapolis, MN: Fortress Press, 1996), p.7.
2. Tacitus, *The Histories* (London: Penguin Books, 1964), p.273.
3. W. Keller, *The Bible as History* (New York: Hodder & Stoughton, 1956), p.350. The prophet Amos (5:26) inveighed against the worship of Saturn, an Akkadian star god. Jeremiah 7:18 and 44:19 refer to an offering to the god, a caked baked in the form of a star – which was the image of Ishtar.
4. K. Critchlow, *Islamic Patterns* (London: Thames & Hudson, 1992), p.154.
5. The three sides of an equilateral triangle are bisected, and each of the six points so created are joined both directly one to the other and via the central point – so creating six Stars of David.
6. Deuteronomy 16:21 and 17:3; 2 Kings 17:16; Jeremiah 19:13. Deuteronomy and Kings record the suppression of Astarte worship. She was a pre- and early Israelite goddess whose symbol was a crescent moon and star.
7. Babylonian Talmud, Shabbat 156a.
8. Joshua Trachtenberg, *Jewish Magic and Superstition* (Philadelphia, PA: University of Pennsylvania Press, 2004), p.69.
9. T. Carmi (ed.), *The Penguin Book of Hebrew Verse* (Harmondworth: Penguin Books, 1981), p.353; and D. Goldstone (ed.), *Hebrew Poems from Spain* (Oxford: The Littman Library of Jewish Civilization, 2007), p.123. P. Cole, *The Dream of the Poem* (Princeton, NJ: Princeton University Press, 2007), p.174.
10. Gershom Scholem, *The Messianic Idea in Judaism* (New York: Schocken Books, 1971), p.260.
11. Shalom Sabar, *King Solomon's Seal*, edited by Rachel Milstein (Jerusalem: Tower of David Museum of the History of Jerusalem, 2002), pp.177–84.
12. Gerbern S. Oegema, *The History of the Star of David* (Frankfurt: Peter Lang, 1996), p.39.
13. Sabar, *King Solomon's Seal*, p.181.

14. Scholem, *Messianic Idea*, p.264.
15. K.S. Painter, *The Mildenhall Treasure* (London: British Museum Publications, 1977), p.76, Plate 31. Whilst there is no evidence of any significant Jewish settlement in the British Isles during the Roman period there are many indicia pointing to small groups of Jews living here. Shimon Applebaum's, *Were there Jews in Roman Britain?* (London: The Jewish Historical Society of England, 1953), Vol. xvii, pp.189–205, answers his question with a contra. We do know of the support given to Julius Caesar by some wealthy Jews of Rome in his worldwide designs (1) and given the substantial number of Jewish Roman citizens (sometimes up to 10 per cent of the population) it is unlikely that none followed the legions that occupied Britain or were among the Roman traders and ex-soldiers who subsequently settled here. Then, too, after the Romans destroyed Israel in 70 CE young Israelites were sold off into slavery and scattered throughout the Roman Empire. A Roman brick found in Mark Lane, London is thought to be Judaic (2), a coin of the Bar Kokhba revolt (132–135 CE) has also been found by archaeologists in London and ornaments excavated in Gaza were certainly made of Irish gold. In the fourth century, St Jerome refers to Jews living in England and Spain (3).

The following three citations signify a not inconsiderable Jewish settlement in England, otherwise these decrees would surely not have been issued. In 740 CE Egbert, Archbishop of York, forbids Christians attending any of the Jewish festivals; in 833 CE the king of Mercia ordered that all the property taken from the Jews be passed over to the monks of Croyland and a couple of hundred years later, Edward the Confessor decrees that all Jews and their property belong to him. Many French Jews, mainly from the Rouen area, including his personal barber-surgeon, supported and accompanied William the Conqueror in his takeover in 1066.

> (1) Israel Abrahams, *Jewish Life in the Middle Ages* (Jerusalem: Jewish Publication Society, 1930). p.242. A. Hyamson, *A History of the Jews of England* (London: Methuen, 1928), p.2.
> (2) Cecil Roth, *A History of the Jews of England* (Oxford: Oxford University Press, 1964), p.2 St Jerome, Commentary, on Isaiah 66:20; Amos 8:12; and Zephaniah 2:8.
> (3) D'Blossiers Tovey, *Anglia Judaica*, edited by Elizabeth Pearl (London: Weidenfeld & Nicolson, 1990 [1738]), pp.1–4.

However, H.G. Richardson, in *The English Jewry under Angevin Kings* (London: Meuthen, 1960), p.1, has suggested that such references to Jews in Anglo-Saxon statistics may simply reflect direct copying of similar documents from mainland Europe and would not therefore demonstrate the existence of significant Jewish communities in England prior to the eleventh century.
16. R. Loewe, *Ibn Gabriol* (London: Peter Halban, 1989), p.103.
17. R. Llopis, *La Villa Santiaguista de Leitor en la Baya Edad Media* (Murcia: Pictografia, 1993), p.59.
18. Joshua Trachtenberg, *The Devil and the Jews* (Philadelphia, PA: Jewish Publication Society of America, 1983), p.231 n.16. Gershom Scholem states that 'the Arabs knew only the Seal of Solomon': see Scholem, *Messianic Idea*, p.264. The star's appearance in Christian religious books of Spain in the fifteenth century perhaps comes about either as a reflection of

Islamic influence on Christian art or merely as a decorative device. F. Spalding, *Mudejar Ornament in Manuscripts* (New York: Hispanic Society of America, 1953), Figs. 23, 36. However, I do not think one can exclude the possible influence of Arab astrological determinism originating in Morocco and, via thinkers such as Yehuda ben Nissim ibn Malka, percolating into the Kabbalah of Spain.

19. S. Dubnov, *History of the Jews* (New Brunswick, NJ: Thomas Yosseloff, 1967–69), pp. 219–20. The tradition had been established earlier. In 1239, following the expulsion of the Moors from Cordova, the pope urged his bishop to introduce the Jewish badge there: Salo Baron, *A Social and Religious History of the Jews* (New York: Jewish Publication Society and Columbia University Press, 1965–67), Vol. 10, p. 121. These badges varied greatly throughout Europe, the most common form being wheel-shaped. In Egypt in the fourteenth century, Jews had to wear a yellow patch; its exact shape is not known. The text reads: '[The] yellow badge is required so that real blood will not be spilt.' N. Stillman, *The Jews of Arab Lands* (Philadelphia, PA: Jewish Publication Society, 1979), p. 270.

20. Scholem, *Messianic Idea*, pp. 243–51. See also his great work, *Major Trends in Jewish Mysticism*, pp. 257–81:

    An epilogue to the Curious History of the Six Pointed Star may today be seen on the US one dollar bill. Above the bald eagle in the right hand circle (the two circles comprise the Great Seal of the United States of America) are thirteen stars representing the thirteen original colonies as well as the thirteen original signatures to the Declaration of Independence. Those stars are configured into a hexagram. What had happened was that George Washington, desperate for funds to finance the War of Independence, approached Hayim Salomon (1740–1785), a wealthy Philadelphian financier for a loan equivalent today to twenty-five million dollars. Salomon, in giving Washington the money, said he wanted nothing for himself—but something for his fellow Jewish Americans. The Star of David was the request. Statues to Salomon are to be seen in New York, Washington and Los Angeles.

21. See Ecclesiastes 12:12.
22. *Institute of Nautical Architecture Newsletter*, 15, 4, p. 15.
23. Eli Barnavi, *A Historical Atlas of the Jewish People* (London: Kuperard, 1998), p. 20.
24. Scholem, *Messianic Idea*, p. 260. See E. Goodenough, *Jewish Symbols in the Greco-Roman Period* (London: Pantheon Books, 1953), Vol. 2, p. 68, citing David Diringer, *Le Inscrizioni antico-Ebraiche Palestinesi* (Florence: Felice de Monnier, 1934), pp. 130–2 and Plate XVI.
25. Jules Harlow, 'Jewish Textiles in Light of Biblical and Post-Biblical Literature', in Barbara Kirshenblatt-Gimblett, *Fabric of Jewish Life* (New York: The Jewish Museum, 1977), p. 31.
26. Goodenough, *Jewish Symbols in the Greco-Roman Period*, Vol. 2, p. 68.
27. A. Eder, *The Star of David* (Jerusalem: Rubin Mass, 1987), p. 9.
28. Goodenough, *Jewish Symbols in the Greco-Roman Period*, Vol. 1, pp. 217ff.
29. Edward J. Keall, 'Brother of Jesus Ossuary', *Biblical Archaeology Review*, 29, 4 (July–August 2003), pp. 55, 70.

30. Goodenough, *Jewish Symbols in the Greco-Roman Period*, Vol. 2, p.96.
31. W. Gunter Plaut, *The Magen David* (Washington, DC: B'nai B'rith Books, 1991), p.27. Bar Kokhba's military skills in his fight against the might of Rome were thorough. For example, prior to the war, merchants would offer to supply the Roman army's procurement officers with weapons, which were then deliberately made substandard. Rejected, therefore, by the Romans, those weapons would then discreetly be made good and used to arm the insurgents.
32. Oegema, *History of the Star of David*, p.28.
33. Ibid., pp.36, 37.
34. Goodenough, *Jewish Symbols in the Greco-Roman Period*, Vol. 3, Fig. 616; Vol. 6, pp.198–201.
35. Cecil Roth in Bezalel Narkiss (ed.), *Jewish Art* (London: Vallentine Mitchell, 1971), p.98.
36. Goodenough, *Jewish Symbols in the Greco-Roman Period*, Vol. 2, p.141–2.
37. Trachtenberg, *Jewish Magic and Superstition*, p.141. G. Vermes, in *The Dead Sea Scrolls in English*, 3rd edn (London: Penguin, 1987), pp.81–99, traces a messianic interpretation of the star in Numbers 24:17 as found in the Damascus Covenant 7:14–21 of the first century BCE community of Qumran.
38. Oegema, *History of the Star of David*, pp.59, 60. Heikhalot, or chariot mysticism, was studied and practised through much of the first millennium CE
39. J.B. Frey, *Corpus Inscriptionum Judaicarum*, New Matter (Vatican City, 1936), Vol. l, Europe. Item No. 621. See also Eder, *Star of David*, p.11.
40. Eder, *Star of David*, p.11.
41. Pessachim 117:6.
42. Git 68 a–b.
43. Oegema, *History of the Star of David*, p.17.
44. Ibid., p.22. The magical and cosmological meanings of the star were embraced as early as the tenth century by the Italian physician, Shabbetai Donnolo (913–982).
45. Plaut, *Magen David*, p.49.
46. Josephine Bacon, *The Illustrated Atlas of Jewish Civilization*, consulting editor Martin Gilbert (London: Andre Deutsch, 1969), p.50. I am uncertain about this. Sir Martin Gilbert, in his later and splendid *The Dent Atlas of Jewish History* (London: J.M. Dent, 1993), p.10, refers only to a yellow patch, not a Star of David. However in his dazzling *Atlas of Jewish Civilisation* (p.50), Martin Gilbert states that the Jews were forced to wear 'a yellow star as an identifying symbol'. Bernard Lewis, *The Jews of Islam* (Princeton, NJ: Princeton University Press, 1987), p.25, states: 'The origins of the yellow badge, first introduced by a caliph in Baghdad in the ninth century'. Kevin Brook, in his fascinating book *The Jews of Khazaria* (Lanham, MD: Rowan & Littlefield, 2006), pp.113, 167, notes that in the ninth to tenth centuries the Star of David form appeared on various burial relics in the tombs of the Khazari, a large and independent, mainly Jewish kingdom stretching above the Black and the Caspian seas. They may, however, have been shamanistic sun discs, despite such being banned by the Jewish Khazar rulers. In present-day northern Serbia, in numbers of undoubtedly Jewish graves of the eleventh century, a Star of David appears on a fragment along with Hebrew writing and menorot.

47. It seems to me, that even where there is no associative context, it would be wrong simply to assume and attribute the symbol as belonging to the majority and not to the minority culture. More often than not, we simply do not know.
48. Scholem, *Messianic Idea*, p.264.
49. A few other Jewish weaves from the sixth century in Egypt have survived. A particularly charming one is a roundel displaying the Joseph story. What makes it Jewish are firstly its Hebrew letters and secondly the images which, as with Hebrew, move from right to left. Alfred Rubens, *A History of Jewish Costume* (London: Peter Owen, 1981), pp.25–6, citing L. Kybalova, *Coptic Textiles* (London: Paul Hamlyn, 1967), p.141.
50. Richard Ettinghausen, 'The Early History, Use and Iconography of the Prayer Rug', in *Prayer Rugs*, exhibition catalogue (Washington, DC: The Textile Museum, 1979), pp.12–15.
51. Jere L. Bacharach (ed.), *Fustat Finds* (Cairo: American University in Cairo Press, 2002), p.141; p.164 Fig. 7; p.225, Fig. 22.
52. Stefan Reif, *A Jewish Archive from Old Cairo* (London: Curzon, 2000), p.226.
53. P. Lambert (ed.), *Fortifications and the Synagogue* (Montreal: Canadian Centre for Architecture, 1994), pp.80, 231.
54. Ibid., p.222.
55. C.J. Lamm, *The Marby Rug and Some Fragments of Carpets Found in Egypt*, p.56, Fig. 2, Plate 1C, in E. Kühnel and L. Bellinger, *Catalogue of Spanish Rugs, 12th Century to 19th Century* (Washington, DC: The Textile Museum, National Publishing Company, 1953), p.7. There is no direct evidence linking this fragment to the synagogue – but equally there is no direct evidence separating it therefrom.
56. Howard Sacher, *Farewell España, The World of the Sephardim Remembered* (New York: Random House, 1995), p.23.
57. Jack Nosseri, 'The Synagogues of Egypt – Past and Present', *Jewish Review*, 25 (1913–14), Plate facing p.40, and in Lambert, *Fortifications and the Synagogue*, p.215.
58. The grille-work of the lamps suspended in the Palestinian Synagogue in Old Cairo quite possibly displayed the Star of David. S.D. Goitein, *A Mediterranean Society* (London: University of California Press, 1999), Vol. 2, p.551, n.16.
59. Goitein, *Mediterranean Society*, Vol. 4, p.134.
60. The Erna Michael Haggadah in the Israel Museum, Jerusalem. Star-shaped Sabbath lamps were known in Germany from the 1450s. *Encylopaedia Judaica* (Jerusalem: Keter Publishing, 1971), Vol. 14, p.570. In *Jewish Art*, second edition ed. Bezalel Narkiss, pp.125, 126, Cecil Roth reports on a fourteenth-century six-pointed Sabbath lamp and on another very old surviving example probably dating back to the eleventh century from Erfurt.
61. The Yahudah Haggadah in the Israel Museum, Jerusalem. Also, the Museum of London has a charming star-shaped Sabbath lamp dated to the twelfth century.
62. Oegema, *History of the Star of David*, p.75. Looking at this carpet page with all its verses extolling the sanctity of the biblical text, so skilfully and purposely embedded in and around the hexagram, with all its symbol power, it cannot be anything but the Star of David.

63. Goitein, *Mediterranean Society*, Vol. 1, p.337.
64. Oegema, *History of the Star of David*, p.75, and see further examples of the use of the Star of David in V.Z. Rabinovitch's *Hebrew Manuscript Ornaments*, Masterpiece of Jewish Art Series (Moscow: Russian National Library, 2003).
65. Scholem, *Messianic Idea*, p.267, disagreeing with the standard references, contends that the most significant point was invented by and added to the text in the first printed edition in Crimea in 1836.
66. Goitein, *Mediterranean Society*, Vol. 4, p.199.
67. Fanny M. Pallister, 'Historic Devices, Badges and War-Cries' (London, 1870), p.139, n.2, cited in Plaut, *Magen David*, pp.38, 45.
68. Haim Beinart, *Atlas of Medieval Jewish History* (New York: Simon & Schuster, 1992), p.51.
69. Victor Klagsbald, *A L'Ombre de Dieu* (Leuven, Belgium: Peeters, 1997), p.27.
70. Trachtenberg, *Jewish Magic and Superstition*, p.296, n.12. In Kabbalah the Star of David also symbolized the directions of space plus the centre – north, south, east, west and the centre – and then under the influence of the Book of Zohar it came to represent the six *sephirot* of the male united with the seventh *sephirot* of the female.
71. Oegema, *History of the Star of David*, p.21.
72. Scholem, *Messianic Idea*, p.269, and Eder, *Star of David*, p.15.
73. Abraham ben Isaac held that the three points forming the vowel *segol* should be placed above the YHVH – the sacred and unpronounceable name of God – and were divine illuminations. These dots were a unity representing the redemptive power and activating messianic impulses. See Dan Cohn-Sherbok, *Jewish Mysticism* (Oxford: Oneworld Publishers, 1998), p.135. The placement of the dots formed an equilateral triangle and so seemed to bring us near to the equilateral triangles of the Star of David.
74. Scholem, *Messianic Idea*, pp.156–201; p.391, n.78.
75. *Facsimiles from an Illustrated Hebrew Bible of the Fifteenth Century* (New York: Hispanic Society of America, 1993), folios 364V and 365.
76. *Cantigas de Santa Maria*, folio 39r, facsimile edition of the copy held in the Bibliotheca del Real Monasterio de San Lorenzo de El Escorial, Madrid, in *Remembering Sepharad* (Madrid: State Corporation for Spanish Cultural Action Abroad, 2003), p.52. The swastika form appears in a number of different cultures, either symbolizing an astral god or representing something that could not be depicted. This second characteristic, it is thought by some, lead to it being used by Jews, and it is to be seen on some ancient synagogues. The *Cantigas de Santa Maria*, among its verses in praise of the Virgin, includes numerous scurrilous anti-Jewish fables.
77. José Ramón Magdalena Nom de Déu, 'The Poblet Haggadah: An Unknown Fourteenth Century Illuminated Sephardi Manuscript', *Jewish Art*, 18 (1992), p.114.
78. H. Ecker, *Caliphs and Kings: The Art and Influence of Islamic Spain* (Washington, DC: Arthur M. Sackler Gallery, Smithsonian Institution; New York: Hispanic Society of America, 2004), pp.76, 147.
79. A. Felton, *Jewish Carpets* (Woodbridge: Antique Collectors Club, 1997), p.179, n.173, citing I. Nusenblatt, *Magen David XIII* (Yivo Bletter, 1942), pp.460–76 (Yiddish).
80. Oegema, *History of the Star of David*, p.81.

81. There is a theory — I have no clear views as to its merit, but is worth noting — as to another factor which may have helped move the star into a more significant nationalist–religious symbol. In the eighth century, the king of Khazaria converted to Judaism and for the next 100 or so years the Khazarian kings ruled over a vast empire stretching from the Black Sea to the Caspian, from the Caucasus to the Volga. But by the twelfth century, the Khazar Empire had been overrun, and in Europe and the Middle East, the Jewish world was in ferment, for in the epic battle between Christianity and Islam, in the First Crusade and in the wars in Germany preceding the Second Crusade, it was the Jews who were being massacred. They cried out for the Messiah — and one appeared in Iraq. David Alroy, proclaiming himself the Messiah — and, it is believed, raising his standard of the Star of David — assembled a large army of Khazar and Kurdish Jews, and planned to march on and to liberate Jerusalem. He was, however, assassinated (possibly by his father-in-law) and his army fell away — but his memory lived on.

   Salo Baron suggests that Alroy's standard of the Star of David, now reinvigorated in the writings of the thirteenth-century German Hasids, appeared both in the Prague synagogue and in the flag given by the Austro-Hungarian Emperor to the Jews of Prague as their identifying symbol. S.W. Baron, *A Social and Religious History of the Jews* (New York: Jewish Publication Society and Columbia University Press, 1965–67), Vol. 3, p.204; Vol. 4, pp.202–4 and notes. See also D. Dunlop, *The History of the Jewish Khazans* (New York: Schocken Books, 1954), p.256, citing Poliak, 'Conversion — The Khazar Conversion to Judaism' (Zion, 1941) (Hebrew). Benjamin Disraeli, himself the son of an unconverted Jew, based his novel *The Wondrous Tale of Alroy* on these events and, when pressed by Queen Victoria as to where he stood in these matters, placed his hand on her Bible at the mid-point between the Old (the Jewish) and the New Testament.
82. *Encyclopaedia Judaica* (Jerusalem: Keter Publishing, 1971), Vol. 11, p.688.
83. E. Bevan and C. Singer (eds), *The Legacy of Israel* (Oxford: Oxford University Press, 1928), p.xxv.
84. Joseph Gutmann, *Beauty in Holiness* (Jerusalem: Ktav Publishing, 1970), p.xxii.
85. D. Friedenberg, *Medieval Jewish Seals from Europe* (Detroit, MI: Wayne State University, 1987), p.269.
86. Scholem, *Messianic Idea*, p.268.
87. C. Descatoire (ed.), *Treasures of the Black Death*, catalogue (London: The Wallace Collection, 2009).
88. Eder, *Star of David*, pp.26, 27, 48, 116.
89. Shabbetai Donnolo, cited in Oegema, *History of the Star of David*, p.22.
90. Friedenberg, *Medieval Jewish Seals from Europe*, p.68.
91. Ibid., p.69 and generally in Dr Friedenburg's fascinating book.
92. Oegema, *History of the Star of David*, p.66.
93. *Remembering Sepharad*, p.104.
94. *Encyclopaedia Judaica*, Vol. 11, p.688.
95. Ibid., Vol. 11, p.695.
96. Gershom Scholem, *Kabbalah* (New York: New York Times Book Co., 1974), pp.362–8. *Encyclopaedia Judaica*, Vol. 11, p.688.
97. Gershom Scholem, *Kabbalah* (Jerusalem: Keter Publishing House, 1977), p.364, cited in

Eder, *Star of David*, p.97.
98. Gershom Scholem, 'The Star of David: History of a Symbol', in Scholem, *Messianic Idea*, p.269.
99. *See and Sanctify*, catalogue (New York: Yeshiva University Museum, 1979), p.46, Exhibit 99.
100. Oegema, *History of the Star of David*, p.58. Sotheby's catalogue (Sale, 18 July 2008, Lot 15) illustrates a fine example of late-fourteenth- to early-fifteenth-century German Kabbalist script with four Stars of David as letters, each containing further Hebrew letters as written characters in their celestial alphabet.
101. It is interesting to see that the teacher (Maimonides?) holds up an astrolobe, an instrument which, combined with certain astronomical tables, helps determine a ship's position at sea. As early as the fourth century, the Jerusalem Talmud (Aboda Zara, 42c) stated that the world was globular in form, and the Zohar (Leviticus 1:3) declared that the world rotated on its own axis like a ball. The Zohar tells us that at the End of Time all the stars, sparkling, will fall down together. Maimonides would have believed the earth to be round – a dangerous heresy in medieval Spain.
102. Oegema *History of the Star of David*, p.84. One such tile may be seen in Heather Ecker's beautiful book, *Caliphs and Kings: The Art and Influence of Islamic Spain* (Washington, DC: Arthur M. Sackler Gallery, Smithsonian Institution; New York: Hispanic Society of America, 2004), pp.102, 160.
103. Matfree D'Ermengaud, *Breviar d'amor*, cited in *Encyclopaedia Judaica*, Vol. 2, p.695.
104. Joseph Caro, *Shulhan Arukh*, Yoreh Deah, 141.1, translated and cited by Vivian Mann, *Jewish Texts on the Visual Arts* (Cambridge: Cambridge University Press, 2000), p.29, n.31.
105. Mishnah, Avodah Zarah 3:5, 4:4.
106. Clifford Pickover, *The Loom of God* (New York: Plenum Trade, 1979), p.168.
107. Mann, *Jewish Texts on the Visual Arts*, citing a Responsa of Moshe Feinstein.
108. I am indebted in this to the wisdom and the generosity of Dr Tali Loewenthal of the Chabad Unit, London.
109. *The Jerusalem Report*, 13 January 2003, p.23.
110. Professor Chimen Abramsky of London most kindly advised me of some other early appearances of the star in addition to those cited in the text: (1) On some Dutch and Italian *Ketubot* (Marriage Contracts); (2) On European *parokhet* (hangings before the Ark); (3) On German kiddush cups (for the benediction of the Sabbath). And the range of the use of the star extended down to the Yemen with a manuscript of 1404 with Massorah and Haphtorah displaying the Star of David within a circle: M. Narkiss, *The Artcraft of the Yemenite Jews* (Jerusalem: The Society of Friends of the Jewish National Museum Bezalel, 1941), p.vi.
111. *Encyclopaedia Judaica*, Vol. 11, p.688 (see n.90).
112. The Talmud explicitly permits five, six or eight branched candelabra. Bab. Tal. Rosh Hashanah 24a, Menahot 28b, Avodah Zarah 43a. See too Dan Barag, 'The Menorah as a Messianic Symbol in Antiquity', in Yael Israeli (ed.), *In the Light of the Menorah: Story of a Symbol* (Jerusalem: The Israel Museum, 1999), p.73. Nine- and eleven-branched menorot have also been recorded in Z. Ma'az, 'The Art and Architecture of the Synagogues of the Golan', in Lee I. Levine (ed.), *Ancient Synagogues Revealed* (Jerusalem: Israel Exploration

Society, 1981), p.111. A medieval gold ring from Regensburg decorated with a silver pointed star and a crescent probably served to identify the owner as holding a specific office within the Jewish community. See also numerous examples of such candelabra in nineteenth- and twentieth-century carpets in Felton, *Jewish Carpets*, and in Chapter 13 of this work.

113. Ferrandis Torres, 1939, p.59, cited in Charles Ellis Grant, *Oriental Carpets in the Philadelphia Museum of Art* (Philadelphia, PA: Herbert, 1988), p.245; and John Mills, 'The Coming of the Carpet to the West', in D. King and D. Sylvester, *The Eastern Carpet in the Western World from the 15th to the 17th Century*, exhibition catalogue (London: Arts Council of Great Britain, 1983), p.51.

114. Mills, 'Coming of the Carpet to the West', p.11. 'When the Black Death struck in 1348 and 1349 Clement VI spoke up courageously and prevented the mob from killing the Jews in the papal enclaves of France.'

115. Ibid., pp.11, 20.

116. So, for example, in Italy two crossed ellipses, double knot forms, appeared frequently on the mosaic floors of many houses near to the synagogue and the cemetery in Brescia. There are various inscriptions in the mosaic referring to the synagogue donors and a specific inscription to the *archisinagogo*, the head of the synagogue, being written in Greek rather than Roman letters, so tracking this neglected Jewish settlement back to the early Roman Imperial period. Those ellipses straightened out form the Star of David! The symbol also appears in a Jewish context in Aquileia, Monasters, Vercelli, Ostia and Sicily. Like the Star, these crossed ellipses are universal signs. Known as the 'Knot of Hercules' in the early Roman Imperial period, and appearing later in Byzantine art, they are also to be seen consistently in Jewish art and artefact and, known as the 'Knot of Solomon', are a Kabbalistic device of divine inscrutability (Hebrew History Federation, New York, Fact Paper No. 34). Significantly the 1460 edition of Maimonides Mishnah Torah displays the Stars of David on Solomon's knot: Victor Klagsbald, *A L'Ombre de Dieu* (Leuven, Belgium: Peeters, 1997), p.31.

Do see Arnold Schwartzman's extraordinarily beautiful book *Graven Images* (Hong Kong: Harry N. Abrams, 1993), p.58, for later examples of the double knot form carved on Jewish graves. The same two crossed ellipses, the double knot forms, interlinked with a complex vertical, horizontal and diagonal grid appear again in fifteenth-century Jewish Bibles. See, for example, the first Hispano-Portuguese Bible in Trinity College, F.120.106, and, as mentioned above, the Spanish Mishnah Torah of 1460, in the National and University Library in Jerusalem, which displays a number of stars within one of the ellipses.

117. Contra Judy Garland in *The Wizard of Oz*.

118. Schuyler V.R. Cammann, 'Symbolic Meanings in Oriental Rug Patterns, Part 1', *Textile Museum Journal*, 3 (December 1972), p.11.

119. May M. Beattie, 'The "Admiral Rugs" of Spain: An Anaysis and Classification of their Field Designs', in Robert Pinner and Walter Denny (eds), *Oriental Carpet & Textile Studies, 2: Carpets of the Mediterranean Countries 1400–1600* (London: Hali Publications, 1986), p.278.

120. Louise W. Mackie, 'Two Remarkable Fifteenth Century Carpets from Spain', *Textile Museum*

Journal, 4, 4 (1977), p.21.
121. W. Denny, Hali, 1, 2 (1978), p.158.
122. Kjeld von Folsach and Anne-Marie Keblow Bernsted, *Woven Treasures – Textiles from the World of Islam* (Copenhagen, The David Collection, 1993), p.51, citing J. Dodds (ed.), *Al-Andalus: The Art of Islamic Spain*, catalogue, Metropolitan Museum of Art (New York: Harry N. Abrams, 1992), Cat. no. 97; Monique King and Donald King, *European Textiles in the Keir Collection, 400 BC to 1800 AD* (London: Faber & Faber, 1990), p.39; Florence Lewis May, *Silk Textiles of Spain* (New York: Hispanic Society of America, 1957), Figs. 63, 89.
123. R. Berliner, 'Remarks on some Tapestries from Egypt', *Textile Museum Journal*, 1, 4 (December 1965), p.40, n.29.
124. Oleg Grabar in Dodds (ed.), *Al-Andalus: The Art of Islamic Spain*, catalogue, p.7.

The Menorah and The *Hamsa* (The Hand)

Light dominates the Jewish symbolic system, and the menorah, a candelabra usually but not necessarily seven-branched, is rich in cosmic symbolism – above all representing the light of the Eternal in the universe. In Genesis the primordial light is described as the first medium of creation, an idea totally in agreement with modern physics, which approaches light as prime energy.[1] Ibn Gabirol (c.1021–c.1056), pursued a not dissimilar and Neoplatonic line of thought when he described light as the first emanation of God, mediating between the complete Transcendent Being, the lower spheres of material forms, and matter itself. His verses are majestic, pre-empting by a millennium the principles of modern physics that hold everything, absolutely everything, to be but part of a cosmic spectrum of wavelengths travelling at different speeds. So, firstly, there is light vibrating fantastically fast, then there is sound resonating more slowly, and lastly there is solid matter oscillating at relatively slower wavelengths.

Josephus saw the menorah as representing the seven stars (that is, the known planets at the time) and Philo (d. 50 CE) saw it as an emblem of the stars. Kabbalah regards many of the qualities of light as helpful analogies to the emanations of the Almighty. Those qualities include its existence, which cannot be denied: it, too, is incorporeal, enlightening and delighting; it is received by the most subtle and tenuous of all the sense perceptions; it is never separate from its source, so if it is cut off from its source it disappears; it spreads instantly, irradiating but not mixing, and never changing; it is essential to life in general and is received and absorbed in relation to the capacity of the recipient. But we are warned by the great Kabbalist, Moses Cordovero (1522–70), not to take any of these metaphors too far: 'For there is no image whatever that can be imagined that is not corporeal.'[2]

The menorah (Figure 26) is the most ancient and powerful Jewish symbol; originally a cultic object, its symmetrical shape and uplifted branches convey both balance and energy. Dating from the Bronze Age, it is described in fine detail in the Bible where its design is revealed by God to Moses.[3] Standing first in the portable Tabernacle and then in the Temple, the menorah illuminated the Ark until the Romans destroyed the Temple in 70 CE and carried off its Golden Menorah in triumph to Rome. Its image is still to be seen there today in the Forum, sculptured on the victory arch of the Emperor Titus. There it was intended to symbolize the end of the Temple and of Israel, but within 100 years or so it became the primary Jewish symbol,[4] compensating the Jews for the loss of the physical object by preserving and perpetuating its meaning and its memory through its image.

That the menorah, as with so many other elements in Judaism, was taken up in Christianity's perceived role as the new or true Israel, did not change its value or meaning in Judaism. In fifteenth-century Spain the Kabbalists, deepening its meaning, saw it as a symbol of the structure of the *Sephirot* (divine attributes), encapsulating and conveying the wisdom of their theosophy in a non-corporeal schematic form (Figure 51). Its use as a teaching diagram for this esoteric scheme of existence, and for contemplation and in worship, continued to spread, and today a Sephardi prayer book informs us that 'whoever looks at the Menorah daily and reflects upon it ... is assured of a place in the world to come'.

On the Vizcaya carpet we see many five-branched figures, a decorative form with no specific Jewish connotation to the world at large. When some of the Admiral carpets were first shown to the public in 1910 at the *Exhibition of Muslim Art* in Munich, the experts readily perceived the five-branched candelabra, but they failed to connect it to its Jewish source.[5] Not all menorot have seven branches (Chapter 12, n.113) and among such early examples is the five-branched menorah found at Capernaum (some have suggested it might have had seven branches originally) and the eleven-branched menorot carved in stone in Kazrin in the Golan.[6] This change in the number of the branches of the menorah had been authorized in the Talmud when – possibly in the face of the oppression following the failure of the bar Kokhba revolt (132–35 CE) – Rabbi Jose ben Rabbi Judah decreed that one may not make 'a Menorah in the form of a Menorah, but rather with five or six branches or eight, but not with seven'. While this ruling fell somewhat into desuetude, it remained there in the teaching section of the Talmud.[7] And five-, six- and eight-branched menorot did not disappear. A five-branched menorah is to be seen carved on the door of the second-century synagogue in Avelim (Israel) and on a fourth-century seal in Avignon; on a fifth-century Spanish tombstone; on a seventh-century epitaph in Narbonne which, in Latin, records the death of three of Paragorus's children and, ending in Hebrew, 'Peace to Israel', displays the five-branched menorah; on many medieval seals and magic formulations; on eighteenth- and nineteenth-century East European tombstones; and embroidered on the dresses of Jewish Ethiopian women and twentieth-century Bezalel and Persian Jewish carpets. Six-branched menorot are still to be seen today, painted on the outside of Jewish houses in Djerba, Tunisia, and it is the eight-branched candelabra – often to be seen in medieval synagogues and mezuzot – that today is still lit annually in celebration of the victory of the Maccabees in freeing the land of Israel from Hellenistic domination (see Chapter 12, n.113).

Those menorot in the Vizcaya carpet may well have been seen as powerful and desperately needed affirmations of the Divine Light in those dark times, each individual light representing a Divine attribute pouring blessings and spiritual radiance downwards through each branch, through the central stem and on down into the world – offering hope of the coming of the Messiah and of personal redemption. That in Christianity the beautiful eleventh-century menorah in the Essen Cathedral or the marvellous twelfth-century medieval menorah in the Milan Cathedral conform exactly to the instructions laid down in Exodus 25:31–6), and that it appears on Islamic coins of the eighth century as a symbol of Jerusalem, did nothing to alter its position as a prime symbol in Judaism.

THE HAMSA (THE HAND)

There is an alternative or parallel meaning to this symbol. In Figure 52 we see two menorot in the Vizcaya carpet, but might their five-fingered form represent another ancient symbol? It may at first seem strange that within one culture a particular symbol can have multiple meanings, but as Schuyler V.R. Cammann, an authority on folk symbols, made clear in his analysis of their use on carpets, 'a single symbol may carry a whole succession of meanings'. He goes on to state – and here he gets to the essence of the point I make in this enquiry – that 'again, it was a matter of the culture as a whole. For this reason, to reach any full understanding of the symbols on the rugs and their meanings, we must carefully consider the environment in which – and for which – they were first produced.'[8] These forms on the Vizcaya carpet are subtle, for another ancient symbol and one reflected in Kabbalah is the protective hand of the Almighty.

Before the dawn of history, hands were being drawn on the walls of caves throughout many Mediterranean countries. To ancient Canaanites, the image would been understood as 'the hand of Baal'; later, to Christians of the region, it would have meant 'the hand of Mary'; then, to many Muslims, especially to the Shi'ah, it was 'the hand of Fatima' – and today to the Greeks it is a savage insult. To Jews, however, it instantly and unconsciously conveys the message of the supreme gift of the Torah and of Divine protection from the cruelty of the world, recalling those words in The Wisdom of Solomon (3:1–3): 'But the souls of the righteous are in the Hand of God. And no torment shall touch them.'

For the hand – that essential tool of mankind which, more succinctly than speech, can signify exclusion or inclusion, war or peace – has, right from the start, been an expression of Divine power.[9] With His right hand He made the heavens, and with His left hand He made the earth. With His right hand He reached out to stay Abraham's hand and save the sacrificial son and with His left He protected the Israelites.[10] The primacy of the hand is spelled out in Psalm 137, verse 5: 'If I forget thee, O Jerusalem, may my right hand lose its cunning.'

Representations of open hands had appeared in Spain as early as in the Palaeolithic period. By the Middle Ages, under Muslim influence, it was used to protect one from the evil eye, for the image can be seen as an instinctive and immediate gesture to ward off danger to oneself. Then, under Christian influence in the later Middle Ages, when the carpet was woven, the open hand had closed into a fist with the thumb sticking out between the index and the middle finger. That this ancient Jewish symbol, predating Islam by many hundreds of years, was taken up by Islam did not lessen its power or change its meaning within Judaism. On the contrary, it seems to me that the consequence of both Christianity and Islam taking up and adapting Jewish symbols to their own communities sometimes served to reinvigorate their meaning and appearance in Jewish culture.

While we have little information about the earliest use of the amuletic hand, it is likely that its image was common among the Jews of medieval Spain and conveyed by them to other countries after the pogroms of 1391 and expulsion of 1492.[11] This symbol is called the *Hamsa*, the word coming from Hebrew for five (*hamesh*) and so clearly linked to four fingers and one thumb of the hand.

Whether painted in the murals of the third-century Dura Europos Synagogue, on the mosaic floor of the sixth-century Beth Alpha Synagogue, in the German Haggadah of around 1320 (Figure 53), the fourteenth-century Spanish Haggadah (Figure 54), or the fifteenth-century Palma prayer book (Figure 55), Jewish art often represents Divine intervention with a hand descending from the heavens. On the Vizcaya carpet (Figure 56, the fourth square to the right), is not that orant figure with its hands raised, its fingers separated, an evocation of the benediction made when the Temple priests would raise their hands bestowing a blessing upon the assembled worshippers?[12] Or might it be Daniel in the lion's den? I will discuss this further in Chapter 18. We see the same hands, only this time it is the back and not the palms, and now adorned with one of the names of the Almighty, at the bottom of the central field of a seventeenth-century synagogue rug (today in the Israel Museum) woven in Chalcis [Greece?] by the Sephardi Moshe ben Costa and inscribed to, or commissioned, by Joseph Nasi, a famous Sephardi nobleman.

The Kabbalists used the Hand of God as a metaphor to explain the cause of evil in the world. The wrath of God was symbolized by His left hand and His love and mercy by His right hand – both qualities are interlinked and in balance with each other. However, when pure justice outweighs mercy it is transformed into evil, into the dark world of Satan. Spiritual strength is signified, in an early seventeenth-century compendium of Kabbalah, by two hands each divided into twenty-eight sections (Figure 57).

Whether as menorot or *hamsa*, these symbols on the Vizcaya carpet in fifteenth-century Spain would for Jews have been profoundly meaningful; for non-Jews they would either have been quite meaningless – or conveyed a quite different meaning altogether.

NOTES

1. Albert Einstein's formulation of E=mc2 tells us that a tiny amount of mass may be converted into an enormous amount of energy – vide the atomic bomb. Light, however, has no mass, because the photon, unlike most other particles, is pure energy. It is, according to the scientists of the twenty-first century, at one and the same time both a wave and a particle: that is (if I understand it, which I don't think I do), at one and the same time it may be at both ends of the universe. And when I read that stars rush around at speeds in excess of tens of thousands of miles per second and that black holes are gateways to alternative universes, I confess I am far more at ease with the verities of the Bible.
2. J. Schochet, *Mystical Concepts in Chassidim* (New York: Kehot, 1988), pp.43, 44.
3. Exodus 25:31–40; 37:17–24; see also Zechariah 4:2–4.
4. Numbers Rabbah, 15:19; Bab. Tal. Berakhot 57a.
5. J. Ferrandis Torres, *Exposicion de Alfombras Antiguas Expañolas* (Madrid: Espasa-Calpe, 1933), p.35.
6. Marilyn Chiat, 'Synagogues and Churches in Byzantine Beit Shean', *Journal of Jewish Art*, 7, p.8, n.21.
7. Babylonian Talmud, Rosh Hashanah 24a, b; Menalot 28 b; Avodah Zarah 43a; and Dan Barag, 'The Menorah as a Messianic Symbol in Antiquity', in Yael Israeli (ed.), *In the Light of the Menorah: Story of a Symbol* (Jerusalem: The Israel Museum, 1999), p.73.
8. Schuyler V.R. Cammann, 'Symbolic Meanings in Oriental Rug Patterns, Part 1', *Textile Museum Journal*, 3 (December 1972), p.21.
9. Exodus 3:20; 15:6, 12; Isaiah 62:8; Psalms 17:7; 21:9; 44:4, and through the ancient ritual of the priestly blessing the hands became the symbol of the priestly class, the Cohenim.
10. L. Ginzberg, *The Legends of the Jews* (Philadelphia, PA: Jewish Publication Society, 1967), Vol. 7.
11. Shalom Sabar, *King Solomon's Seal*, edited by Rachel Milstein (Jerusalem: Tower of David Museum of the History of Jerusalem, 2002), p.12, citing J. Herber, 'La Main de Fathma', *Hesperis*, 7 (1927), p.218; W.L. Hildburgh, 'Images of the Human Hand as Amulets in Spain', *Journal of the Warburg and Courtauld Institutes*, 18 (January–June 1955), pp.78–9.
12. Numbers 6: 23, 24, 26.

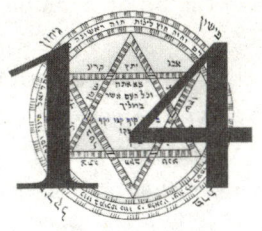

Pomegranates and Walnuts

THE POMEGRANATE

Not all the images on the Vizcaya carpet are sufficiently recognizable for us to interpret their symbolic meanings to the Jews of Spain 500 years ago. Figure 58 is one such image. I think it represents a pomegranate but it could be a walnut.

Of all the fruits of the land flowing with milk and honey, it was the pomegranate that held pride of place in Jewish symbolism. Its beautiful flowers, its shapely structure, its ruby red colour, its sweet flavour and its prodigious number of seeds made it a symbol of fertility and prosperity. Right from the beginning and up to today, the pomegranate has occupied a central role in Jewish iconography.

In the Middle Ages, a Jew looking at the Spanish synagogue carpet may well have seen the mystical pomegranate with all its promises in the circular shapes in the horizontal band under the triangular roof and either side of the lower central door (Figure 13). And those circular shapes on our Vizcaya carpet (Figure 58), with their internal spiralling compartments also echoing the pomegranate's cross section, may well have meant far more to him than the overt image.[1]

We look to the Bible. The Israelites have escaped from Egypt and the Almighty is instructing them as to the modalities. He requires the priestly robes to be made with 'pomegranates of blue, purple and scarlet yarn around the hem ... with gold balls between them' (Exodus 28:33). Later, Solomon's crown is modelled on the pomegranate and his Temple is adorned 'with pomegranates in two rows encircling each network to decorate the capitals on top of the pillars' (1 Kings 7:18). In the Song of

Songs (4:3, 13; 6:7, 11; 8:2) the pomegranate figures prominently in the imagery of love and sensuality; its colour is associated with fire and passion. Today, science tells us that pomegranates are packed with oestrogen.[2]

The only relic believed by some to have survived from Solomon's Temple is a small ivory pomegranate, today in the Israel Museum in Jerusalem. And still today adorning the staves of the Torah scrolls in synagogues throughout the world, the pomegranate decorates the festive tables of Jewish homes greeting the New Year – a festival whose prayers include a wish or a promise that one's merits may be as numerous as the seeds of the pomegranate. Throughout Jewish history it appears in allegories and poetry and is to be seen on a host of everyday objects from lamps to carpets. Finally, it appears today on the coins and stamps of the State of Israel.

As for the significance and importance of the pomegranate in medieval Spain, we need look no further than Granada, for it is embedded in the word 'pomegranate' ('apple of Granada'); and when conquered by the Arabs in 711 CE, Granada was known as *Gharnata al-Yahud*, or 'Granada of the Jews'.

Endowed with ancient mystical properties, this fruit became a major metaphor in Kabbalist writings, an affirmation of faith with the numerical values of the Hebrew, 'Pomegranate Garden' sharing the numerical value and so the meaning of 'The One Lord God'. Its very shape oddly echoes the *Sephirot*. 'The Book of the Pomegranate' (*Sefer ha-Rimmon*) was written by Moses ben Shem Tov de Leon (c.1240–1305), a leading Kabbalist of Castile. Two hundred and fifty-odd years later, Moses de Cordovero (1522–70), an outstanding Sephardi Kabbalist of Safed, wrote 'The Pomegranate Garden' (*Pardes Rimmonim*).

As suggested in Chapter 4, that we see the same Sephardi pomegranate appearing later on the carpets of Samarkand may (or may not) be mere coincidence.[3] But the image of the pomegranate, as with all the other symbols on the Vizcaya carpet, with one set of messages to the *conversos* and different messages to the churchmen, was part and parcel of the complicated double lives of the Sephardim of Spain.

THE WALNUT

This image may possibly be a cross section of a walnut – an ancient symbol first referred to in the Song of Songs when the Almighty goes into the nut (walnut) garden – and since taken to represent the Jewish people. Nahmanides, the towering biblical scholar of medieval Spain, took the walnut as a metaphor for the Jew, for in nature a walnut may be surrounded by and covered in dirt without its inner kernel being sullied. Equally, moving but a single walnut in a pile of walnuts will affect them all.

Later, Joseph Gikatilla, the great Spanish Kabbalist, in *Ginat Egoz* saw the nut with its hard outer shell and leathery coating as representing the Torah, for it too is protected by a cover and kept safely in a covered Ark. The metaphors multiply, for even the walnut tree, some of whose roots must usually remain exposed, to the Kabbalist tells us that our sins may only be expiated if they are equally explicitly revealed.

Finally there is also just a possibility that this symbol portrays a rose, but while the form would fit, I am uncertain about the colours. However, it is worth mentioning here that the rose, a common mystical symbol, entered Jewish culture in the early years of the Common Era. Its transient and fragile beauty as it unfolds in the late spring, linking it to the festival of Shavuot, gave it symbolic values of love, perfection and Torah. Its role as a metaphor in the Talmud and the Zohar lead to its appearance on ritual objects, illuminated *Ketubot* and other Judaica, including possibly the Vizcaya carpet. As with all the symbols on this carpet, its beauty also lay in its secret and private Judaic meanings.

NOTES

1. I am greatly indebted to Enzo and Roberto Danon of Textilia of Rome for their extraordinary book *The Garden of Pomegranates*; of the many very beautifully designed books on Oriental carpets and Jewish Art, their book surely has pride of place. This chapter on the pomegranate owes everything to them.
2. S. Bigg, *The Forbidden Fruit* (Jewish American Medical Association, 1967), p.199.
3. The influence of the Jews of Bukhara on its carpets may go back to the Middle Ages. Their traditional accounts of their return to Bukhara after it had been laid waste by Genghis Khan in the thirteenth century do possibly point to some presence and involvement. One such story is of Tamerlane bringing ten Jewish families of silk weavers to Samarkand in the fourteenth century. Another tells us of expert Jewish carpet weavers 'given' to the king of Bukhara by the Afghan king to teach their skills to the latter's local craftsmen. Yet another is they had come from Spain prior to Tamerlane's reign. Audrey Burton, 'Bukharan Jews, Ancient and Modern', *Transactions of the Jewish Historical Society of*

England (edited by J. Schonfield), 34 (1994–96), p.46, citing M. Zand, 'Bukharan Jews', in *Encyclopaedia Iranica*, IV fasc. 5 (1990), p.530–45. A.Z. Idlesohn, 'Aus dem Leben der Bucharischen Juden', *Hebraisch-Orientalischer Melodienschatzz* III (1992), p.13.

Birds

It was no surprise to see so many different types of birds, both abstract and composite, in the Vizcaya carpet; their images are widespread in Jewish art and artefact. Unfettered by gravity, birds symbolize grace, freedom and the soul striving towards God (Figure 17). In Jewish mythology the souls of one's ancestors in the form of birds cluster around the Divine Throne, interceding on behalf of their loved ones here on earth.[1] Isaiah drew upon this image in describing God's concern for Israel: 'As birds hovering, so will the Lord of Hosts protect Jerusalem.'[2] The great early-seventeenth-century Christian Hebraist, Buxtorf the Elder (1564–1629), noted that Torah Ark hangings (*parokhet*) often displayed birds, for they too had hovered over the Ark of the Covenant.[3]

Let us look at those birds on the carpet that can be identified – the peacock, dove, rooster, goose and the demon bird – and review each of their symbolic meanings and their sources, so that armed with that knowledge we may have a sense of what they meant to a *converso* looking at this carpet.

The most clearly identified bird is the peacock. Long associated with beauty and incorruptibility, it is mentioned twice in the Bible as being brought by King Solomon's ships from Tarshish – identified by many with Tartessos, in southern Spain. As a bird of paradise it signified hope for redemption of the soul and so appeared quite frequently on plaques (Figure 60) and tombstones, in synagogues and on many other Jewish carpets.[4] Here, on the Vizcaya carpet (Figure 59), it is identified by its stylized tail, which seems to branch out into familiar six-sided figures. The tradition continued, for we see similar peacocks/birds of paradise on a seventeenth-century Jewish wall hanging from Azemmour, a coastal town near Casablanca. Such embroideries were woven there solely by Sephardi Jews specializing in that craft and were decorated with the motifs they had brought with them from Spain and Portugal.[5] By contrast, the Yezidi Kurds, seeing the peacock as a sign of Satan, held it in great awe and respect.[6]

The dove and the turtledove are also there in the Vizcaya carpet (Figure 61) and like so many of the birds on the carpet their tails fan out in flight. Doves are monogamous and unlike most birds that fight beak and claw are thought (incorrectly, as it happens) to prefer flight to fight. The dove is usually depicted as white, so symbolizing purity, vulnerability and innocence: fittingly, it became an early symbol for the Jewish people.[7] Since biblical times the turtledove has been noted for its sweet song and colourful plumage. Its return to the Land of Israel heralds each spring – 'And the song of the turtledove is heard in our land'[8] – and, symbolizing hope and rebirth, like the dove, it became an emblem of love and of the Jewish people. But we hear also the cry of Psalm 55, verse 6, echoing throughout Jewish history: 'Oh, that I had the wings of a dove! I would fly away and be at rest.' Carvings of doves, emblematic of the souls of the departed, appear on Jewish-Roman tombstones and on the walls of their catacombs.

Their role in the Israelite economy – for dove-rearing on a large scale, both for meat and fertilizer, was common – added to the values of their images. Later, either singly or in pairs, they became a characteristically Jewish design in the decorative arts of North Africa, brought there by the Sephardim who had fled from Spain. In Christian iconography the dove represents the Holy Spirit and also symbolizes a faithful marriage.[9] In the Hindu tradition, however, it is a messenger from the Death-God.[10]

The next bird adorning the carpet is the rooster (or cockerel) (Figure 63), an ancient Jewish symbol going back to at least the tenth century BCE and so to the kings of Judah.[11] Its use as a symbol of protection goes back at least as far as the third century BCE, when a rooster appeared on the grave of Apolophanes who had been the head of the Jewish community in Merissa, Israel. And it is because the rooster foresees the ending of darkness and the dawning of light that he became a symbol of fruitfulness and special wisdom. Because of his association with the messianic light of redemption, a benediction to the rooster's wisdom is included in the daily morning prayer.[12]

Roosters also symbolized all those qualities much needed if the Jews of the Middle Ages were to survive: foresight, wisdom,[13] courage,[14] fertility[15] and the expectation of messianic redemption.[16] Further, the Talmud describes the rooster as loyal and faithful to his mate. A charming example of a rooster is to be seen in the thirteenth- to fourteenth-century Ashkenazi Haggadah (Figure 62), and in Figure 63 we see a pair of roosters, or perhaps a rooster and a hen, facing each other on the Vizcaya carpet. For in the Sephardi tradition a hen and a rooster would be kept a while in a new house, so that it might gain some of their qualities before it was to be occupied. In the case of newlyweds, the birds would be flung above the heads of the bride and groom that their union might be blessed. That the rooster occupied an important symbolic position in other cultures – for example, appearing in Greco-Roman culture as a wake-up call to the dead; in Zoroastrianism heralding the dawn; in Christianity symbolizing the resurrection of Christ – was all of great value, for on the Vizcaya carpet these different meanings obscured their very specific messages to Jews. On some Persian rugs the rooster offers protection against the evil eye and on Armenian rugs it signifies Christian faith and fruitfulness. The rooster is featured on Jewish seals from the late medieval period and, as we have seen (Chapter 11), already in fourteenth-century Germany the symbol of the white rooster was used on Jewish seals to 'express thoughts which were to remain hidden to the hostile Christians'.

There is another symbolic aspect to roosters and hens, for despite opposition from some important Spanish rabbis, they could take over the role of the scapegoat. The belief was that the human soul might relocate itself in the bird, so rendering it a sacrificial substitute for the miscreant, who thereby hoped to evade punishment. Verses from Psalms and Job were recited as the bird was swung three times around the head of the recanting sinner, then slaughtered and given to the needy.

The goose (or possibly the duck) is no stranger to us (Figure 64). Just like the Star of David and the sheep, it can be seen on the Spanish synagogue carpet (Figures 13, 14 and 15) and further strengthens the evidence that both carpets share the same cultural tradition.[17] Are these images geese or ducks? Although they look a little more like some species of ducks, I think it likely the designers had geese rather than ducks in mind – both are, of course, members of the swan family. Ducks do make an appearance in Jewish iconography in the Hellenic period; the water fowl in the mosaic floor of Beth Alpha (Figure 17) could well be ducks and those in the mosaic floor of the synagogue at Hamman Lif in Tunisia can only be ducks, but without any biblical or Talmudic authority or subsequent symbolic use their meaning is obscure. Geese, on the other hand, have a solid base in Israelite culture. Extensively bred in ancient Egypt they are to be seen being fattened in a ninth-century-BCE tablet found at Megiddo and are among the delicacies enjoyed by King Solomon and his guests. The Talmudic references to geese point to a number of values. One is to wisdom, for it is written that if in a dream you see a goose, you may hope for wisdom. Certainly geese had a special place in medieval Jewish culture, with a general disinclination to kill them over the winter solstice – the time that demons were at the height of their power. The image can also function as a warning, since geese would act as guard dogs; if disturbed they make a ferocious noise. Or the message can be a messianic reminder, for they will be served on the banquet table for the righteous at the End of Days.

But the next bird is strange. It may be a stylized peacock (Figure 65) but this abstracted form echoes the bird-like demons on the protective amulet in the *Sefer Raziel*, a book of Jewish magic published in Holland in 1701–02, recording earlier practices (Figure 66). In the heart of the bird on the carpet are two concentric diamond lozenges, well-known Jewish symbols in the sixth to ninth centuries in the Land of Israel, and those we see here with the dot in the middle are reflective of the resurrection of the dead. A similar demon bird of practical Kabbalah is to be seen on an amulet in the sixteenth-century book *Shaar ha-Yihud* by Hayyim Vital, where, as a further defence against unseen danger, we also see the Kabbalist protective hand (Figure 67).

Finally, among the battery of birds, do we spy a sparrow, thought to be essential in the process of cleansing oneself from leprosy, a terrible illness endemic in the Middle Ages?[18] Or is it the phoenix, a mythological but major figure in Graeco-Roman iconography and later of importance in Christian art as a symbol of the Resurrection? When it migrated into Judaic imagery the phoenix acquired a different meaning. Living for 1,000 years, eating nothing, martyred in an auto-da-fé funeral pyre and then emerging renewed, it became a symbol of the martyrdom and of the rebirth of the *conversos*.[19]

All living symbols answer contemporary needs. When we bring all the themes of these bird images together we see, encapsulated, all the elements that the Jews of Spain longed for: protection, wisdom, redemption and peace. It is these yearnings that are the predominant themes of the Jewish symbols in the Vizcaya carpet, woven in a world where the natural and the supernatural were as one, and the rage and the power of the demons was as real as that of the mob. These symbols were invaluable to the *conversos*, for none, save one versed in Talmud and Kabbalah, would understand them for what they were.

NOTES

1. A. Kanof, *Jewish Symbolic Art* (New York: Gefen, 1990), p.74, n.16, citing Ber Sanhedrin 91a, quoted in T.H. Gaster, *Myth, Legend and Custom in the Old Testament* (New York: Harper & Row, 1969), p.881.
2. Isaiah 31:5.
3. Franz Landsberger, 'Old Time Torah Curtains', in Joseph Gutmann, *Beauty in Holiness* (Jerusalem: Ktav Publishing, 1970), p.158.
4. A. Felton, *Jewish Carpets* (Woodbridge: Antique Collectors Club, 1997), pp.57–151.
5. Vivian Mann (ed.), *Morocco, Jews and Art in a Muslim Land* (New York: The Jewish Museum, 2000), p.184, citing Bibliography Paris, Le Petit Palais, 1999, No. 383, and in the Collection of Isabelle C. Denamur.
6. Count Bobrinskoy, *Peacocks from Heaven: A Kurdish Yezida Tale* (Aurora, OR: Two Rivers Press, 1983, reissued by James Opie).
7. Psalms 74:19, and the later Talmudic ruling that 'One should ever be of the persecuted but not of the persecutors.' *Encyclopaedia Judaica* (Jerusalem: Keter Publishing, 1971), Vol. 15, p.1467.
8. Song of Songs 2:12.
9. J. Chevalier and A. Gheerbrant, *The Penguin Dictionary of Symbols*, trans J. Buchanan-Brown (London: Penguin Books, 1996), p.306.
10. Giulio Busi, 'Common Symbolic Patterns in Hebrew and in Sanskrit Literature', *Journal of Indo-Judaic Studies*, VI (2003), p.67.
11. *Encyclopaedia Judaica*, Vol. 5, p.418.
12. L.Y. Rahmani, 'Three Desk Seals in the Jewish Museum, London', *Jewish Art*, 19–20 (1993–94), p.160.
13. Jewish exegesis interpreted the *sekhvi* in Job 38:36 as referring to the cockerel, who was thus imbued with special wisdom (Bab. Tal. Rosh Hashanah 26a; and Pal. Tal. Berakhot 9:2). Rahmani, 'Three Desk Seals', p.159.
14. Rahmani, 'Three Desk Seals', pp.159–60; Bab. Tal., Beiza 25B; Ex. Rabbah, 42:9.
15. Rahmani, 'Three Desk Seals', pp.159–60; Bab. Tal., Gittin 57A.
16. Rahmani, 'Three Desk Seals', pp.159–60; Bab. Tal., Sanhedrin 98.
17. Babylonian Talmud, Berachot 57a; Ketubot 27a; Baba Batra 73b–74a.

18. Leviticus 14:4.
19. Job 29:18; Babylonian Talmud, Sanhedrin 108b, trans. H. Freedman (London: Soncino Press, 1935).

Sheep

Sheep (rams, lambs and ewes)[1] are referred to more than 100 times in the Bible and, as symbols in Judaic iconography, were almost bound to appear on both the Vizcaya (Figures 68, 69) and the Spanish synagogue carpet (Figures 13, 14, 15), reflective of their unique place in Israelite and Jewish history. Earlier representations are to be seen in the catacombs and synagogues of the Talmudic era, and by the Middle Ages sheep had a solid role in the iconographic repertoire of the Jews of Spain.

Sheep are a part of a metaphor for God, as the divine shepherd caring for his flock, and the Bible is filled with such cherished verses as 'The Lord is my shepherd, I shall not want' (Psalm 23:1). Right from the beginning, a ram was there when Abraham's hand was stayed and, replacing Isaac on the sacrificial pyre, it signalled the transformation from human to animal sacrifice – a change reversed some 3,000 years later by the Inquisition. Many of the greatest Jewish heroes – Jacob, Moses and King David – were shepherds. It is the sheep's innocence, their defencelessness and their contribution – their donation – to man's welfare that marks them out as symbols of the Jewish people: 'Nay, for Thy sake we are slain all the day long, and accounted as sheep for the slaughter' (Psalm 44:22).

For the sheep gave its all to the Israelites. I earlier explored its role in ritual: the ram's horn formed the trumpet; their fleece was woven into the prayer shawl; their shank-bone was served at the Passover festival and their hide was used for the Torah scroll. Indeed, there was little of a sheep's body that was not used in biblical Israelite life – its meat (Isaiah 53:7), its milk (Deuteronomy 32:14), its wool for textiles and carpets (Hosea 2:7) and its hide for belts, straps, shoes and clothing (Exodus 25:5). The hides were also used to carry wine or water, or, when inflated, as floats to cross water. Many of the organs were also used: the gut for stringed instruments and fine bindings, and the bones for glue and paint. Even its dung was preserved and used for fuel. In return, along with the offspring of the goat (the biblical term *zon* refers to both sheep and goats), sheep received the ruling in Exodus (23:19; 34:26) and Deuteronomy (14:21): 'Thou shalt not seethe a kid in its mother's milk', which then grew into the broader prohibition against mixing milk with meat. Only recently has archaeology suggested that as boiling a kid in its mother's milk was a popular pagan fertility rite, the prohibition was part of the process of preserving a separate cultural identity.

The sheep on the Vizcaya carpet are surely the direct offspring of the rams on the Spanish synagogue carpet, being part of the same tradition and sharing those same symbolic meanings and associations. The ram's horn, visible on both carpets, is a particularly poignant sign, for its blast, heard every year for the last 2,000 years and more, recalls a solemn moment as it announces the arrival of the New Year, reminding us too that at the End of Days it is its last trump that will finally be heard, heralding the coming of the Messiah.

These would be but some of the conscious and unconscious responses of a Spanish Jew in the Middle Ages to the sheep and the ram's horn on these two carpets. Today, however, peering through our monocultural secular spectacles, we may well miss the point – for it was their point, it is not ours.

NOTE

1. E. Frankel and B.P. Teutsch, *The Encyclopaedia of Jewish Symbols* (Northvale, NJ: Jason Aronson, 1992), p.154.

Torah Arks

After the Romans destroyed the Temple in 70 CE, Torah Arks (cabinets to house the Scrolls of the Law) came to represent and replace the Temple, so becoming a constant theme in Jewish art (Figures 14, 17, 18 and 19) – often directly portrayed, sometimes more discreetly hinted at. In this respect the penultimate border of the Vizcaya carpet (Figure 70) is particularly interesting, as the unknown artist who designed this carpet worked at a time when Jews would see Hebrew letters and Jewish symbols everywhere: in the shapes of the clouds in the heavens above and in the countless formations of man and nature. Christians, too, at the edge of their vision would see cherubs, angels, devils and saints.

If we look at this border neither from our modern perspective nor through the eyes of a Christian or a Muslim of fifteenth-century Spain but through those of a Jew of that time, we may just see things differently. With diamond shapes atop a gabled roof and hooked forms protruding from its sides, those narrow pointed perpendicular forms, evocative of the angelic letters used in the writing of practical Kabbalah, do perhaps convey something of the form of Torah Arks, as do the triangular gabled rooftops protruding from the inner border into the penultimate border. These forms hark back to the Torah Arks we have seen on the Spanish synagogue carpet (Figures 13, 14, 15), for their half-diamond shapes form the roof of the Arks with their six bands; two of these are in turn made of half-diamond shapes, and they mirror the inner border of the Vizcaya carpet. These pyramidal forms convey a sense of fire and of spiritual ascent.

The design of the double doors of the Ark flows from the pictorial tradition that prevailed after the destruction of the second Temple. Examples can be seen in clay oil lamps and tombstones from the second, third and fourth centuries CE (Figure 71);[1] gold glass bases from the fourth century (Figure 72); the mosaic floor of the Beth Alpha Synagogue of the sixth century (Figure 17);[2] and in stylized form in the St Petersburg Pentateuch of 1008 CE.[3] As for the lozenge shapes, they are found on the frescos in the synagogue at Dura Europos, on the tomb door from Kfar Yassif and often on ossuaries. Again we see the same double diamond form on one panel of the eight-sided glass bottles made in Jerusalem for Jewish pilgrims from the fourth to the seventh centuries. Erwin Goodenough states that these lozenges symbolize the resurrection of the dead, and the palm tree the revival of the righteous. The forms on the other sides of these glass bottles include the palm tree, the menorah, the shofar and the chalice.[4]

The blue of the Vizcaya carpet may also be significant. Blue is the most important colour in the hierarchy of Jewish colour symbolism because, as the colour of the infinite sky, it represents the Eternal.[5] When juxtaposed with white, it echoed the colours of the prayer shawl and to the sophisticated Jews of Spain it was expressive of the human dynamic – for white represented the rational and blue the mystical sides of our nature.[6] In the magic of the masses, white denoted purity and repelled the Evil Eye by dazzling it; blue was also an antidote to evil.

Against a wide blue background the designer of the carpet set slender vertical, horizontal and angled straight off-white lines that form a regular pattern. The contrasting colours of these forms against their backgrounds strike us, and are further enhanced by their reddish-brown outlines. Very similar designs can be seen in the textiles of Sicily and of Egypt – countries that for a time also enjoyed a *Convivencia* of Christians, Muslims and Jews. Their vestigal Kufic, commonly seen in other carpets of that era, convey the sense of a great Muslim invocation. There is, too, a suggestion of a perimeter fence safeguarding what lies within, being built up of all those lines parallel to the four sides of the carpet, framing a base for the inward-pointing isosceles triangles and their right-angled barriers. That same sense is conveyed in the minute serrating at the edges of the 'V' shapes at the innermost border; they are suggestive of a sharp, saw-like protective barrier guarding the central field against the evil eye and defining the inner and sacred space with the sides aligned to the cardinal directions.

NOTES

1. This tombstone, found in Monteverde to the north of Murcia, bears the following inscription: 'Here lies Samuel, an infant of one year five months. May he rest in peace! Be brave Samuel! No one is immortal.'
2. Yaffa Levy, 'Ezekiel's Plan in an Early Karaite Bible', *Jewish Art*, 19–20 (1993–94), p.73.
3. Paul Figueras, *Decorative Jewish Ossuaries* (Leiden: Brill, 1983), pp.57, 69.
4. D. Harden, *Glass of the Caesars* (Milan: Olivetti, 1987), p.177.
5. In Catholic Spain, the colour blue seems to have acquired a specific symbolic meaning, for priests were not permitted ever to wear that colour on any day other than on the annual feast of the Immaculate Conception. A brilliant red colour became the colour of the cardinal's robe and, being made from the Kermes bug, was called Vermilion – the early Spanish word for 'little worm'.
   The muddy brown colour called 'Isabella' was named after Queen Isabella of Castile's bodice. Isabella (cousin of our Enriquez and signatory, with her husband Ferdinand, king of Aragon, to the edict expelling the Jews in 1492), on learning that one of her towns was besieged, swore a solemn oath that she would not change her bodice until it was relieved. However, it took six months or more before the town (and presumably Isabella, Ferdinand and anybody else close to her) was relieved. Victoria Finlay, *Colour* (London: Sceptre, 2002), p.113.
6. R. Solovietchik, 'The Symbolism of Blue and White', in A. Besdin (ed.), *Man of Faith in the Modern World* (Jerusalem: Ktav, 1989). Quoted on P'til Tekhelet website, www.tekhelet.com.

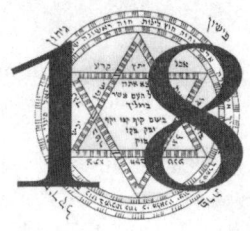

Other Symbols, Numerology and Orant Figures

I think there may be other Jewish symbols embedded in both the Spanish synagogue and the Vizcaya carpet. Rosettes, crowns, hanging lamps, zigzag lines, double diamond-shaped lozenges, stylized trees, shofar, eye writing, cuneiform writing, double circular forms, myrtle flowers (symbols of peace and joy): all seem to appear and then disappear, only to reappear. In this chapter, apart from the clearly identifiable orant figure and the three-point marks, I discuss some other symbols that I looked for but did not find in the Vizcaya carpet.

For the Kabbalist, everything is a symbol for something else – mere decoration does not really exist – for everything has meaning and relationship to the whole; their world is filled with subtle connections, for our reality is but a web of invisible threads binding together ideas and events. In Kabbalah, the letters of the Hebrew alphabet are akin to the building blocks of the cosmos. So the Kabbalist will look behind the surface of a text, seeking out its deeper meaning and, manoeuvring letters, words and numbers, will produce new text. A good example of this is seen in the five books of Moses, known collectively as the Torah, in Hebrew 'vru,'.

It is quite odd, really, and works like this. In the first book of Genesis, take the first time the letter T appears in the Hebrew version of the book, then take the fiftieth subsequent letter: it is the letter O. Then take the fiftieth letter after the O, which is the letter R, and then take the fiftieth letter after the R: it is an H – TORH. Exactly the same formula applied to the second book of Exodus produces the same word. Now skip the next book of Leviticus for the moment, and turn to the fourth and fifth books of Numbers and Deuteronomy, where the same formula applies as for the first two books – only the word TORH is now spelt backwards! In other words it *faces* rather than follows on from the coded word in the third book of Leviticus. To find out what that coded word is, mark the first time the letter J appears and proceed seven letters further on to see the letter H; seven letters after that is the letter V, and finally seven letters after that is an H – so spelling JHVH, the Hebrew name for God.[1]

Every one of the twenty-two letters of the Hebrew alphabet has a numerical value[2] and their placement is reviewed either in geometric or arithmetic terms and, being reinstated into letters, forms new words, so yielding a way of looking behind the explicit and into the implicit meaning of the texts. Hidden words, too, are revealed by an arithmetic or geometric selection of the initial letters of words in the text, as well as by other complex permutations of the Hebrew alphabet.[3] Acrostics – a device whereby the initial, final or other prearranged letters in each line of a text when taken together spell out a new word or words – appear in the Bible, and acquired mystical significance in Kabbalistic literature. I could not, however, trace any letters inscribed on the Vizcaya carpet.

As for numbers, Bevis Longstreth has made some interesting suggestions regarding the possible use of Jewish magical numbers on a fourth- to fifth-century-BCE carpet, but I find this form of numerology a bit befuddling.[4] By counting both the number of like symbols and their various placements in each of the four major borders on the Vizcaya carpet, one can produce significant numbers such as seven – the most auspicious number in the Bible. 'Perfect' numbers like twenty-eight (which is divisible by one, two, four, seven and fourteen – all of which, added together, come to twenty-eight) may also be traced. It is also possible that even the magical ratio pi (22/7) is there to be found. Number eight is more easily traced in the design: its special meaning in Kabbalah is to represent what is beyond the norm, beyond the boundary of the physical world. Eight is quite an extraordinary number, being a cube number, that is, a number which can be created by multiplying another number twice by itself. So, for example, $2 \times 2 \times 2 = 8$. It is also a Fibonacci number – that is, a member of the sequence of numbers such that each number is the sum of the preceding two. So the first seven numbers are 1, 2, 3, 5, 8 and 13.[5] Of course, in any design, one may very easily see numbers that had no relation whatsoever to the knowledge or intent of the designers. But it is because such numerology was an element in Kabbalah, it seems to me, that we face both the possibility of the use of magic numbers on the Vizcaya carpet and the impossibility of coming to any rational and objective conclusions in that regard.

The same question of plausibility applies to the small three-point marks found in the carpet. Are they simply an accident – or perhaps the serendipity – of the weavers? Do they, as in some Kabbalist works, represent the letter shin, the initial letter of 'Shaddai', one of the names of the Almighty? Or, as G. Busi proposes, do they represent the three branches of the Tree of Life?[6] And are those triangular forms in the margin magical triangles? By repeatedly reducing the size of an inscription within a series of triangles of the same size, one would squeeze out evil spirits. That there is no Hebrew script in the triangles may not necessarily have negated the associative response in the mind of a devout Jew of the time: to a Kabbalist, the Hebrew alphabet is part of the building blocks of the world; every one of its twenty-four letters and may be read into the Star of David. Then too, a points-mark to a Kabbalist brought with it a profound meaning – that of creation from nothing. The analogy is the points-mark in geometry, which has no dimensions but whose movement creates lines and circles and concepts. And three circles, particularly if, as we see in Figure 71, resting within a horizontal rectangle, evoke memories of the row of six scrolls laid on a shelf in the Torah Ark.

There are some deteriorated images of animals on the carpet, which may be sheep or lions, and given that the two Admiral carpets most closely associated with our Vizcaya carpet seem to display lions, one should not ignore the possibility that these impaired images were originally lions. A pre-Judaic symbol, figuring significantly in Solomon's Temple, the lion was more often drawn, painted, sculpted, sealed in glass or woven in and on Jewish artefacts than any other animal. The lion, the badge of the tribe of Judah, symbolized physical and spiritual strength, protection, justice and redemption.[7] And in Figure 72 we see, on a fourth-century glass vase, five lions protecting the Ark, with its six scrolls above two menorot.

There is, however, a far more credible image on the Vizcaya carpet (see Figure 56). It is of a man and very closely resembles images of Daniel in the lion's den found on the base of a Torah shrine and in the mosaic floors of a number of fifth- and six-century synagogues, and frequently seen on Jewish artefacts such as oil lamps from that time onwards. Daniel, who did not always appear with the lions at his side, was usually depicted as an orant, or man at prayer. Here he appears in his classic pose with his arms bent at the

Other Symbols, Numerology and Orant Figures

elbows, the palms of his hands open and raised to the heavens, which posture may reflect the position for prayer of the Jews in late antiquity. Daniel would be a totally appropriate figure for the Vizcaya carpet for, from the Maccabean period onwards, he symbolized the man of such pure faith that death held no terrors for him.[8] For the Jews of Spain, with their history of discrimination leading to a sense that the past is ever contingently present, the linkage to Daniel is inescapable. For it was Daniel in sixth-century-BCE Babylon who rather than worship another god was thrown into a lion's pit – and survived. His story, the Book of Daniel, was first inscribed in the second century BCE when Antiochus IV Epiphanes, the Seleucid overlord of Judea, ordered the Jews to worship his gods, so sparking off the successful Maccabean revolt. Just like the other images on the carpet that we have discussed, this symbol of Daniel also appears in Christian and Muslim traditions.

As discussed earlier, the prohibition in the Second Commandment against replicating the image of major life forms (animals, fishes, humans) was variously complied with – or not at all. It all depended on the response of the viewer. So, for example, a German Haggadah of 1430 CE portraying a naked woman with long hair echoes Ezekiel 16:7. Maimonides had no objection to the human figure being woven in a carpet so long as it was not the complete form, and his view was codified in the sixteenth-century Shulhan Arukh.[9] The central concern was that God alone and no other may be an object of reverence and worship.[10] The later adoption of the figure of Daniel in Christian culture did not take away from its meaning in Judaism, and as with so many of the symbols on our carpet, their use in Christian iconography served to conceal their primary symbolic value for the Jews of Spain.

Of course, we all see what we want to see (or do not see what we do not want to see), projecting our desires on to the world around us. Viewing the Vizcaya carpet through the eyes of Spanish Jews and *conversos* of some 500 years or more ago, and apprised of the metaphysical meanings of its symbols we may, with sensitivity and empathy, occasionally glimpse what they saw. I may, of course, be misinterpreting any one or more of these lesser symbols, but the conjunction of their appearance alongside the obvious major Judaic symbols, with the particular history of the carpet and of the Enriquez, and the strong evidence for the weavers being *conversos*, suggests that they should not be summarily dismissed as Islamic or Christian symbols or as mere decorative devices without symbolic meaning. The overall coincidence of those elements is too clear to be denied.

This constellation of Judaic symbols on the carpet, all bearing the same basic message of hope and of faith, combined with the absence of any *exclusively* Christian or Islamic messages is significant. Even the few crosses on the carpet – with all four arms of the same length – were valued symbols in the magic tradition of Judaism, for those arms would disperse the effect of the Evil Eye to the four winds. The point to restate is that these crosses and all the other symbols on the Vizcaya carpet would be familiar to Christians and to Muslims either as specific symbols in their own cultures or as ordinary decorative devices. In those intensely suspicious and superstitious times, they would not point to the private and personal life of a *converso*.

NOTES

1. G. Schroeder, *Genesis and the Big Bang* (New York: Bantam, 1991), p.182.
2. The Hebrew alphabet itself demands interpretive skills because it has no vowels, only consonants, so that the same group of letters with different vocalizations may yield very different meanings. By analogy in English the consonants B and G might, depending upon the context, be interpreted as bag or beg or big or bog or bug.
3. Clifford A. Pickover, *The Loom of God* (New York: Plenum Trade, 1979), p.196.
4. Bevis Longstreth, 'The Riddle of the Pazyryk', *Hali*, 137 (November–December 2004), pp.49–51, who also suggests that this ancient and sophisticated carpet was woven by a Jewish master weaver of Sardis.
5. Remer Daniel, 'Pieces of Eight', *Jewish Chronicle*, 3 December 2004, p.33.
6. G. Busi, *Simboli del Pensiero Ebraico* (Torino: G. Einaudi, 1999), p.328.
7. E. Frankel and B.P. Teutsch, *The Encyclopaedia of Jewish Symbols* (Northvale, NJ: Jason Aronson, 1992), p.98.
8. Joan Goodnick Westenholz (ed.), *Images of Inspiration*, catalogue of the Bible Lands Museum (Jerusalem, 2001), pp.116, 117, 129, 130.
9. Mishneh-Torah Avodat Kochavim, 3:10, 11; and Shulhan Arukh, Yoreah Deah 141:47.
10. Franz Landsberger, *Development of Jewish Art* (Cincinnati, OH: Union of American Jewish Congregations, 1944), p.208.

PART 5

SUMMING UP

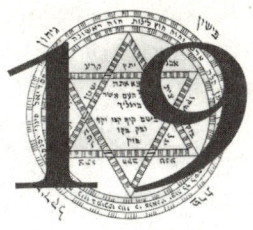

Conclusion

To best answer the question as to whether any of the Admiral carpets might be Judaic, and focussing on the Vizcaya carpet, I have asked what evidence, if any, is there:

A. that the Enriquez who commissioned the carpet might have been *conversos* who continued in private to follow the Jewish faith?
B. that the designers and weavers of the carpet might also have been crypto-Jewish *conversos*?
C. that the symbols on the Vizcaya carpet might have had particular religious values for Spanish Jews and crypto-Jewish *conversos* of the time?

In approaching the problem I have kept in mind the Socratean principle of following the evidence, wherever it leads. My answers to the three questions follow:

A. *What is the evidence that the Enriquez who commissioned the carpet might have been conversos who continued in private to follow their Jewish faith?*

A.1. What is known is that Fadrique Enrique, twin brother of the Enrique Trastamara, king of Castile, married a *conversa*, as did their son and their grandson, Fadrique – he who commissioned the Vizcaya carpet – who also had his heir by a Jewish noble lady. That the majority of conversions were made for social or political reasons or under life-threatening pressure did not usually alter one's private beliefs and traditions – at least for a generation or two and, in the view of the Spanish Inquisition, for many, many generations thereafter. What is also known is that Enrique Trastamara used anti-Semitism as a political tool to gain the throne in Castile but, once in power, he changed from being a persecutor to a protector of the Jews. The motivation for this extraordinary about-turn was partly economic, for the Jews generated much of the wealth – as well as the administrative structures to tax that wealth. Medieval kings, however, were not renowned for acting solely in their economic best interests and at the time most were preoccupied, aided by the church and the populace, in persecuting and expelling their Jewish citizens. It was therefore possible that Fadrique and his wife, dona Juana, were influential in this unusual about-turn, which of itself proves little – but is the first step in a pattern which emerged as I went on to examine the unusual philo-Semitic history of these three generations of the Enriquez.

A.2. Murcia, one of the Enriquez domains (and where the carpet was woven), was a haven from persecution for Jews and *conversos*. To save their own and their children's lives, many Jews in other parts of Spain were baptized but, as soon as they could, would flee to the sanctuary of Murcia where, in the synagogues renouncing their false and forced baptisms, they would publicly declare their true faith as Jews. In turn, the Jews of Murcia sent emissaries to support their fellow Jews, and raised the ransom monies needed to pay for the lives of those imprisoned and tortured in other parts of Spain. This would not have happened without the compliance of the Enriquez.

A.3. Jewish law and the custom of the *conversos* determined that the children of a Jewish woman must be brought up in the Jewish faith – albeit discreetly during a time of persecution. If, therefore, dona Juana were to have been a practising crypto-Jew, it is likely that her son Alfonso, would have been one too.

A.4. Alfonso in turn married dona Juana Mendoza, also a fabulously wealthy *conversa*. It is of course quite possible that he married her solely for love or money (or both) – or that she was no longer a practising crypto-Jew – but the pattern of the Enriquez *converso* intermarriage is now beginning to emerge. For only through such marriages were the parties confidentially and confidently best able to continue to follow in their faith. Their son Fadrique, in accordance with the tradition of the Spanish Jews, was named after his paternal grandfather.

A.5. In turn Fadrique also married a fabulously wealthy *conversa*, dona Marina de Ayala, and it is their coats of arms that adorn the carpet. It seems they had no children. But Fadrique had a relationship with a beautiful noble Jewish lady, so continuing the pattern of Jewish and *converso* affiliations, and their son became Fadrique's heir. What is unusual is not necessarily untrue, and the Enriquez *converso* life was really not that unusual at all; indeed, it was very common. In the next century the king's secretary reported that there was hardly a noble Castilian family that was not related to or descended from *conversos*. Nor is it surprising that conversions based upon social and economic pressures are likely to be fragile or false and that, for a few generations, it is clear that many *converso* families remained discreetly true to the faith of their fathers. As much as one may deplore the methods employed by the Inquisition in this regard, their understanding of the tenacity of the Jewish faith cannot be questioned.

A.6. The unusual support given by the Enriquez to the Jews combined with their three-generational pattern of marrying only *conversos* did not, in itself, prove that they were crypto-Jews. The Enriquez conversions may all have been totally authentic and those three generations might have been devout Christians – but for the following critical point. Death is the time of truth, and the disposition of one's earthly remains in medieval society was a matter of supreme importance. Alfonso's and dona Juana's requirements in this respect taking them right out of Christian culture put them squarely into Jewish culture. Their absolute rejection of the essential Christian nobles funerary iconry – the statue at rest atop of the tomb, crucifixes, and pictures of Jesus and the apostles et al. Were they to have been Catholic, this remarkable failure to conform to the rules and rituals of their faith would have been condemned them to burn in hell for eternity! If they had been agnostics or even atheists, it is less likely that they would have rejected the Christian funerary requirements. For only Jews, whether discreetly so or not, would feel compelled to comply with the Second Commandment which absolutely forbids such graven images. I see no other explanation. The Catholic visions of Hell to which the vast majority were condemned for eternity lead many *conversos* to follow the well-established pattern of deathbed reversion to a Judaism whose sense of the afterlife was infinitely less punitive.

A.7. In the next century the Inquisition busied itself opening up the tombs of important Christians with Jewish forebears to check whether they had been buried in accordance with Jewish or with Christian law – for they considered that burial in the Jewish tradition was prima facie evidence that the descendant was a heretic. In a pre-emptive move, the Enriquez grandson, heir to most of their lands and titles, broke open Alfonso's and dona Juana's divergent sepulchres. He had their mortal remains buried elsewhere and their telltale tombs disappear from history. I cannot think of any other good reason why he should desecrate their tombs unless it was to conceal their Jewish burials.

A.8. In the second half of the fourteenth century, the increasing power of the church and of the emerging middle classes, general civil instability and finally the pogroms of 1391 at least 100,000 Jews, from the highest to the lowest, to convert. Whilst all became Christian in form, many in substance remained embedded in the culture and faith of their fathers. The 1449 Purity of Blood laws split the people of Castile and Leon into those who had and those who did not have Jewish forebears; the powerful Enriquez, being of royal blood, were specifically exempted from these laws.

The above facts, fully detailed and referenced in Chapter 7, establish a strong case for the probability that through dona Juana (the sister-in-law of the king of Castile), her son Alfonso and his wife, and in turn Alfoso's son Fadrique and his wife, the Enriquez for three generations remained to a considerable extent within their Jewish tradition.

B. *What is the evidence that the designers and weavers of the carpet might also have been conversos?*

B.1. There is a quite unfounded assumption embedded in the corpus of our received knowledge about Jews and carpets that Jews, while creating the dyes, were almost exclusively traders, not weavers. It is this assumption, especially in relation to the Jewish weavers of the Middle Ages, that by looking to the facts I seek to correct.

We now have all the building blocks in place with the facts, coming from a wide range of material including, from Jewish sources: the Bible, the Talmud, the *Responsa* of the great rabbis, the court records and commercial documents of the Genizah, the journals of the medieval travelling merchants, the writings of the Kabbalists, the prose and poetry of the Sephardim, illuminated manuscripts, marriage contracts, wills, synagogue inventories and carpets and carpet fragments. From Christian sources: the New Testament, the

Conclusion

writings of the saints and sages, Papal Bulls, the edicts and records of the churchmen and the Spanish Inquisition. Other research sources include the taxation records, the censuses, petitions and royal edicts as well as the accounts of medieval Muslim geographers and chroniclers and the reports and ordinances of the Ottoman Empire.

The facts were presented in their separate contexts. So Chapter 1 started with the history of weaving in Murcia of Spain and Chapter 2 reviewed the history of 'The Jews of Spain'. Chapter 3 discussed 'Carpets in Jewish Culture', which was given greater focus in Chapter 4, 'The Jewish Weavers of Spain and North Africa'.

In Chapter 5 we turned to look at the Vizcaya carpet itself and went on, in Chapter 6, to see the same Judaic imaging in the earlier 'Spanish Synagogue Carpet'. Chapter 8 examined both what was happening to the Jews and the New Christians in the 100 years leading up to the expulsion in 1492. The importance and the numbers of Jewish weavers in Spain and their close involvement with the Jewish weavers of the Maghreb and Egypt are looked at closely, for during much of the Middle Ages virtually every major textile centre surrounding the Mediterranean was also home to a major Jewish community – so casting light for us on the culture and practices of the Jewish and *converso* weavers of Murcia.

These background studies also established three critical points:

(i) The Jews were very successful commercially; at one time they were producing from 35 to 60 per cent of the revenue of every one of the Iberian kingdoms.
(ii) Murcia's economy was based on its huge volume of quality carpet production.
(iii) The commercial success of the Jews of Murcia was such that they paid the greatest amount of tax of all the Jewish communities in Spain.

Bringing together these facts, it is a safe assumption that there were large numbers of highly skilled Jews and *conversos* working in the carpet industry in Murcia.

B.2. Then, in Chapter 9, the facts pointing to the Admiral carpet then being woven by *conversos* in Murcia may be summarized as follows:

(i) As a consequence of and in the years following the Christian conquest of Murcia, skilled Muslims moved to Muslim held Granada.

(ii) From the middle of the fifteenth century, there were very few Muslim weavers in Murcia and none at all in the Hellin district.

(iii) The Jewish weavers, now New Christians, had every good reason to seek refuge in the Hellin district – and they did so, as evidenced, too, by the taxation and the Inquisitions records reporting the extraordinary large number of Judaizing New Christians living there.

(iv) The huge sums of money needed to buy a certificate attesting to the 'purity' of one's blood are indicative both of the numbers and commercial success of the crypto-Jewish weavers.

(v) The skills of the large numbers of Spanish-Jewish weavers fleeing Spain created the exponential expansion of the carpet weaving industry in the Ottoman Empire.

Finally, given also that the Vizcaya carpet was commissioned by the *converso* Enriquez, and given the *conversos'* hunger for covert Judaic symbols, I think the carpet was far less likely to have been woven by Old Christians or Muslims than by Judaizing New Christians.

C. *What is the evidence that the symbols in the Vizcaya carpet might have particular religious values for Spanish Jews and crypto-Jewish conversos of the time?*

If, for all the reasons set out in the text and summarized in A and B above, we accept that both the commissioning owners and the weavers of the carpet, along with many tens of thousands of other *conversos*, while Christian in form did not in fact cut themselves off from Jewish culture, we see in the Vizcaya carpet rich, meaningful and much-needed Jewish symbols – the selfsame symbols we have seen in ancient Israelite craft, in medieval Sephardi art, artefact and literature, and today in the iconography of the State of Israel. We also see the same Judaic iconography in the earlier Spanish synagogue carpet – the sheep, the ducks, the Star of David – and in the later Sephardi carpets. It would be an act of ignorance to ignore all these linkages – they are all too clear. The meaning of the symbols on the Vizcaya carpet within Jewish, Christian and Muslim cultures were analysed and the critical point made that minority cultures, particularly those under pressure from the majority, develop symbols, signs and phrases that convey one meaning to the minority and another to the majority. We looked at examples of this from the writings of de Rojas, Cervantes and others, at *converso* catchphrases and at a *converso* Hannukiah. We considered the causes and the nature of the church's increasing pressure put on the Jews and *conversos* and its impact on Jewish symbols.

The critically important point is that 500 years ago, the covert and powerful meanings of these symbols as Jewish would not clearly have been such to anyone but Jews. To non-Jews they would have been seen as straightforward Christian or Muslim symbols or as mere decorative devices – and perhaps that still remains true today.

Perhaps the Vizcaya carpet's true history having remained hidden for so long tells as much about the need for discretion at that time as it does about our own cultural limitations today, which cause us to miss the meanings in the material cultures of worlds other than our own.

In concluding, I am troubled in this attempt to answer Ita Aber's question by the word 'certainty'. It is said by some that ultimately the only certainty is uncertainty, and to affirm, therefore, that the Vizcaya carpet is Judaic without acknowledging a degree of uncertainty would be less than candid. But to affirm only what is fashionably thought to be certain would be (apart from being craven) to omit the flood of facts discussed and analysed in this book. Some of that evidence is solid, some is circumstantial – but it is substantial. Any incompleteness in the evidence does not amount to evidence against. Plausibility is not proof, but if facts are not the product of the most probable explanation, what are they?[1]

For all the reasons set out in the text and summarized here, I think the Vizcaya carpet, on the strongest balance of probability, is an extraordinary and beautiful encoded statement of Jewish faith and survival. As primary evidence of the stress of Jewish life in fifteenth-century Spain, it is a transcendent cultural chronicle yielding insights into the lives of humble and of noble crypto-Jewish *conversos*. It is an important document, as importantly historically as any royal charter of the time, and this story of a society at odds with itself, as seen through the history of the Vizcaya carpet, of those for whom it was made and of those who made it, surely echoes down the ages with meanings and messages for us today.

NOTE

1. Ockham's Razor – a methodological principle dictating a bias towards simplicity in theory construction.

Postscript

From glory to decadence: it is no accident that in the years following 1492, the quality of the carpets of Spain steadily deteriorated. Eventually, little was produced save degenerate and sad reminders of the great craft that was no more. With the exception of one early sixteenth-century carpet, the end of the fifteenth century brought an end to the Admiral carpets of Spain.

Finally, before we close, there is yet another carpet I would like to share with you (Figure 73). It is a synagogue carpet, a *parokhet* for hanging before the Ark. Its structure is that of a Cairene carpet, and while its language portrays Mamluk, Ottoman and European influences, and despite the ingenious interpretations of a number of authorities, it cannot be anything other than a Jewish carpet – with the menorah, the flaming brazier, the Crown of the Torah. Above all, in the beautifully drawn Hebrew characters, commonly to be seen on the title page of Hebrew books as well as on synagogue entrance doors, we read the inscription of Psalm 118, verse 20: 'This is the gate of the Lord through which the righteous shall enter.' Whilst there is no direct evidence, this carpet might well have been made by a great master weaver who had lived in Cairo and in 1490 moved to Ferrara where, under the protection of Duke Alfonso I d'Este, he ran a famous carpet workshop employing many weavers. He was Sabadino, a Jewish name given by Sephardim to a boy born or circumcised on the Sabbath. Whether Sabadino learned his craft among the Jewish weavers of Murcia who had fled to Cairo, or whether he was born into the Cairo community of carpet weavers, we shall not know. But his wonderful carpet provides physical confirmation of the quality of Jewish carpets and the high skills of their Jewish carpet weavers.

The Spanish synagogue carpet (Chapter 6), the Vizcaya carpet (Chapter

5), the carpet of the Seville congregation (page 50), Joseph Nasi's carpet, a seventeenth-century magnificent piece inscribed to Joseph Nasi who was Duke of Naxos, Lord of Tiberius, Knight of the Roman Empire, friend of both Emperor Maximilian and Suleiman the Magnificent – and a *converso*, and Sabadino's carpet are the material proof, amply backed by the plethora of evidence cited here, of the continuous and high tradition of Sephardi carpet weaving. Today, viewing these carpets as cultural chronicles, we may learn something of the lives and deaths, of the yearnings and religious imperatives of the Jews of Spain. These carpets, these few survivors of the countless devotional carpets that have not survived, gave expression to the Jews' hopes and expectations of the coming of the Messiah – ushering in for them, and for us all, a new era in which peace would reign supreme.

Appendix

A Summary of the Main References to Stars, Rosettes and Star Forms in the Text

Where the star form was not almost incontrovertibly Judaic – that is, it had not been located in Bibles, Haggadot and other Jewish writings, or in synagogues, or was not juxtaposed to other clearly Jewish symbols or Hebrew script, or located in Greek, Roman, Christian and Islamic writings and illustrations directly pertaining to Jews – such reference have been followed by a question mark. Those references range from ones whose Judaic association are entirely speculative to ones closely pertinent but, lacking the above described criteria of near certain proof, have been excluded from the first category.

Century BCE	Place	Item
15th–13th	Canaan/Egypt	Four- and eight-pointed stars (?)
8th	Israel	A workshop producing limestone seals with stars
8th	Assyria	On Shalmaneser III black obelisk (?)
7th	Lebanon	On the seal of Joshua ben Asayahu
7th	Lebanon	On the seal of Yosine Arcohen, Head Priest

Century BCE	Place	Item
7th	Israel	Hezekiah adopts the rosette
6th and on	Israel	On numerous seals, pots and jars
5th	Israel	On an oil cruse belonging to the Temple
5th and on	Carthage	On oil lamps
3rd and on	Israel	On tombs, ossuaries and sarcophagi
3rd and on	Israel	On jars
2nd	Israel	On the Temple facade
1st	Israel	On lamps
1st	Israel	On an Herodian building
1st	Israel	On a coin of Alexander Yannai
1st	Israel	On a coin of Herod the Great
1st	Israel	On coins of the Hasmonean period
1st	Israel	In writings (Josephus – the Seal of Solomon)
1st	Israel	On the textile hanging in the Temple (?)
1st	Israel	On synagogue walls
1st	Israel	On the tomb of Herod the Great
1st–3rd	Spain	On tombstones and ossuaries (?)
1st–5th	Israel	On lamps
1st–5th	Israel	On tables
1st–5th	Israel	On sarcophagi
1st–5th	Israel	On mosaic floors
1st–5th	Israel	On lamps
1st–5th	Israel	On bread stamps
1st–5th	Israel	In a catacomb
2nd	Israel	On the coins of Bar Kokhba
2nd	Israel	On a weight of Bar Kokhba
2nd–3rd	Israel	On a synagogue frieze

The Main References to Stars, Rosettes and Star Forms

Century CE	Place	Item
2nd–3rd	Iran	On seals, with the crescent moon
2nd–6th	Spain	On tombstones
3rd–4th	Israel	On mosaic floors of synagogues
3rd–8th	Israel	On magic bowls
3rd–4th	Israel	On tombstone
4th	England	On a Roman bowl (?)
4th	Israel	On a tombstone
4th	Israel	On a synagogue lintel
4th	Israel	On late Roman silver vessels
4th	Israel	On pottery lamps
5th	Israel/Diaspora	Referred to in early post-Talmudic incantations
6th	Spain	On architectural friezes
6th	Spain/Italy	On tombstones
6th	Israel/Diaspora	Referred to in the Talmud
7th and on	The Diaspora	On amulets
7th and on	The Diaspora	In literature
8th	Khazariah	On the Flag of David (?)
8th	Egypt	On a Coptic band
8th and 9th	Egypt	On a Coptic weave
9th	Iraq	On a badge
10th	Egypt	In a child's reader
10th	Egypt	In the Ben Ezra Synagogue
10th	Egypt	In Bibles
10th	Egypt	On a carpet
10th	Syria	In the Aleppo Synagogue
10th	Spain	Added to mezuzot
10th	Spain	On amulets
10th	France	On silver bowls and on rings

Century CE	Place	Item
10th	Germany	On silver bowls and on rings
11th	Egypt	A mould to stamp onto glass
11th	Egypt	On a cotton sampler
11th	Egypt	In a child's jottings
11th	Egypt	On the grille of synagogue lamps
11th	Egypt	On dowry lamps
11th	Egypt	In Bibles
11th	Egypt	On a merchant's seal
11th	Egypt	On betrothal rings
11th	Spain	In Bibles (?)
11th	Serbia	On a burial fragment
11th–12th	Babylon/Persia	In a Bible (?)
11th–13th	Mediterranean	On silks
11th–13th	Mediterranean	In Bibles
11th–13th	Mediterranean	In literature
12th	Egypt	In a Bible
12th	Egypt	On marriage and Sabbath lamps
12th	Germany	On coins
12th	Germany	In Bibles
12th	Germany	In synagogue windows
12th	Poland	On coins
12th	Spain	In Kabbalist and other writings
13th	Spain	In books commissioned by the king of Castile
13th	Spain	In mezuzot
13th	Czech/Slovakia	In a synagogue window
13th	Czech/Slovakia	On the metal work of the ark
13th	Czech/Slovakia	On a flag granted by the emperor
13th	Germany	In synagogue

The Main References to Stars, Rosettes and Star Forms

Century CE	Place	Item
13th	Germany	On wedding stones
13th	Spain	In Bibles
13th	Spain	In signatures
13th	Spain	In Kabbalist writings
13th	Spain	On Passover table decorations
13th	England	Sabbath lamps
13th onwards	Spain, England, France, Germany, Switzerland	On seals
13th onwards	France	On signet rings
13th onwards	Spain	In numerous Bibles, Haggadot, Kabbalist and other writings
13th onwards	Spain	In signatures
14th	Tunisia	To mark goods
14th	Djerba	Woven on clothing (?)
14th	Djerba	On trunks, cupboards, tables (?)
14th	Czech/Slovakia	On the standard of the Prague Synagogue
14th	Czech/Slovakia	In the Budweiss Synagogue
14th	Czech/Slovakia	In book title pages
14th	Czech/Slovakia	On a coin
14th	Spain	On a matzah press
14th	Spain	On synagogue tiles
14th	Spain	On a synagogue ceiling
14th	Spain	On a leather brooch
14th	Spain	On a buckle of a belt
14th	Spain	In signatures
14th	Spain	In family badges
14th	Spain	On dishes and bowls

Century CE	Place	Item
14th	Spain	On Passover plates
14th–15th	The Diaspora	In books, seals, mantels and binders
14th–15th	Hungary	On a flag
14th–15th	Portugal	On the king of Portugal's map
14th–15th	Spain	In numerous Bibles, books and book covers
14th–15th	Spain	Household silver
14th–15th	Spain	On synagogue walls
15th	Germany	Lamps
15th	Germany	Haggadot
15th	Portugal	In a painting
15th	Czech/Slovakia	On flag
15th	Italy	On a boundary post ordered by the Doges of Venice
15th	Italy	On an illustration of the stoning of St Stephen
15th	Yemen	On a micrographic biblical illustration
16th	Switzerland	In Paracelsus's writings

Glossary

Aggadah:	Stories and tales relating to the Bible.
Apocrypha:	The fourteen books being an appendix to, but not part of, the Hebrew Scriptures.
Arabesque:	Seemingly endless design form of circular or spiral tendrils.
Ark:	Cabinet or chest in the synagogue to house the Scrolls of the Law.
Auto-da-Fé:	Public ceremony of the carrying out of the Death Sentence, often by roasting alive, by the Inquisition.
Ayyubids:	Islamic dynasty of sultans in Egypt and Syria 1171–1250.
Bar mitzvah:	The term and celebration applies to a boys attainment of legal and religious maturity at age 13.
BCE:	Before the Common Era; BC in the Christian calendar.
Border:	A design or designs framing and defining the field and controlling implicit movement inside that frame.
Cairo Genizah:	Depository for sacred books and artefacts in the Ben Ezra Synagogue.
Caliph:	Title of the successors of Muhammad as rulers of the Islamic world.
CE:	Common Era; AD in the Christian calendar.
Central Field:	Area of carpet within the borders.
Chuppah:	Wedding canopy.
Converso:	One converted from the Jewish or Muslim faith, especially the former, to Christianity in Christian Spain or Portugal and applied to all their descendants. Female version: *conversa*.
Copt:	An Egyptian descended from the ancient Egyptians or a member of the Coptic Egyptian church.
Cortes:	Local assemblies or parliaments in Spain.

Cross Panel:	Broad horizontal strip across the top or the bottom of a field of a carpet.
Decalogue:	The Ten Commandments, the Tablets of the Law.
Diaspora:	Jewish communities outside the land of Israel.
Eucharist:	Christian sacrament commemorating Christ's last supper by the consecration of bread and wine.
Familiar:	Lay official of the Inquisition.
Fatimids:	Islamic rulers of North Africa and Egypt 909–1171.
Field:	Area of carpet within the border.
Finials:	Decorative terminals.
Fostat:	Ancient city near modern Cairo.
Genizah:	A depository (usually in an attic) for sacred books and artefacts.
Guard Strip:	Weaving outside the final border of a carpet.
Haggadah:	The book recalling the events of Exodus, retold every year at the Passover Seder; plural: Haggadot.
Halakhah:	Jewish law.
Hamsa:	The Hand of God, a decorative device offering protection.
Hannukah:	Festival celebrating the Hasmonean victory of 165 BCE which re-established religious freedom in Israel.
Hannukiah:	A eight-branched candelabra with an additional master light, from which one candle is lit every day over the eight days of the Hannukah festival.
Hasids:	Devotees of the spiritual side of Jewish life.
Heikhalot:	Apocalyptic mysticism aspiring to a perception of the phenomenon of the Throne on its Chariot and its divine glory as attested in the Book of Enoch.
Hue:	Pure colour.
Inquisition:	Ecclesiastical tribunal of the Catholic Church dedicated to rooting out heresy.
Ka'ba:	Cubic meteorite stone in the centre of Mecca, the focus of Muslim prayer and pilgrimage.
Kabbalah:	Jewish metaphysical system which seeks to draw down spiritual energies into the material world, exchanging reason for intuition and the known for the unknown in pursuit of the eternal.

Karaite:	Jewish sect originating in the eight century reliant solely on the scriptures and rejecting all Talmudic and rabbinic exegesis.
Kashrut:	Jewish dietary laws.
Kelim:	A pileless carpet woven in a slit – tapestry technique.
Ketubbah:	Pre-nuptial contract.
Kiddush:	The prayer recited over a cup of wine consecrating the Sabbath or a festival.
Kufic:	One of the oldest forms of Arabic script.
Lattice:	A decorative feature of lines crossing one another at regular intervals, leaving spaces between them.
Levite:	A descendant of the tribe of Levi consecrated to serve the priests in the Temple.
Lozenge:	A four-sided motif having two oblique and two obtuse angles.
Maghreb:	The extreme part of north-west Africa including Morocco, Algeria, Tunisia and sometimes Libya.
Main Border:	The longest and largest border, often containing its own motifs.
Maimonides:	Moses ben Maimon (1135–1204), generally acknowledged to be the greatest Jewish thinker, Talmudist and codifier in the Middle Ages.
Mamluks:	Egyptian based Islamic dynasty 1251–1517 CE.
Marbadiah Carpets:	Rugs woven in Israel in the period from the 1920s to the 1950s in the style of the Bezalel rugs.
Marranos:	Pejorative name for *conversos*, literally 'swine'.
Matzah:	Unleavened bread eaten during the eight days of Passover.
Medallion:	Large motif, often the focus or forming the focus of a rug.
Menorah:	Seven-branched candelabrum that stood in the Tabernacle and the Temple in Jerusalem; plural: menorot. The term also applies to the Hannukiah.
Merino:	A breed of sheep with particularly long fine hair.
Mezuzah:	Parchment scroll containing Deuteronomy 6:4–9 and 11:13–21 in a case fixed onto the door posts of a building.

Mihrab:	Arched niche in the wall of a mosque, being a directional finder to Mecca; often appearing as an arch or gate-shaped motif on Islamic prayer rugs.
Mitzvah:	A good deed, a commandment.
Mizrach:	Wall decoration, often a rug, indicating the direction to Jerusalem for prayer.
Moriscos:	Muslim converts to Christianity.
Motif:	Single or multiple shapes used as a design element.
Mudejars:	Muslims living under Christian rule.
Nahmanides:	Moshe ben Nahman, an outstanding Talmudist (1194–1290) who won respectability for the Spanish Kabbalah.
New Christians:	Conversos.
Old Christians:	Christians who claimed they had no Jewish ancestors.
Palette:	Overall colour scheme.
Parokhet:	Curtain hanging behind the Ark in the Sephardi tradition, and before the Ark in the Ashkenazi tradition. It follows the injunction of Exodus 26:31, so linking the original Tabernacle to the Temple and on to the Synagogue.
Passover:	Festival celebrating the Exodus from Egypt.
Pentateuch:	The five books of Moses.
Pile:	Ends of the thousands of individual knots tied to the warp and the weft, so forming the surface of the rug.
Ply:	Two or more yarns twisted together.
Pogrom:	An organized massacre for the destruction or annihilation of a body or class – chiefly applied against the Jews.
Practical Kabbalah:	The practice or belief that the mysteries of the Kabbalah could harness higher power to change the laws of nature. A legitimate form of white magic.
Purim:	Festival celebrating the defeat of Haman's plan to exterminate the Jews.
Rabbi:	Teacher of Judaism, qualified to render decisions in Jewish law.
Rashi:	Solomon ben Isaac (1040–1105) one of the greatest biblical and Talmudic commentators.

Glossary

Repeat Call:	Same overall pattern.
Responsa:	Written answers by authoritative rabbis to questions of legal and religious matters.
Romaniots:	Original Jewish population of the Byzantine Empire.
Safavids:	Islamic dynasty in Persia 1502–1736 CE.
Samaritans:	Descendants from the tribes of Ephraim and Manasseh who intermarried with non-Israelite colonialists and continue living today in Israel.
Sassanids:	Persian dynasty 226–641 CE.
Secondary Borders:	Supplementary borders, usually either side of the main border.
Seder:	First night of Passover.
Sephardim:	Jews originating from the Mediterranean region.
Sephirot:	Kabbalist term for the ten emanations or manifestations of God, expressed schematically.
Shavuot:	Festival commemorating the handing down of the Law on Mount Sinai. Also known as Pentecost.
Shema, The:	The most familiar and important of all Jewish prayer, a confession of faith, declaring the Oneness of God.
Shofar:	Ram's horn sounded in the synagogue on Rosh Hashanah, new moons and other occasions.
Star of David:	The six-pointed star formed by two (usually equilateral) interlocking triangles.
Sukkot:	Festival celebrating the Divine protection given to the Israelites during their wanderings following the Exodus; coming, too, at harvest time it is particularly celebratory.
Shpanyer: (Spanish)	Textile decoration of stylized foliate designs in silver or gold, a speciality of the Sephardi.
Tabernacle:	Portable structure housing the Tablets of the Law during the Israelites' wanderings in Sinai.
Tablets of the Law:	The Ten Commandments.
Tallit:	Prayer shawl.
Talmud:	Code of Jewish law of the second century with later rabbinic commentary. The Jerusalem version was redacted circa 425 CE, the Babylonian version circa 500 CE. Layer upon layer of biblical interpretation

	evolving into a synthesis of moral, criminal and civil law encompassing many rich and varied folk legends of biblical characters, rabbis, angels and demons.
Temple, The:	The great building in Jerusalem where the people of Israel would worship the Almighty. Built by Solomon in the tenth century BCE and destroyed by Nebuchadnezzer in 584 BCE, rebuilt in 515 BCE, reconstructed by Herod from 20 BCE and destroyed by the Romans in 70 CE.
Tints:	The range from a pure hue to white.
Tones:	The range from a pure hue to very grey.
Torah Ark:	See Ark.
Torah:	Literally 'Teaching'. Depending upon the content it can refer to the first five books of the Hebrew Bible (the Pentateuch) or to all of scripture, or to all revelation, written or oral, in Judaism.
Warp:	Longitudinal threads forming the base of a rug.
Weft:	Latitudinal threads inserted sinuously after each row of knots so binding all the threads into a cohesive structure.
Yeshiva:	Academy devoted to the study of the Talmud and its subsequent commentaries.

Bibliography

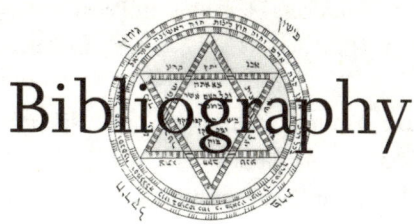

Abajo, M., *Documentos de la Catedral de Palencia* (Salamanca: Gráficas Cervantes, 1986).

Aber, Ita, 'Are the Spanish Carpets Jewish?' *Jewish Art*, 18 (1992), pp.87–99.

Abrahams, Israel, *Jewish Life in the Middle Ages* (Jerusalem: Jewish Publication Society, 1930).

Adb al-Rahman b. Nasr al Shayzari, *The Book of the Islamic Market Inspector*, trans. R. Buckley (Oxford: Oxford University Press, 1999).

Adler, Elkan, 'Notes of a Journey to the East', *Jewish Chronicle*, December 1888.

Adler, Elkan, *The Itinerary of Benjamin of Tudela* (Oxford: Oxford University Press, 1907).

Adler, Elkan, *Jewish Travellers in the Middle Ages* (New York: Dover Publications, 1946).

Albright, William, *From the Stone Age to Christianity: Monotheism and the Historical Process* (New York: Doubleday Anchor Books, 1957).

Alighieri, Dante, *The Divine Comedy*, trans. P. Dale (London: Anvil Press Poetry, 1996).

Alpert, M., *Secret Judaism and the Spanish Inquisition* (Nottingham: Five Leaves Publications, 2008).

Amador de los Rios, *Toledo: Monumentos Ariquetectonicos de España* (Impreta de Antonio Cr. Izquicerdo, 1905).

Anquetel, J., *Carpets, Techniques, Traditions and History* (Paris: Octopus, 2003).

Appelbaum, S., 'The Minor Arts of the Talmudic Period' in Cecil Roth, *Jewish Art*, second edition ed. Bezalel Narkiss (London: Vallentine Mitchell, 1971).

Aristotle, *The Politics*, ed. Betty Radice (Harmondsworth: Penguin Books, 1958).

Asaf, S., *Mekorot l-toledot hahinnuk b'Israel* (Tel Aviv, 1936).

Ashtor, Eliyahu, *The Jews of Moslem Spain*, 3 vols (Jerusalem: Jewish Publication Society, 1973–84).

Aston, M., *Faith and Fire* (London: Hambledon Press, 1993).
Bacharach, Jere L. (ed.), *Fustat Finds* (Cairo: American University in Cairo Press, 2002).
Bacon, Josephine, *The Illustrated Atlas of Jewish Civilization*, consulting editor Martin Gilbert (London: Andre Deutsch, 1969).
Baer, Y., *A History of the Jews in Christian Spain*, 2 vols (Philadelphia, PA: Jewish Publication Society, 1992).
Baigent, M. and Leigh, R. *The Inquisition* (London: Penguin Books, 2000).
Baker, K.B., *Conquerors and Chroniclers of Early Medieval Spain* (Liverpool: Liverpool University Press, 1999).
Banquero Almansa, A., *La Literatura en Murcia desde Alfonso X a los Reyes Catolicos* (Madrid: T. Fortanat, 1877).
Barag, D., 'Glass Pilgrim Vessels from Jerusalem', Parts 1, 2 and 3, *Journal of Glass Studies*, 12 (1970) and 13 (1971).
Baraz, D., *Medieval Cruelty* (Ithaca, NY: Cornell University Press, 2003).
Barber, E., *Prehistoric Textiles* (Princeton, NJ: Princeton University Press, 1991).
Barclay, John, *Jews in the Mediterranean Diaspora* (London: University of California Press, 1996).
Barnavi, Eli, *A Historical Atlas of the Jewish People* (London: Kuperard, 1998).
Baron, S., *A Social and Religious History of the Jews*, 10 vols (New York: Jewish Publication Society and Columbia University Press, 1965–67).
Barthes, R., *Mythologies*, trans. A. Lavers (New York: Hill & Wang, 1972).
Barton, S. (ed.), *Cross, Crescent and Conversion: Essays on Medieval Spain and Christendom in Memory of Richard Fisher* (Leiden: Brill, 2007).
Beattie, M., 'The "Admiral" Rugs of Spain: An Analysis and Classification of their Field Designs', in Robert Pinner and Walter Denny (eds), *Oriental Carpet & Textile Studies, 2: Carpets of the Mediterranean Countries 1400–1600* (London: Hali Publications, 1986).
Beinart, Haim, *Conversos on Trial: The Inquisition in Cuidad Real* (Jerusalem: Magnes Press, 1981).
Beinart, Haim, *Atlas of Medieval Jewish History* (New York: Simon & Schuster, 1992).
Beinart, H., *The Expulsion of the Jews from Spain* (Oxford: The Littman Library of Jewish Civilization, 2005).
Benbassa, Esther and Rodrique, Aron, *Sephardi Jewry* (Berkeley: CA: University of California Press, 2000).
ben David, Yehuda, 'The Golden Age, Expulsion and Inquisition', in *The Sephardic*

Journey 1492–1992, exhibition catalogue (New York: Yeshiva University Museum, 1992).

Ben Shimon Halevi, Z'ev, *Kabbalah: Tradition of Hidden Knowledge* (London: Thames & Hudson, 1979).

Berg, P., *The Essential Kabbalah* (New York: Bell Tower, 2002).

Biale, D., *Cultures of the Jews* (New York: Schocken Books, 2002).

Bialer, Y., *Jewish Life in Art and Tradition* (London: Putnam, 1976).

Bibles: The Revised Standard Bible (London: Wm Collins, 1971); *The Illustrated National Family Bible* (United Presbyterian Church); *The Self Interpreting Bible* (Bungay, 1814); *The Holy Scriptures: New Jewish Publication Society Translation* (Philadelphia, PA: New Jewish Publication Society, 1959).

Blanquez-Perez, Juan, *Arqueologia en Albacete* (Madrid: Artes Gráficas, 1993).

Blazquez, Miguel, *La Inquisicion en Albacete* (Albacete: Gráficas Panadero, 1985).

Bontempi, F., *Il Ferro e la Stella* (Brescia: Circolo Cultural S. Alessandro, 1994).

Boralevi, A., 'Three Egyptian Carpets in Italy', in Robert Pinner and Walter Denny (eds), *Oriental Carpet and Textile Studies, 2: Carpets of the Mediterranean Countries 1400–1600* (London: Hali, 1986).

Braude, B. and Lewis, B., *Christians and Jews in the Ottoman Empire: The Functioning of a Plural Society*, 2 vols (New York: Holmes & Meier, 1982).

Brook, Kevin, *The Jews of Khazaria* (Lanham, MD: Rowan & Littlefield, 2006).

Bronstein, L., *Kabbalah and Art* (Waltham, MA: Brandeis University Press, 1980).

Broshi, Magen, *Bread, Wine in Arks and Scrolls* (Israel: Academic Press, 2001).

Browne, Lewis, *The Story of the Jews* (London: Jonathan Cape, 1926).

Buber, M., *Moses, the Revelation and the Covenant* (New York: Harper Torchbooks, 1936).

Burman, E., *Inquisition* (Stroud: Sutton Publishing, 2004).

Burns, R., *Muslims, Christians and Jews in the Crusader Kingdom of Valencia* (Cambridge: Cambridge University Press, 1984).

Busi, G., *Simboli del Pensiero Ebraico* (Torino: G. Einaudi, 1999).

Cammann, Schuyler V.R., 'Symbolic Meanings in Oriental Rug Patterns, Part 1', *Textile Museum Journal*, 3 (December 1972), pp. 5–22.

Capsali, E., *Seder Eliyahu Zuta*, edited by A. Schmuelevitz, S. Simonsohn and M. Benayahu, 3 vols (Israel: Ben Zvi Institute, 1975; Tel Aviv University, 1977; and Jerusalem University, 1983).

Capsali, E., *Chronique de l'Expulsion*, trans. S. Sultan-Bohbot (Paris: Les Editions de Cerf, 1994).

Carmi, T. (ed.), *The Penguin Books Book of Hebrew Verse* (Harmondsworth: Penguin Books, 1981).

Carroll, D., *Looms and Textiles of the Copts* (San Francisco, CA: California Academy of Sciences, 1985).

Casar, María Fuencisla García, 'Jewish Participation in Castilian Fairs: The Example of Medina del Campo in the Fifteenth Century', in A.M. Ginio (ed.), *Jews, Christians and Muslims in the Mediterranean World after 1492* (London: Frank Cass, 1992).

Castro, Americo, *The Structure of Spanish History*, trans. Edmund King (Princeton, NJ: Princeton University Press, 1954).

Castro, Americo, *The Spaniards* (Berkeley, CA: University of California Press, 1971).

Castro, A., *El Real Monasterio de Santa Clara de Palencia y los Enriquez, Almirantes de Castilla* (Valladolid: Sever-Cuesta, 1982).

Catalogue of Spanish Rugs (Washington: The Textile Museum, 1953).

Cervantes, Miguel de, *The Adventures of Don Quixote*, trans. J.M. Cohen (London: Penguin Books, 1954).

Chaucer, Geoffrey, *The Canterbury Tales*, trans. N. Coghill (London: Penguin Books, 2003).

Chazan, R., *The Jews of Medieval Western Christendom* (Cambridge: Cambridge University Press, 2006).

Chevalier, J. and Gheerbrandt, A., *The Penguin Dictionary of Symbols*, trans. J. Buchanan-Brown (London: Penguin Books, 1996).

Child, W.R., *Anglo-Castilian Trade in the Later Middle Ages* (Manchester; Totowa, NJ: Manchester University Press; Rowan and Littlefield, 1978).

Cirlot, J., *Dictionary of Symbols* (New York: Philosophical Library, 1962).

Cohen, J., *The Friars and the Jews: The Evolution of Medieval Anti-Judaism* (Ithaca, NY: Cornell University Press, 1982).

Cohen, M., *Under Crescent and Cross: The Jews in the Middle Ages* (Princeton, NJ: Princeton University Press, 1994).

Cohn-Sherbok, D., *The Blackwell Dictionary of Judaica* (Oxford: Blackwell, 1992).

Cohn-Sherbok, Dan, *Jewish Mysticism* (Oxford: Oneworld Publishers, 1995).

Cole, P., *The Dream of the Poem* (Princeton, NJ: Princeton University Press, 2007).

Collins, Roger, *Visigoths of Spain 407–711* (Oxford: Blackwell, 2004).

Collins, R. and Goodman, A. (eds), *Medieval Spain: Culture, Conflict & Coexistence* (Basingstoke: Palgrave Macmillan, 2002).

Constantino, C., *La Republica de Genova* (Torino, 1986).

Critchlow, K., *Islamic Patterns* (London: Thames & Hudson, 1992).

Crow, John A., *Spain, the Root and the Flower* (Berkeley, CA: University of California Press, 2005).

Dan, J. and Liebes, E., *The Library of Gershom Scholem* (Jerusalem: The Hebrew University, 1999).

Danon, Enzo and Danon, Roberto, *The Garden of Pomegranates* (Rome: Textilia, 2004).

David, A., *To Come to the Land* (Tuscaloosa, AL: University of Alabama Press, 1999).

Davis, E. and Davis, D., *Jewish Folk Art Over the Ages* (Jerusalem: Rubin Mass, 1977).

Davis, N., *Europe* (London: Pimlico, 1997).

de Bofarull y de Sartoria, Manuel D., *Gremios y Cofradias de la Corona de Aragon* (Barcelona: Barcelona Impr. Del Archivo, 1866).

de la Torre, F., *Albacete en Textos Geograficos Anteriors a la Creación de la Provincia* (Albacete: Talleres, 1985).

de Nicolay, N., *Les Navigations, Pérégrinations et Voyages fait en Turqyai* (Antwerp, 1577).

de Rojas, Fernando, *The Spanish Bawd*, trans. J.M. Cohen (London: Penguin Books, 1964).

de Rojas, Fernando, *La Celestina*, edited by M. Marciales, 2 vols (Urbana and Chicago, IL: University of Illinois Press, 1985).

Denny, W., *The Classical Tradition in Anatolian Carpets*, exhibition catalogue, Textile Museum, Washington (Washington, DC: Scala, 2002).

Descatoire, C. (ed.), *Treasures of the Black Death*, catalogue (London: The Wallace Collection, 2009).

Diâz-Mas, Paloma, *Sephardim*, trans. George Zucker (Chicago, IL: University of Chicago Press, 1992).

Diccionario Geográfico de España (Madrid: Hvali, Ediciones Movimiento, 1959), Vol. 2.

Dilley, Arthur, *Oriental Rugs and Carpets*, revised by M.S. Dimand (Philadelphia, PA: Lippincott & Co., 1959).

Dimand, M., 'An Early Cut-Pile Rug from Egypt', *Metropolitan Museum Studies* (Metropolitan Museum of Art), 4, 2 (March 1933), pp.151–61.

Dimand, M. and Mailey, J., *Oriental Rugs in the Metropolitan Museum of Art* (New York: Metropolitan Museum of Art, 1973).

Dimont, Max, *Jews, God and History* (London: New American Library, 2003).

Dodds, J. (ed.), *Al-Andalus: The Art of Islamic Spain*, catalogue, Metropolitan Museum of Art (New York: Harry N. Abrams, 1992).

Dodds, J., Menocal, M. and Balbale, A., *The Arts of Intimacy* (New Haven, CT: Yale University Press, 2008).

Drob, S., *Symbols of the Kabbalah* (Northvale, NJ: Jason Aronson, 2000).
Dubnov, S., *History of the Jews*, 3 vols (New Brunswick, NJ: Thomas Yosseloff, 1967–69).
Echeandia, T., *Atlas Grafico del Reino de Murcia* (Aguilar S.A. de Ediciones-Grupo Santillana, 1979).
Ecker, H., *Caliphs and Kings: The Art and Influence of Islamic Spain* (Washington, DC: Arthur M. Sackler Gallery, Smithsonian Institution; New York: Hispanic Society of America, 2004).
Eder, A., *The Star of David* (Jerusalem: Rubin Mass, 1987).
Edwards, C., *The Persian Carpet* (London: Duckworth, 1953).
Edwards, John, *Inquisition* (Stroud: Tempus, 1999).
Eiland III, Murray, *Starting to Collect Antique Oriental Rugs* (Woodbridge: Antique Collectors Club, 2003).
Elliot, J.H., *Imperial Spain 1469–1716* (Harmondsworth: Penguin Books, 2002).
Ellis, C., *Oriental Carpets in the Philadelphia Museum of Art* (Philadelphia, PA, 1988).
Emmanuel, I.S., *Histoire de l'Industrie de Tissus de Israélites de Salonique* (Paris, 1935).
Empereur, J.-Y. *Alexandria* (New York: Harry Abrams, 2001).
Encyclopaedia Judaica, 16 vols (Jerusalem: Keter Publishing, 1971).
Enrique, Alonso, *Honras y Obsequios que hizo al Catolico, y Christianisimo Rey Don Felipe Tercero Muestro Señor fue muy noble y muy leal Ciudad de Murcia* (Murcia: Luys Beros: 1622–32).
Erasmus, Desiderius, *In Praise of Folly* (New York: Dover Thrift, 2003).
Erdmann, K., *Seven Hundred Years of Oriental Carpets* (London: Faber & Faber, 1970).
Ettinghausen, Richard, 'The Early History, Use and Iconography of the Prayer Rug', in *Prayer Rugs*, exhibition catalogue (Washington, DC: The Textile Museum, 1979).
Fabre-Vasson, C., *The Singular Beast*, trans. C. Volk (New York: Columbia University Press, 1997).
Facsimiles from an Illuminated Hebrew Bible of the Fifteenth Century (New York: Hispanic Society of America, 1993).
Feldman, Louis and Reinhold, Meyer, *Jewish Life and Thought Among Greeks and Romans: Primary Readings* (Minneapolis, MN: Fortress Press, 1996).
Felton, A., *Jewish Carpets* (Woodbridge: Antique Collectors Club, 1997).
Fernandez, L., *Real Academia de la Historia: Monarquia Hispana y Revolución Trastámara* (Madrid: Real Academia de la Historia, 1994).
Fernandez, Mitre, *Los Judios de Castilla en Tiempos de Enrique III: el Pogrom de 1391* (Zaragoza: Co op Artes: Gráficas Libreria General, 1994).

Ferrandis Torres, J., *Exposicion de Alfombras Antiguas Expañolas* (Madrid: Espasa-Calpe, 1933).

Ferrer, J., *Alfrombas Antiguas de la Provincia de Albacete* (La Roda: Artes Gráficas Quintanilla, 1986).

Figueras, Pau, *Decorative Jewish Ossuaries* (Leiden: Brill, 1983).

Fletcher, Richard, *Moorish Spain* (London: Phoenix, 2004).

Fontes, Juan Torres, *Los Judios Murcianos en el Reinado de Juan II* (Murcia: Academia Alfonso X El Sabio, Sucesores de Nogues, 1965).

Fontes, Juan Torres, *Los Judios Murcianos en el Siglio XIII* (Murcia: Academia Alfonso X El Sabio, 1965).

Frank, D. (ed.), *The Jews of Medieval Islam: Society, Community and Identity* (Leiden: Brill, 1995).

Frank D. (ed.), *The Jews of Medieval Islam: Proceedings of an International Conference held by the Institute of Jewish Studies, University College, London, 1992* (Leiden: Brill, 1995).

Frankel, E. and Teutsch, B.P., *The Encyclopaedia Of Jewish Symbols* (Northvale, NJ: Jason Aronson, 1992).

Freehof, Solomon, *The Responsa Literature* (Philadelphia, PA: Jewish Publication Society, 1955).

Freehof, S., *A Treasury of Responsa* (Philadelphia, PA: Jewish Publication Society, 1963).

Freehof, L. and King, B., *Embroideries and Fabrics of Synagogues and Home* (New York: Heathside Press, 1966).

Frey, J., *Corpus Inscriptionum Judaicarum* (Vatican City, 1936).

Friedenberg, D., *Medieval Jewish Seals from Europe* (Detroit, MI: Wayne State University, 1987).

Friedenberg, Daniel, *Sasanian Jewry and its Culture* (Champaign, IL: University of Illinois Press, 2009).

Gage, J., *Colour and Culture* (London: Thames & Hudson, 1993).

Gantzhorn, V., *The Christian Oriental Carpet* (Cologne: Benedikt Taschen, 1991).

Garcia Guinea, M., *Viajes y viajeros en la España Medieval* (Madrid: Grafinas Soto Impresor, 1984).

Garcia, Luis Rubio, *Los Judíos de Murcia en la Beja Edad Media (1350–1500)* (Murcia: Universidad de Murcia, 1992).

Gaster, T., *Myth, Legend and Custom in the Old Testament* (New York: Harper & Row, 1969).

Gerber, Jane, *The Jews of Spain* (London: Free Press, 1994).

Gerli, Michael E. (ed.), *Medieval Iberia: An Encyclopedia* (New York and London:

Routledge, 2003).
Gil, Moshe, *A History of Palestine* (Cambridge: Cambridge University Press, 1997).
Gilbert, M., *The Jews of Arab Lands* (London: Board of Deputies of British Jews, 1976).
Gilbert, Martin, *The Dent Atlas of Jewish History* (London: J.M. Dent, 1993).
Gillis, C. and Nosch, M.-L., *Ancient Textiles* (Oxford: Oxbow Books, 2007).
Gilman, Stephen, *The Spain of Fernando de Rojas* (Princeton, NJ: Princeton University Press, 1972).
Gilmour, G., 'An Iron Age II Pictorial Inscription from Jerusalem Illuminating Yahweh and Asherah', *Palestine Exploration Quarterly*, 141, 2 (July 2009), pp.87–103.
Ginio, Alisa Meyuhas (ed.), *Jews, Christians and Muslims in the Mediterranean World after 1492* (London: Frank Cass, 1992).
Ginsberg, L., *The Legends of the Jews* (Philadelphia, PA: Jewish Publication Society, 1967).
Gitlitz, D., *Secrecy and Deceit* (Philadelphia, PA: Jewish Publication Society, 1996).
Glick, Thomas F., *Islamic and Christian Spain in the Early Middle Ages* (Princeton, NJ: Princeton University Press, 1979).
Goitein, S.D., *Letters of Medieval Jewish Travellers* (Princeton, NJ: Princeton University Press, 1973).
Goitein, S.D., *A Mediterranean Society*, 6 vols (London: University of California Press, 1999).
Goitein, S.D., *A Mediterranean Society: An Abridgement In One Volume*, edited by J. Lassner (London: University of California Press, 1999).
Gonzalez, J., *Historia de Palencia, Edades Antigua y Media*, Vol. 1 (Madrid: J. Soto Impresor, 1984).
Goodenough, E., *Jewish Symbols in the Greco-Roman Period*, 8 vols (London: Pantheon Books, 1953).
Goodman, M., *Judaism in the Roman World* (Leiden: Brill, 2007).
Goodman, M., *Rome and Jerusalem* (London: Penguin Books, 2007).
Goodnick Westenholz, Joan, *Images of Inspiration*, catalogue (Jerusalem: Bible Lands Museum, 2001).
Grabar, Oleg, *The Formation of Islamic Art* (New Haven, CT and London: Yale University Press, 1987).
Graetz, H., *History of the Jews, 1894–1945*, 5 vols (Jerusalem: Jewish Publication Society, 1956).

Grant, Charles Ellis, *Oriental Carpets in the Philadelphia Museum of Art* (Philadelphia, PA: Herbert, 1988).
Gross, N., *The Economic History of the Jews* (Jerusalem: Keter Publishing, 1975).
Gubbay, L. and Levy, A., *The Sephardim* (London: Carnell, 1992).
Gui, B., *The Inquisition's Guide*, trans. Janet Shirley (Welwyn Garden City: Ravenhall, 2006).
Gutmann, Joseph, *Beauty in Holiness* (Jerusalem: Ktav Publishing, 1970).
Halevi, J., *The Kuzari* (New York: Schocken Books, 1964).
Halkin, A. and Hartman, D. (eds), *Crisis and Leadership: Epistles of Maimonides* (Philadelphia, PA: Jewish Publication Society, 1985).
Hamilton, R., *Khirbat al-Mafjar* (Oxford: Oxford University Press, 1959).
Harden, D., *Glass of the Caesars* (Milan: Olivetti, 1987).
Harlow, Jules, 'Jewish Textiles in Light of Biblical and Post-Biblical Literature', in Barbara Kirshenblatt-Gimblett, *Fabric of Jewish Life* (New York: The Jewish Museum, 1977).
Harris, M., *History of the Medieval Jews from the Moslem Conquest of Spain to the Discovery of America* (New York: Bloch Publishing Co., 1916).
Harvey, L.P., *Islamic Spain 1250–1500* (London: University of Chicago Press, 1990).
Hildburgh, W.L., 'Images of the Human Hand as Amulets in Spain', *Journal of the Warburg and Courtauld Institutes*, 18 (January–June 1955), pp.78–9.
Housego, Jenny, 'Literary References to Carpets in North Africa', in Robert Pinner and Walter Denny (eds), *Oriental Carpet & Textile Studies, 2: Carpets of the Mediterranean Countries 1400–1600* (London: Hali Publications, 1986), pp.103–7.
Hyamson, A., *A History of the Jews of England* (London: Methuen, 1928).
Idachs, Luis Marco, *Los Judiós de Cataluña* (Barcelona: Ediciones Destino, 1985).
Inman, N. (ed.), *Spain* (New York: Dorling Kindersley, 2002).
Irwin, Robert G., 'Egypt, Syria and their Trading Partners 1450–1550', in Robert Pinner and Walter Denny (eds), *Oriental Carpet & Textile Studies, 2: Carpets of the Mediterranean Countries 1400–1600* (London: Hali Publications, 1986).
Isaac, Benjamin, *The Invention of Racism in Classical Antiquity* (Oxford: Princeton University Press, 2004).
Israeli, Yael (ed.), *In the Light of the Menorah: Story of a Symbol* (Jerusalem: The Israel Museum, 1999).
Jacob, H.S., *Idealism and Realism* (Leiden: Brill, 1954).
Jenkins, David, *The Cambridge History of Western Textiles* (Cambridge: Cambridge University Press, 2003).

The Jewish Encyclopaedia, edited by I. Singer, 12 vols (New York: Funk & Wagnalls, 1916).
Johnson, Paul, *A History of the Jews* (London: Weidenfeld & Nicolson, 1987).
Josephus, *Jewish Wars* (London: W. Whiston, 1737).
Juhasz, E., 'Textiles for the Home and Synagogue', in E. Juhasz (ed.), *Sephardi Jews in the Ottoman Empire* (Jerusalem: The Israel Museum, 1990), pp.65–119.
Jung, C., *Man and his Symbols* (London: Aldus Books, 1972).
Kagan, Richard and Dyer, Abigail, *Inquistorial Enquiries* (Baltimore, MD: John Hopkins University Press, 2004).
Kamen, H., *The Spanish Inquisition* (London: Phoenix, 2003).
Kanof, A., *Jewish Symbolic Art* (New York: Gefen, 1990).
Kaplan, G.B., *The Evolution of Converso Literature* (London: University Press of Florida, 2002).
Keats, V., *Chess, Jews and History* (Oxford: Oxford Academic Publishers, 1994).
Kedourie, E., *The Sephardi Experience 1492 and After* (London: Thames & Hudson, 1992).
Keller, W., *The Bible as History* (New York: Hodder & Stoughton, 1956).
King, D. and Sylvester, D., *The Eastern Carpet in the Western World from the 15th to the 17th Century*, exhibition catalogue (London: Arts Council of Great Britain, 1983).
King, Monique and King, Donald, *European Textiles in the Keir Collection, 400 BC to 1800 AD* (London: Faber & Faber, 1990).
Kirshenblatt-Gimblett, Barbara, *Fabric of Jewish Life* (New York: The Jewish Museum, 1977).
Klagsbald, Victor, 'The Menorah as Symbols: Its Meaning and Origin in Early Jewish Art', *Jewish Art*, 12–13 (1986–87), pp.126–34.
Klagsbald, Victor, *A L'Ombre de Dieu* (Leuven, Belgium: Peeters, 1997).
Kochan, Lionel, *Beyond the Graven Image* (London: Macmillan Press, 1997).
Kruger, S., *The Spectral Jew* (Minneapolis, MN: University of Minnesota Press, 2005).
Kubiak, W. and Scanlon. G., *Fustat Expedition: Final Report* (Lake Winona, IN: American Research Center in Egypt, 1989).
Kühnel, E. and Bellinger, L., *Catalogue of Spanish Rugs, 12th Century to 19th Century* (Washington, DC: The Textile Museum, 1953).
Kybalova, L., *Coptic Textiles* (London: Paul Hamlyn, 1967).
Lambert, P. (ed.), *Fortifications and the Synagogue* (Montreal: Canadian Centre for Architecture, 1994).

Landsberger, Franz, *Development of Jewish Art* (Cincinnati, OH: Union of American Jewish Congregations, 1944).
Landsberger, F., *Beauty in Holiness: Studies on Jewish Customs and Ceremonial Art*, edited by J. Gutmann (New York: Thomas Yoseloff, 1970).
Lea, H.C., *A History of the Inquisition of Spain*, 4 vols (New York: Macmillan, 1906–08).
Leroy, Beatrice, *The Jews of Navarre in the Late Middle Ages*, Hispania Judaica Vol. 4 (Jerusalem: Magnes Press, 1985).
Le Tourneau, R., Vajda, G., Chouraqui, A., Corcos, D. and Housego, Jenny, 'Mamluk Carpets and North Africa', in Robert Pinner and Walter Denny (eds), *Oriental Carpet & Textile Studies, 2: Carpets of the Mediterranean Countries 1400–1600* (London: Hali Publications, 1986).
Levey, M., *Die Sephardim in Bosnien* (Sarajevo, 1911).
Levy, Yaffa, 'Ezekiel's Plan in an Early Karaite Bible', *Jewish Art*, 19–20 (1994).
Lewis, B., *The Jews of Islam* (Princeton, NJ: Princeton University Press, 1987).
Llopis, Rodriguez, *La Villa Santiaguista de Leitor en la Baya Edad Media* (Murcia: Pictographia, 1993).
Loeb, L.D., *Outcast: Jewish Life in Southern Iran* (New York: Gordon & Beach Science Publishers, 1977).
Loewe, R., *Ibn Gabriol* (London: Peter Halban, 1989).
Longstreth, Bevis, 'The Riddle of the Pazyryk', *Hali*, 137 (November–December 2004), pp.49–51.
Lopez, R. and Raymond, W., *Medieval Trade in the Mediterranean World* (New York: W.W. Norton, no date).
Ma'az, Z., 'The Art and Architecture of the Synagogues of the Golan', in Lee I. Levine (ed.), *Ancient Synagogues Revealed* (Jerusalem: Israel Exploration Society, 1981).
McCall, A., *The Medieval Underworld* (Stroud: Sutton Publishing, 2004).
MacKay, Angus, 'Popular Movements and Pogroms in Fifteenth Century Castile', *Past and Present*, 55 (1972).
MacKay, A., *Spain in the Middle Ages* (Basingstoke: Macmillan, 1977).
Mackie, L., *Weaving through Spanish History: Thirteenth–Seventeenth Centuries* (Washington, DC: Textile Museum, 1972–73).
Mackie, L.W., 'Two Remarkable Fifteenth Century Carpets from Spain', *Textile Museum Journal*, 4, 4 (1977), pp.15–32.
Maimonides, M., *The Guide to the Perplexed*, trans. M. Friedlander (London: Routledge, 1928).

Maimonides, M., *Epistles*, edited by Abraham Halkin and David Hartman (Philadelphia, PA: Jewish Publication Society, 1985).

Mann, V., *Jewish Texts on the Visual Arts* (Cambridge: Cambridge University Press, 2000).

Mann, V. (ed.), *Morocco, Jews and Art in a Muslim Land* (New York: The Jewish Museum, 2000).

Mann, V., Glick, T. and Dodds, J. (eds), *'Convivencia', Jews, Muslims and Christians in Medieval Spain* (New York: George Braziller in conjunction with the Jewish Museum, 1992).

Mañueco, J., *Jornadas Sobre el Arte de las Ordenes Religiousas en Palencia* (Palencia: Gráficas Iglesias, 1990).

Markoe, G., *The Phoenicians* (London: British Museum Press, 2000).

Martin, Frederick Robert, *A History of Oriental Carpets Before 1900* (Vienna: Martin, 1908).

Martz, Linda, *A Network of Converso Families in Early Modern Toledo: Assimilating a Minority* (Ann Arbor, MI: University of Michigan Press, 2003).

Marx, A., *Studies in Jewish History and Booklore* (New York: The Jewish Theological Seminary of America, 1994).

Masson, G., *Courtesans of the Italian Renaissance* (London: St Martin's Press, 1975).

Mattingley, H., *Coins of the Roman Empire in the British Museum* (London: British Museum, 1936).

May, F., *Hispano-Moresque Rugs* (New York: Hispanic Society of America, 1945).

May, Florence Lewis, *Silk Textiles of Spain* (New York: Hispanic Society of America, 1957).

Mehrdad, R. Izady, *The Kurds: A Concise Handbook* (London: Taylor & Francis, 1992).

Melammed, Renée Levine, *Heretics or Daughters of Israel* (Oxford: Oxford University Press, 1999).

Melville, C. and Ubaydli, A., *Christians and Moors in Spain*, Vol. 3 (Warminster: Aris & Phillips, 1992).

Menocal, Maria Rosa, *The Ornament of the World* (New York: Little, Brown & Co., 2002).

Meyerson, M., *A Jewish Renaissance in Fifteenth Century Spain* (Princeton, NJ: Princeton University Press, 2004).

Meyerson, A. and English, E. (eds), *Christians, Muslims and Jews in Medieval and Early Modern Spain* (Notre Dame, IN: University of Notre Dame Press, 2000).

Mills, John, 'The Coming of the Carpet to the West', in D. King and D. Sylvester, *The Eastern Carpet in the Western World from the 15th to the 17th Century*, exhibition catalogue (London: Arts Council of Great Britain, 1983), pp.11–23.

Morena, A. (ed.), *La España Gotica*, 12 vols (Madrid: Ediciones Encuentro, 1997).

Motley, J. *The Rise of the Dutch Republic* (New York: Harper Bros, 1900).

Muchembled, R., *A History of the Devil*, trans. J. Birrell (Cambridge: Polity Press, 2003).

Namenyi, E. *The Essence of Jewish Art*, Popular Jewish Library (New York, London: Thomas Yoseloff, 1957).

Nepaulsingh, Colbert I., *Apples of Gold in Filigrees of Silver* (New York: Holmes & Meier, 1995).

Nepaulsingh, C., *Jewish Writing in the Eye of the Inquisition* (New York: Holmes & Meier, 1995).

Netanyahu, B., *The Marranos of Spain from the late XIVth to the Late XVth I Century According to Contemporary Hebrew Sources* (New York: American Academy for Jewish Research, 1966).

Netanyahu, B., *Toward the Inquisition: Essays on Jewish and Converso History in Late Medieval Spain* (Ithaca, NY: Cornell University Press, 1997).

Netanyahu, Benzion, *The Origins of the Inquisition in Fifteenth Century Spain*, 2nd edn, (New York: New York Review of Books, 2001).

Neuman, Abraham, *The Jews in Spain*, Vol. 1 (Philadelphia, PA: Jewish Publication Society, 1948).

Norwich, John Julius, *The Kingdom in the Sun* (London: Longmans, 1970).

Nusenblatt, I., *Magen David XIII* (Yivo Bletter, 1942) (Yiddish).

O'Callaghan, J., *Reconquest and Crusade in Medieval Spain* (Philadelphia, PA: University of Pennsylvania Press, 2004).

OCTS, *Oriental and Textile Studies II*, eds. R. Pinner and W. Denny (London: Hali, 1986).

Oegema, G., *History of the Shield of David* (Frankfurt: Peter Lang, 1996).

Oegema, Gerbern S., *The History of the Star of David* (Frankfurt: Peter Lang, 1996).

Okumura, Sumiyo, *The Influence of Turkic Culture in Mamluk Carpets* (Istanbul: Centre for Islamic History, Art and Culture, 2007).

O'Shea, Stephen, *The Perfect Heresy* (London: Profile Books, 2001).

Painter, K., *The Mildenhall Treasure* (London: British Museum Publications, 1977).

Panofsky, Erwin, *Tomb Sculpture* (New York: Thames & Hudson, 1964).

Paradinas, Lavado P.J., *Alfombres del Almirante o Alfombras de Tierea di Campos*, Actas de las II Journadas de Cultima Arabe e Islamic (1980) (Madrid: Institute Hispano-Arabe de Culture, 1985).

Parfitt, Tudor, *The Lost Tribes of Israel* (New York: Orion Books, 2002).
Paris, Matthew, *Historia Major* (London: Excudebat Richardus Hodgkinson, 1640).
Pastoureau, M., *Blue: The History of a Colour* (Princeton, NJ: Princeton University Press, 2001).
Patai, R., *The Children of Noah* (Princeton, NJ: Princeton University Press, 1998).
Payne, S., *Historia de España: La España Medieval* (Madrid: Editorial Player, 1985).
Peskowitz, M., *Spinning Fantasies* (Berkeley, CA: University of California Press, 1997).
Pfister, R. and Bellinger, L., *The Excavations at Dura-Europos: Final Report 4: Part 2 – The Textiles* (New Haven, CT: Yale University Press, 1945).
Pickover, Clifford A., *The Loom of God* (New York: Plenum Trade, 1979).
Pinner, Robert and Denny, Walter (eds), *Oriental Carpet & Textile Studies, 2: Carpets of the Mediterranean Countries 1400–1600* (London: Hali Publications, 1986).
Plaut, W. Gunter, *The Magen David* (Washington, DC: B'nai B'rith Books, 1991).
Poncé, Charles, *Kabbalah* (San Francisco, CA: Straight Arrow Books, 1977).
Quesada, Miguel-Angel, 'Mudéjares and Repobladores in the Kingdom of Granada (1485–1501)', in A.M. Ginio (ed.), *Jews, Christians and Muslims in the Mediterranean World after 1492* (London: Frank Cass, 1992).
Rabinovitch, V.Z., *Hebrew Manuscript Ornaments*, Masterpiece of Jewish Art Series (Moscow: Russian National Library, 2003).
Raby, Julian, 'In Vitro Veritas: Glass Pilgrim Vessels from 7th Century Jerusalem', in J. Johns (ed.), *Bayt Al-Maqdis: Jerusalem and Early Islam*, Oxford Studies in Islamic Art (Oxford: Oxford University Press, 1999).
Rahmani, L.Y., 'Three Desk Seals in the Jewish Museum, London', *Jewish Art*, 19–20 (1993–94).
Raphael, H., *The Sephardi Story* (London: Vallentine Mitchell, 1991).
Ray, J., *The Sephardic Frontier* (Ithaca, NY: Cornell University Press, 2006).
Reif, Stefan, *A Jewish Archive from Old Cairo* (London: Curzon, 2000).
Reilly, Bernard F., *The Medieval Spains* (Cambridge: Cambridge University Press, 2001).
Remembering Sepharad (Madrid: State Corporation for Spanish Cultural Action Abroad, 2003).
Richardson, H.G., *The English Jewry Under Angevin Kings* (London: Methuen, 1960).
Rodriguez de la Torre, F., *Albacete en Textos Geográficos Anteriors a la Creacion de la Provincia* (Talleres Tip-offset G.A. Albacete, 1985).
Rodriquez Garcia, D., *Documentation de Don Alfonso de Trastamara en el Archivo General de Simancia* (Valladolid: Gráficas Andrés Martín, 1981).
Rogers, Clive (ed.), *Early Islamic Textiles* (Brighton: Rogers & Podmore, 1983).

Roth, Cecil, *The Jewish Contribution to Civilization* (Cincinnati, OH: Union of American Hebrew Congregations, 1940; London: East and West Library, 1956).

Roth, C., *The Duke of Naxos* (Philadelphia, PA: Jewish Publication Society, 1948).

Roth, Cecil, *A History of the Jews of England* (Oxford: Oxford University Press, 1964).

Roth, Cecil, *Jewish Art*, second edition ed. Bezalel Narkiss (London: Vallentine Mitchell, 1971).

Roth, Cecil, *The Spanish Inquisition* (London: W.W. Norton, 1996).

Roth, H.L., *Studies in Primitive Looms* (Carlton, Bedford: reprinted by Ruth Bean, 1977).

Roth, N., *Conversos, Inquisition and the Expulsion of the Jews from Spain* (Madison, WI: University of Wisconsin Press, 2002).

Rubens, A., *A History of Jewish Costume* (London: Peter Owen, 1981).

Rubin, Miri, *Gentile Tales* (New Haven, CT: Yale University Press, 1999).

Ruiz, T.F., *From Heaven to Earth* (Princeton, NJ: Princeton University Press, 2004).

Sabar, Shalom, *King Solomon's Seal*, edited by Rachel Milstein (Jerusalem: Tower of David Museum of the History of Jerusalem, 2002).

Sabar, Shalom, *The Hand of Fortune* (Tel Aviv: The Eretz Israel Museum, 2002).

Sacher, H., *Farewell España, The World of Sephardim Remembered* (New York: Random House, 1995).

Sahula, Isaac ibn, *Meshal Haqadmoni*, 2 Vols, trans. R. Loewe (Oxford: Littman Library, 2004).

Samuel, Edgar, *At the End of the Earth* (London: Jewish Historical Society of England, 2004).

Sanchez Ferrer, J., *Alfombras Antiguas de la Provincia de Albacete* (Albacete: Artes Gráficas Quintanilla, 1986).

Sanchez Torres, F., *Historia de Albacete* (Albacete: Imprenta de Eliseo Ruiz, Artes Gráficas Quintanilla, 1916).

Sarre, F., 'A Fourteenth Century Spanish Synagogue Carpet', *Burlington Magazine*, 56 (1930), pp. 88–95.

Sarre, F. and Martin, F., *Die Ausstellung von Meisterwerken Muhammedanischer Kunst in München*, Vol. 1 (Munich, 1912), 'Die Teppiche', Tafel 86.

Schochet, J., *Mystical Concepts in Chassidim* (New York: Kehot, 1988).

Schoeser, Mary, *World Textiles: A Concise History* (London: Thames & Hudson, 2003).

Scholem, G., 'The Curious History of the Six Pointed Star', *Commentary* (New York) (1949), pp. 243–51.

Scholem, G., *On the Kabbalah and its Symbolism* (New York: Schocken Books, 1965).

Scholem, G., *Major Trends in Jewish Mysticism* (New York: Schocken Books, 1995).

Scholem, Gershom, *The Messianic Idea in Judaism* (New York: Schocken Books, 1971).

Scholem, Gershom, *Kabbalah* (New York: New York Times Book Co., 1974).

Scholem, Gershom, *Kabbalah* (Jerusalem: Keter Publishing House, 1977).

Schroeder, G., *Genesis and the Big Bang* (New York: Bantam, 1991).

Schwartz-Be'eri, O., *The Jews of Kurdistan*, catalogue (Jerusalem: The Israel Museum, 2000).

Schwartz, D., *Studies in Astral Magic in Medieval Jewish Thought* (Leiden: Brill, 2004).

Schwartz, S., *Imperialism in Jewish Society 200 BC–640 CE* (Princeton, NJ: Princeton University Press, 2001).

Arnold Schwartzman, *Graven Images* (Hong Kong: Harry N. Abrams, 1993).

Sed-Rajna, G., *Ancient Jewish Art* (New Jersey: Chartwell Books, n.d.).

See and Sanctify, catalogue (New York: Yeshiva University Museum, 1979).

The Sephardic Journey 1492–1992, exhibition catalogue (New York: Yeshiva University Museum, 1992).

Serjeant, R.B., *Islamic Textiles: Material for a History up to the Mongol Conquest* (Beirut: Librarie du Liban, 1972).

Shah, Idries, *Oriental Magic* (London: Octagon, 1993).

Sherrill, S., *Carpets and Rugs of Europe and America* (New York: Abbeville Press, 1996).

Soloveitchik, R., 'The Symbolism of Blue and White', in A. Besdin (ed.), *Man of Faith in the Modern World* (Jerusalem: Ktav, 1989).

Spalding, F., *Mudejar Ornament in Manuscripts* (New York: Hispanic Society of America, 1953).

Spuhler, F., *Oriental Carpets in the Museum of Islamic Art, Berlin* (London: Faber and Faber, 1988).

Stanzer, W., *Foreign Influence in the Ait Ouauzguite Textiles*, First International Conference on Oriental Carpets in Marrakesh, 1995; *Oriental Carpet and Textile Studies* (London: Hali).

Stauffer, A.M, *Textiles of Late Antiquity* (New York: Metropolitan Museum of Art, 1995).

Stillman, N., *The Jews of Arab Lands* (Philadelphia, PA: Jewish Publication Society, 1979).

Strauss, L., *Persecution and the Art of Writing* (Glencoe, IL: Free Press, 1952).

Suarez Fernandez, L., *Historia de España: Los Trastamara y Los Reyes Católicos* (Madrid: Gredos, 1985).

Tacitus, *The Histories* (London: Penguin Books, 1964).

Taylor, R. 'Spanish Rugs at Vizcaya', *Hali*, 52 (August 1990), pp.101–10.

Thomas, H., *Rivers of Gold* (London: Phoenix, 2003).

Thomas, Oliver, *A History of Sin* (Edinburgh: Canongate, 1993).
Thompson, D., *Coptic Textiles in the Brooklyn Museum* (New York: Brooklyn Museum, 1971).
Thompson, J., *Milestones in the History of Carpets* (Milan: Tabibnia, 2006).
Thompson, W., 'Hispano-Moresque Carpets', *Burlington Magazine*, 18 (1910–11).
Tovey, D'Blossiers, *Anglia Judaica*, edited by Elizabeth Pearl (London: Weidenfeld & Nicolson, 1990 [1738]).
Trachtenberg, J., *Jewish Magic and Superstition* (Philadelphia, PA: University of Pennsylvania Press, 2004).
Trachtenberg, Joshua, *The Devil and the Jews* (Philadelphia, PA: Jewish Publication Society of America, 1983).
Ungerleider-Mayerson, J., *Jewish Folk Art from Biblical Days to Modern Times* (New York: Summit Books, 1986).
Unterman, A., *The Wisdom of the Jewish Mystics* (London: Sheldon, 1986).
Valdéon Baruque, J., *Los Judios de Castilla y la Revolucion Trastamara* (Valladolid: Gráficas Andrés Martín, 1968).
Van de Put, A., *Hispano-Moresque Ware of the XV Century*, catalogue, Agnew & Co Ltd (London: Bradbury, 1904).
Van de Put, A., 'Some Fifteenth Century Spanish Carpets', *The Burlington Magazine*, 19, C11 (September 1911), pp.345–9.
Vermes, G., *The Dead Sea Scrolls in English*, 3rd edn (London: Penguin, 1987).
Vivanco, Laura, *Death in Fifteenth Century Castile: Ideologies of the Elites* (Rochester, NY: Tamesis, Boydell & Brewer, 2004).
Von Bode, W., *Vorderasiatische Knupfteppiche aus Alterer Zeit*, Monographien des Kunstgewerbes (Leipzig: Monographie des Bankgewerbes, 1902).
Von Folsach, Kjeld and Keblow Bernsted, Anne-Marie, *Woven Treasures – Textiles from the World of Islam* (Copenhagen, The David Collection, 1993).
Von Soden, W., *The Ancient Orient: An Introduction to the Study of the Ancient Near East*, trans. D. Schley (Grand Rapids, MI: William B. Eerdmans, 1994).
Walker, B., *The Woman's Dictionary of Symbols and Sacred Objects* (New York: Harper & Row, 1988).
Weitzman, Steven, *Surviving Sacrilege: Cultural Persistence in Jewish Antiquity* (Cambridge, MA: Harvard University Press, 2005).
Westenholz, J. (ed.), *Seals and Sealing* (Jerusalem: Bible Lands Museum, 1993).
Whitechapel, Simon, *Flesh Inferno* (London: Creation Books, 2003).
Wischnitzer, M., *A History of Jewish Crafts and Guilds* (New York: Jonathan David, 1965).

Wolff, Anne, *How Many Miles to Babylon* (Liverpool: Liverpool University Press, 2003).
Woolley, L., 'Pagan Classical Christian–Egyptian Hangings of the 4th to 7th Centuries', *Hali*, 48 (December 1989).
Yadin, Yigael, *The Finds from the Bar Kokhba Period in the Cave of Letters* (Jerusalem: Israel Exploration Society, 1963).
Ziffer, Irit, 'O my Dove, that art in the clefts of the rock', catalogue (Tel Aviv: Eretz Israel Museum, 1998).

JOURNALS

Biblical Archaeology Review, Washington, 1970.
Ghereh, Ghereh Textile Art Publications, Turin, 1995 on.
Hali, 1981 on.
Jewish Chronicle, Fetter Lane Publishers, London, 1870s on.
Journal of Jewish Art, Spertus College of Judaica Press, Chicago, The Hebrew University, Jerusalem 1974 on – title changed to *Jewish Art*.
Hebrew History Federation Newletter, New York, History Federation 1990–2003 [Hebrew].
Palestine Exploration Quarterly, Maney Publishing, Leeds, England, 1984 on.
Textile Museum Journal, Washington, DC, The Textile Museum, 1962 on – title changed to *Journal of the Textile Museum*.

Index

Please note that page numbers relating to Notes will have the letter 'n' following the page number. The prefix 'al' is ignored in filing order.

'Abbasids (749–1258), 43
'Abd al-'Aziz, 3
'Abd al-Rahman III, 8n, 21n
Aber, Ita, xvi, xviiin, 237
ablutions, religious, 138
Abraham, Biblical figure, 23, 55, 168; Shield of, 172
Abrahams, Israel, 194n
Abramsky, Chimen, 200n
Abravanel, don Isaac, 135
Abu'l-Walid ibn Rushd, 130
acrostics, 225
acts of faith, 165n
Adler, E., 57n, 77n
Admiral carpets, xvi–xvii, 52, 66, 67–8, 70n, 92, 143, 204, 226; end of, 239; whether Judaic, 231; stars in, 191–2; weaving of, 101, 129, 140, 235–6; *see also* Vizcaya carpet
afterlife, 89–90, 100n; in Christianity, 90, 93, 94, 99n, 108
Aggadah (biblical stories), 126n, 247
Ahmadinejad, Mahmoud, 127n
Aholiab (son of Ahisamach of tribe of Dan), 24, 29
Akhenaten (Pharoah), 30n
Akkad, Iraq, 23
Alahdab, Yitzhaq, 48
Alba Bible, Castilian, 148
Albacete region, Spain, xvii
Albali, Baruch (master weaver), 12, 13
Alboraiques (insincere converts), 145n
Alcarez, Murcia, 140

Alconqui, Çag, 18
Aleppo Synagogue, Syria, 179–80
Alexander the Great, 37
Alexandria, 39; Jewish weavers of, 29, 37–8, 41, 42
Alfonso Enriquez of Castile (1354–1429), xvi, 67, 69, 82, 85, 86, 88, 90, 92, 93, 94, 95, 96, 137, 232, 233
Alfonso I d'Este, Duke, 239
Alfonso VI of Castile and Leon (1040–1109), 129
Alfonso X of Castile and Leon (the Wise), 7, 19, 73, 131, 148, 159, 182
Alfonso XI of Castile and Leon, 19, 81
Algeria, 33
Algiers, 35
Alharizi, Judah, 148
allegorical meaning, of Bible, 147, 149
Almeria port, Spain, 4, 42
Almohads, 18, 106
Almoravids (1055–1149), 106, 129; Almoravid silk lampas textiles, 4
Alpert, Michael, 145n
Alphonso IV of Portugal (1325–57), 174
Alsh, Murcia, 7
altar, 6
Altica, Atta, 14
Altneu Synagogue, Prague, 186
alum (mordant to fix dye into wool), 3
Alvarez, Leonar, 152
American Journal of Human Genetics, 120, 135
Amidah prayer, 172
ammunition, manufacture, 49
amulets, 160, 174, 177, 178, 216
Anatolia, 23, 50, 54, 60n
Angel of Death, 107

Anilaeus, 28
animals, as metaphors, 147
Antichrist, Jews perceived as servants of, 102
Antiochus IV Epiphanes, 227
anti-Semitism, 81, 82, 107, 159; see also ill treatment/expulsions of Jewish people
Apocalypse, 115
apocrypha, 26, 40, 247
Apostles, Acts of, 32n
Aquila (follower of St Paul), 32n
Aquitaine, expulsion of Jews from, 17
arabesque (design form of circular/spiral tendrils), 66, 247
Aragon, 18, 19
Aramaic words, 74
Arcohen, Yosine, 175
Arianism (form of Christianity), 14, 15
Aristotle, 114, 125n
Ark, 6, 29, 221–3, 247, 250; Spanish synagogue carpet, 71–2, 74
Armenian carpets, 126n, 162, 215
Armorial carpets see Admiral carpets
Arragel, Rabbi Moses, 148
Art Institute, Chicago, 67
Artabanus III, Parthian King, 28
artefacts, dual-purpose, 151
artisans, 46, 47, 55, 115, 131
Asaf, Simha, 154n
Ashbea, house of, 26
Ashdod (coastal town in Land of Israel), 24
Asherah, 171
Ashkenazi Haggadah, 215
Ashtor, Eliyahu, 9n, 58n
Asia Minor, carpet production in, 4
Asinaeus, 28
assimilation, 133, 158
Assur (Assyrian god), 175
Assyrian power, 175
astral magic, 174
astrological tradition, 168
astrology, central dilemma, 170
Astruc, 185–6
atheism, 165n
Augustine, Saint, 102, 111
Auschwitz, 32n
auto-da-fé (public ceremony for carrying out of death penalty), 46, 111, 120, 247
Ayala, Marina Diez de Cordova, xvi, 66–7, 85, 86, 94, 232–3
ayyubids (Islamic dynasty of sultans 1171–1250), 247
Azemmour (carpet trading centre), 34, 42, 213–14

Bacharach, Jere L., 197n

Bacon, Josephine, 58n, 196n
badge, of identity, 110–11, 174, 181
badges of trades, 44
Baer, Y., 99n, 144n, 145n, 146n
Baghdad, 40, 55
Baigent, M., 124n
Banda, Order of, xvi
Baqrat, Rabbi Abraham, 145n
bar Gedaliyah, Scholomo, 185
Bar Kokhba revolt (132–135 CE), 194n, 204
Bar Kokhba, Shimon (Son of the Star), 176–7, 196n
bar mitzvah, 126n, 247
bar Shemuel Halevi, Todros Halevi, 185
bar Yonai, Rabbi Shimon, 116
Barbary Coast, 15
Barclay, John, 21n, 124n
Barnavi, Eli, 195n
Baroja, Caro, 145n
Baron, Salo, 199n
Barthes, Roland, 164n
Bayazid II, Sultan, 49
BCE (prior to Common Era), 247
Beattie, May, 69n, 191, 192, 201n
Beaujour, Felix, 55
Beinart, Haim, 56n, 127n, 145n, 198n
Beit al-sha'r (tent), 25
Beit Jibrin, Marisa, 176
Beit Mirsim (town), 25
Beit Shearim, 28, 177
Bellinger, L., 9n, 10n, 31n, 59n, 197n
Bellini prayer rug, 53
Belmonte, Portugal, 120–1
ben Abdalla Hadshi Halfa, Mustafa, 55
ben Asayahu, Joshua, 175–6
ben Asher, Judah, 75
ben Avraham ibn Malek, Menachem, 180
ben Barzilay ha Bargeloni, Judah, 133
ben David of Posquières, Rabbi Abraham, 115
ben David, Yehuda, 103–4, 123n
ben Eliezer Bonfils, Joseph, 187
ben Elijah Hadassi, Yehudah, 180
Ben Ezra Synagogue, Cairo Genizah, 29, 35, 41, 42, 67, 179–80, 247; Jeremiah's tomb, 39
ben Isaac, Abraham (of Granada), 182, 198n
ben Isaac of Worms, Eliezer, 188
ben Isaac, Solomon (biblical commentator, 1040–1105) see Rashi (Solomon ben Isaac)
ben Jonah, Benjamin, 39, 40
ben Judah, David, 188
ben Judah Messer Leon, David, 188
ben Maimon, Moses (1135–1204) see Maimonides (Moses ben Maimon)
ben Meir Halevi, Samuel, 185, 188

Index

ben Moses Arama, Rabbi Isaac, 118, 189
ben Nahman, Moshe (Talmudist 1194–1290)
  see Nahmanides (Moshe ben Nahman)
ben Rabbi Judah, Rabbi Jose, 204–5
ben Samuel Abulafia, Abraham, 181–2
ben Shem Tov de Leon, Moses, 210
Ben Sirach, 26
ben Solomon Luria, Isaac, 189
ben Ya'akov, Moshe, 183
ben Yehiel, Asher, 43, 44, 75
ben Yehuda ibn Merwas, Joseph (of Toledo), 182
ben Yiju, Abraham, 36
ben Yosi I, Eleazar, 31n
ben Zemah Duran, Rabbi Simon, 84
Benbassa, Esther, 145n
Benedict XIII, Pope, 20
Benjamin II, 40
Ben-Sasson, M., 57n
Berbers, 15
Berliner, Rudolph, 38, 57n, 202n
Berruguete, Pedro, 120
Beth Alpha synagogue, sixth-century, 28–9, 72, 73, 207, 215, 222
Beth Hatefutsoth Museum, 38
Beth Shean, 28
Beth Shean Synagogue, 27, 29, 74
Beth Yerah Synagogue, 73
Beth-El, nr. Ramallah, 176
Bevan, E., 199n
Bible, 12, 13, 38, 39, 72, 115; Hebrew see Hebrew Bible; ways of reading, 147
Bier, Carol, 60n
Bigg, S., 211n
Bill of Sale (1248), 181
birds, 74, 213–18; on Vizcaya carpet, 73, 213, 214, 215
bishops, of Castile, 102–3
Black Death (1348–50), 81, 102, 103, 123n, 130, 143n, 145n, 184
Black Death (1391), 103
Black Prince (Edward of Woodstock), 82, 98n
Blanquez-Perez, J., 146n
blazons, Vizcaya carpet, 66, 67
Blazquez, Miguel, 145n, 146n
Blecua, Alberto, 150
Bobrinskoy, Count, 217n
Bohemia, 186
Bonafous, Solomon, 181
Bône, 35
Bontempi, Francis, 128n
'Book of Games' (Alfonso X), 73, 74, 192
Book of Tahkemoni (Alharizi), 148
Book of the Boundary, The (David ben Judah), 188
Boralevi, Alberto, 77n

borders, 50, 247; main and secondary, 249, 251; Vizcaya carpet, 65, 66, 192–3, 221, 225
Borja, Salamanca: Jewish workshop, 45
Bosch, Hieronymus, 152, 154n
Braude, Benjamin, 22n, 60n
Braziller, George, 143n
Brescia region, 118
British Museum, 178
Bronze Age, Israelite imaging, 171
Brook, Kevin, 196n
Browne, Lewis, 22n
Budapest, 186
Bukhara, Jews of, 211–12n
Burgos, 190
burials, 90–2, 136–7
Burman, Edward, 146n
burning alive, 102, 119
Bursa, 55
Busi, Giulio, 217n, 228n
Buxtorf the Elder (1564–1629), 213
Byzantine Empire, 22n, 29, 54, 126n, 251
Byzantine synagogue, Cairo, 37

caballero mayor (title), 18
Cain, marks of, 158, 174
Cairene carpets, 35, 239
Cairo, 35, 36, 37, 38, 43
Cairo Genizah, Ben Ezra Synagogue, 29, 35, 41, 42, 67, 179–80, 247
Cairo Museum, 43
Cairo Synagogue, Middle Ages, 180
Calatayud district, 46
Caliph, 6
Cammann, Schuyler V.R., 201n, 205–6, 208n
Canaanites, 175, 206
canon law, 104, 110
Capernaum Synagogue, 177
Capsali, Eliyahu (of Crete), 49, 60n, 86, 98n
Carmi, T., 193n
Caro, Joseph, 78n, 188, 200n
carpet centres, 34–5, 40, 140
carpets, xv, 6, 21n, 32n, 54, 69n, 162; Admiral see Admiral carpets; Cairene, 35, 239; kelim (pileless), 26, 249; Maghreb region, 34, 35, 45, 51; Mamluk see Mamluk carpets/rugs; Marbadiah, 73, 249; parts, definitions, 247, 248; piled, 23, 30n, 36, 68, 250; purple, of Alexandria, 37–8; role in Islamic culture, 45; role in Jewish culture, 23–32, 45; synagogue see Spanish synagogue carpet; Turkestan, 61n, 69n; Vizcaya see Vizcaya carpet; wall-to-wall carpeting, 36; see also rugs
Carroll, D.L., 39
Cartagena region, 11, 13

Carthage, 11, 13
Carthaginians (descendants of Canaanites and Phoenicians), 11
cartoons (graph-type paper), 68
Castile, Spain, xvi, 5, 7, 8, 130; Jewish population in, 18, 113, 145n; rulers of, 17–18
Castilian currency, debasing (fifteenth century), 5
Castro, Americo, xvi, xviiin, 66, 69n, 98n, 99n, 100n, 101, 128n
Cathars of Languedoc, 109, 110, 116, 124n, 139
Catherine of Lancaster (widow of Enrique III), 113
Catholic Encyclopaedia, 110
Catholicism, 15, 90, 104, 109, 111, 118, 123n, 146n, 152, 153, 163; anti-*converso* tract of 1449, 89; and Judaism, 108; theology, 107; *see also* Christianity
Caucasia, Jewish weavers of, 41
Cave of Letters, 13
Cave of the Warrior, nr. Dead Sea, 23
CE (Common Era: AD in Christian calendar), 247
celestial bodies, 168, 169
censorship, 147
central field, carpets, 50, 247; Vizcaya carpet, 65–6, 192
Cerro del Castillo, 139
Cervantes, Miguel de, 150, 151, 154n
Chagall, Marc, 29
Chanukah *see* Hannukah
Charlemagne the Great, 16
Charles IV, Emperor of Prague, 186
Chaucer, Geoffrey, 82, 97n, 98n
chess symbol, 73, 77n
Chevalier, J., 217n
Chiat, Marilyn, 32n, 208n
Chincilla carpets, Murcia, 6
Chios, 34
Christ *see* Jesus Christ
Christian knights, 7–8, 17, 18, 19, 39, 47, 130
Christian symbols, 94, 151, 157, 158, 168, 174; cross, 157, 160–1, 176; rooster, 215; star, 183–4
Christianity, 16, 73, 115, 122, 162, 205, 214; afterlife in, 90, 93, 94, 99n, 108; Arianism form, 14, 15; Catholicism *see* Catholicism; and devil, 101, 102, 107; funerary requirements, 90–1, 92, 136–7; Muslims living under rule of (Mudejars), 7, 250; Old Christians, 87, 105, 127n, 131, 133, 138, 250; Protestantism, 120, 124n, 152, 163; washing, significance of, 138; *see also conversos/conversas* (persons converted

from Jewish or Muslim faith to Christianity); Jesus Christ; *moriscos* (Muslim converts to Christianity)
Christian–Jewish relationship, medieval Spain, 108–9
Christ-killers, Jews perceived as, 104
Chronicle of Rassis, the Moor (tenth-century work), 4
Chrysostom, St John, 104
Chuppah (wedding canopy), 24, 247
Church of Rome *see* Catholicism
circle symbol, 174, 209, 226
City of God, The (St Augustine), 111
civil wars (1440s and 1450s), 113
Claudius Claudianus, 27
Clement of Alexandria, 38
Clement VI, Pope, 67, 191
clothing, identifying, 110
coats of arms, Vizcaya carpet, 66, 67, 86, 94, 233
Cohen, Alonso, 106–7
Cohn-Sherbok, Dan, 60n, 125n
Cole, P., 22n, 59n, 128n, 146n
colour symbolism, Jewish, 46
Columbus, Christopher, 127n, 128n
Common Era, 211, 247
communion service, 112
Concaro, Edoardo, 54, 61n
concealment of faith, 162–3
Constantine, Emperor, 14
Constantinople, 180; fall to Islam (1453), 113
Constitution pro Judeis, 104
convents, Spanish, 69
conversos/conversas (persons converted from Jewish to Christian faith), xviii, 15, 68, 74, 105, 106, 112, 117, 131, 132, 133–4, 147, 148, 152, 247; deathbed reconciliations to Judaism, 90; designers and weavers of carpet as, 234–6; Enriquez family, xvii, 83–4, 85, 86, 87, 88, 89, 92, 97, 127n, 231–4; and Jewish weavers of Spain/North Africa, 34, 46, 48, 51; religious lives, 94–5; and symbols, 160, 161; *see also* crypto-Jews
Convivencia (living at peace with your neighbours), 87, 88, 163
copt, 247
Coptic tradition, 38–9, 66, 74, 75, 76, 162, 179
Cordovero, Moses, 204, 210
corpse, ritual washing, 91
cortes (local Spanish assemblies), 247
Corvinus, Matthias, 186
Cosmas Indicopleustes of Alexandria, 38
Cossa, Balthazar, 124n
Council of the Doges, 138, 183–4

Index

craft guilds, 26, 27, 38; Sephardic, 29
crescent moon symbol, 159, 165n
Cresques, Abraham, 181
Critchlow, K., 193n
cross panel, carpet, 248
cross symbol, 157, 160–1, 176; see also under symbols
crucifixion, 12, 26, 94
cruelty, allegations of, 102
crypto-Jews, 81–2, 87, 94, 97, 106, 152, 153, 232; see also conversos/conversas (persons converted from Jewish to Christian faith)
Cuenca, Murcia, 140; Bishop of, 7
cypress tree motif, 52
Cyrenaica, Jewish community in, 28

Dagger of Faith, The (Martin), 102
Damascus, 51
Daniel, Book of, 126n, 168, 226–7
Daniel, Remer, 228n
Danon, Enzo and Roberto, 61n, 211n
Dante Alighieri, 93, 99n
David, Abraham, 60n
David, Shield of, 173, 174, 177, 182, 188
Dávila, Juan Arias, 96
d'Avila, Judah, 50
Davin, Crescias, 144n
Davis, Norman, 8n
Day of Judgement, 89, 93, 137
de Barrientos, Lope, 85
de Cordovero, Moses, 54
de Guzman, Enrique, 85
de Montemayor, Jorge, 150
De Occulta Philosophia (Paracelsus), 189
de Rais, Marshal Gilles, 112
De Reinoso, Alonso Núñez, 150
de Rio, Anton, 46
de Rojas, Fernando, 147, 148–9, 150, 151, 153n, 154n
de Unger, Edmund, 60n
Dead Sea, 13
death, 111; auto-da-fé see auto-da-fé (public ceremony for carrying out of death penalty); in medieval Spain, 89, 93; see also afterlife; hell; soul
Debou town, Morocco, 47
decalogue see Ten Commandments
deism, 165n
della Vida, Isac, 55
demonizing of Jewish people, 102, 112
Denny, Walter, 9n, 53, 60n, 69n, 192, 202n
Descatoire, C., 199n
Deuteronomy, 69n, 106, 170, 186–7, 193n, 220, 225
devil, 93, 101, 102, 107, 123n

Di Giovanetti, Matteo, 191
dialectics, 122
diaspora, 248
Diaz de Toledo, Fernán, 85
dietary laws, 150, 161, 249
Dilley, Arthur, 10n, 21n, 57n, 58n
Dimand, M.S., 10n, 57n, 78n
Diocletian (Roman emperor), Edict of Maximum Prices, 27
Divine Comedy (Dante), 93, 99n
Divine Light, 46, 205
Djerba, nr. Tunisia, 180–1
Dodds, J., 9n, 77n, 78n, 143n, 165n
Domitian, Emperor, 21n
Don Quixote de la Mancha (Cervantes), 150
Donates, Jaco, 119
Donnolo, Shabbetai, 199n
Douai, Flanders: weavers' strike in (1245 and 1320s), 4
dove, 214
du Guesclin, Bertrand, 82
Dubnov, S., 125n, 195n
ducks, 73, 215
Dunlop, D., 199n
Dura Europos Synagogue, Syria, 27, 31n, 74, 207, 222
Duran, Profiat, 57n
dyes and dyers, 3, 11, 13, 27; Jewish weavers of Spain and North Africa, 40, 44, 45, 61n

ecclesiastic law, 111
Echeandia, T., 146n
Ecker, Heather, 143n, 154n, 198n
Eder, A., 195n
Edict of Expulsion (1492), 118
Edict of Faith (1519), 137
Edmison, Susan, 57n
Edward I of England, 7
Edward the Confessor, 194n
effigies, 90–1
Egbert, C.E., 194n
Egypt, 4, 179, 181; carpet production/trading, 35, 45, 76
Eiland III, Murray, 52
Einstein, Albert, 208n
El Tránsito Synagogue, Toledo, 72, 185, 188
Eleanor, Princess of Castile, 7
Eleazar, High Priest of Jerusalem, 37
elite, cult of, 114, 115, 125n
Elizabeth I of England, 98n
ellipses, crossed (Italy), 201n
End of Days, 108, 115
England: expulsion of Jews from, 17; Roman site, Midlenhall, 172; yellow star to be worn by English Jews (1222), 183

Enrique de Trastamara (Enrique II, son of Alfonso XI), 81–3, 84, 231–2
Enriquez family, xvi, xvii, 47, 67–8, 81–100, 128n, 131, 133, 142; as *conversos* (people converting to Christian faith), xvii, 83–4, 85, 86, 87, 88, 89, 92, 97, 127n, 231–4; Murcia region under, 84, 107, 112; public lives, 89; role in struggle for power, 88; *see also specific members, such as Alfonso Enriquez of Castile (1354–1429)*
Enriquez II of Castile (1334–1379), 112
Enriquez III of Castile (1379–1406), 84, 110–11, 112–13
Erasmus, Desiderius, 122, 128n
Erdmann, Kurt, 52, 61n
Erna Michael Haggadah, 197n
esoteric actuality, 160
esparto weaving, 3, 47
Essen Cathedral, 205
Esther, Biblical Queen, 95
Estrada, Francisco López, 150
Eternal Flame, 179
eternal salvation, quest for, 89
ethnic cleansing, of Muslims, 130
ethnography, 71
Ettinghausen, Richard, 56n, 197n
Eucharist (Christian sacrament), 94, 112, 248
Eve (Biblical figure), 23
exegesis, 24, 147, 176, 217n
Exodus, 24, 30n, 57n, 99n, 106, 208n, 209, 220
exoteric reality, 159–60

Fadrique Alfonso of Castile, twin brother of Enrique de Trastamara (1334–1358), 81, 82, 83, 231–2
Fadrique Enriquez de Cabrera (1485–1538), 96
Fadrique Enriquez of Castile (1390–1473), xvi, 66, 67, 85, 86, 88, 89, 94, 231, 232–3
Familiars (lay officials of the Inquisition), 142, 248
Fars, 40
fatimids (Islamic rulers 909–1171), 248
Feder, Theodore, 193n
Feinstein, Rabbi, 189
Ferandez, Antonio, 6
Ferdinand II of Aragon, 48, 88, 97, 135, 145n
Ferdinand III of Castile, 19
Ferrandis Torres, J., 146n
Ferrara city, 119
Ferrara synagogue, fifteenth-century, 72
Ferrer, Sanchez, 144n
Ferrer, Vincent, 113
festivals, Jewish *see* Hannukah; Passover; Purim; Rosh Hashanah; Shavuot; Sukkot

feudal Europe, 4
Feyjoso, Doctor, 136
Fez (carpet trading centre), 34
Fiddler on the Roof, 154n
field, carpet, 248
Figueras, Pau, 78n
Fine Arts Museum, San Francisco, 38
finials (decorative terminals), 248
First Commandment, 122
First Crusade, 126n, 199n
First Temple, Jerusalem (c. 961–586 BC), 25, 74, 210; destruction by Nebuchadnezzar (586 BC), 11, 114
fish symbol, 161
Flavius Josephus, 25, 28, 31n, 126n, 172, 176, 203
flesh, Christian view of, 108–9
Fletcher, Richard, 9n
fleur de lis, 169
folk memory, 25
folklore music, Sephardi, 53
fostat (ancient city nr. Cairo), 248
France, expulsion of Jews from, 17
Frank, Daniel, 22n
Frankel, E., 220n, 228n
Franses, M., 60n
Frederick II (Holy Roman Emperor), 45, 58n
free will, 170
Freehof, L., 20n
Freehof, Solomon, 98n
Freud, Sigmund, 30n
Frey, J.B., 196n
Friedenburg, Daniel, 159, 165n, 185, 199n
fundamentalism, Islamic, 16
funerary portraits, 21n
funerary requirements: Christian, 90–1, 92, 136–7; Jewish, 91–2, 99n, 136–7
Fustat rug, 38

Gamliel, Rabbi, 91
Gampel, Benjamin R., 21n
Garcia, Pedro, 119
Garcia de Lucio, Ruy, 119
Garden of Earthly Delights, The (Bosch), 152
Gates of Righteousness, The (Gikatilla), 182
geese, 73, 215, 216
Genesis, 91, 172, 203, 224
Genizah, Cairo, 29, 35, 247
Genoa, 46, 127n
Gerber, Jane S., 21n, 22n, 49, 58n, 100n, 124n
Gerizim, Mount, 31n
Germany, 69n, 180, 184
Gervers, V., 77n
al-Ghawri, Qansuh, 55

Index

Gheerbrant, A., 217n
Ghent and Bruges, rebellion of weavers in (1379), 4
Gibralter, Rock of, 15
Gikatilla, Joseph, 182, 211
Gilbert, Martin, 56n, 196n
Gilman, Stephen, 153n
Ginzberg, L., 208n
Giovanetti da Viterbo, Matteo, 67
Glick, T., 9n, 10n, 59n, 77n, 78n, 143n, 144n, 165n
Gnosticism, 115, 116
goats' hair, 68, 142
God: caring shepherd as metaphor for, 73, 219; hand of, 205–7, 248; shields, likened to, 172–3
Goitein, S.D., 8n, 9n, 56n, 57n, 58n, 198n
gold, 12, 46, 47
Golden Haggadah (of Barcelona), 182
Golden Menorah, 204
Gonclaves, Nuno, 174
Gonzales, Maria, 152
Goodenough, Erwin, 14, 72, 77n, 176, 195n, 196n
Goodnick Westenholz, Joan, 228n
Gordian knot, 21n
Gordium, 21n
gospels, 104
Gough, Sean, 57n
Grabar, Oleg, 3, 8n, 33, 56n, 129, 143n, 163–4, 165–6n, 202n
Graetz, H., 97n, 112–13, 125n
Granada, southern Spain, 7, 130, 131, 134, 140
Granger-Taylor, Hero, 20n
grapes/grapevines, 95
graven images, 93
Greco-Roman period, 168, 176, 215, 216
Gregory the Great, Pope, 15
guard strip, carpet, 248
Gui, Bernard, 112
Guide to the Perplexed (Maimonides), 188
Guild of Carpet Weavers and Purple Dyers of Hierapolis, Phryrgia, 21n
guilds, 44, 55; *see also* craft guilds
Gujarat, 36
Gunter Plaut, W., 178, 196n
Gutmann, Joseph, 57n, 199n
Gutwirth, Eleazer, 59n

ha'Cohen, Jacob, 59n
Haggadah (book recalling events of Exodus), 30n, 180, 187, 193, 197n, 215, 248
halakhah (Jewish law), 248
Halevi, Judah, 17, 100n

Halevi, Solomon, 117
Hamadan, 40
Hamelin Synagogue, Germany, 184
Hammurabi (King of Akkad), 23, 30n
Hamsa (Hand of God), 205–7, 248
ha-Nagid, Samuel, 43
hand symbol, 205–7, 248
Hannukah, 151, 248
Hannukiah, 72, 151, 186, 248; *see also* menorah
Harden, D., 77n
al-Harizi, Judah, 40
Harlow, Jules, 31n, 195n
Harvey, L.P., 144n
Hasdai ibn Shaprut, Abu Yusuf, 21n
hasids, 116, 126n, 184, 248
Hasmonean period (167–37 BCE), 171; Hasmonean victory (165 BCE), 248
Hassan, Falah, 69–70n
hat, as symbol, 159
heavenly bodies, 168, 169
Hebrew alphabet, 225, 226, 228n
Hebrew Bible, 13, 72, 91, 127n, 161, 163; of 1299–1300, 182
Hebrew letters, 41
Hebrew University of Jerusalem, 171
Heikhalot (apocalyptic mysticism), 177, 248
hell, 90, 93, 94, 99n, 101
Hellenistic rule, 27, 38, 85, 176, 205
Hellin district, Murcia region, 137, 139, 140, 142, 143, 144n
hemp frame, knots, 68
Henry III of England, 158
Henry V of England, 124n
Henry VII of England, 119
hens, 215
heresy, 102, 108, 110, 111, 136, 138, 141
Hermippos, 11
Hernandez of Hellin, Pedro, 138
Herod, King, 13
Herod the Great (73–4 BCE), 171, 176
hexagons, Vizcaya carpet, 65, 66
hexagrams, 67, 163, 167, 169, 176–8, 181, 185, 191; early use, 180; geographic limits of use, 192; and Judaism, 171–2; *see also* Star of David; star symbol
Hezekiah, King (727–698 BCE), 175
hidden meanings, 147–8
Hierapolis, Phrygia, 27
al-Himyari, ibn 'Abd al-Munin, 6, 10n
Hirsch, Udo, 30n
Hisham (Umayyad Caliph), 43
Hispanic Society of America, New York, 67, 182
Hispanic–Moresque carpet, xvii, 51
Hispanus, 20n
homiletic values, of Bible, 147

horizontal loom, 5, 9n
Horn of Africa, 36
Housego, Jenny, 51, 56n, 59n
Howard, Pamela, 154n
hue, 248
Humani Generis Inimicus (bull of Pope Nicholas V), 105
hygiene practices, 138
Hyksos (Semitic tribe), 24

Iberian Peninsula: conquered by Germanic tribes (fifth century), 14; conquered by Islam (eighth century), 3, 33; conquered by Rome (200 BCE), 12; Jewish population/Jewish ancestry, 21n, 135; present population, 120
Ibero-Roman period, 165n
Ibn al-Faqih, 58n
Ibn al-Walid Isma'il ibn Muhammad al-Shakundi, 6–7
Ibn Arabi (Sufi poet), 87, 99n
ibn Ezra, Abraham, 16, 121, 170
Ibn Ezra, Isaac, 16–17
Ibn Gabirol, 173, 203
ibn Gan, Jacob, 43
Ibn Khurdadhbih, 9n
ibn Muhammad al-Idrisi, Muhammad, 6
ibn Muhammad al-Makkari, Ahmad, 10n
ibn Musa ibn Sa'id, Abi, 6, 10n
Ibn Nuwairi, 15
ibn Sahula, Isaac, 147–8, 153n
ibn Verga, Rabbi Yehuda, 117
ibn Zaid, Tariq, 15
iconography, 68, 92; Christian, 214; Islamic, 52; Judaic, 46, 52, 67
Idachs, Luis Marco, 98n
al-Idrisi, Muhammad ibn Muhammad, 6
ill treatment/expulsions of Jewish people, 17, 134–5; expulsions of 1492, 12, 48, 68, 88, 97, 101, 118, 126n; pogroms *see* pogroms; *see also* anti-Semitism
infidels, banning of trade with, 45
Inman, N., 146n
Innocent III, Pope, 104, 110
Inquisition, 88, 133, 136, 138, 146n, 152, 233–4, 248; period from 1391 to 1492, 102, 103, 110, 117, 120; towns and villages affected by, 141–2; trial records, 186
Inquisitor's Guide,The (Gui), 112
intention, 104–5, 146n
inter-community travel, 41
intermarriage, 85
Iraq, 178
Irwing, Robert G., 57n
Isaac the Blind, 115, 116

Isabella I of Castile, 48, 88, 97, 135, 145n
Isaiah, 126n, 217n
Isfahan, 40
Ishmael (oldest son of Abraham), 4
Islam, 7, 45, 49, 113, 129; and Christianity, 122; and Spanish Jews, 15, 16; symbols, xvii, 168, 174; *see also* Muslims
Islamic Museum, Berlin, xvii
Islamic symbols, xvii
Israel Museum, Jerusalem, 23, 197n, 210
Israelites, ancient, 26, 27, 29, 169, 170, 209, 219
Istanbul, 50–1
Italy, 45; star symbol, 183–4, 201n

Jacob, 168
James I of Aragon, 7
James the Greater, Saint, 12
Jare, Obadiah, 40
Jativa, Valencia, 116
Jean of France, Duke of Berry, 7, 191
Jehu, King of Israel (842–814 BCE), 175
Jehudah, Rabbi, 14
Jerba (carpet trading centre), 34, 42, 53
Jeremiah, 26, 30n, 31n
Jeremiah's tomb, Ben Ezra Synagogue, 39
Jerome, Saint, 14, 104
Jerusalem: Exiles of, 12; fall to Romans (70 CE), 26, 27; Israel Museum, 23, 197n, 210; Temple in *see* Temple, The
Jesus Christ, 48, 90, 91, 102, 104, 108, 109, 157; crucifixion, 12, 26, 94
Jewish Academy of Baghdad, head of, 36
Jewish culture, role of carpets in, 23–32, 45
Jewish Dyers Guild of Barcelona, 44
Jewish history, 167
Jewish Museum of London, 187
Jewish Museum of New York, 163
Jewish people of Spain, 11–22, 104, 227; contradictory treatment by Enrique de Trastamara (Enrique II), 81, 82, 83, 84; expulsion from Spain (1492), 12, 48, 68, 88, 97, 101, 118, 126n; hidden meanings in writings of, 147; ill-treatment under Visigoths, 15; inducements to stay, 18; and mysticism, 116–17; as People of the Book, 19; perceived as Christ-killers, 12; symbols of *see* Jewish symbols; taxes paid by, 19–20, 135; trades and professions, 131–2; *see also* anti-Semitism; ill treatment/expulsions of Jewish people
Jewish symbols, 46, 94, 157–8, 159, 228; Ten Commandments, 24, 124n, 158, 248; *see also* hexagrams; menorah; pentagrams; Star of David; star symbol; symbols

Index

Jewish Symbols in the Greco-Roman Period (Goodenough), 176
'Jewish veils', 27
Jewish weavers, 13, 14, 24, 26, 27–8, 29, 30; apprenticeships/family businesses, 36; of North Africa and Spain, 33–62; see also weaving/weavers
Job, Book of, 168
Job's lament, 26
John of Gaunt, Duke of Lancaster, 98n
John XXII, Pope, 67, 124–5n
Jonathan (weaver), 28
Joseph (Jewish weaver), 38
Josephus, Flavius, 25, 28, 31n, 126n, 172, 176, 203
Josiah, 170
Juan I of Castile (1358–1390), 112, 174
Juan II of Aragon (1398–1479), 97
Juan II of Castile (1405–1454), 88, 113, 131
Juana, dona (Jewish wife of Fadrique Alfonso of Castile), 83–4, 98n, 232
Juana, dona (wife of Alfonso of Castile) see Mendoza, Juana de (wife of Alfonso Enriquez of Castile)
Jubilees, Book of, 170
Judaism: on afterlife, 99n, 100n; and Catholicism, 108; deathbed reconciliations to, 90; descent, bloodlines, 84, 85; and dialectics, 122; enigmatic history, 17; funerary requirements, 91–2, 99n, 136–7; hidden meanings in writings, 147; honouring of skilled carpet designers and weavers, 7; life, preservation of, 161–2; magical practices/superstitions, 115; Orthodox vs. Kabbalah, 126–7n; structures of, 55
Judea/Judean desert, 12, 23, 27
Judenstern (star-shaped lamp), 180
Juhasz, Esther, 60n
Jung, C.J., 32n
Juster, J., 31n

ka'ba (cubic meteorite stone, Mecca), 248
Kabbalah, 54, 81, 100n, 147, 160, 248; colour system, 192; on light, 203; mystical theosophical system of, 115; and numerology, 225–6; vs. Orthodox Judaism, 126–7n; practical, 114, 182, 250; and symbols, 187–8, 207, 224; theosophical, 191; Zohar, 55, 116, 148; see also Tree of Life symbol
Kabbalists, 51, 109, 126n, 170
Kahana, Queen, 15
Kahana, Rabbi, 28
Kairouan (carpet trading centre), 34, 42
Kamen, Henry, 99n
Kanof, A., 217n

Kaplan, Gregory B., 99n
karaite (Jewish sect), 249
Kashan, 152
kashrut, 150, 161, 249
Keall, Edward J., 195–6n
Keats, Victor, 77n
Keblow Bernsted, Anne-Marie, 202n
kelim (pileless carpet), 26, 249
Keller, W., 193n
Kennicott Bible, Bodleian Library (Oxford), 182
Kermes beetle, 3
Ketuba (pre-nuptial contract), 36, 249
Ketubot (wills), 36–7
Khazar tribe, 21n, 100n, 196n, 199n
Khazaria, King of, 199n
Khirbat Shura synagogue, Galilee region, 172
Khizghilov, Tyilo, 41, 58n
Khotan carpets, east Turkestan, 54
kiddush, 249
Kienaptel, Frau, 76–7n
King, B., 20n
King, D., 69n, 77n
King David's Flag, 186
Kirshenblatt-Gimblett, Barbara, 31n, 162, 165n
Kitaj, tapestry of, 32n
Klagsbald, Victor, 164n, 198n
knights, Christian see Christian knights
Knights Castile soap, 133, 144n
'Knot of Hercules', 201n
knots, 21n, 50, 69n, 76; warp, 50, 66, 68; see also piled (knotted) textiles/carpets
kohen (priest), 50
Kirshenblatt-Gimblett, Barbara, 31n, 162, 165n
kufic (form of Arabic script), 249
Kühnel, E., 9n, 10n, 59n, 197n
Kuran see Qu'an
Kurdistani Jews, 40
Kybalova, Ludmila, 162, 165n

La Celestina (de Rojas), 147, 148–9
La Villa Santiaguista de Leitor en la Baya Edad Media (Llopis), 131
Lainez, Gregorio, 119
lamb metaphor, 73
Lambert, P., 197n
Lamm, C.J., 197n
lamp symbol, 151, 171, 180, 197n
Land of Israel, 51; wars of independence (66–72 CE), 12
Landsberger, Franz, 30n, 31n, 57n, 217n, 228n
Languedoc, Cathars of, 109, 110, 116, 124n, 139
Lateran Council, 110, 125n
lattice, 249
Lea, H.C., 59n, 97n, 135
Lebanon, 175

Leigh, R., 124n
Leitor, 131, 140, 141, 143
Leon, Moses ben Shemtov de, 116
Lerida, 190
Leroy, Beatrice, 22n
letters, Hebrew, 41
Letur, 131, 140, 141, 143, 144n
Levite, 249
Leviticus, 69n, 179, 218n, 224–5
Levy, Yaffa, 77n
Lewis, Bernard, 196n
life, preservation of (in Judaism), 161–2
light, 203
lions, 226–7
literacy, of Jews of Spain, 19
literal reading, of Bible, 147
Little, Donald P., 56–7n
Llopis, Rodriquez, 131, 144n, 194n
Loewe, R., 194n
Longstreth, Bevis, 21n, 225, 228n
looms, 23, 27; horizontal, 5, 9n; silk, 52; two-beamed vertical, 24, 68; vertical, 5, 14, 143
Lopez, Inez, 153
Lopez, R., 56n
lozenge (four-sided motif), 249
Lubavitcher Rebbe, 189
Lydda, 27

Maccabee, Judah, 151
Maccabees, fourth book of, 168
Machiavelli, Niccolò, 109, 124n
MacKay, A., 10n, 98n, 99n, 144n
Mackie, A., 59n
Mackie, L., 56n, 75, 192, 202n
Magen David (as Hebrew word for hexagram shape), 172, 189
Maghreb region: carpet production in, 34, 35, 45, 51; description, 33, 249; Jewish communities in, 41, 42, 61n; whether oldest surviving Spanish carpet in, 71
magical practices/superstitions, 115
Mailey, J., 57n, 78n
Maimonides (Moses ben Maimon), 42–3, 46, 76, 91, 99n, 105, 124n, 126n, 161, 187, 188, 227, 249; Aristotelian rationalism of, 114, 125n
main border, 249
al-Makkari, Ahmad ibn Muhammad, 10n
Mamluk carpets/rugs, 29, 45, 51, 52, 55, 68; origins of, 53, 61n
Mamluk dynasty (1251–1517), 52, 249
Mangalore, south India, 36
Mann, V., 9n, 58n, 77n, 78n, 143n, 165n, 217n
al-Mansur (military dictator), 43
manta (rug), 55; *see also* rugs

Mañueco, J., 99n, 100n
Manuel I of Thebes, 40
maravadis (currency), 135
Marbadiah carpets, 73, 249
Maria (spinner and weaver), 12–13
Maria of Castile, xvi, 67
Mariana, Juan de, 118, 128n
Marinid kingdom (1286–1465), 5, 34
Mark, Saint, 26
Markoe, G., 20n
Marrakesh, 35
Marranos (*conversos*), 60n, 120–1, 151, 249
Martin, Raymond, 102
Martin I of Aragon, 191
Martin of Leon, Saint, 124n
Martin V, Pope, 113
Mártinez, Ferrant, 83
martyrdom, 105, 160, 168, 184
Marx, Karl, 127n
Masada, 13
Masson, Georgina, 125n
Master of the Order of Calatrava, 139
matzah (unleavened bread), 112, 182, 185, 249
May, Florence Lewis, 8n, 58n, 59n, 144n
Mazel tov, 171
McCall, Andrew, 99n
medallion, rugs, 249
Medina del Campo Treaty (1464), 88
Mediterranean, Jewish merchants as major textile merchants in, 4
Melammed, Renée Levine, 100n, 123n, 154n
memory, xv, xvi
Mendoza, Juana de (wife of Alfonso Enriquez of Castile), 85, 90, 92–3, 94, 95, 96, 128n, 137, 232, 233
Mendoza y Bobadilla, Francisco, 85
Menocal, Maria Rosa, 22n, 154n
menorah, 39, 65, 72, 158, 203–5, 249; in Christianity, 205; and star symbol, 177, 179, 181, 200–1n; *see also* Hannukiah
Merchant of Venice (Shakespeare), 110–11, 125n, 131
Merino wool, 5, 51, 249
Mesha, king of Moab, 25
Meshhad, 152
Messiah, 92, 114, 115, 122, 205
metaphors, 147, 160
metaphysical realm, 125–6n
Metropolitan Museum of Art, New York, 67
Meyuhas Ginio, Alisa, 59n
mezuzot, 187, 249
Middle Ages, 11, 68, 75; from 1391 to 1492, 101–28; Enriquez family, 89, 93; weaving in, 4, 27, 45; *see also* Spain, medieval

mihrab (arched niche in mosque wall), 179, 250
Milan Cathedral, 205
Mildenhall, England: Roman site, 172
Miletus sheep, 37
Mills, John, 69n, 70n, 78n, 201n
mitzvot (good deeds), 96, 250
Mizrach (wall decoration), 250
Moabite Stone (850 BCE), 25
monasteries, Spanish, 69
Monk's Tale, The (Chaucer), 82
Morena, A., 8n, 146n
moriscos (Muslim converts to Christianity), 250
Morocco, 33, 47
mosaics, 28, 29, 73
Moses (biblical figure), 55, 170; five books of (Pentateuch) see Pentateuch (five books of Moses); Law of, 122
Moshe, Gil, 22n
mosques, 6, 50, 75, 129–30
motifs, 41, 52, 71, 74, 160, 250
Motley, John, 128n
Mudejars (Muslims under Christian rule), 7, 129, 130, 146n, 250
Muhammad (Prophet), 4
multicultural societies, 54–5
Murcia region, xvii, 82, 87, 113, 232; Enriquez family, under, 84, 107, 112; Hellin district, 137, 139, 140, 142, 143, 144n; Jewish people in, 18, 19, 29; medieval centre, 139; whether oldest surviving Spanish carpet in, 71; town plan (1481), 47, 133; weaving in, 3–10, 35, 45, 48, 54, 131, 134; see also Vizcaya carpet
Murciano, 47
Muslim revolt (1264), 131
Muslims: under Christian rule (Mudejars), 7, 129, 130, 146n, 250; conversion to Christianity (moriscos), 250; ethnic cleansing of, 130; expulsion from Spain, 12; 'New Muslims,' 154n
mysticism, 102, 114, 116–17, 125–6n, 159; star symbol, 184–5, 190

Naamah (first spinner and weaver), 23
Naarinx synagogue, 73
Nablus, 51
Nahmanides (Moshe ben Nahman), 116, 188, 211, 250
Najera, Castile, 42
Nasi, Joseph, 207, 240
Natan, Moshe, 142
National Library, Lisbon, 182
Navarra, 96
Nazi era, 32n

Nebuchadnezzer, 11, 20n, 252
Nehardea, Babylon, 28
Neolithic Age, 3
Neoplatonic philosophy, 115, 116, 203
Nepaulsingh, Colbert I., 146n, 147, 153n, 154n
Nerva, Emperor, 21–2n
Netanyahu, Benzion, 22n, 81, 97n, 98n, 123n
Netherlands, Spanish, 120
Neuman, Abraham, 22n, 131–2, 144n
New Christians see conversos/conversas (persons converted from Jewish or Muslim faith to Christianity)
'New Muslims,' 154n
Nicholas V, Pope, 105
Nimrod, black obelisk at, 175
North Africa and Spain, Jewish weavers of, 33–62; closeness of communities, 42, 179
Norwich, John Julius, 57n
Nosseri, Jack, 197n
Nuestra Senora de las Esperanza, Convent, 96
Numbers, 73, 186, 208n, 225
numerology, 225–6
Nuzi, nr. Kirkuk, 175

Obadiah Jare, 40
Obadiah of Bertinoro, 51
Ochsenschlager, E.L., 30n
Ockham's Razor, 146n, 237n
octagons, Vizcaya carpet, 65, 66
Oegema, Gerban, 177, 193n, 196n, 197–8n, 200n
Okumura, Sumiyo, 61n
Old Christians, 87, 105, 127n, 131, 133, 138, 250; see also conversos/conversas (persons converted from Jewish to Christian faith)
Old Testament, 39
Olmedo, Battle of (1445), 88
oral tradition, 25, 26
ordinances (1412), 113
Origen (Christian theologian), 109
Orihuela, 107
Ot (Hebrew word for alphabetical letter), 157
Ottoman Empire, 30, 49, 50, 51, 54, 55, 119
Oxyrhynchus, 27

pacifist tradition, Christian, 111
Painter, K.S., 194n
Palace of the Popes, Avignon, 67
Palencia, northern Spain, 69–70n, 87
Palestinian synagogue, Cairo, 37
palette (overall colour scheme), 250
Pallister, Fanny M., 198n
palm tree motif, 52
Paloma bat Gedaliah, 86, 98n

panegyric, biblical, 26
Paracelsus, 189
Paradinas, Lavado, 92, 140, 146n
parokhet (curtain), 25, 26, 27, 75, 176, 250
Passover, 29, 74, 121, 185, 219, 250; Seder, 72, 251
Patai, R., 20n
patching of Spanish carpets, 68
Patricius, 28
Paul, Saint, 12, 29, 90, 162–3
Pazyryk carpets, 21n
peacock symbol, 14–15, 216
Pedro IV of Aragon, 44
Pedro of Castile (the Cruel), 81–2, 83, 97–8n
Pena, Diego de la, 119
pentagrams, 171, 172, 176, 181, 185
Pentateuch (five books of Moses), 26, 37, 163, 180, 222, 250; *see also* Deuteronomy; Exodus; Genesis; Leviticus; Numbers
Persia, 22n, 53
Persian rugs/carpets, 4, 40, 215
Pesach *see* Passover
Petachia, Rabbi, 40
Peter the Venerable, 9n
Pfister, R., 31n
Philadelphia Museum of Art, 67
Philo (Jewish philosopher), 38, 203
Phoenicians, 13
Phrygian weavers, 21n
Pickover, Clifford, 200n, 228n
pictorial symbols, 157
piled (knotted) textiles/carpets, 23, 30n, 36, 68, 250
Piloti, Emanuel, 42, 58n
Pinner, Robert, 9n, 57n, 60n, 69n
Plato, 30n
Plautus, Roman playwright, 37–8
Pliny (62–133 CE), 38
ply (two or more yarns twisted together), 250
poetry, 16–17, 87, 103–4, 121–2, 170, 173
pogroms, 84, 103, 105, 106–7, 113, 127n, 150, 159, 234, 250; and Jewish weavers of Spain/North Africa, 35, 46, 49, 52; *see also* ill treatment/expulsions of Jewish people; riots
pomegranate symbol, 53, 61n, 65, 209–10
Pompeii, volcanic eruption (79 CE), 12
Pompey the Great (Roman general), 12
Portugal, Jewish community of, 174
practical Kabbalah, 114, 182, 250
Prague, 186
Prague Synagogue, 72
prayer rugs, 6, 33, 50; Bellini, 53
predestination, 170
primordial light, 203
Priscillian (Spanish bishop), 111

prophetic tradition, 116
Protestantism, 120, 124n, 152, 163
Psalms, 50, 168, 169, 172, 178, 189, 214, 217n, 239
Ptolemaic period (230–30 BCE), 24, 37
Ptolemy II Philadelphus, 37
Punic rugs, 13
Purim, 250
Purity of the Blood law (1449), 84, 85, 87
Pythagorean tetractys, 169

Qu'an, 19
Quesada, Miguel-Angel, 130, 144n
Quesne, C. Le, 57n

Rabat rugs, 54
rabbonim, 55, 122
Raby, Julian, 77n
Radhanites (Spanish Jewish merchants), 5, 9n
Ragusa, 34
Rahmani, L., 162, 165n, 217n
ram, symbol of, 72–3, 219
Rambam Synagogue, Cordoba, 180
Raphael, Chaim, 58n
Rashba Bible, 182
Rashi (Solomon ben Isaac), 5, 29, 250
al-Rashid, Harun, 16, 43
Ratisbon Synagogue, Germany, 184
Rav Huna, 28
Raymond, W., 56n
Reccared, Visigoth King, 15
redemption, messianic, 159
Reformation, 163, 164
Regensburg community (1356), 159
Reif, Stefan, 57n, 197n
Reilly, Bernard F., 8n, 56n, 144n
Renaissance, 75
repeat call, 251
responsa, rabbinic, 28, 43, 84, 189, 251
Rhodes, 34
Richardson, H.G., 194n
riots, 103, 112, 113, 133, 174; *see also* pogroms
ritual sacrifice, 111
Robbins, R.H., 124n
Rodrig, Juana (of Toledo), 132
Rodrique, Aron, 145n
Roger II (Sicilian king), 39
Roman baths, 137–8
Roman Empire, 27
Romaniots (original Jewish population of Byzantine Empire), 49, 251
Rome, conquering of Iberian Peninsula (200 BCE), 12
rooster, 214–15

Index

rose window symbol, 151
rosette symbol, 52, 151, 175; six-pointed, 14, 176; summary of references, 241–6
Rosh Hashanah, 251
Roth, Cecil, 9n, 128n, 146n, 153n, 194n, 196n
Roth, N., 98n, 100n, 124n, 125n, 145–6n, 145n
Royal Guild (*La Mesta Real*), 5
Rubens, Alfred, 197n
Rubio Garcia, Luis, 47, 59n, 84, 98n
rugs, 4, 13, 24–5, 38, 40, 54, 215, 249, 250, 252; Mamluk *see* Mamluk carpets/rugs; prayer, 6, 33, 50, 53; *see also* carpets
Ruiz, Elvira, 186
Russian National Library, St Petersburg, 180

Sabadino, 239
Sabar, Shalom, 171, 173, 189, 193n, 194n, 208n
Sabbath, 152, 161, 169, 171
Sabbath lamps, 180
Sacher, Howard, 127n, 197n
sacrifice, 111
Safavids (Islamic dynasty, Persia 1502–1736 CE), 52, 251
Safed, Israel, 5, 51
saffron flower, 3
Sagunto, Valencia, 11
Salomonula, Annia, 14
Salonica, 49, 50, 51, 55
Samaritans (descendents from tribes of Ephraim and Mansseh), 31n, 251
Samarkand carpets, 54
Samuel, Alfonso Fernández, 137
Samuel, Edgar, 98n, 124n
San Pedro, Diego de, 150
San Rocco, Catholic school, 55
Sancho IV, King of Castile, 18
Sancho Panza, 151
Sancho the Fat, 21n
Santa Clara de Palencia (convent), 69, 88, 92, 94
Santa Maria La Blanca synagogue, Toledo, 95
Saragossa, 44, 92
Sarre, Friedrich, 76n
Sasanian rule, 28, 159
sassanids (Persian dynasty 226–641 CE), 251
Satan, 93, 101, 102
Saturn (planet), 169
Savejero Haggadah, 30n
Schneemelcher, W., 31n
Schochet, J., 208n
Schoeser, Mary, 8n, 20n, 57–8n
Scholem, Gershom, 153n, 172, 187, 193n, 194n, 195n, 198n, 199n, 200n

Schroeder, G., 228n
Schwartz-Be'eri, O., 58n
Schwartzman, Arnold, 201n
science, methodology, 165n
Scrolls of the Law, 71, 72
Scuola Cataluna Roman synagogue, 72
Scythopolis, 29
sea snail, murex, 11
Seal of Solomon, 159, 172, 173, 174, 176, 177, 182, 191
seals, Jewish, 173, 175–6, 185–6, 215
Second Coming, 108
Second Commandment, 75, 91, 93, 122, 171, 227, 233
Second Temple, Jerusalem (515 BCE–70CE), 25, 74, 168, 176; destruction by Romans in 70 CE, 28, 71, 158, 204
secondary borders, 251
secondary evidence, 13
Seder, 72, 251
Sefer Gematriaot (Kabbalist work), 181
Sefer Raziel (compendium of Jewish magic), 188
Sefer Yetzirah (Book of Creation), 170
Sefran, 35
segol (vowel), 198n
Seleucids, 171
Seneor, Abraham, 88
Senior, Abraham, 145n, 190
Sephardim, 5, 49, 50, 52, 54, 71, 251; acculturation process, 53; origins of term, 12
sephirot, 251
Sepphoris, 27
Septuagint (biblical title), 37
Seville, 42, 47; Synagogue, 50
Sfax (Gafsa), 45
Shaddai (Almighty), 185, 226
Shakespeare, William, 110–11, 125n, 131
Shalmaneser III, Lord of Assyria, 175
Shavuot, 251
sheep, 4–5, 25, 37, 73, 74, 219–20, 249; *see also* wool
Shema, The, 251
shepherd, caring: as metaphor for God, 73, 219
Sherrill, S., 8n, 9n, 10n, 76n, 77n, 78n
shields: Abraham, Shield of, 172; David, Shield of, 173, 174, 177, 182, 188; God likened to, 172–3; Vizcaya carpet, 66
Shiraz, 40
shofar (ram's horn), 72, 251
Shpanyer (textile decoration of stylized foliate designs), 251
Shpanyer Arbeit (Spanish weaving), 60n
shrouds, in Judaism, 99n
Shulhan Arukh, 78n

shuls *see* synagogues
Sicily, 39–40
Silius Italicus, 13
silk production, 5, 45, 46, 47, 49, 131; in Granada, 130
silver, 46, 47
sin, 93, 123n
Singer, C., 199n
Smyrna (Izmir), 55
Socrates, 25
Solomon, Biblical King, 11, 25, 213, 216; Seal of Solomon, 159, 172, 173, 174, 176, 177, 182, 191
Solomon, Rabbi, 85
Solomon, Vidal, 181
Song of Songs, 210–11, 217n
soul, 90, 92, 99–100n, 108
Sovereign Carpets (Concaro), 54
Spain, medieval: Christian–Jewish relationship, 108–9; Granada, southern Spain, 7, 130, 131, 134, 140; Jewish people of *see* Jewish people of Spain; Murcia region *see* Murcia region; Palencia, northern Spain, 69–70n, 87; Vizcaya carpet *see* Vizcaya carpet; *see also* Castile, Spain; Inquisition; Spanish synagogue carpet; Spanish weavers
Spalding, F., 195n
Spanish Inquisition *see* Inquisition
Spanish knot, 69n
Spanish synagogue carpet, 71–8, 209; lower cabinet, 73; upper cabinet, 72–3; *see also* Admiral carpet; Vizcaya carpet
Spanish weavers, 3–10; and North African, 33–62, 179; *see also* Spain, medieval
spinning, process of, 25
spiritual experiences, 114
St Augùstine, 102, 111
St James the Greater, 12
St Jerome, 14, 104
St John Chrysostom, 104
St Mark, 26
St Martin of Leon, 124n
St Paul, 12, 29, 90, 162–3
St Stephen, 184
St Vincent, church of, 174
Star of David, 14, 34, 38, 118, 128n, 159, 163, 167–202, 226, 251; abstract geometry of, 169; ascent as Jewish symbol, 169–70; hexagram shape, 171; origins of, 171; six-pointed star, significance, 169; Spanish synagogue carpet, 73, 74; Vizcaya carpet, 65, 66, 168, 178–9, 192
Star of Joseph, 186
star symbol, 159, 165n, 168; on Admiral carpet, 191–2; in England, 183; history, 167, 174–90; in Italy, 183–4; mystical meanings, 184–5; research problems, 167–8; in Sephardi manuscripts, 183; summary of references, 241–6; *see also* Star of David
State Corporation for Spanish Cultural Action Abroad, 135
Statute of Expulsion (Ferdinand and Isabella), 48
Stauffer, Anne Marie, 165n
Stein, Sir Aurel, 76
Stephen, Saint, 184
Stone, Caroline, 61n
Strauss, Leo, 153n
Sufis, 116
Sukkot, 24, 30n, 132, 251
Sunday trading, 48
supernatural, 99n, 107
superstition, 115, 172
Suriano, Francesco, 51
Sushan Sodot, 188
swastika, 198n
Sylvester, D., 69n, 77n
symbols, 157–66; abstract element, 157; of Christianity *see* Christian symbols; concrete element, 157; culture, effects on, 176; hand, 205–7; Islamic, xvii, 168, 174; of Judaism *see* Jewish symbols; migration of, 160; pomegranate, 53, 61n, 65, 209–10; star *see* Star of David; star symbol; of Vizcaya carpet, 65, 66, 67, 73, 147, 153, 159, 160, 168, 178–9, 192, 204–7, 209, 213–17, 220, 224–8, 236–7; walnut, 210–11
synagogues, 94–5; Egyptian, 46, 180; in Prague, 72; in Seville, 50; Spanish synagogue carpet, 71–8; specific synagogues named, 27, 28–9, 29, 31n, 37, 72, 73, 74, 95, 172, 176, 177, 179–80, 180, 184, 185, 186, 188, 207, 215, 222; *see also* Ben Ezra Synagogue
Syria, 34, 51

Tabernacle, 24, 25, 74, 204, 251
Tablets of the Law *see* Ten Commandments
Tacitus (anti-Jewish historian), 169, 193n
tallit, 251
Talmud, 19, 26, 27, 44, 95–6, 115, 161, 170, 177, 200n, 215; Babylonian, 28, 32n, 57n, 193n, 208n; burning of books, 116; definition, 251–2; hidden meanings, 147; and menorah, 204, 205
Tantalya carpets, Murcia, 6–7
tapestries, pictorial, 38
taqiyya, Islamic doctrine, 163
Tarsim, 27
Tarsus, 27
Tartessus (ancient Phoenician seaport), 11

tassel (fringe of prayer shawl), 73
Taylor-Schechter Collection, Cambridge, 35
Temple, The, 26, 171, 204, 252; *see also* First Temple, Jerusalem (c. 961–586 BC); Second Temple, Jerusalem (520 BCE–70 CE)
Ten Commandments, 24, 124n, 158, 169, 248; *see also* First Commandment; Second Commandment
Ten Sephirot, 54
Tenth legion, Roman, 13
tents, 25, 32n
Teutsch, B.P., 220n, 228n
Textile Museum, Washington, 67, 74
textiles: contribution of Jews to, xv–xvi, 20, 24, 27; piled, 23; *Shpanyer* (textile decoration of stylized foliate designs), 251; Spain, 4, 6, 11, 20; *see also* gold; silk
Thebes, Greece, 39
Theodemer, Count, 3
theological Jew, 107–8
Theophrastus (372–288 BCE), 168–9
Thirty Years War, 126n
Thomas, H., 144n
Thompson, John, 52, 61n
Thompson, W.G., 9n
threads, 5, 12, 44
Tiberias, 27
tints, 252
Titus (Roman general), 12
Tlemcen (carpet trading centre), 34, 42
Tobit, book of, 26
Todros Halevi bar Shemuel Halevi, 185
Toledo, Jewish settlement in (Middle Ages), 11, 12
Toledo revolt (1449), 86–7
tombstones, 14, 40, 92–3, 95–6
tones, 252
Torah, 77n, 78n, 252; *see also* Pentateuch (five books of Moses)
Torah Ark *see* Ark
Torquemada, Cardinal Juan de, 105
Torquemada, Fray Tomás de, 96, 136, 142, 145n
Torre, Fernando de la, 121
Torres, Ferrandis, 201n
Torres, Louis de, 117, 128n
Torres Fontes, Juan, 22n, 125n
Tortosa, Jewish Iberian tombstone in, 14
torture, 102, 111, 112, 123n
Tower of David, 164
Trachtenberg, Joshua, 104, 123n, 193n, 194–5n, 196n, 198n
trade, importance of handing down in families, 44
Tree of Life symbol, 14–15, 45, 72, 181

triangles and Star of David, 171, 172
Tripoli, 35
truth, 159, 178
Tunis, 35, 45
Tunisia, 33, 34, 180
Turkestan carpets, 61n, 69n
Turkey, 27, 50–1
Turkish 'Holbein' rugs, 54
Turkish knot, 50
turtle dove, 214
Tustar, 40

Umayyads (755–976), 3, 16, 43
Unitary Declaration, 186
Ur (Biblical city), 23
Ushak rugs, Anatolia, 54

Valdéon Baruque, J., 59n, 98n
Valencia, 5, 190
Vebius Tamudianus (spinner and weaver), 12–13
Venice, use of star, 183–4
vertical loom, 5, 14, 143
Vespasian, Emperor, 12
Virgin Mary, 26, 149
Visigoth rulers, 3, 14, 15, 16, 106, 137
Vizcaya carpet, 5, 20, 47, 61n, 65–70, 76, 92, 95, 96; birds on, 73, 213, 214, 215; blazons on, 66, 67; borders, 65, 66, 192–3, 221, 225; coats of arms on, 66, 67, 86, 94, 233; colour system, 222; Daniel in lion's den image on, 226–7; dating of weaving, 140, 141; five-branched figures on, 204; geometric layout, 65, 67; hands on, 206, 207; identity of weavers, 140; maintenance, 68–9; menorah on, 205; messages written into, 149–50; sheep on, 220; Star of David on, 65, 66, 168, 178–9, 192; symbols on, 65, 66, 67, 73, 147, 153, 159, 160, 168, 178–9, 192, 204–9, 213–17, 220, 224–8, 226–7, 236–7; weaving of, 129–46
Vizcaya Museum, Miami, xvi–xvii, xviii, 65
Von Folsach, Kjeld, 192, 202n
von Karben, Victor, 95

wall-to-wall carpeting, 36
walnut symbol, 210–11
al-Wansharishi, fatwa, 130
warp/warp knot, 50, 66, 68, 252
washing, significance of, 138
weaves, Coptic, 39
weaving factories, crisis (fourth century), 29
weaving/weavers, xv, 11; of Admiral carpet *see* Admiral carpet; craft guilds *see* craft guilds; iconographic link with mosaic floor, 73;

importance of, 4, 12, 25, 27; Jewish *see* Jewish weavers; in Murcia region, 3–10, 35, 45, 48, 54, 131, 134; process of weaving, 25; of Vizcaya carpet *see* Vizcaya carpet
welf, 252
Western Europe, significance of Star of David to, 184
wheel symbol, 176, 182
whorl, 44
wife, ideal, 26
William the Conqueror, 194n
wills, 36–7, 92, 94
Wischnitzer, M., 31n, 32n, 57n, 58n, 59n, 60n, 61n, 62n, 125n
Wisdom of Solomon, 105, 123n, 168, 206
witch persecutions, 101–2
Wolff, Anne, 22n, 58n
Wolsey, Cardinal, 54
wool, 23, 25, 26, 30n, 46, 68, 142; goats' hair compared, 68; Merino, 5, 51, 249; trade war over (Spain and England, fifteenth century), 8–9n; *see also* sheep
woollen rugs, 40
Woolley, Leonard, 30n
Woolley, Linda, 144n
words/word play, 157, 159

Yadin, Yigael, 20n
Yafa Synagogue, 176
Yahudah Haggadah, 197n
Yahweh, 171
Yannai, Alexander, 171
Yemen, 180
yeshiva, 46, 252
Yonah, Avi, 31n
Yusuf III of Granada, 130

Zacharias (Jewish weaver), 38
Zohar, 55, 116, 148
Zoroastrianism, 215
Zvi, Sabbatai, 126n